Lecture Notes in Computer Science 4776

Commenced Publication in 1973
Founding and Former Series Editors:
Gerhard Goos, Juris Hartmanis, and Jan van Leeuwen

Nikita Borisov Philippe Golle (Eds.)

Privacy Enhancing Technologies

7th International Symposium, PET 2007
Ottawa, Canada, June 20-22, 2007
Revised Selected Papers

 Springer

Volume Editors

Nikita Borisov
University of Illinois at Urbana-Champaign
Department of Electrical and Computer Engineering
1308 West Main Street, Urbana, IL 61801-2307, USA
E-mail: nikita@uiuc.edu

Philippe Golle
Palo Alto Research Center
3333 Coyote Hill Road, Palo Alto, CA 94304, USA
E-mail: Philippe.Golle@parc.com

Library of Congress Control Number: 2007938055

CR Subject Classification (1998): E.3, C.2, D.4.6, K.6.5, K.4, H.3, H.4

LNCS Sublibrary: SL 4 – Security and Cryptology

ISSN   0302-9743
ISBN-10   3-540-75550-0 Springer Berlin Heidelberg New York
ISBN-13   978-3-540-75550-0 Springer Berlin Heidelberg New York

Typesetting: Camera-ready by author, data conversion by Scientific Publishing Services, Chennai, India
Printed on acid-free paper   SPIN: 12171590   06/3180   5 4 3 2 1 0

Foreword

The PET community has grown in size considerably since the first PET workshop was held in 2000. With this growth came an increase in the number and quality of submissions. PET has become a premier venue for publishing original research on privacy enhancing technologies, and the current acceptance ratio puts PET in the same league as other highly selective security and privacy venues. To appropriately reflect this evolution, the PET workshop is changing its name to the *Privacy Enhancing Technologies Symposium.*

PET 2007 was held at the University of Ottawa, Canada, on June 20–22, 2007. We received 84 full-paper submissions, of which 16 were selected for presentation at the symposium. PET also included a keynote address and two panel discussions. PET was once again collocated with the IAVoSS Workshop on Trustworthy Elections (WOTE 2007), with a full day of plenary sessions. All participants were free to attend sessions from both events.

The program chairs would like to thank, first of all, the authors, speakers, and panelists for their contribution to the content of the workshop. We would also like to thank the program committee for their hard work of a month of reviews and two more weeks of intense discussions, helping to ensure a program of high scientific quality. As well, we would like to acknowledge the contribution of the external reviewers, who assisted the program committee with the reviews. A special thanks is due to the designers of the Websubmission and Webreview software at K.U. Leuven for allowing us to use their software to help with the selection process, and to Thomas Herlea for his help in getting the software up and running.

Our general chair, Carlisle Adams, did an outstanding job taking care of the local arrangements and making sure the symposium ran smoothly. We also would like to thank Jeremy Clark for designing and maintaining the PET 2007 Website. We are very grateful to Josh Benaloh, the chair of WOTE 2007, for his help in coordinating the two events. Finally, PET 2007 was made possible, and more affordable, thanks to our sponsors: Microsoft, ORNEC, Bell Privacy Centre of Excellence, PGP Corporation, and Google. We are extremely grateful for their generous support.

The Award for Outstanding Research in Privacy Enhancing Technologies was given this year to Stephen C. Bono, Matthew Green, Adam Stubblefield, Ari Juels, Aviel D. Rubin, and Michael Szydlo for their paper "Security Analysis of a Cryptographically-Enabled RFID Device." The award is sponsored by Microsoft and by the Office of the Information and Privacy Commissioner of Ontario and the winners were selected through an independent prize committee headed by George Danezis to whom we are thankful.

July 2007   Nikita Borisov
                                                                                   Philippe Golle

Organization

Organizers

General Chair	Carlisle Adams (University of Ottawa, Canada)
Program Chairs	Nikita Borisov (University of Illinois at Urbana-Champaign, USA)
	Philippe Golle (Palo Alto Research Center, USA)
PET Prize	George Danezis (K.U. Leuven, Belgium)
Stipends	Roger Dingledine (The Tor Project, USA)

Program Committee

Alessandro Acquisti (Carnegie Mellon University, USA)
Mikhail Atallah (Purdue University, USA)
Michael Backes (Saarland University, Germany)
Alastair Beresford (University of Cambridge, UK)
Jean Camp (Indiana University, USA)
George Danezis (K.U. Leuven, Belgium)
Claudia Díaz (K.U. Leuven, Belgium)
Roger Dingledine (The Tor Project, USA)
Cynthia Dwork (Microsoft Research, USA)
Simson Garfinkel (Harvard University, USA)
Ian Goldberg (University of Waterloo, Canada)
Susan Hohenberger (Johns Hopkins University, USA)
Dennis Kügler (Federal Office for Information Security, Germany)
Bradley Malin (Vanderbilt University, USA)
David Martin (University of Massachusetts at Lowell, USA)
Nick Mathewson (The Tor Project, USA)
David Molnar (University of California at Berkeley, USA)
Steven Murdoch (University of Cambridge, UK)
Andreas Pfitzmann (Dresden University of Technology, Germany)
Mike Reiter (University of North Carolina at Chapel Hill, USA)
Andrei Serjantov (The Free Haven Project, UK)
Vitaly Shmatikov (University of Texas at Austin, USA)
Paul Syverson (Naval Research Laboratory, USA)
Matthew Wright (University of Texas at Arlington, USA)

External Reviewers

Mike Bergmann
Alexander Böttcher
Katrin Borcea-Pfitzmann
Sebastian Clauß
Richard Clayton
Markus Duermuth
David Evans
Anna Lisa Ferrara
Elke Franz
Bikas Gurung

Thomas Heydt-Benjamin
Yong Ho Hwang
Ponnurangam Kumaraguru
Haim Levkowitz
Benyuan Liu
Matteo Maffei
Sasha Romanosky
Sandra Steinbrecher
Carmela Troncoso
Lasse Øverlier

Sponsors

Microsoft
ORNEC
Bell Privacy Centre of Excellence
PGP Corporation
Google

Table of Contents

Attacking Unlinkability:
The Importance of Context

Matthias Franz[1], Bernd Meyer[1], and Andreas Pashalidis[2]

[1] Siemens AG, Corporate Technology,
Otto-Hahn-Ring 6, 81739 München, Germany
{matthias.franz,bernd.meyer}@siemens.com
[2] NEC Europe Ltd, Network Laboratories
Kurfürsten-Anlage 36, 69115 Heidelberg, Germany
andreas.pashalidis@netlab.nec.de

Abstract. A system that protects the unlinkability of certain data items (e. g. identifiers of communication partners, messages, pseudonyms, transactions, votes) does not leak information that would enable an adversary to link these items. The adversary could, however, take advantage of hints from the context in which the system operates. In this paper, we introduce a new metric that enables one to quantify the (un)linkability of the data items and, based on this, we consider the effect of some simple contextual hints.

1 Introduction

A number of privacy-preserving systems, such as mix networks, anonymous credential systems, and secret voting schemes, protect the unlinkability of certain data items of interest. Mix networks, in particular, protect the unlinkability of the messages that enter the network with respect to their recipients, the messages that leave the network with respect to their senders, and, hence, the identifiers of communicating parties with respect to communication sessions. Since their introduction [9], a number of different mix network variants have been proposed (see, for example, [4,19,26,33,34]), some of which have also been implemented and deployed. Anonymous credentials, on the other hand, protect the unlinkability of the pseudonyms and the transactions with respect to the users they correspond to. Since their introduction into the digital world [10], a number of anonymous credential systems have been proposed (see, for example, [7,8,11,12,13,14,29,32,38]). Secret voting schemes protect the unlinkability of votes with respect to the users who cast them. Such schemes have evolved from ostracism [24] to sophisticated cryptosystems; for an overview of the current state of the art the reader is referred to [1].

The problem of analysing how well the above types of system protect unlinkability has received some attention during recent years. The focus of most works is, however, on mix networks (see, for example, [2,15,16,25,27,30]). This is not surprising since mix networks provide the basis for anonymous communication

N. Borisov and P. Golle (Eds.): PET 2007, LNCS 4776, pp. 1–16, 2007.

and are, as such, necessary for preserving privacy in a number of settings, including the setting of anonymous credentials [17] and, sometimes, the setting of voting systems (see, for example, [6]).

An adversary that wishes to link the protected items may use information that is leaked by the system during its operation, or hints from the environment in which the system operates. In contrast to existing literature, the focus of this paper is on the latter. That is, we study a number of simple contextual hints and their effect on unlinkability. Our results apply to *all* types of unlinkability-protecting system, including mix networks, anonymous credentials, and secret voting schemes. The rest of the paper is organised as follows. Section 2 introduces the metric for unlinkability that is used throughout the paper. Section 3 examines seven different types of hint and their effect on unlinkability. Finally, Section 4 concludes.

2   Measuring Unlinkability

Consider a set of elements A and a partition $\pi \vdash A$ of that set. Note that we do not distinguish between π and the equivalence relation it defines. In the sequel, we write $a_1 \equiv_\pi a_2$ if the elements $a_1, a_2 \in A$ lie in the same equivalence class of π, and $a_1 \not\equiv_\pi a_2$ otherwise. Let $\tau \vdash A$ denote a 'target' partition, chosen uniformly at random. We use entropy as a metric for unlinkability. That is, the unlinkability of the elements in a set A against an adversary $\mathcal{A}$ is defined as

$$\mathcal{U}_A(\mathcal{A}) = - \sum_{\pi \in \Pi} \Pr(\pi = \tau) \log_2(\Pr(\pi = \tau)),$$

where $\Pi = \{P : P \vdash A\}$ denotes the set of partitions of A and $\Pr(\pi = \tau)$ denotes, in $\mathcal{A}$'s view, the probability that π is the target partition τ. We further define the *degree* of unlinkability of the elements in A against an adversary $\mathcal{A}_H$ with access to a hint H about τ as

$$\mathcal{D}_A(\mathcal{A}_H) = \frac{\mathcal{U}_A(\mathcal{A}_H)}{\mathcal{U}_A(\mathcal{A}_\emptyset)},$$

where $\mathcal{A}_\emptyset$ denotes the adversary without any hints. That is, $\mathcal{A}_\emptyset$ knows A but has no information about τ. The set of candidate partitions for $\mathcal{A}_\emptyset$ is therefore $\Pi_A(\mathcal{A}_\emptyset) = \Pi$, i.e. the set of all partitions of A. The number $|\Pi_A(\mathcal{A}_\emptyset)| = B_{|A|}$ of such partitions, a Bell number [3,35], is given by the recursive formula

$$B_{n+1} = \sum_{k=0}^{n} \binom{n}{k} B_k \tag{1}$$

where $B_0 = 1$.[1] Since τ is chosen uniformly at random, the unlinkability of the elements in A is therefore at its maximum, i.e. $\mathcal{U}_A(\mathcal{A}_\emptyset) = \log_2(B_{|A|})$ bits. This

---

[1] The first few Bell numbers are 1, 1, 2, 5, 15, 52, 203, 877, 4140, 21147.

is the best case from a privacy point of view: all partitions of A are equally likely to be the target partition τ.

Remark 1: In the setting of unlinkability-protecting systems, the goal of the adversary is to identify a target partition from an 'anonymity set' of candidate partitions. The fact that the information-theoretic metric we use for unlinkability is identical to the metric introduced for anonymity in [18,36], is therefore natural.

Remark 2: $\mathcal{U}_A$ is a measure of the information that is contained in the probability distribution that the adversary assigns to the set of all partitions of A. Since we assume that τ is selected uniformly at random, this distribution is, a priori, uniform. However, a hint may enable the adversary to change his view such that, a posteriori, some partitions are more likely than others. The hints we consider in this paper enable the adversary to exclude a number of candidate partitions (i.e. to reduce the size of the 'anonymity set') while the remaining partitions remain equally likely.

Example: Consider an anonymous help line where a clerk offers advice over the telephone. Suppose that, one day, the clerk receives four calls, denoted $A = \{\lambda_1, \lambda_2, \lambda_3, \lambda_4\}$. Without any additional information, all $B_4 = 15$ partitions of A constitute valid ways to link these calls. Since without any additional information all these partitions are equally likely, the unlinkability of the calls is, in this case, $\log_2(15) \simeq 3.9$ bits, and the degree of unlinkability is $\log_2(15)/\log_2(15) = 1$.

The clerk, however, has some additional information: he realised that the calls λ_1 and λ_2 were made by men, and that the calls λ_3 and λ_4 by women (however, the clerk does not know whether or not the same person called twice). This hint effectively rules out all partitions where λ_1 or λ_2 appears in the same equivalence class as λ_2 or λ_4. In particular, only four partitions remain valid, namely $\{(\lambda_1, \lambda_2), (\lambda_3, \lambda_4)\}$, $\{(\lambda_1, \lambda_2), (\lambda_3), (\lambda_4)\}$, $\{(\lambda_1), (\lambda_2), (\lambda_3, \lambda_4)\}$, and $\{(\lambda_1), (\lambda_2), (\lambda_3), (\lambda_4)\}$. Since these four partitions are equally likely, the unlinkability of the calls is, in this case, $\log_2(4) = 2$ bits, and the degree of unlinkability is $\log_2(2)/\log_2(15) \simeq 0.52$.

3   The Importance of Context

In this section, we examine seven types of hint that an adversary may obtain from the operational context of the system. In particular, we examine hints that reveal to the adversary (a) the number of equivalence classes in τ, (b) the cardinality of equivalence classes in τ, (c) the fact that all equivalence classes in τ have a given cardinality, (d) a 'reference partition' the equivalence classes of which have exactly one representative in each equivalence class in τ, (e) a set of element pairs that are equivalent in τ, (f) a set of element pairs that are not equivalent in τ, and (g) a combination of (e) and (f).

3.1   The Number of Equivalence Classes

Consider an adversary $\mathcal{A}_{H_1}$ with a hint $H_1 = (\alpha)$, where $\alpha \in \mathbb{N}$ and $1 \leq \alpha \leq |A|$, that reveals how many equivalence classes τ has. $\mathcal{A}_{H_1}$ can restrict its attention to $\Pi_A(\mathcal{A}_{H_1}) = \{P : P \vdash A, |P| = \alpha\}$, i.e. the partitions that divide A into exactly α equivalence classes. The number of such partitions, which is a Stirling number of the second kind [22], is given by

$$|\Pi_A(\mathcal{A}_{H_1})| = \frac{1}{\alpha!} \sum_{k=0}^{\alpha} (-1)^k \binom{\alpha}{k} (\alpha - k)^{|A|}.$$

Since τ is chosen uniformly at random, the unlinkability of the elements in A is $\mathcal{U}_A(\mathcal{A}_{H_1}) = \log_2(|\Pi_A(\mathcal{A}_{H_1})|)$ bits. Figure 1 shows the degree of unlinkability $\mathcal{D}_A(\mathcal{A}_{H_1})$ as a function of $|A|$.

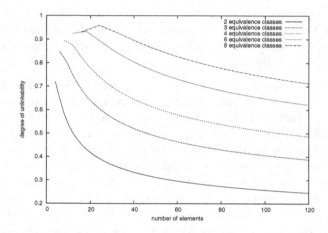

Fig. 1. Degree of unlinkability $\mathcal{D}_A(\mathcal{A}_{H_1})$ of elements in a set A as a function of $|A|$, if it is known that they must be divided into α equivalence classes

How to obtain this hint: The number α typically is the number of users in a system. In the setting of mix networks, this number may be known to the operator of the network if users are required to register themselves or pay a fee. Otherwise, obtaining such a hint may be tricky due to the possibility of sybil attacks [20]. Whether or not it is straightforward to obtain this hint in the setting of anonymous credentials depends on the application. In the case of cash, for example, the financial institution is very likely to know how many users participate in the system. Similarly, in the case of demographic or personal credentials (such as age certificates or driving licences), the issuing authority is also likely to know the number of users in the system. In the setting of secret voting, there exist multiple ways to obtain the number of voters. The number of cast ballots, for example, may be conclusive about the number of voters.

3.2   The Cardinality of Equivalence Classes

Consider an adversary $\mathcal{A}_{H_2}$ with a hint $H_2 = (\beta_1, \beta_2, \ldots, \beta_\alpha)$, where $\sum_{i=1}^{\alpha} \beta_i = |A|$ and $1 < \alpha < |A|$, that reveals the sizes of the equivalence classes in τ. That is, if $\tau = \{T_1, T_2, \ldots, T_\alpha\} \vdash A$, H_2 reveals that $|T_1| = \beta_1$, $|T_2| = \beta_2$, and so on. $\mathcal{A}_{H_2}$ can restrict its attention to $\Pi_A(\mathcal{A}_{H_2}) = \{P : P = \{T_1, T_2, \ldots, T_\alpha\} \vdash A, \forall 1 \leq i \leq \alpha, |T_i| = \beta_i\}$, i.e. the partitions that divide A into exactly α equivalence classes with cardinalities $\beta_1, \beta_2, \ldots, \beta_\alpha$. The number of such partitions is given by

$$|\Pi_A(\mathcal{A}_{H_2})| = \frac{|A|!}{\prod_{i=1}^{\alpha}(\beta_i!) \prod_{i=1}^{|A|}(\gamma_i!)} \tag{2}$$

where, for all $1 \leq i \leq |A|$, $\gamma_i = |\{\beta \in H_2 : \beta = i\}|$ (for a proof see Appendix B). That is, γ_i is the number of equivalence classes in τ that have cardinality i. Since τ is chosen uniformly at random, the unlinkability of the elements in A is $\mathcal{U}_A(\mathcal{A}_{H_2}) = \log_2(|\Pi_A(\mathcal{A}_{H_2})|)$ bits. It is perhaps worth noting that there exist hints of type H_2 which do not reveal any information as to whether any two given elements are equivalent or not. This is in contrast to what is claimed in [37] (see Appendix A).

As a special case, consider an adversary $\mathcal{A}_{H_3}$ with a hint $H_3 = (\alpha)$, where $\alpha \in \mathbb{N}$ divides $|A|$, that reveals the fact that τ has α equivalence classes *of the same cardinality* $|A|/\alpha$. $\mathcal{A}_{H_3}$ can restrict its attention to $\Pi_A(\mathcal{A}_{H_3}) = \{P : P \vdash A, \forall p \in P, |p| = |A|/\alpha\}$, i.e. the partitions that divide A into exactly α equivalence classes of equal cardinality $|A|/\alpha$. The number of such partitions is given by

$$|\Pi_A(\mathcal{A}_{H_3})| = \frac{|A|!}{\alpha!((|A|/\alpha)!)^\alpha} \tag{3}$$

(for a proof see Appendix B). Since τ is chosen uniformly at random, the unlinkability of the elements in A is $\mathcal{U}_A(\mathcal{A}_{H_3}) = \log_2(|\Pi_A(\mathcal{A}_{H_3})|)$ bits. Figure 2 shows the degree of unlinkability $\mathcal{D}_A(\mathcal{A}_{H_3})$ as a function of $|A|$.

How to obtain this hint:[2] In the setting of mix networks, this hint may be obtained if it is known how many messages each user sends in each session. In the setting of anonymous credentials, it is possible to obtain this hint if it is known how many pseudonyms each user has. In the setting of secret voting, this hint may be obtained if it is known how many ballots each user has cast.

3.3   A Reference Partition

Consider an adversary $\mathcal{A}_{H_4}$ with a hint $H_4 = (\rho)$, consisting of a 'reference partition' $\rho = \{R_1, R_2, \ldots, R_{|A|/\alpha}\} \vdash A$ such that, for all $1 \leq i \leq |A|/\alpha$, $|R_i| = \alpha$ (note that α divides $|A|$), and that reveals the fact that each of the equivalence classes of τ contains exactly one element from R_i. $\mathcal{A}_{H_4}$ can restrict its attention to $\Pi_A(\mathcal{A}_{H_4}) = \{P : P \vdash A, P \text{ is a transversal of } \rho\}$, i.e. the partitions that divide A into α equivalence classes of equal cardinality $|A|/\alpha$, where each class contains exactly one element from each of $R_1, R_2, \ldots, R_{|A|/\alpha}$. The number of such partitions is given by

$$|\Pi_A(\mathcal{A}_{H_4})| = (\alpha!)^{(|A|/\alpha)-1} \tag{4}$$

---

[2] This paragraph refers to hints of both type H_2 and H_3.

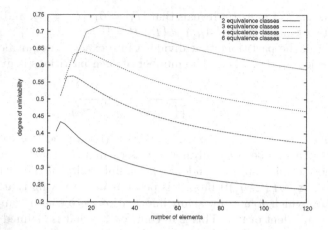

Fig. 2. Degree of unlinkability $\mathcal{D}_A(\mathcal{A}_{H_3})$ of elements in a set A as a function of $|A|$, if it is known that they must be divided into α equivalence classes of equal cardinality $|A|/\alpha$

(for a proof see Appendix C). Since τ is chosen uniformly at random, the unlinkability of the elements in A is $\mathcal{U}_A(\mathcal{A}_{H_4}) = \log_2(|\Pi_A(\mathcal{A}_{H_4})|)$ bits. Figure 3 shows the degree of unlinkability $\mathcal{D}_A(\mathcal{A}_{H_4})$ as a function of $|A|$.

How to obtain this hint: In the setting of mix networks this hint may be obtained if each of the α users sends exactly one message through the network in β communication sessions. An adversary that wishes to divide the set of messages that leave the network (there are $\alpha \cdot \beta$ of them) into α subsets of equal cardinality β, such that each subset contains the messages sent by a single user,

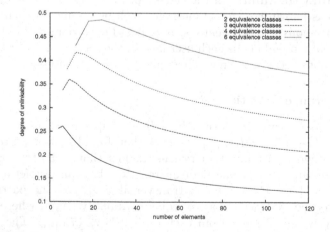

Fig. 3. Degree of unlinkability $\mathcal{D}_A(\mathcal{A}_{H_4})$ of elements in a set A as a function of $|A|$, if it is known that they must be divided into α equivalence classes of equal cardinality $|A|/\alpha$, such that each class contains exactly one element from each equivalence class of a given partition

can construct a reference partition $R_1, R_2, \ldots, R_\beta$ by grouping the messages that leave the network according to communication sessions (i.e. such that, for all $1 \leq i \leq \beta$, R_i contains the messages that leave the network in session i). In the setting of anonymous credential systems, this hint may be obtained if each user has established exactly one pseudonym with each organisation in the system; an adversary that controls the organisations knows the reference partition as a side effect of normal operation. In the setting of secret voting, this hint may be obtained in special cases, such as the case of a combined election where each of the α voters is asked to answer β different questions on separate ballots. An adversary that wishes to divide the set of cast ballots (there are $\alpha \cdot \beta$ of them) into α subsets of equal cardinality β, such that each subset contains the ballots cast by a single user, can construct a reference partition by grouping the ballots according to the question they correspond to.

3.4   Breach of Privacy: Linking Case

Consider an adversary $\mathcal{A}_{H_5}$ with a hint $H_5 = (L)$, where the set L consists of distinct pairs $\{a_1, a_2\} \subseteq A$, and that reveals the fact that, for all $\{a_1, a_2\} \in L$, $a_1 \equiv_\tau a_2$. Note that $|L| \leq |A|(|A| - 1)/2$. $\mathcal{A}_{H_5}$ can restrict its attention to $\Pi_A(\mathcal{A}_{H_5}) = \{P : P \vdash A, \forall \{a_1, a_2\} \in L, a_1 \equiv_P a_2\}$. That is, the adversary can restrict its attention to those partitions that divide A such that, for all $\{a_1, a_2\} \in L$, a_1 and a_2 are equivalent. The number of such partitions is given by

$$|\Pi_A(\mathcal{A}_{H_5})| = B_{\Phi(A,L)} \tag{5}$$

where $\Phi(A, L)$ denotes the number of connected components in the graph (A, L) with vertices the elements in A and edges the elements in L. For a fixed L, and since τ is chosen uniformly at random, the unlinkability of the elements in A is $\mathcal{U}_A(\mathcal{A}_{H_5}) = \log_2(|\Pi_A(\mathcal{A}_{H_5})|)$ bits. If, on the other hand, L is chosen at random, then the expected value of (5) is given by

$$\mathrm{E}(|\Pi_A(\mathcal{A}_{H_5})|) = \mathrm{E}(B_{\Phi(A,L)}) = \sum_{k=1}^{|A|} B_k \Pr(\Phi(A, L) = k)$$

where $\Pr(\Phi(A, L) = k)$ denotes the probability that the graph (A, L) consists of exactly k connected components. Figure 4 shows the expected degree of unlinkability $\mathrm{E}(\mathcal{D}_A(\mathcal{A}_{H_5})) = \log_2(\mathrm{E}(B_{\Phi(A,L)}))/\log_2(B_{|A|})$ as a function of $|A|$ and $|L|$, for the case where the elements in L are selected uniformly at random. Note that, in this case, the graph (A, L) is a random graph with $|L|$ edges,[3] and the probability $\Pr(\Phi(A, L) = k)$ depends only on $|A|$ and $|L|$. Due to lack of an exact formula for $\Pr(\Phi(A, L) = k)$ (but see [21,28]), the values shown in the figure are based on simulation. It is, of course, by no means necessary that the elements in L are selected uniformly at random; depending on the context and the power of the adversary, these elements may be selected by some other process that may lead to a faster or slower decrease in unlinkability.

---

[3] See, for example, [5,23] for a treatment of such graphs.

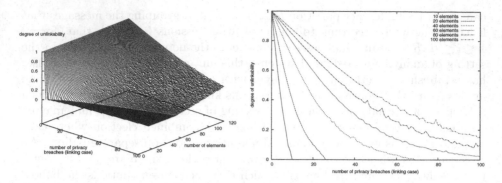

Fig. 4. Expected degree of unlinkability $E(\mathcal{D}_A(\mathcal{A}_{H_5}))$ as a function of the number of elements $|A|$ and the number of privacy breaches (linking case) $|L|$. The elements in L are selected uniformly at random.

How to obtain this hint: Each element $\{a_1, a_2\} \in L$ can be seen as a privacy breach that tells the adversary that a_1 and a_2 are linked. In the setting of mix networks, a_1 and a_2 could be messages that leave the network; an adversary can link them based on e.g. their content or recipient. In the setting of anonymous credential systems, a_1 and a_2 could be transactions; an adversary can link them based on contextual information such as credential type [31], timing, location, or an identical piece of information that is attached to both transactions, e.g. a telephone number or an email address. In the setting of a combined election, a_1 and a_2 could be ballots; an adversary can link them based, for example, on the handwriting they may contain.

3.5   Breach of Privacy: Unlinking Case

Consider an adversary $\mathcal{A}_{H_6}$ with a hint $H_6 = (U)$, where the set U consists of distinct pairs $\{a_1, a_2\} \subseteq A$, and that reveals the fact that, for all $\{a_1, a_2\} \in U$, $a_1 \not\equiv_\tau a_2$. Note that $|U| \leq |A| \cdot (|A| - 1)/2$. $\mathcal{A}_{H_6}$ can restrict its attention to $\Pi_A(\mathcal{A}_{H_6}) = \{P : P \vdash A, \forall \{a_1, a_2\} \in U, a_1 \not\equiv_P a_2\}$. That is, the adversary can restrict its attention to those partitions that divide A such that, for all $\{a_1, a_2\} \in U$, a_1 and a_2 are in different equivalence classes. The number of such partitions is given by

$$|\Pi_A(\mathcal{A}_{H_6})| = \sum_{U' \subseteq U} (-1)^{|U'|} B_{\Phi(A,U')} \qquad (6)$$

where $\Phi(A, U')$ denotes the number of connected components in the graph (A, U') with vertices the elements in A and edges the elements in U' (for a proof see Appendix D). For a fixed U, and since τ is chosen uniformly at random, the unlinkability of the elements in A is $\mathcal{U}_A(\mathcal{A}_{H_6}) = \log_2(|\Pi_A(\mathcal{A}_{H_6})|)$ bits. If, on the other hand, U is selected at random, the expected value of (6), for a given number n of elements in U, is given by

$$E(|\Pi_A(\mathcal{A}_{H_6})|) = \sum_{\substack{U \subseteq Z \\ |U|=n}} \Pr(U) \sum_{U' \subseteq U} (-1)^{|U'|} B_{\Phi(A,U')} \qquad (7)$$

where Z denotes the set of all distinct pairs $\{a_1, a_2\} \subseteq A$ and $\Pr(U)$ denotes the probability that U is selected. Figure 5 shows the expected degree of unlinkability $E(\mathcal{D}_A(\mathcal{A}_{H_6})) = \log_2 E(|\Pi_A(\mathcal{A}_{H_6})|)/\log_2(B_{|A|})$ as a function of $|A|$ and $|U|$, for the case where the elements in U are selected uniformly at random.[4] It is, of course, by no means necessary that the elements in U are selected uniformly at random; depending on the context and the power of the adversary, these elements may be selected by some other process that may lead to a faster or slower decrease in unlinkability.

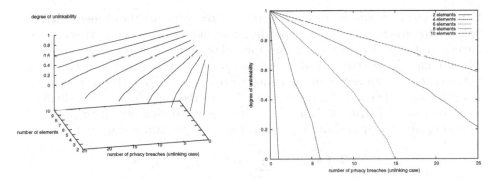

Fig. 5. Expected degree of unlinkability $E(\mathcal{D}_A(\mathcal{A}_{H_6}))$ as a function of the number of elements $|A|$ and the number of privacy breaches (unlinking case) $|U|$. The elements in U are selected uniformly at random.

How to obtain this hint: Each element $\{a_1, a_2\} \in U$ can be seen as a privacy breach that tells the adversary that a_1 and a_2 are not linked. In the setting of mix networks, a_1 and a_2 could be messages that enter the network; an adversary can unlink them based on e. g. their content or sender. In the setting of anonymous credential systems, a_1 and a_2 could be transactions; an adversary can unlink them based on contextual information such as credential type, timing, location, or a piece of information that is attached to both transactions, e. g. two differing telephone numbers or email addresses. In the setting of a combined election, a_1 and a_2 could be ballots; an adversary can unlink them based, for example, on the handwriting they may contain.

Example: Let us briefly revisit the example from Section 2 at this point. Since the clerk knows that the calls λ_1 and λ_2 were made by men, and the calls λ_3

---

[4] Since evaluating (7) takes time exponential in $|U|$, the results shown in Figure 5 were obtained by simulation.

and λ_4 by women, he can effectively unlink λ_1 and λ_2 from λ_3 and λ_4. That is, he has a hint $H_6 = (U) = (\{(\lambda_1, \lambda_3), (\lambda_1, \lambda_4), (\lambda_2, \lambda_3), (\lambda_2, \lambda_4)\})$. In order to evaluate (6) the value of $\Phi(A, U')$ must be determined for each subset $U' \subset U$. In this example, we have

- the case where $U' = U$ and $\Phi(A, U') = 1$,
- four cases where $|U'| = 3$ and $\Phi(A, U') = 1$,
- six cases where $|U'| = 2$ and $\Phi(A, U') = 2$,
- four cases where $|U'| = 1$ and $\Phi(A, U') = 3$, and
- the case where $U' = \emptyset$ and $\Phi(A, \emptyset) = 4$.

That is, (6) evaluates to $B_1 - 4B_1 + 6B_2 - 4B_3 + B_4 = 1 - 4 + 12 - 20 + 15 = 4$, which coincides with the result from the elementary approach in Section 2.

3.6   Breach of Privacy: Combined Case

Consider an oracle which answers questions of the form 'are the elements (a_1, a_2) linked?' by either 'yes' or 'no', depending on whether $a_1 \equiv_\tau a_2$ or $a_1 \not\equiv_\tau a_2$. An adversary $\mathcal{A}_{H_7}$ with access to such an oracle obtains, in effect, a hint $H_7 = (L, U)$, where L and U are as described above. Note that $L \cap U = \emptyset$ and $|L| + |U| \leq |A| \cdot (|A|-1)/2$. $\mathcal{A}_{H_7}$ can restrict its attention to $\Pi_A(\mathcal{A}_{H_7}) = \{P : P \vdash A, \forall\{a_1, a_2\} \in L, a_1 \equiv_P a_2 \land \forall\{a_1, a_2\} \in U, a_1 \not\equiv_P a_2\}$, i.e. to those partitions that divide A such that, for all $\{a_1, a_2\} \in L$, a_1 and a_2 are equivalent and, for all $\{a_1, a_2\} \in U$, a_1 and a_2 are not equivalent. The number of such partitions is given by

$$|\Pi_A(\mathcal{A}_{H_7})| = \sum_{U' \subseteq \tilde{U}} (-1)^{|U'|} B_{\Phi(\tilde{A}, U')} \tag{8}$$

where $\tilde{A}$ denotes the set of components of the graph (A, L), the set of edges $\tilde{U}$ contains the edge $\{c_1, c_2\}$, where $c_1, c_2 \in \tilde{A}$ and $c_1 \neq c_2$, if and only if U contains a pair $\{a_1, a_2\}$ such that either $(a_1 \in c_1$ and $a_2 \in c_2)$, or $(a_1 \in c_2$ and $a_2 \in c_1)$, and $\Phi(\tilde{A}, U')$ denotes the number of components in the the graph $(\tilde{A}, U')$ with vertices the elements in $\tilde{A}$ and edges the elements in U'. In effect, the difference between equations (6) and (8) lies in the fact that the latter operates on a quotient graph — induced by L — of the graph on which the former operates.

For a fixed set of oracle calls, i.e. a fixed L and U, and since τ is chosen uniformly at random, the unlinkability of the elements in A is $\mathcal{U}_A(\mathcal{A}_{H_7}) = \log_2(|\Pi_A(\mathcal{A}_{H_7})|)$ bits. If, on the other hand, τ and the oracle calls are selected at random, the expected value of (8), if exactly $n = |L| + |U|$ oracle calls are made, is given by

$$E(|\Pi_A(\mathcal{A}_{H_7})|) = \sum_{\substack{L, U \subseteq Z \\ |L|+|U|=n}} \Pr(L \land U) \sum_{U' \subseteq \tilde{U}} (-1)^{|U'|} B_{\Phi(\tilde{A}, U')} \tag{9}$$

where Z denotes the set of all distinct pairs $\{a_1, a_2\} \subseteq A$ and $\Pr(L \land U)$ denotes the probability of selecting τ and oracle calls such that L and U are the results of the oracle's answers. Figure 6 shows the expected degree of unlinkability $E(\mathcal{D}_A(\mathcal{A}_{H_7})) = \log_2 E(|\Pi_A(\mathcal{A}_{H_7})|)/\log_2(B_{|A|})$ as a function of $|A|$ and $|L \cup U|$, for the case where τ and the elements in $L \cup U$ are selected uniformly at random.[5] It is, of course, by no means necessary that τ and the elements in $L \cup U$ are selected uniformly at random; depending on the context and the power of the adversary, these elements may be selected by some other process that may lead to a faster or slower decrease in unlinkability.

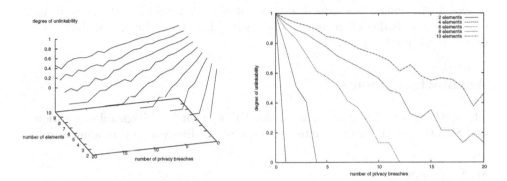

Fig. 6. Expected degree of unlinkability $E(\mathcal{D}_A(\mathcal{A}_{H_7}))$ as a function of the number of elements $|A|$ and the number of privacy breaches $|L \cup U|$. The target partition τ and the elements in $L \cup U$ are selected uniformly at random.

How to obtain this hint: See sections 3.4 and 3.5.

4   Conclusion

In this paper, we considered the setting of a system that protects the unlinkability of certain elements of interest, and an adversary with the goal to nevertheless link these elements. We studied how a number of contextual hints, if disclosed to the adversary, affect its ability to link the elements. We conclude that an adversary that knows only the number or the cardinality of the equivalence classes that the elements must be divided into (or a 'reference partition' as described in Section 3.3), is, in most cases, unable to link the elements with certainty. However, as Figures 1, 2, and 3 demonstrate, such knowledge nevertheless reduces the degree of unlinkability of the elements to a significant extent.

By contrast, an adversary that breaches privacy by linking and/or by unlinking pairs of elements, is able to identify the target partition (i.e. uniquely link all elements) after a certain number of breaches have occurred. However, if the adversary is limited to linking (resp. unlinking), then this required number of privacy breaches can occur only in the extreme case where all elements are equivalent (resp. if each element constitutes a separate equivalence class) in the

---

[5] Since evaluating (9) takes time exponential in $|U|$, the results shown in Figure 6 were obtained by simulation.

target partition. Figures 4, 5, and 6 demonstrate the significance of such breaches in an 'average' case, i.e. in the case where randomly selected pairs are linked or unlinked. Note that linking (Figure 4) has a significantly more dramatic effect on unlinkability compared to unlinking (Figure 5). This however, is not surprising, since 'belonging to the same equivalence class' is a transitive relation, while 'belonging to different equivalence classes' is not.

Finally, note that the list of hints studied in this paper is by no means exhaustive and that some types of hint may be of more practical relevance than others. Identifying other, practical types of hint that help an adversary to link otherwise unlinkable elements, and studying their effect on unlinkability, is a direction for further research.

Acknowledgements

The authors would like to thank Michael Braun for his insightful suggestions, and Svante Janson for his pointers to some of the literature on random graphs.

References

1. Adida, B.: Advances in cryptographic voting systems. PhD thesis, Massachusetts Institute of Technology (2006)
2. Agrawal, D., Kesdogan, D., Penz, S.: Probabilistic treatment of mixes to hamper traffic analysis. In: 2003 IEEE Symposium on Security and Privacy (S&P 2003), Berkeley, CA, May 11-14, 2003, pp. 16–27. IEEE Computer Society, Los Alamitos (2003)
3. Bell, E.T.: Exponential numbers. American Mathematical Monthly 41, 411–419 (1934)
4. Berthold, O., Federrath, H., Köpsell, S.: Web mixes: A system for anonymous and unobservable internet access. In: Federrath, H. (ed.) Designing Privacy Enhancing Technologies. LNCS, vol. 2009, pp. 115–129. Springer, Heidelberg (2001)
5. Bollobás, B.: Random Graphs. In: Cambridge Studies in Advanced Mathematics, 2nd edn., vol. 73, Cambridge University Press, Cambridge (2001)
6. Boneh, D., Golle, P.: Almost entirely correct mixing with applications to voting. In: Atluri, V. (ed.) Proc. of the 9th ACM Conference on Computer and Communications Security, pp. 68–77. ACM Press, New York (2002)
7. Camenisch, J., Lysyanskaya, A.: An efficient system for non-transferable anonymous credentials with optional anonymity revocation. In: Pfitzmann, B. (ed.) EUROCRYPT 2001. LNCS, vol. 2045, pp. 93–118. Springer, Heidelberg (2001)
8. Camenisch, J., Lysyanskaya, A.: Signature schemes and anonymous credentials from bilinear maps. In: Franklin, M. (ed.) CRYPTO 2004. LNCS, vol. 3152, pp. 56–72. Springer, Heidelberg (2004)
9. Chaum, D.: Untraceable electronic mail, return addresses, and digital pseudonyms. Communications of the ACM 24(2), 84–90 (1981)
10. Chaum, D.: Security without identification: transaction systems to make big brother obsolete. Communications of the ACM 28(10), 1030–1044 (1985)

11. Chaum, D.: Showing credentials without identification: transferring signatures between unconditionally unlinkable pseudonyms. In: Seberry, J., Pieprzyk, J.P. (eds.) AUSCRYPT 1990. LNCS, vol. 453, pp. 246–264. Springer, Heidelberg (1990)

12. Chen, L.: Access with pseudonyms. In: Dawson, E., Golic, J.D. (eds.) Cryptography: Policy and Algorithms. LNCS, vol. 1029, pp. 232–243. Springer, Heidelberg (1996)

13. Chen, L., Enzmann, M., Sadeghi, A.-R., Schneider, M., Steiner, M.: A privacy-protecting coupon system. In: Patrick, A.S., Yung, M. (eds.) FC 2005. LNCS, vol. 3570, pp. 93–108. Springer, Heidelberg (2005)

14. Damgård, I.: Payment systems and credential mechanisms with provable security against abuse by individuals. In: Goldwasser, S. (ed.) CRYPTO 1988. LNCS, vol. 403, pp. 328–335. Springer, Heidelberg (1990)

15. Danezis, G., Serjantov, A.: Statistical disclosure or intersection attacks on anonymity systems. In: Fridrich, J. (ed.) IH 2004. LNCS, vol. 3200, pp. 293–308. Springer, Heidelberg (2004)

16. Díaz, C., Preneel, B.: Reasoning about the anonymity provided by pool mixes that generate dummy traffic. In: Fridrich, J. (ed.) IH 2004. LNCS, vol. 3200, pp. 309–325. Springer, Heidelberg (2004)

17. Díaz, C., Preneel, B.: Security, Privacy and Trust in Modern Data Management, chapter Accountable Anonymous Communication. Springer, Berlin, 2006 (in print)

18. Díaz, C., Seys, S., Claessens, J., Preneel, B.: Towards measuring anonymity. In: Dingledine, R., Syverson, P.F. (eds.) PET 2002. LNCS, vol. 2482, pp. 54–68. Springer, Heidelberg (2003)

19. Dingledine, R., Mathewson, N., Syverson, P.F.: Tor: The second-generation onion router. In: Proceedings of the 13th USENIX Security Symposium, August 9-13, 2004, San Diego, CA, USA, USENIX, pp. 303–320 (2004)

20. Douceur, J.: The sybil attack. In: Druschel, P., Kaashoek, M.F., Rowstron, A. (eds.) IPTPS 2002. LNCS, vol. 2429, pp. 251–260. Springer, Heidelberg (2002)

21. Erdös, P., Rényi, A.: On random graphs I. Publicationes Mathematicae Debrecen 6, 290–297 (1959)

22. Graham, R.L., Knuth, D.E., Patashnik, O.: Concrete Mathematics: A Foundation for Computer Science. ch. 6.1, 2nd edn., pp. 257–267. Addison-Wesley, Reading (1994)

23. Janson, S., Łuczak, T., Ruciński, A.: Random Graphs. In: Interscience Series in Discrete Mathematics and Optimization, John Wiley & Sons, Inc., Chichester (2000)

24. Kagan, D.: The origin and purposes of ostracism. Hesperia 30(4), 393–401 (1961)

25. Kesdogan, D., Agrawal, D., Penz, S.: Limits of anonymity in open environments. In: Petitcolas, F.A.P. (ed.) IH 2002. LNCS, vol. 2578, pp. 53–69. Springer, Heidelberg (2003)

26. Kesdogan, D., Egner, J., Büschkes, R.: Stop-and-go-mixes providing probabilistic anonymity in an open system. In: Aucsmith, D. (ed.) IH 1998. LNCS, vol. 1525, pp. 83–98. Springer, Heidelberg (1998)

27. Klonowski, M., Kutylowski, M.: Provable anonymity for networks of mixes. In: Barni, M., Herrera-Joancomartí, J., Katzenbeisser, S., Pérez-González, F. (eds.) IH 2005. LNCS, vol. 3727, pp. 26–38. Springer, Heidelberg (2005)

28. Ling, R.F.: The expected number of components in random linear graphs. The Annals of Probability 1(5), 876–881 (1973)

29. Lysyanskaya, A., Rivest, R.L., Sahai, A., Wolf, S.: Pseudonym systems. In: Heys, H.M., Adams, C.M. (eds.) SAC 1999. LNCS, vol. 1758, pp. 184–199. Springer, Heidelberg (2000)

30. Mathewson, N., Dingledine, R.: Practical traffic analysis: Extending and resisting statistical disclosure. In: Martin, D., Serjantov, A. (eds.) PET 2004. LNCS, vol. 3424, pp. 17–34. Springer, Heidelberg (2005)
31. Pashalidis, A., Meyer, B.: Linking anonymous transactions: The consistent view attack. In: Danezis, G., Golle, P. (eds.) PET 2006. LNCS, vol. 4258, pp. 384–392. Springer, Heidelberg (2006)
32. Persiano, G., Visconti, I.: An efficient and usable multi-show non-transferable anonymous credential system. In: Juels, A. (ed.) FC 2004. LNCS, vol. 3110, pp. 196–211. Springer, Heidelberg (2004)
33. Reiter, M.K., Rubin, A.D.: Crowds: anonymity for Web transactions. ACM Transactions on Information and System Security 1(1), 66–92 (1998)
34. Rennhard, M., Plattner, B.: Introducing morphmix: peer-to-peer based anonymous internet usage with collusion detection. In: Jajodia, S., Samarati, P. (eds.) Proceedings of the 2002 ACM Workshop on Privacy in the Electronic Society, WPES 2002, Washington, DC, USA, November 21, 2002, pp. 91–102. ACM, New York (2002)
35. Rota, G.C.: The number of partitions of a set. American Mathematical Monthly 71, 498–504 (1964)
36. Serjantov, A., Danezis, G.: Towards an information theoretic metric for anonymity. In: Dingledine, R., Syverson, P.F. (eds.) PET 2002. LNCS, vol. 2482, pp. 41–53. Springer, Heidelberg (2003)
37. Steinbrecher, S., Köpsell, S.: Modelling unlinkability. In: Dingledine, R. (ed.) PET 2003. LNCS, vol. 2760, pp. 32–47. Springer, Heidelberg (2003)
38. Verheul, E.R.: Self-blindable credential certificates from the Weil pairing. In: Boyd, C. (ed.) ASIACRYPT 2001. LNCS, vol. 2248, pp. 533–551. Springer, Heidelberg (2001)

A   Counterexample to the Theorem in [37]

Theorem 1 in [37] claims that it cannot be reached that, for all arbitrarily chosen pairs $\{a_1, a_2\} \subseteq A$, $\Pr(a_1 \equiv_\tau a_2) = \Pr(a_1 \not\equiv_\tau a_2) = 1/2$, from the point of view of $\mathcal{A}_{H_2}$.[6] This is wrong as the claim does not hold, for example, if $|A| = 4$ and $H_2 = (1, 3)$. We remark that, more generally, the claim does not hold for all solutions of the system of equations

$$\sum_{\beta \in H_2} \beta = |A|, \qquad \sum_{\beta \in H_2} \beta^2 = \frac{|A|^2 + |A|}{2}.$$

B   Proof of (2) and (3)

Consider the task of dividing the elements in a set A into α subsets such that, for all $1 \leq i \leq \alpha$, the ith subset contains exactly β_i elements. One can perform this task by first ordering the elements in A, and then putting the first β_1 elements into the first subset, the next β_2 elements into the second subset, and so on. If one performs this task for all $|A|!$ orderings of A, one ends up with only $|A|!/(\beta_1! \cdot \beta_2! \cdots \beta_\alpha!)$ different outcomes, because permuting the elements in each

---

[6] The claim has been rephrased in order to fit our notation.

subset does not make a difference. Moreover, since the equivalence classes of a partition are *not* ordered, i.e. one can permute the equivalence classes of the same size without changing the partition, the number of *distinct* partitions that divide A into α subsets of cardinality $\beta_1, \beta_2, \ldots, \beta_\alpha$, is given by (2). Equation (3) follows as a special case. $\qquad\square$

C   Proof of (4)

Consider a set A, a partition $\{R_1, R_2, \ldots, R_\beta\} \vdash A$ that divides A into $\beta = |A|/\alpha$ subsets of equal cardinality α, and the task of dividing A into α subsets of equal cardinality β, such that each subset contains exactly one element from $R_1, R_2, \ldots, R_\beta$. For ease of presentation, assume that, for all $1 \leq i \leq \beta$, there exists an ordering on the elements in R_i. Then one can perform this task by grouping the first element in each of $R_1, R_2, \ldots, R_\beta$ into Q_1, the second element in each of $R_1, R_2, \ldots, R_\beta$ into Q_2, and so on. By doing this, one ends up with a partition $\{Q_1, Q_2, \ldots, Q_\alpha\} \vdash A$ that meets the requirements.

It is possible to construct another partition $\{Q_1, Q_2, \ldots, Q_\alpha\} \vdash A$ that meets the requirements by permuting the elements in $R_1, R_2, \ldots, R_\beta$ and then repeating the above procedure. Indeed, one can construct all partitions that meet the requirements by repeating the above procedure for all combinations of permutations of the elements in $R_1, R_2, \ldots, R_\beta$. If one does this for all such combinations, of which there exist $\kappa = |R_1|! \cdot |R_2|! \cdots |R_\beta|! = (\alpha!)^\beta$, each of the resulting κ partitions will appear exactly $\alpha!$ times, namely once for each permutation of the sets $Q_1, Q_2, \ldots, Q_\alpha$. Thus, the number of *distinct* partitions that divide A into α subsets of equal cardinality β, such that each subset contains exactly one element from $R_1, R_2, \ldots, R_\beta$, is given by (4). $\qquad\square$

D   Proof of (6)

Let (A, U) be a graph, and let $X(A, U)$ be the number of partitions of A such that each edge $e \in U$ connects two vertices in the same equivalence class, and $\Psi(A, U)$ the number of partitions such that no edge connects two vertices in the same equivalence class. We know from (5) that

$$X(A, U) = B_{\Phi(A,U)},$$

where $\Phi(A, U)$ denotes the number of connected components of (A, U) and B_n the n-th Bell number, i.e., the number of partitions of a set with n elements, see (1).

For a partition $\pi \vdash A$ and an edge $e \in U$ set $f_e(\pi) = 1$ if the vertices connected by e lie in the same equivalence class of π, and $f_e(\pi) = 0$ otherwise. Clearly,

$$X(A, U) = \sum_{\pi \vdash A} \prod_{e \in U} f_e(\pi)$$

because the product evaluates to 1 unless an edge connects two different equivalence classes, in which case it does not contribute to the sum. Similarly,

$$\Psi(A, U) = \sum_{\pi \vdash A} \prod_{e \in U} \left(1 - f_e(\pi)\right)$$

$$= \sum_{U' \subseteq U} (-1)^{|U'|} \sum_{\pi \vdash A} \prod_{e \in U'} f_e(\pi)$$

$$= \sum_{U' \subseteq U} (-1)^{|U'|} X(A, U'),$$

as was to be shown.   □

A Fresh Look at the Generalised Mix Framework

Andrei Serjantov

The Free Haven Project
schnur@gmail.com

Abstract. Anonymity systems designed to handle anonymous email
have been implemented with a variety of different mixes. Although many
of their properties have been analysed in previous work, some are still
not well understood and many results are still missing.

In this paper we reexamine the generalised mix framework and the
binomial mix of [7]. We show that under some parameterizations the
binomial mix has undesirable properties. More specifically, for any constant parameterization of the binomial mix, there is a minimum number
of messages beyond which it acts as a timed mix. In this case the number of messages inside it is no longer hidden from the adversary and the
mix is vulnerable to easy active attack. We suggest ways to avoid this
in the generalised mix framework. Secondly, we show that the binomial
distribution used in the framework produces distribution of pool sizes
with low variance and show how to improve on this.

Finally, we present a technique from queueing theory which allows us
to analyse this property for a class of mixes assuming Poisson message
arrivals.

1 Introduction

Anonymous email systems are commonly implemented using mixes [2]. To provide
anonymity a mix has to follow a cryptographic protocol which ensures bitwise unlinkability to prevent attackers linking messages based on their bit patterns and a
batching or reordering strategy to prevent timing attacks, i.e. adversaries linking
messages by simply watching them coming in and out of the mix.

In this paper we consider batching strategies of mixes used in real message-
based anonymity systems such as Mixmaster and Mixminion. In the remailer
community which runs these systems there is an ongoing debate about the properties of different batching strategies; we hope this work not only contributes to
this debate, but also helps influence the design of deployed systems and hence
improve the anonymity properties for their users. We start off by describing what
is perhaps the most sophisticated mix to date, the binomial mix.

The binomial mix has been proposed in [7] and further analysed in [4]. The
batching strategy of this mix is as follows: if the mix contains M messages, then
the number of messages to be forwarded on to their next hops (or destinations)
is determined by the number of heads obtained from tossing a biased coin for
each message. The bias of the coin is obtained from the function $g(M)$ which is
the cumulative normal distribution function.

N. Borisov and P. Golle (Eds.): PET 2007, LNCS 4776, pp. 17–29, 2007.

The rest of the paper is organized as follows: first we review the generalised mix framework. Then we look at the expected number of messages to be kept in the pool as a function of the number of messages in the mix for some existing mixes. We find that as the number of messages in the existing binomial mix increases, the expected size of the pool approaches zero and argue that this is undesirable. Another consequence of this is that the binomial mix loses its desirable property of hiding the number of messages inside it at high traffic volume. We then show that by altering the $g(M)$ function and the distribution from which the number of messages to be forwarded is drawn we can alter the expected size of the pool mix and its variance and hence retain the desirable properties of the binomial mix at high traffic volumes. Finally, we turn our attention to the distribution of the number of messages in the mix. We present a technique which allows us to calculate the distribution of messages inside the Stop and Go mix and to slight variants of the timed dynamic pool mix and the binomial mix assuming message arrivals are Poisson distributed.

2   The Generalised Mix Framework

The generalised mix framework and the binomial mix have evolved from the pool and the timed dynamic pool mixes [12]. The framework introduced two innovations: unlike in the case of the pool mixes where the number of messages to be forwarded is deterministic, it is now a random variable chosen from the binomial distribution[1], $\text{Bin}(M, g(M))$. The expectation of this random variable is determined by a function g of the number of messages in the mix. Before we proceed, let us set up the terminology explicitly.

- M is the number of messages in the mix at the start of the round
- X is the number of messages retained in the mix
- $P = g(M)$ where $g : [0, \infty) \rightarrow [0, 1]$ is the probability of forwarding each message

Hence a mix is specified almost entirely[2] by the function $g(M)$. Whilst this is enough to express the mix strategy in a concise manner, we argue that it is more insightful to look at $P(X = x|M)$, the conditional distribution of the number of messages retained in the pool and its expectation and variance. Clearly, the number of messages which stay in the mix follows a binomial distribution $\text{Bin}(M, 1 - g(M))$.

$$P(X = x|M) = \binom{M}{x} g(M)^{(1-x)}(1 - g(M))^x$$

$$\mathbb{E}[P(X = x|M)] = M(1 - g(M))$$

---

[1] Hence in most cases the attacker cannot tell with certainty how many messages are in the mix [7], but note [10].

[2] The only remaining parameter is t, how often the mix flushes.

$$\text{Var}[P(X = x|M)] = Mg(M)(1 - g(M))$$

We now proceed to look closely at the expectation of the size of the pool in various existing mixes[3] defined in the generalised mix framework, i.e. via $g(M)$ and compare their properties.

3   Expected Pool Size of Various Mixes

We start by comparing the relatively simple mixes from [12] which were further analysed in [10,11].

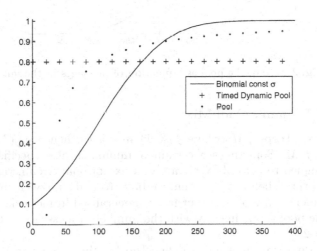

Fig. 1. The function $g(M)$ for some existing mixes

3.1   Timed Pool Mix

This mix always keeps n messages and outputs $M - n$. Note that although it is impossible to express exactly this behaviour in the binomial mix framework, it will suffice that the expected number of retained messages is n. See Figures 1 and 2 for a graphical representation of the properties of existing mixes.

$$g_p(M) = \begin{cases} 0 \text{ if } M \le n \\ \frac{M-n}{M} \text{ otherwise} \end{cases}$$

$$P(X = x|M) = \begin{cases} 0 \text{ if } M \le n \\ M - n \text{ otherwise} \end{cases}$$

---

[3] More precisely, their randomized versions.

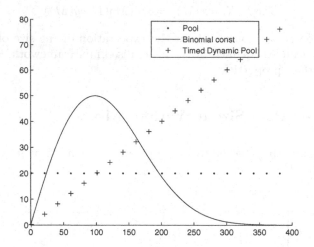

Fig. 2. Size of the pool as a function of messages in the mix

3.2   Timed Dynamic Pool Mix

This mix always keeps fM (where $f < 1$) messages, hence $g_{dp}(M) = f$ and outputs $(1 - f)M$. Sometimes a certain minimum is also specified, but this should be designed to act only very rarely in exceptional circumstance without changing the overall behaviour. Again, we have to make do with this being the expected number of messages output in our generalised framework. This clearly shows that the pool grows linearly with the number of messages in the mix. See Figures 1 and 2.

Clearly, the existing pool mixes define the limiting cases – a constant and a linear function. Let us now look at the binomial mix and see how it can be parameterized to behave as either of these.

4   The Binomial Mix

As mentioned above, the weight of the biased coin in the case of the binomial mix is determined from a cumulative distribution function of the normal distribution. The question that has not been addressed in the literature so far is *which* normal distribution. A normal distribution is uniquely defined by its mean and variance, $N(\mu, \sigma)$ hence the $g(M)$ of the binomial mix is as follows.

$$g(M, \mu, \sigma) = \int_{-\infty}^{M} \frac{1}{\sqrt{2\pi}\sigma} e^{-\frac{(M-\mu)^2}{2\sigma^2}}$$

Up to now it has been implicitly assumed that in $g(M, \mu, \sigma)$ μ and σ are independent of M (simply constants).

The function does not have a closed form representation; we illustrate functions with $\sigma = 100, \sigma = 0.3M, \sigma = 0.5M, \sigma = M$. The difference between these

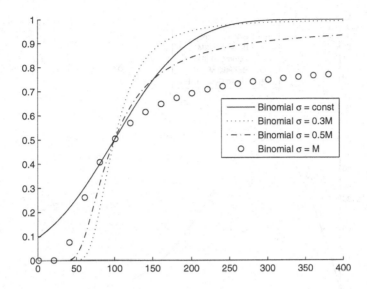

Fig. 3. Different parameterizations of the cumulative normal distribution function

may not seem significant, however, it is clearer when we examine the expected pool size as a function of M. This is illustrated in Figure 4.

Clearly, a binomial mix with a constant σ parameter $\lim_{M\to\infty} \mathbb{E}[P(X|M)] = 0$ approaches zero very quickly – the normal distribution has very thin tails. Hence at large M the constant-σ mix has turned into a simple timed mix. This is clearly undesirable: such a mix can be flushed in one round given a sufficiently high number of messages and hence admits an easy active attack [12].

The binomial parameterizations where σ is linear in M are much better. First, they retain the property of having a quickly increasing pool for small values of M, this can be adjusted via the μ parameter of the cumulative normal distribution function and behave like the timed dynamic mix at large values of M – linear pool size growth.

It is interesting to note that there are several alternatives, also expressed in the binomial mix framework. Hence below we present 3 mixes with 3 different properties: $\mathbb{E}[P(X|M)]$ approaching a non-zero constant (though this hardly helps with the active attack, the $g(M)$ function is simple and analytically tractable); logarithmic or square root growth. We show that in terms of the generalised mix definition they look quite similar, hence looking at the growth of the size of the pool has been an insightful exercise.

Properties of the new mixes are shown in Figure 5. Because the mixes are all expressed in the generalised framework, their anonymity and delay properties (although not in closed form) follow directly from [7,4,5]; we do not restate them here.

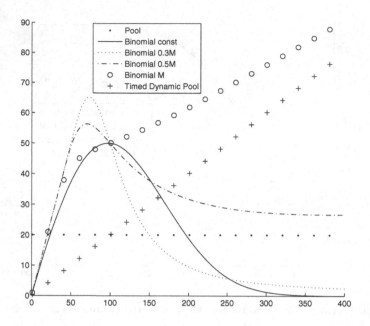

Fig. 4. Expected pool size for existing mixes and various parameterizations of the binomial mix

4.1 Binomial+ Mix

First we try to find a mix which is similar to the binomial mix, but can be adapted so that $\lim_{M\to\infty} P(M) = n$, i.e. it has a pool of at least n messages. We find the following function to be suitable:

$$g(M) = 1 - \frac{(M - n)e^{-kM} + n}{M}$$

$$\mathbb{E}[P(X|M)] = (M - n)e^{-kM} + n$$

Figure 5 uses $k = 0.01$. Indeed, $\mathbb{E}[P(X|M)]$ has a similar shape to that of the binomial mix.

4.2 Logarithmic and Square Root Mixes

If we seek to have slow growth of the pool size, we can have a logarithmic or a square root function for $\mathbb{E}[P(X|M)]$ and hence have $g_{\log}(M) = 1 - \frac{\log(M)}{M}$ and $g_{\mathrm{sqrt}}(M)) = 1 - \frac{1}{\sqrt{(M)}}$. Their behaviour is shown in Figure 5. A practical implementation may have lower bound on the size of the pool in either case; here we are concerned with the asymptotic properties only. Clearly, these mixes have higher expected delay but also higher anonymity.

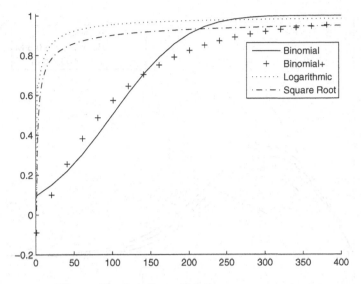

Fig. 5. The function $g(M)$ for some new mixes

5   Distribution of the Number of Messages to Forward

One of the benefits of introducing the binomial framework as presented in [7] is the fact that the binomial mix hides the number of messages inside it which makes it (slightly) more difficult to mount a blending attack on it[4]. And yet the obvious parameterization implies that (as the authors of the original paper conjecture) by sending a sufficiently high number of messages during a single round, all messages can be flushed from the mix with a high probability. Making this more precise, the probability of having a message retained in the mix is:

$$P(X \geq 1|M) = 1 - (g(M))^M$$

It is evident that this probability approaches 1 for the Logarithmic, the Square root and the Binomial+ mixes, and hence it is impossible to flush the mix in a single round and mount an easy active attack. What is less obvious (due to the lack of closed form representation of $g(M)$) is that this probability asymptotically approaches 0 for the binomial mix with constant σ[5]. Clearly, as we have seen above, this is not the case when σ is a function of M.

Attacking the same problem from a slightly different angle, if we examine the variance of the distribution $P(X|M)$, we find that while the variance for the number of messages sent out by the constant-σ binomial mix approaches zero with increasing M, it increases in the case of the other mixes. The expectation $\mathbb{E}[P(X|M)]$ and values of one standard deviation around it for the Binomial with constant σ, Binomial with $\sigma = 0.5M$ are shown in Figure 6.

---

[4] For a thorough analysis of similar issues for the existing mixes see [10].

[5] The reader is invited to verify this either by analytical or empirical means.

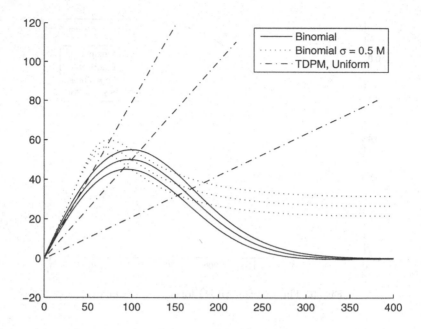

Fig. 6. Comparing Expectations and Standard Deviations of Pool Size

It is also clear that the variance of the pool size in the other mixes does not grow significantly as M increases. This naturally suggests a rethink of the generalised mix framework; instead of specifying $g(M)$, the mix should be defined by the probability distribution of the number of messages to be forwarded given the number of messages in the pool, $P(X = x|M)$, with $x \in \{0 \dots M\}$[6]. We have already seen the case where $P(X = x|M) = \text{Bin}(M, 1 - g(M))$, however there are many alternatives: the Hypergeometric distribution, the Uniform distribution, the Maximum Entropy Distribution which we describe further below or (the inelegant) discretized versions of the scaled Beta or the Normal distributions. Note, however, that from above we already have good candidates for the expectation of such distributions, namely the linear σ binomial, square root or logarithmic mix $g(M)$ functions.

We do not delve into the question of distributions too deeply, but show by example that the difference in the variance of the pool size is substantial and present the maximum entropy distribution which maximizes variance. We conjecture that such a distribution is optimal at hiding the number of messages in the mix.

Example 1. In this paper we described a version of the timed dynamic pool mix which had

$$[P(X|M)] = 0.5M$$

---

[6] Given X, we construct a random permutation of messages and forward the first X.

$$P(X = x|M) = \binom{M}{x} f^{(1-x)}(1-f)^x$$

Instead, we could have a timed dynamic pool mix with the same $[P(X|M)] = 0.5M$ but $P(X = x|M) = \text{Uniform}[0, M]$. The expectation value and the values one standard deviation away from it of such a timed dynamic pool mix are also shown on Figure 6.

The variance of the uniform distribution is $\frac{(M+1)^2-1}{12}$ which is greater than that of the binomial distribution, $M/4$. Note that given a set of values $\{0 \ldots M\}$, and a given expected value μ the maximum entropy distribution is of the following form:

$$P(X = x) = Cr^x$$

Using the facts that the sum of the probabilities equals 1 and the expectation equals μ allows us to determine the values for constants C and r. For example, if we have 100 messages in the mix, we may flush between zero and 100. We wish to use the maximum entropy distribution to determine how many should be flushed, with the expected number set at 20 messages. Using numerical methods to obtain C and r, we find that the distribution to use is as follows:

$$P(X = x) = 1.58342(-0.986546)^x$$

Naturally, if $\mu = M/2$, the maximum entropy distribution is simply the uniform distribution.

6   Distribution of the Number of Messages in Mixes

The number of messages inside simple mixes during operation is well understood. For example, the threshold mix contains no more than N messages, the timed mix contains quite simply all the messages which have arrived since the last flush, the timed pool mix contains all the messages which have arrived since the last flush plus n, the size of the pool. For more complex mixes, this number or rather, the distribution of the number of messages inside the mix is not so clear. Yet a mix can only store a finite number of messages, so this distribution needs to be understood in order to minimize the probability of a message having to be dropped. This, in part, has originally motivated the choice of $g(M)$ of the binomial mix which makes it behave as a simple timed mix at high loads.

In the first part of this paper we showed that both the timed dynamic pool mix and the improved parameterization of the binomial mix retain a constant fraction of messages – they both have the property that $lim_{M \to \infty} g(M) = c$ for $c < 1$. In this section we present a method for determining the distribution of the number of messages inside various mixes, in particular the Timed Dynamic Pool Mix. Such a method allows us to to determine the probability of the mix running out of space and hence select a suitable parameterization to avoid this.

First, we consider Stop and Go Mix introduced by Kesdogan in [9]. It delays each message individually by an amount picked from an exponential distribution.

Assuming Poisson distribution of message arrivals, we can model it as an $M/M/n$ process and use standard queuing theory techniques [3] as we informally outline below.

We proceed by denoting a mix as an n-state system where $n - 1$ is the maximum possible number of messages in the mix. We assume message arrivals are distributed with a Poisson distribution with parameter λ and the time between flushes is distributed exponentially with parameter μ. The system changes state when either one message arrives (with probability λ) or one message leaves (with probability μ). For example, take a mix which can hold a maximum of three messages. The rates of transitions between states 0 to 3 (0,1,2 or 3 messages inside the mix) are as follows:

$$
A_{sg} = \begin{pmatrix} -\lambda & \mu & 0 & 0 \\ \lambda & -(\lambda + \mu) & \mu & 0 \\ 0 & \lambda & -(\mu + \lambda) & \mu \\ 0 & 0 & \lambda & -\mu \end{pmatrix}
$$

The rows represents the state of the mix. We see that the rate of transition out of state 0 and into to state 1 is λ – this is the probability that a message arrives at the mix. Similarly, the rate of transition into state 0 from state 1 is μ. Reading row 2, the rate of transition into state 1 is λ from state 0, μ from state 3 and $-(\lambda + \mu)$ to account for the probabilities of a message arriving or leaving while the mix is in state 2.

Now, we seek a vector of probabilities P such that the system is in equilibrium, i.e. there is no net inflow or outflow from each state. Our last constraint is that the probabilities sum to 1. We now solve the system of linear equations $AP = 0$ together with $\sum P = 1$ and obtain P, the probabilities of finding the system in each state. For instance, when $\lambda = 1/3$ and $\mu = 1/2$, the distribution of messages in the 4 state mix defined above is: $[0.4154, 0.2769, 0.1846, 0.1231]$.

The same technique can be used directly for a mix with exponential inter-flush times but which, like the timed dynamic pool mix, flushes deterministic batches of messages. The transition matrix for this mix ($f = 0.5$) differs from the one above only by the position of the μ in the right hand column – the mix transitions from having 3 messages inside it to having 1.

$$
A_{tdpm} = \begin{pmatrix} -\lambda & \mu & 0 & 0 \\ \lambda & -(\lambda + \mu) & \mu & \mu \\ 0 & \lambda & -(\mu + \lambda) & 0 \\ 0 & 0 & \lambda & -\mu \end{pmatrix}
$$

The vector of probabilities is now $[0.4737, 0.3158, 0.1263, 0.0842]$. The probabilities of high states are lower because more messages get forwarded on some of the flushes, hence fewer remains in the mix. As a further example of the capabilities of this technique, we calculated the distribution of the number of messages inside a pool and a timed dynamic pool mixes, each with maximum capacity 100 messages. These are illustrated in Figure 7.

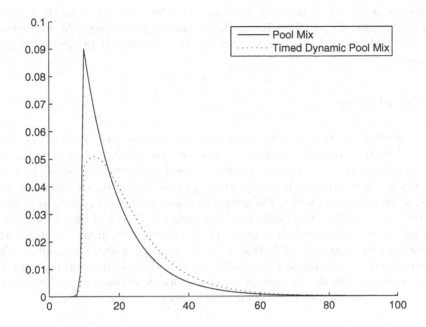

Fig. 7. Distributions of the number of messages inside mixes. $\lambda = 5$, $\mu = 0.5$

This technique is efficient and allows us to calculate the probability distribution of the number of messages inside mixes with arbitrary $P(X = x|M)$ with exponential inter-flush times in an environment with Poisson-distributed inter-arrival times. Hence a slight modification of the binomial mix with exponential inter-flush times falls into this category and can now be analysed.

More advanced queueing theory tools are needed to consider other known mixes. To be more precise, mixes with Poisson arrivals and arbitrary distributions of inter-flush times can be described by a $M/G/n$ model and those with deterministic inter-flush times (for instance Pool or Timed Dynamic Pool mixes) fit the $M/D/s$ model. The interested reader is invited to refer to [3].

In this section we assumed that message inter-arrival times are Poisson distributed. To the best of our knowledge, the only work investigating the issue is [6]; there the authors find a large structural break in their data sample. We briefly reexamined the same data and looking at shorter time horizons we find the distribution broadly Poisson; though a full empirical investigation of inter-arrival times is long overdue we do not consider the issue here. From the theoretical point of view, the number of messages inside a mix which forwards a constant fraction of messages (such as the linear-σ binomial or the timed dynamic pool mix) follows a mean reverting Ornstein-Uhlenberg stochastic process with non-Gaussian increments (the increments model the distribution of the number of messages arriving in one batch). Theories of such processes with arbitrary increments exist[7]; in particular it is reassuring that under reasonable assumptions the implied distributions inside the mixes are stationary. The mathematically inclined reader is referred to [1,8] for (very complex) properties of such processes.

7   Conclusion

In this paper we drew attention to the asymptotic properties of mixes. By considering how the size of the pool mix grows with the number of messages in the mix, we showed that the obvious previously used parameterization of the binomial mix has some undesirable properties and proposed a fix. We have also suggested some new mixes within the generalised mix framework. Next, we showed that the variance of the previously used binomial mix is zero at high loads, hence it no longer has pool size hiding properties. Furthermore, mixes which use the generalised mix framework all have small variance of pool size. We propose using arbitrary distributions for pool size and show how this can increase the variance of the pool size. Finally, we present a method for determining the distribution of messages inside various mixes assuming Poisson message arrivals.

References

1. Barndorff-Nielsen, O.E., Shepard, N.: Non-gaussian OU based models and some of their uses in financial economics and modelling by Levy processes for financial econometrics. Economics Papers 1999-w9/2000-w3, Economics Group, Nuffield College, University of Oxford (2000)
2. Chaum, D.: Untraceable electronic mail, return addresses, and digital pseudonyms. Communications of the ACM 4(2) (February 1981)
3. Cooper, R.: Introduction to Queueing Theory. North-Holland, New York (1981)
4. Díaz, C.: Anonymity and Privacy in Electronic Services. PhD thesis, Katholieke Universiteit Leuven, Leuven, Belgium (December 2005)
5. Díaz, C., Preneel, B.: Reasoning about the anonymity provided by pool mixes that generate dummy traffic. In: Fridrich, J. (ed.) IH 2004. LNCS, vol. 3200, Springer, Heidelberg (2004)
6. Díaz, C., Sassaman, L., Dewitte, E.: Comparison between two practical mix designs. In: Samarati, P., Ryan, P.Y A, Gollmann, D., Molva, R. (eds.) ESORICS 2004. LNCS, vol. 3193, Springer, Heidelberg (2004)
7. Díaz, C., Serjantov, A.: Generalising mixes. In: Dingledine, R. (ed.) PET 2003. LNCS, vol. 2760, Springer, Heidelberg (2003)
8. James, L.F.: Laws and likelihoods for Ornstein Uhlenbeck-Gamma and other BNS OU stochastic volatilty models with extensions (2006),
   ⟨http://www.citebase.org/abstract?id=oai:arXiv.org:math/0604086⟩
9. Kesdogan, D., Egner, J., Büschkes, R.: Stop-and-go MIXes: Providing probabilistic anonymity in an open system. In: Aucsmith, D. (ed.) IH 1998. LNCS, vol. 1525, Springer, Heidelberg (1998)

---

[7] They turn out to be useful in modeling stochastic volatility and electricity prices(!).

10. O'Connor, L.: On blending attacks for mixes with memory. In: Barni, M., Herrera-Joancomartí, J., Katzenbeisser, S., Pérez-González, F. (eds.) IH 2005. LNCS, vol. 3727, Springer, Heidelberg (2005)
11. Serjantov, A.: On the Anonymity of Anonymity Systems. PhD thesis, University of Cambridge (June 2004)
12. Serjantov, A., Dingledine, R., Syverson, P.: From a trickle to a flood: Active attacks on several mix types. In: Petitcolas, F.A.P. (ed.) IH 2002. LNCS, vol. 2578, Springer, Heidelberg (2003)

Two-Sided Statistical Disclosure Attack

George Danezis, Claudia Diaz, and Carmela Troncoso

K.U. Leuven, ESAT/COSIC,
Kasteelpark Arenberg 10,
B-3001 Leuven-Heverlee, Belgium
{George.Danezis,Claudia.Diaz,Carmela.Troncoso}@esat.kuleuven.be

Abstract. We introduce a new traffic analysis attack: the Two-sided Statistical Disclosure Attack, that tries to uncover the receivers of messages sent through an anonymizing network supporting anonymous replies. We provide an abstract model of an anonymity system with users that reply to messages. Based on this model, we propose a linear approximation describing the likely receivers of sent messages. Using simulations, we evaluate the new attack given different traffic characteristics and we show that it is superior to previous attacks when replies are routed in the system.

1 Introduction

Anonymous communications systems have been studied since 1981, when David Chaum first proposed the mix [2]. Yet, it has been known for some time that anonymity systems, not offering full unobservability, are insecure against long term Disclosure [1] and Statistical Disclosure Attacks [3] (SDA).

In this work, we extend Statistical Disclosure Attacks [3] in order to model user's behavior that deviates from the standard model considered so far in the literature. We consider that users not only *send messages* to a list of contacts, but also *reply to received messages* with some probability. Despite the real-world significance of modeling systems that allow anonymous replies, this is the first in-depth study of their security.

An adversary deploying our *Two-sided Statistical Disclosure Attack* (TS-SDA) takes into account the fact that some messages sent by a target user Alice are replies, in order to infer information on the set of Alice's contacts, and trace individual messages more effectively. This is done by combining information from sender and receiver anonymity sets when tracing replies.

We show through simulations that the Two-sided Statistical Disclosure Attacks give much better results than the traditional Statistical Disclosure Attacks, when tracing anonymized traffic that contains replies. We also evaluate how the effectiveness of our attacks is influenced by users' behavior (e.g., how often users reply, or how long it takes them to reply).

This paper is organized as follows: We review the relevant previous work concerning Disclosure Attacks in Sect. 2. Section 3 describes our model of the network and the users' behavior. Section 4 introduces our attacks, which are

N. Borisov and P. Golle (Eds.): PET 2007, LNCS 4776, pp. 30–44, 2007.

evaluated through simulations in Sect. 5. Finally, some thoughts on extending the attacks are discussed in Sect. 6, and we offer our conclusions in Sect. 7.

2   Background and Related Work

The field of anonymous communications started in 1981 with David Chaum's mix [2]. A mix is a relaying router that ensures, through cryptography and reordering techniques, that input messages cannot be linked to output messages, therefore providing anonymity. Based on these ideas, specialized cryptographic communication protocols exist for 'remailing' email messages, and the latest standard, Mixminion [4], allows users not only to send, but also to anonymously reply to email messages.

Despite the level of protection that mix networks provide, they still leak some information. An external observer is able to find out the identities (or at least network addresses) of mix users sending or receiving messages, as well as the exact time messages are sent and received. We can find in the literature a powerful family of *Disclosure Attacks* [1], first proposed by Kesdogan *et al.* [8]. These attacks allow an observer to learn the correspondents of each user and, in the long run, de-anonymize their messages. To counter these attacks, there is new research towards unobservable mix networks, such Nonesuch [7], where the users send their messages to the anonymity system as stegotext hidden inside Usenet postings.

The Disclosure Attack relies on a simple model for anonymous communications and user behavior. The target user, Alice, communicates only with her contacts (a subset of all possible recipients), while the other users send to all possible recipients with uniform probability. All users send their messages through a simple threshold mix [2]. This type of mix collects a certain number of messages (the threshold), and sends them to their destinations in a random order. An adversary only learns the public parameters of they system, and, in each round, who is sending and receiving messages. With no further information, the adversary can learn the set of contacts of Alice.

The two key shortcomings of the Disclosure Attack are its reliance on solving an NP-complete problem, and its sensitivity to deviations from the simple user behavior and communication models considered. The computational efficiency of the attack has been reduced by the Hitting Set Attack [9] where simple heuristics are used to evaluate the most likely set of Alice's contacts, which are tested to see if they are acceptable solutions. This leads to quick and exact results, yet the Hitting Set attack is still sensitive to even slight changes in the model. Allowing flexible models for user behavior and communication is key to understanding the security of real-world anonymous systems, since neither the systems nor the users' behavior fit perfectly idealized models.

A different style of attack, the Statistical Disclosure Attack (SDA) [3], considers the same user behavior and communication model, but reduces the computation complexity by using statistical models and approximations to reveal the same information to an attacker. The Statistical Disclosure Attack has been extended to situations where the anonymity system is a pool mix, instead of a simple threshold mix [5]. This demonstrates that its underlying principles provide enough flexibility to successfully model complex anonymity systems. Even more complex models were evaluated by simulation in [10]. In this paper, we present a variant of the Statistical Disclosure Attack to de-anonymize traffic containing replies.

3   Mix Networks with Anonymous Replies

Building systems that allow full bi-directional anonymity, as first suggested by David Chaum in 1981, has been a key goal for anonymous communication designers. The latest remailer, Mixminion, offers this feature through the use of *single use reply blocks* (SURBs), cryptographic tokens that can be used to anonymously route back reply messages through a mix network. One of the key requirements of the Mixminion reply mechanism was to make replies indistinguishable from normal messages: an adversary observing a message leaving a user is not able to tell, from the bit string of the message or the processing that is applied to it in the first few mixes, if it is a reply or a normal message.

Our objective is to study the anonymity of messages in a network, such as Mixminion, that allows anonymous replies. For this reason, we modify the user behavior model of the Disclosure Attacks to accommodate replies, while considering that they are semantically indistinguishable from normal forward messages. In our new models, users send messages to the anonymity network either to initiate a discussion with one of their contacts, or to reply to a message they have received.

Following the spirit of previous Statistical Disclosure Attacks we describe many aspects of the system, such as the choice of conversation partners, the fact of replying to a message, and the time taken to send replies, as being sampled from *independent* probability distributions. We model users' initiation of new discussions as a Poisson process, and their choice of conversation partners is a sample out of a distribution of contacts. Messages are replied to with a known probability, and the time it takes to send the reply is exponentially distributed.

3.1   A Formal Model for Message Replies

We assume that there are N users in the system that send and receive messages. Each user $n \in [0, N-1]$ has a probability distribution D_n of sending to other users. We consider that the target user Alice has a distribution D_A of sending to a subset of her $k \in N$ contacts with uniform probability $1/k$. We have considered two models for the rest of the users: in the first case, they send with uniform probability $1/N$ to the N users. In the second case, they send to a subset $k \in N$, as Alice does. All users initiate discussions according to a Poisson process with rate λ_I. An array notation denotes the probability user n initiates a conversation with user m (i.e., $D_n[m]$), and the distribution over all users should sum up to one (i.e., $\sum_{\forall m \in N} D_n[m] = 1$). Figure 1 depicts our system model.

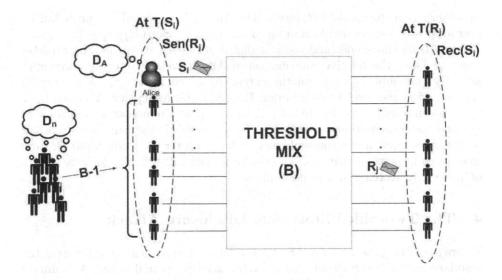

Fig. 1. System model

Alice, the target of the attack, is the only user that we initially model as replying to messages. She replies to received messages with probability r. If a reply is to be sent, it is done some time after the message it replies to was received. The reply delay is a sample from an exponential distribution with parameter (rate) λ_r. We have also considered a model in which all users reply to messages. We note that relationships are not symmetric in our system, and therefore the set of senders to which users reply to is not the same as the set of receivers considered in D_n.

The adversary knows the overall replying behavior of Alice, namely the probability of a reply r and the reply delay rate λ_r. He also knows the number of users in the system N and the rate λ_I at which discussions are initiated by them. The objective of the adversary is to uncover D_A.

A passive observer of the system can see when users send or receive messages. In our analysis, we only look at the messages received and sent by Alice. We denote K_s and K_r the total number of messages sent and received by Alice, respectively, within the time window $[0, t_{max}]$ in which the system is observed. An adversary has accurate information about the time each message was sent or received, denoted as $T(S_i)$ and $T(R_j)$ for sent message i and received message j, respectively.

We consider that the adversary is observing all messages going in and out of the anonymity system, and can therefore calculate the probabilities describing the likely receivers or senders of each message. We denote the distribution over all N potential senders for a received message R_j as $\mathbf{Sen}(R_j)$, and over the receivers of a sent message S_i as $\mathbf{Rec}(S_i)$. We use an array notation to denote the probability of individual senders or receivers (e.g., $\mathbf{Sen}(R_j)[n]$ for the probability that user n sent the message R_j received by Alice). As expected, the probabilities over all possible users should sum up to one ($\sum_{\forall n \in N} \mathbf{Sen}(R_j)[n] = 1$).

Aside from the sender and receiver distributions for messages, the attacker needs to know the relative contribution of Alice's messages to the anonymity sets. By contribution we mean the extent to which inputs S_i from Alice in the mix affect the receiver distribution $\mathbf{Rec}(S_i)$. Assuming that Alice sends α_r messages in round r, we denote the relative contribution messages from Alice as $\frac{\alpha_r}{B}$, and the contributions for others as $\frac{B - \alpha_r}{B}$, as this is the contribution of her α_r messages input into a threshold mix with parameter (i.e., threshold) B. Note that an equivalent quantity can be calculated without difficulty for other types of anonymity systems such as pool mixes.

4   The Two-Sided Statistical Disclosure Attack

Before presenting the Two-sided Statistical Disclosure Attack we will present the standard Statistical Disclosure Attack in terms of our formal model. A summary of all the notation is given in Table 1:

Table 1. Variables used in the model and the attacks

Name	Description
N	Number of users in the system
D_A	The distribution of contacts of Alice
D_n	The distribution of contacts of other users
λ_I	The rate of message initiations
r	Probability a message is replied to
λ_r	The rate at which messages are replied to
B	The threshold of the mix
t_{max}	The total observation time
K_s, K_r	The total number of messages Alice sends and receives
$S_i, T(S_i)$	Alice's i^{th} sent message and the time it was sent
$\mathbf{Rec}(S_i)$	The receiver distribution for message S_i
$R_j, T(R_j)$	Alice's j^{th} received message and the time it was received
$\mathbf{Sen}(R_j)$	The sender distribution for message R_j
α_r	The number of messages sent by Alice in batch round r
Z_I	The expected volume of discussion initiations for each unit of time
Z_r	The expected volume of replies for a unit of time
Z_{rj}	The expected volume of replies to R_j
I_{ij}	The intersection of distributions ($\mathbf{Sen}(R_j)$ and $\mathbf{Rec}(S_i)$) of messages R_j and S_i

4.1   The 'Traditional' Statistical Disclosure Attack

The traditional Statistical Disclosure Attack (SDA) works by observing the receiver anonymity sets of all messages sent by Alice, and aggregating them to infer the probability distribution D_A. The messages in the receiver anonymity set $\mathbf{Rec}(S_i)$ of each message sent by Alice are assumed to be drawn from a distribution that is a mixture between the contacts of Alice (D_A) and the contacts of everyone else D_n:

$$\mathbf{Rec}(S_i) \sim \frac{1}{B} D_A + \frac{B-1}{B} D_n \tag{1}$$

The distributions describing the contacts of the rest of the users are approximated by using a uniform distribution U over all the possible senders. The adversary estimates the distribution D_A after a number observations K_s as:

$$\widehat{D_A} \approx \frac{1}{K_s} \sum_{\forall i \in [0, K_s - 1]} [B \cdot \mathbf{Rec}(S_i) - (B-1) \cdot D_n] \tag{2}$$

The estimation $\widehat{D_A}$ can then be used to infer the likelihood of the receiver corresponding to Alice in each round, by calculating:

$$\mathbf{Rec}(S_i)' = \frac{\mathbf{Rec}(S_i) \cdot \widehat{D_A}}{|\mathbf{Rec}(S_i) \cdot \widehat{D_A}|} \tag{3}$$

The key advantage of the statistical versions of the Disclosure Attack is their speed. It requires $\mathcal{O}(K_s)$ vector additions to estimate D_A, and a further $\mathcal{O}(K_s)$ vector inner product calculations to get the estimates for the receiver of each round. Since vectors $\mathbf{Rec}(S_i)$ are sparse, both operations can be done very efficiently, and in parallel.

The downside of statistical attacks is that they are not exact. They do not take into account the basic constraint that a message can only be sent by one sender. This may lead to wrong results if too few samples are used to estimate D_A.

4.2   The Two-Sided Statistical Disclosure Attack

The *Two-sided Statistical Disclosure Attack* (TS-SDA) takes into account the messages received by Alice (and the information about their potential senders), as well as the time of reception and sending of all messages. The aim of the attack is twofold: to estimate the distribution of contacts of Alice D_A, and to infer the receivers of all the messages sent by Alice (i.e., forward messages she has initialized, and replies to messages she has received).

As in the Statistical Disclosure Attack (SDA), we will consider the output of each round of mixing (i.e., the distribution of potential receivers corresponding to each message) as the outcome of a mixture distribution. The components of this mixture are: the distribution D_A of contacts of Alice, the distribution D_n of the other senders, and the potential recipients of replies. Therefore, we need to *approximate* the relative weight of the contribution of each of these distributions to compute the receiver distribution.

Weight of normal messages. Let us consider a specific message, S_i sent by Alice. What is the relative probability of it being a discussion initiated by Alice, versus the probability of being a reply? We approximate this probability Z_I by calculating the estimated number of discussions initiated by Alice that should occur at time $T(S_i)$, which is equal to:

$$\mathbb{E}(\text{Initiated discussion at } T(S_i)) = \frac{K_s}{\lambda_I \cdot t_{\max}} \equiv Z_I \qquad (4)$$

The rationale behind this approximation is the following: the adversary observes Alice sending K_s messages which are a-priori equally likely to be an initiated discussion. Given that Alice initiates messages with rate λ_I, we expect an average of $\lambda_I \cdot t_{\max}$ discussions to be initiated by her over the total observation time $t_{\max}$.

Weight of replies. Similarly, we want to estimate the expected number of replies that would be sent at time $T(S_i)$. This expectation depends on the times messages R_j have been received by Alice before $T(S_i)$, and it is approximated by:

$$\mathbb{E}(\text{Reply to } R_j \text{ at } T(S_i)) = r \cdot \frac{\exp_{\lambda_r}(T(S_i) - T(R_j))}{\sum_{\forall k. T(R_j) < T(S_k)} \exp_{\lambda_r}(T(S_k) - T(R_j))} \equiv Z_{rj}$$

$$(5)$$

$$\mathbb{E}(\text{Replies at } T(S_i)) = \sum_{\forall j. T(R_j) < T(S_i)} Z_{rj} \equiv Z_r \qquad (6)$$

A reply to message R_j is only generated with probability r. If it is generated, then it corresponds to S_i with a certain probability Z_{rj}. This probability is computed by considering the likelihood that the reply was sent at $T(S_i)$, normalized by the likelihood of the reply corresponding to any message S_k, sent after R_j was received (i.e., $T(R_j) < T(S_k)$). We have assumed that messages are answered after a delay distributed exponentially with parameter λ_r (i.e., $\exp_{\lambda_r}(t) = \lambda_r \cdot e^{-\lambda_r t}$). Summing over all messages R_j in the past gives us the likelihood Z_r of message S_i being a reply.

Full model. If message S_i is a reply to message R_j, then we can get even more of information about its destination. We intersect the receiver distribution $\mathbf{Rec}(S_i)$ for sent message, S_i, and the sender distribution $\mathbf{Sen}(R_j)$ for received message R_j, and thus obtain a probability distribution I_{ij} which describes the likely receiver of S_i:

$$I_{ij} = \frac{\mathbf{Rec}(S_i) \cdot \mathbf{Sen}(R_j)}{|\mathbf{Rec}(S_i) \cdot \mathbf{Sen}(R_j)|} \qquad (7)$$

Given the different weights Z_I, Z_r and Z_{rj}, we can model the distribution of receivers corresponding to the round of a message S_i. We do so by combining the distributions $\mathbf{D_A}$, $\mathbf{D_n}$ and the intersection I_{ij} for the replies, while taking into account that Alice sends a total of α_r messages in round r:

The figure below depicts the rationale behind our model. We look at the receivers at the output of the round r of mixing when Alice sends messages $S_i \ldots S_{i-\alpha_r-1}$, and consider what information they convey about her. Each message coming out of this round of mixing could correspond a message sent by Alice,

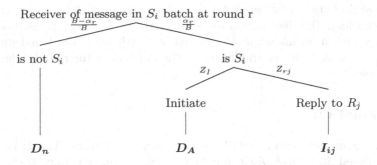

Fig. 2. An illustration of the components of equation 8

or to a message sent by another participant (drawn at random from D_n). If the message corresponds to S_i, then it can either be a discussion initiation, drawn from D_A, or a reply. Analytically we approximate the distribution $\mathbf{Rec}(S_i)$ as:

$$\mathbf{Rec}(S_i) \sim \frac{\alpha_r}{B} \frac{Z_I \cdot D_A + \sum_j Z_{rj} I_{ij}}{Z_I + Z_r} + \frac{B - \alpha_r}{B} D_n \qquad (8)$$

The probabilities $\frac{\alpha_r}{B}$ and $\frac{B-\alpha_r}{B}$ describe the relative weight of Alice's α_r messages, versus the messages of the other senders (modeled by the distribution D_n). The distributions I_{ij} are the normalized intersection of the potential set of senders of R_j with the set of possible receivers of S_i. Each of the I_{ij} are weighted by the factor Z_{rj}, which describes the likelihood S_i is indeed a reply to R_j.

As in the Statistical Disclosure Attack, we solve (8) for D_A and average the (very noisy) estimates for all sent messages S_i, in order to get the estimate $\widehat{D_A}$:

$$D_A \sim \frac{(B \cdot \mathbf{Rec}(S_i)) - (B - \alpha_r) \cdot D_n)(Z_I + Z_r) - \sum_j Z_{rj} I_{ij}}{\alpha_r Z_I} \equiv C_i \qquad (9)$$

$$\widehat{D_A} \approx \frac{1}{K_s} \sum_{\forall i} C_i \qquad (10)$$

Finally, the estimate $\widehat{D_A}$ is in turn used to calculate the distribution of potential receivers for each message S_i:

$$\mathbf{Rec}(S_i)' \sim \left(\frac{\alpha_r}{B} \frac{Z_I \cdot \widehat{D_A} + \sum_j Z_{rj} I_{ij}}{Z_I + Z_r} + \frac{B - \alpha_r}{B} D_n \right) \cdot \mathbf{Rec}(S_i) \qquad (11)$$

Our best guess for the actual receiver of message S_i is the intersection of the a-priori distribution of senders (given the volume of normal messages and replies sent by Alice) as well as their timing (the first term of (11)) and the actual receiver anonymity set for the round, $\mathbf{Rec}(S_i)$.

All the quantities needed to estimate $\mathbf{Rec}(S_i)'$ are known except for the distributions D_n describing the background traffic generated by other users. The traditional Statistical Disclosure Attack, following the model of the Disclosure Attack, considers this distribution to be uniform U ($U[i] = 1/N$). Instead, in the TS-SDA we use a technique, first proposed by Mathewson and Dingledine [10], that estimates D_n from the traffic seen in the network in the rounds when Alice is not present.

5   Evaluation

We evaluate our new Two-Sided Statistical Disclosure Attack (TS-SDA) against the traditional Statistical Disclosure Attack (SDA) under various traffic conditions. In order to compare them and understand which parameters of the system affect their performance, we define a set of *standard parameters* that are summarized in Table 2.

Table 2. Standard parameters of the experiments

Name	Value	Description
N	1000	Number of participants
k	20	Number of contacts of Alice
B	100	Threshold of the mix
t_{max}	4000	Observation time
λ_I	0.1	Initiation rate
r	0.5	Reply probability
λ_r	0.5	Reply delay rate

These parameters were chosen to depict an average system: the threshold is large enough to accommodate a good fraction of senders and receivers (about 1/10) and nodes send enough messages and replies to illustrate our techniques. Note that the rate at which replies are sent ($\lambda_r = 0.5$) is higher than the rate at which discussions are initiated ($\lambda_I = 0.1$). The choice of this parameter was based on the intuition that replies are sent much faster (with respect to the time of reception of the message that originated them) than messages initiated by a user (with respect to the last initiation).

In our analysis so far we have assumed nothing about Alice's distribution D_A. For the sake of simplifying our experiments, we have assumed that the probability mass is distributed equally between k contacts of Alice, meaning that Alice chooses at random between them when she wants to initiate a discussion. Again, the ratio between the number of Alice's contacts k and the total number of users N reflects values observed in a medium size systems ($k/N = 2\%$). It is important to note though, that the statistical attacks should work with arbitrary D_A (although the time needed to discard the unlikely components of D_A would be larger.)

The final output of the TS-SDA attack is a probability distribution $\mathbf{Rec}(S_i)'$ for each message S_i that Alice has sent. These distributions describe the belief of the adversary as to who is the receiver of message S_i. We evaluate our attacks by looking at the *rank* that the real receivers of S_i have in the distributions $\mathbf{Rec}(S_i)'$. The rank is the *number of receivers* in distribution $\mathbf{Rec}(S_i)'$ that have at least the same probability as the real receiver, and would therefore mislead the adversary in its attempts to trace the message[1]. Intuitively, this is equivalent to ordering receivers according to their probabilities, and using the position of the real receiver as a metric. Low ranks show that the attack is more successful.

In each round of the attack, we have a collection of ranks, one for each message S_i the adversary wants to trace. This distribution of ranks is represented in our graphs using box plots containing information about their maximum value, first quartile (Q_1), median, third quartile (Q_3) and maximum value. The box plots also depict outliers; i.e., ranks p that are very far from the rest of the distribution ($p > Q_3 + 1.5(Q_3 - Q_1)$ or $p < Q_1 - 1.5(Q_3 - Q_1)$). The box plots and outliers give a good overview of the tails of the rank distribution, which is crucial in our evaluation.

Fig. 3, compares the performance of the Statistical Disclosure Attack (SDA) to the Two-Sided Statistical Disclosure Attack (TS-SDA), as a user is observed for more time using the standard parameters. While the accuracy of both attacks increases with time, the TS-SDA always provides better results than the SDA. After 4000 ticks the TS-SDA classifies the correct sender within the 20 first candidates 3/4 of the time (for the SDA it is within ~ 35, 3/4 of the time).

It is important to explain why the key difference between the TS-SDA and the SDA can only be seen at the tail of the distributions, while their first quartile (Q_1) and median are about the same. For this, we need to understand better the strengths of each attack. Figure 4 shows the effectiveness of both attacks in tracing discussion initiation messages and replies (in a system using the standard parameters). We we can see that the TS-SDA and the SDA perform equally well in de-anonymizing discussion initiations (the SDA often performs slightly better). However, the main strength of the TS-SDA is its effectiveness in uncovering the recipients of replies, while the simple SDA is remarkably bad at it.

This explains in Fig. 3 the fact that the two attacks have the same first quartile and median: most messages in the system are discussion initiations, and therefore the attacks perform equally well for them. The difference appears only for the minority of messages that are replies, giving the SDA distribution of ranks a much heavier tail.

As we have seen, the TS-SDA outperforms the SDA mostly in its ability to trace replies. In Fig. 5 we show the sensitivity of both the SDA and TS-SDA to the reply parameters. We can see in the first graph that in the absence of

---

[1] Why not use metrics based on Information Theory? The traffic analysis models we use in the (TS-)SDA are only approximations of the real-world as well as the theoretical sending models. Therefore the distributions $\mathbf{Rec}(S_i)'$ give us only partial information about the actual receivers and are sometimes (as we show) just wrong. before applying the information theoretic metrics for anonymity, one would need to look at the mutual information between $\mathbf{Rec}(S_i)'$ and the actual receivers to understand the biases in the approximations.

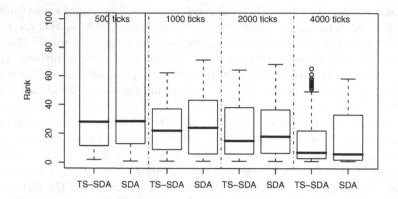

Fig. 3. Distribution of the ranks of the actual receivers after the Statistical Disclosure and Two-sided Statistical Disclosure attacks were applied. The estimation of $\widehat{D_A}$ was after $500, 1000, 2000$ and 4000 ticks, and has a dramatic effect on the effectiveness of the attack. (Some outliers are not shown.)

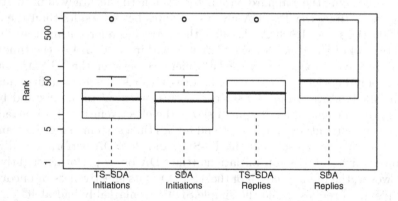

Fig. 4. (*Note the logarithmic scale.*) The effectiveness of the Two-sided Statistical Disclosure and traditional Statistical Disclosure attacks in de-anonymizing discussion initiation messages opposite to replies. The key advantage of the TS-SDA is its ability to correctly handle replies.

replies both attacks yield similar results. The graph labeled "Normal" shows the results for the standard parameters of our simulations, where our attack is more accurate that the SDA.

As messages are replied to at a slower rate ($\lambda_r = 0.025$), both attacks become less effective, since discussion initiations and replies become difficult to distinguish using timing information. The TS-SDA does not benefit any more from being able to intersect receiver and sender anonymity sets, and the standard SDA is subject to more noise. The consequences of this worsening are rather important, since it gives us a idea on how to resist the TS-SDA, and make use of the noise generated by the replies defensively.

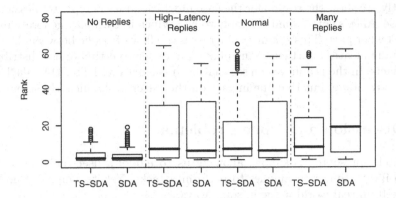

Fig. 5. The effectiveness of the Two-sided Statistical Disclosure and traditional Statistical Disclosure attacks for different types of traffic. With no replies, at high latency times ($\lambda_r = 0.025$), standard conditions and many replies ($r = 0.95$).

When we have more replies (graph "Many Replies," with probability of reply $r = 0.95$) the TS-SDA performs even better. The higher number of replies introduces noise for the SDA, worsening its performance, while the TS-SDA can de-anonymize them more effectively.

Finally, in Fig.6 we show the effects of changing the background traffic. The SDA is sensitive to other users having a non-uniform behaviour (all users send only to a limited set of $k = 20$ contacts – just as Alice does – instead of uniformly to all other $N = 1000$ users in the system), which worsens its accuracy. The TS-SDA, however, can handle this sort of traffic due to its estimation of the background noise.

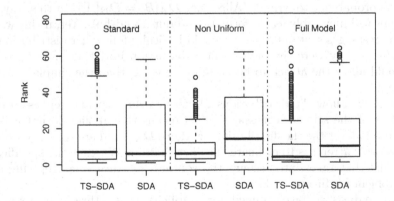

Fig. 6. The effect of the background traffic on the Two-sided Statistical Disclosure and traditional Statistical Disclosure Attacks. In the Non-Uniform case everyone sends to contacts only, and in the Full Model everyone replies.

Lastly, we show the results for the case in which all users reply to messages. In this case, Alice's correspondents reply to her, which in turn may generate further replies by her part. This symmetry increases the flow of traffic between Alice and her communication partners, thus making it easier to estimate her distribution of contacts. In the graph we can see that both the SDA and TS-SDA take benefit of this advantage, but that the impact on the latter is significantly stronger.

6   Discussion and Open Problems

The model presented is simple, allowing us to model a user replying to email and to illustrate our techniques to perform attacks. Yet its simplicity makes it deviate from real world usage in some ways.

First of all, we do not expect real users to initiate discussions in a way that can be approximated by a single Poisson process. There will definitely be fluctuations in the rate new discussions are initiated according to the time of day, the week day, the environment of the user and the user himself. The same is true for fluctuations in the reply delay and the probability of replying to messages.

Secondly, the parameters of the system are not likely to be independent of each other. Users are likely to read, write and reply to emails in bursts and not as they arrive.

Yet in some aspects the greatest shortcoming of the proposed model is that the probability of replying to an email is considered independent of the identity of the sender of the message. This is rather counterintuitive: one would expect Alice to be preferring to reply to her contacts rather than strangers (or even spammers) writing to her. Our model does not capture this aspect of two-way communication.

One way of modeling this aspect is to require contacts to be symmetric, meaning that if Alice has a certain probability to talk to Bob, then Bob should have the same probability to write to Alice (i.e. $D_A[B] = D_B[A]$). In this way, conversations will inevitably leak information about friendships. Yet, if this was the case, the messages sent out by Alice would basically follow her distribution D_A no matter if they were the product of a discussion initiation or a reply. This case would allow the attack to be no more complex than the simple statistical disclosure.

Instead, we allow the distributions D_n to be arbitrary, and replies to be independent of the sender of messages. This means that replies do not leak any information about the the distribution of Alice (D_A), and are rather noise when the adversary attempts to estimate this distribution. We leave the specification of a model that takes into account the contacts of Alice when replying as an open problem for future work.

In our analysis we have assumed, for simplicity, that a threshold mix is used. Since only the probability distributions describing the likely senders and receivers of messages contribute to the attack, it should be possible to extend our analysis to any other anonymity system (not offering full unobservability).

Finally, our model presupposes that there can be only one reply per message, forcing the total volume of replies to be at most a fraction of the discussion initiations. This may not be the case for many users that have reactive rather than proactive email habits, and prefer to reply to messages rather than initiating a discussion. In certain environments (like tech-support desks) this may be a more appropriate model. Again, extending the model to take into account such traffic patterns is an open problem.

7   Conclusions

The Two-sided Statistical Disclosure Attack (TS-SDA) is the first traffic analysis attack to be explicitly targeted at anonymous communication systems that allow anonymous, and indistinguishable, replies. It takes into account the existence of replies and the timing of messages to estimate the correspondents of a target user and to trace the messages they send. The attack we show is very fast, as it operates in time linear in the number of messages ($O(K_s)$) and only requires simple operations on vectors. It is also possible to execute it in parallel or in specialised hardware very efficiently.

We have assessed the effectiveness of the TS-SDA under different conditions. It performs best when the volume of replies is high, and the time it takes users to reply is short. In this case, it uses the timing correlations between the received messages and sent replies to de-anonymize them. On the other hand, it performs as well as the Statistical Disclosure Attack (SDA) when few or no replies are present.

An important observation is that the timing of the replies is critical to the security of the anonymity system. When users send replies long time after receiving a message, it is difficult to correlate them with the originating message. This means that the replies act as cover traffic for the discussion initiation and both TS-SDA and SDA perform worse than in the absence of replies. Therefore, our key conclusion is that secure anonymity systems should make replies not only cryptographically indistinguishable from normal messages, but also difficult to correlate in time with the messages that are being replied.

User contacts in our study are not symmetric: Alice initiating discussions with Bob, does not mean that Bob also initiates discussions with Alice. Yet real social networks are likely to exhibit such symmetries. In this case, replies leak information about a user's contacts that contribute to the success of both the TS-SDA but also the simple SDA.

Acknowledgements

This work was partially supported by the IWT SBO ADAPID project (Advanced Applications for e-ID cards in Flanders), the Concerted Research Action (GOA) Ambiorics 2005/11 of the Flemish Government and by the IAP Programme P6/26 BCRYPT of the Belgian State (Belgian Science Policy). George Danezis is funded by a research grant of the Katholieke Universiteit Leuven.

References

1. Agrawal, D., Kesdogan, D.: Measuring anonymity: The disclosure attack. IEEE Security & Privacy 1(6), 27–34 (2003)
2. Chaum, D.: Untraceable electronic mail, return addresses, and digital pseudonyms. Commun. ACM 24(2), 84–88 (1981)
3. Danezis, G.: Statistical disclosure attacks. In: Gritzalis, D., De Capitani di Vimercati, S., Samarati, P., Katsikas, S.K. (eds.) SEC of IFIP Conference Proceedings, vol. 250, pp. 421–426. Kluwer, Dordrecht (2003)
4. Danezis, G., Dingledine, R., Mathewson, N.: Mixminion: Design of a type iii anonymous remailer protocol. In: IEEE Symposium on Security and Privacy, pp. 2–15. IEEE Computer Society Press, Los Alamitos (2003)
5. Danezis, G., Serjantov, A.: Statistical disclosure or intersection attacks on anonymity systems. In: Fridrich [6], pp. 293–308
6. Fridrich, J. (ed.): IH 2004. LNCS, vol. 3200, pp. 23–25. Springer, Heidelberg (2004)
7. Heydt-Benjamin, T.S., Serjantov, A., Defend, B.: Nonesuch: a mix network with sender unobservability. In: 2006 Workshop on Privacy in the Electronic Society, ACM Press, New York (2006)
8. Kesdogan, D., Agrawal, D., Penz, S.: Limits of anonymity in open environments. In: Petitcolas, F.A.P. (ed.) IH 2002. LNCS, vol. 2578, pp. 53–69. Springer, Heidelberg (2003)
9. Kesdogan, D., Pimenidis, L. : The hitting set attack on anonymity protocols. In: Fridrich [6], pp. 326–339
10. Mathewson, N., Dingledine, R.: Practical traffic analysis: Extending and resisting statistical disclosure. In: Martin, D., Serjantov, A. (eds.) PET 2004. LNCS, vol. 3424, pp. 17–34. Springer, Heidelberg (2005)

A Family of Dunces: Trivial RFID Identification and Authentication Protocols

Gene Tsudik*

Computer Science Department
University of California, Irvine
gts@ics.uci.edu

Abstract. Security and privacy in RFID systems is an important and active research area. A number of challenges arise due to the extremely limited computational, storage and communication abilities of a typical RFID tag. This paper describes a step-by-step construction of a family of simple protocols for inexpensive untraceable identification and authentication of RFID tags. This work is aimed primarily at RFID tags that are capable of performing a small number of inexpensive conventional (as opposed to public key) cryptographic operations. It also represents the first result geared for so-called *batch mode* of RFID scanning whereby the identification (and/or authentication) of tags is delayed. Proposed protocols involve minimal interaction between a tag and a reader and place very low computational burden on the tag. Notably, they also impose low computational load on back-end servers.

1 Introduction

RFID technology is rapidly becoming ubiquitous. In the near future, it is expected to replace barcodes as the most common means of product and merchandise identification. Current and emerging applications range from toll transponders, passports and livestock/pet tracking devices (on the high end) to miniscule stealthy tags in everyday items, such as clothing, pharmaceuticals, library books and so on. Unlike barcodes, RFID tags do not require close physical proximity between a reader and a scanned object and also do not require a line-of-sight communication channel. Furthermore, RFID tags' smaller form factor takes up less valuable packaging "real estate". However, current and emerging RFID proliferation into many spheres of everyday life raises numerous privacy and security concerns.

One of the main issues has to do with malicious tracking of RFID-equipped objects. While tracking RFID tags is typically one of the key features and goals of a legitimate RFID system (e.g., in a supply-chain environment) *unauthorized* tracking of RFID tags is viewed as a major privacy threat.

In general, in-roads recently made by the RFID technology have prompted some public discontent and controversy. Privacy advocates have pointed out some sinister consequences of malicious tag tracking.

---

* An earlier (and much shorter) version of this paper appeared in [1]. This paper includes **substantial** revisions, enhancements and extensions to [1].

N. Borisov and P. Golle (Eds.): PET 2007, LNCS 4776, pp. 45–61, 2007.

This paper describes a protocol family for inexpensive untraceable identification and authentication of RFID tags. *Untraceable* means that it is computationally infeasible to infer – from interactions with a tag – information about the identity of the tag or link multiple authentication sessions of the same tag. Proposed protocols are inexpensive, requiring as little as one light-weight cryptographic operation on the tag and storage for one key. They are particularly well-suited for the **batch mode** of tag identification whereby a reader interrogates a multitude of tags and later identifies/authenticates them in bulk. Furthermore, real-time computational load on the back-end sever is minimal due to the simple pre-computation technique described below.

1.1   Operating Environment

The *adversary*, in our context, can be either passive (e.g., eavesdropper) or active (e.g., impersonator). It can corrupt or, attempt to impersonate, any entity and we assume that its primary goal is to track RFID tags. (In other words, we say – informally – that the adversary succeeds if it manages, with non-negligible probability over 50%, to link multiple authentication sessions of the same tag.) We point out from the start that we **do not** initially consider *forward security* – adversary's inability to link or trace prior manifestations of a tag in the event of complete tag compromise. At the same time, compromise of a set of tags should not lead to the adversary's ability to track other tags (except by distinguishing among the two sets). Furthermore, our initial goals **do not** include resistance to denial of service (DoS) attacks, e.g., attacks that aim to disable the tags. However, we outline out some DoS-resistant solutions later in the paper.

The legitimate entities are: tags, readers and servers. A reader is a device querying tags for identification information. A server is a trusted entity that knows and maintains all information about tags, their assigned keys and any other such information. A server is assumed to be physically secure and not subject to attacks. Multiple readers are assigned to a single server. A server only engages in communication with its constituent readers. For simplicity, we assume a single logical server that might resolve to multiple physically replicated servers. All communication between a server and its readers is assumed to be over private and authentic channels. Furthermore, servers and readers maintain **loosely synchronized clocks**. Both readers and server have ample storage, computational and communication abilities. (However, in some cases, readers may not be able to communicate with servers in real time; see below.)

We assume that an RFID tag has no clock and small amounts of ROM (e.g., to store a key) and non-volatile RAM (to store ephemeral state, such as a counter or time-stamp). With power supplied by a reader – whether contact or contactless – a tag is able to perform a modest amount of computation and commit any necessary state information – of small constant length – to non-volatile storage.

1.2   Goals

As usual, our goals are to *minimize everything*, including:

1. non-volatile RAM on the tag
2. code (gate count) complexity
3. tag computation requirements
4. number of rounds in reader-tag interaction[1]
5. message size in reader-tag interaction
6. server real-time computation load
7. server storage requirements

It is easy to see that the first three items directly influence tag cost. Also, the 4th item (number of rounds and messages) is important since more rounds imply more protocol logic and, hence, higher complexity and gate count. In fact, having more than two rounds in reader-tag interaction implies that the tag MUST keep soft state while the protocol executes. This would necessitate either bigger non-volatile RAM or continuous power from the reader (while the protocol executes) to store soft state in volatile RAM.

Finally, we need to avoid features currently not realistic for most low-cost RFID tags, such as public key cryptography, tamper-resistant shielding or an on-board clock.

1.3   Modes of Operation

We consider two modes of tag identification: *real-time* and *batch*. Here we make an assumption that the back-end server is necessary as a reader is unable to identify/authenticate tags on its own, primarily because of the scale, i.e., large numbers of deployed tags. In situations where this assumption is false, the discussion in this section does not apply. For example, one could imagine an RFID-equipped driver's license reader carried by law enforcement officers which is capable of storing information about all locally-issued driver's licenses, e.g., on the order of tens of millions. (Also, some recent work [16] shows how to perform, under some circumstances, *serverless* RFID authentication.)

The *real-time* mode is the one typically considered in the literature: it involves on-line contact between the reader and the server, in order to quickly identify (and, optionally, authenticate) the tag in question. If immediate feedback about a tag is needed – e.g., in facility access, retail or library check-out scenarios – the server must be contacted in real time.

In *batch* mode, a reader scans numerous tags, collects replies and sometime later performs their identification (and optionally, authentication) in bulk. From the security perspective, the batch mode seems relevant wherever immediate detection of fraudulent/counterfeit tags is not the the highest-priority issue and,

---

[1] We use the term "interaction" – as opposed to "protocol" – since the actual tag authentication protocol may involve interaction between a reader and a server, in addition to that between a tag and a reader. We are understandably less concerned about the complexity of the former.

instead, emphasis is on security against fraudulent readers. In practical terms, however, the batch mode is appropriate when circumstances prevent or inhibit contacting the back-end server in real time. For example, consider an inventory control application, where readers are deployed in a remote warehouse and have no means of contacting a back-end server in real time. More generally, some of the following factors might prompt the use of the batch mode:

- The server is not available in real time, either because it is down, disconnected or because readers do not have sufficient means of communication.
- The server is available, but is over-loaded with requests, causing response time to be jittery, thus making each tag interrogation instance unacceptably slow.
- The server is available and not over-loaded but is located too far away, causing response time to be too long. (Or, the network is congested, which cause unacceptable delays).
- A mobile/wireless reader has limited resources and, in order to conserve battery power, simply can not afford to contact the server for each scanned tag.

1.4   Tag Requirements

Each tag $RFID_i$ is initialized with at least the following values:

$$K_i, T_0, T_{max}$$

K_i is a tag-specific value that serves two purposes: (1) tag identifier, and (2) cryptographic key. Thus, its size (in bits) must be the greater of that required to uniquely identify a tag (i.e., a function of the total number of tags) and that required to serve as sufficiently strong cryptographic key for the purposes of Message Authentication Code (MAC) computation. In practice, a 160-bit K_i will most probably suffice.

T_0 is the initial timestamp assigned to the tag. This value does not have to be a discrete counter, *per se*. For example, T_0 can be the time-stamp of manufacture. T_0 need not be tag-unique; an entire batch of tags can be initialized with the same value. The bit-size of T_0 depends on the desired granularity of time and the number of times a tag can be authenticated. T_{max} can be viewed as the highest possible time-stamp. Like T_0, T_{max} does not need to be unique, e.g., a batch of tags can share this value.

Each tag is further equipped with a sufficiently strong, uniquely seeded pseudo-random number generator (PRNG). In practice, it can be resolved as an iterated keyed hash (e.g., HMAC) started with a random secret seed and keyed on K_i. For a tag $RFID_i$, $PRNG_i^j$ denotes the j-th invocation of the (unique) PRNG of that tag. No synchronization whatsoever is assumed as far as PRNG-s on the tags and either readers or servers. In other words, given a value $PRNG_i^j$, no entity (including a server) can recover K_i or any other information identifying $RFID_i$. Similarly, given two values $PRNG_i^j$ and $PRNG_j^k$, deciding whether $i = j$ must be computationally infeasible.

2 A Family of Dunces: YA-TRIP, YA-TRAP and YA-TRAP*

In this section, we introduce our main idea, based on the use of monotonically increasing time-stamps. We then present three protocols, starting with YA-TRIP which only offers efficient tag identification, continuing with YA-TRAP which also provides tag authentication, and concluding with YA-TRAP* which, in addition, incorporates DoS resistance features.

2.1 The Main Idea

The main idea of our proposal is the use of monotonically increasing time-stamps[2] to provide tracking-resistant (anonymous) tag authentication. The use of timestamps is motivated by the old result of Herzberg, et al. [6], which we briefly summarize next.

The work in [6] considered anonymous authentication of mobile users who move between domains, e.g., in a GSM [13] cellular network or a wired Kerberos-secured [12] internetwork. The technique in [6] involves a remote user identifying itself to the host domain by means of an ephemeral userid. An ephemeral userid is computed as a (collision-resistant, one-way) hash of current time and a secret permanent userid.

A trusted server in the user's "home" domain maintains a periodically updated hash table where each row corresponds to a traveling user. The length of the update interval is a system-wide parameter, e.g., one hour. The table can be either pre-computed or computed on-the-fly, as needed. Each row contains a permanent userid and a corresponding ephemeral userid. When a request from a *foreign* agent (e.g., Kerberos AS/TGS[3] in a remote domain or VLR[4] in a GSM setting) comes in, the home domain server looks up the ephemeral userid in the current table. (Since hash tables are used, the lookup cost is constant.) Assuming that timestamp used by the (authentic) traveling user to compute the ephemeral userid is reasonably recent (accurate), the hash table lookup is guaranteed to succeed. This allows a traveling user to be authenticated while avoiding any tracing by foreign agents or domains.

One of the main advantages of this approach is that the home domain server does not need to compute anything on demand, as part of each request processing. Instead, it pre-computes the current hash table and waits for requests to come in. The cost of processing a request amounts to a table lookup (constant cost) which is significantly cheaper than a similar approach using nonces or random challenges. In the latter case, the server would need to compute an entire table on-the-fly in order to identify the traveling user. As time goes by, an ephemeral userid table naturally 'expires' and gets replaced with a new one. This is the main feature we would like to *borrow* for tag authentication purposes.

---

[2] No other type of counters or sequence numbers will do.
[3] Authentication Server / Ticket Granting Server.
[4] Visitor Location Registry.

Although the technique from [6] works well for traveling/mobile users, it is not directly applicable to the envisaged RFID environment. First, a mobile user can be equipped with a trusted personal device that keeps accurate time. It can be as simple as a wristwatch or as sophisticated as a PDA. (Moreover, even without any trusted device, a human user can always recognize grossly incorrect time, e.g., that which is too far into the future.) Such a device can be relied upon to produce reasonably accurate current time. An RFID tag, on the other hand, cannot be expected to have a clock. Thus, it is fundamentally unable to distinguish among a legitimate and a grossly inaccurate (future) time-stamp.

However, if the tag keeps state of the last time-stamp it "saw" (assuming it was legitimate), then it can distinguish between future (valid) and past (invalid) time-stamps. We capitalize on this observation and rely on readers to offer a putatively valid timestamp to the tag at the start of the identification protocol. A tag compares the time-stamp to the stored time-stamp value. If the former is strictly greater than the latter, the tag concludes that the new time-stamp is probably valid and computes a response derived from its permanent key and the new timestamp. A tag thus never accepts a time-stamp earlier than – or equal to the one stored. However, to protect against *narrowing* attacks[5], even if the timestamp supplied by the reader pre-dates the one stored, the tag needs to reply with a value indistinguishable from a normal reply (i.e., a keyed hash over a valid timestamp). In such cases, the tag replies with a random value which is meaningless and cannot be traced to the tag even by the actual server.

2.2   YA-TRIP: Yet Another Trivial RFID Identification Protocol

We now present the first protocol (YA-TRIP) which provides only the very basic service – efficient tag identification. The protocol is illustrated in Figure 1.

Remark: We note that MACs based on keyed hashes are a fairly simple and general technique which has been used in other RFID-related contexts, e.g., [19]. Although YA-TRIP and its extensions described below use such standard MACs, it is worth noting that more efficient constructs have been proposed, e.g., Juels' light-weight MAC scheme in [19]. Also, the use of PRNGs to obfuscate the tag identity was first introduced by Weis, et al. [18].

The important part of the protocol encompasses steps 1-3. It consists of only two rounds and two messages. The size of the first message determined by T_r and the second – by H_{id}. In each case, the size is no greater than, say, 160 bits.

Note that H_{id} computed in step 2.3.2 and sent in step 3 does not actually authenticate the tag in the sense of the tag actually being present. What step 2.3.2 achieves is a weaker notion which we call "identification". It proves that *at some point*, perhaps far in the past, the tag was involved in a protocol (with a legitimate or a rogue reader) wherein it received, and replied to, the value T_r.

---

[5] Informally, a *narrowing attack* occurs when the adversary queries a tag with a particular timestamp and then later tries to identify the same tag by querying a candidate tag with a timestamp slightly above the previous one.

[1] Tag $\longleftarrow$ Reader: T_r
[2] Tag:[a]
   - [2.1] $\delta = T_r - T_t$
   - [2.2] if $(\delta \leq 0)$ or $(T_r > T_{max})$
   -      [2.2.1] $H_{id} = PRNG_i^j$
   - [2.3] else
   -      [2.3.1] $T_t = T_r$
   -      [2.3.2] $H_{id} = HMAC_{K_i}(T_t)$
[3] Tag $\longrightarrow$ Reader: H_{id}
   In real-time mode, the following steps take place immediately
   following Step 3. In batch mode, they are performed later.
[4] Reader $\longrightarrow$ Server: T_r, H_{id}
[5] Server:
   - [5.1] $s = LOOKUP(HASH\_TABLE_{T_r}, H_{id})$
   - [5.2] if $(s == -1)$
   -      [5.2.1] MSG=TAG-ID-ERROR
   - [5.3] else
   -      [5.3.1] MSG=TAG-VALID /* can return $G(K_s)$ instead */
[6] Server $\longrightarrow$ Reader: MSG

---

[a] Note that it is **imperative** for the respective times taken by steps 2.2 and 2.3 to be as close as possible. This is needed to prevent obvious timing attacks by malicious readers (aimed at distinguishing among the two cases). This is the reason for $PRNG$ to be resolved as described in Section *"Tag Requirements"* above.

Fig. 1. YA-TRIP: Tag Identification

In other words, the tag's reply in step 3 could be pre-recorded and replayed by the adversary.

Recall that we assume private and authentic channels between readers and the back-end server. Moreover, a server is assumed to "talk" only to non-compromised (non-malicious) readers. This pertains to steps 4 and 6 above. Note also that the specifics of step 5.3 depend on the application requirements. If the application allows genuine readers to identify/track valid tags, the server could return a meta-id of the tag: $G(K_s)$ where $G(.)$ is a suitable cryptographic hash with the usual features. Otherwise, it suffices to simply inform the reader that the tag in question is valid, as shown in Step 5.3.1 in Figure 1.

In batch mode, the reader interrogates a multitude of tags, collects their responses and, at a later time, off-loads the collected responses, along with the corresponding T_r value(s) to the server. (Note that, if tag responses are collected over multiple time intervals, the reader needs to group responses according to the T_r value used.) The server then needs to identify the tags. In this setting, YA-TRIP is highly advantageous. Even currently most efficient techniques such as the MSW protocol [2], require the server to perform $O(\log n)$ pseudo-random function (PRF) operations to identify a single tag. This translates into $O(n * \log n)$ operations to identify n tags. Whereas, YA-TRIP only needs $O(n)$ operations for the same task (since the same T_r-specific hash table is used for all lookups and each lookup takes constant time).

2.3 Drawbacks

The YA-TRIP protocol, as presented above, has some potential drawbacks.

First, YA-TRIP does not provide tag authentication – it merely identifies a tag. In order to authenticate itself, a tag needs to reply to a random challenge by the reader. Obviously, T_r is not random, thus, the reply in step 3 only identifies the tag. To remedy this, we extend the protocol in section 2.4.

Second, YA-TRIP is susceptible to a trivial denial-of-service (DoS) attack: an adversary sends a wildly inaccurate (future) time-stamp to a tag and incapacitates it either fully (if the time-stamp is the maximal allowed) or temporarily. Although DoS resistance is not one of our initial goals, it is an important issue. We address it in section 2.5.

Third, the protocol does not offer reader authentication or identification. We do not consider this to be a drawback but a feature. Viewed from the application perspective, the main purpose of reader/tag interaction is to identify (and, optionally, authenticate) the tag. While a number of previously proposed protocols manage (or attempt) to let the tag authenticate the reader, we claim that this is ultimately a waste of time and resources. The reason for this claim is two-fold:

1. **MORE ROUNDS:** Authenticating a reader requires at least a three rounds and three protocol messages; whereas, YA-TRIP is a two-round two-message protocol. It is easy to see why a minimum of three rounds would be needed: the reader always initiates interaction (round 1), the tag generates a challenge and sends it to the reader (round 2), and, the reader replies to the challenge (round 3). Moreover, if the tag does not identify (and authenticate) itself to the reader until the reader first authenticates itself to the tag, a fourth round (and a fourth) message becomes necessary.
2. **TAG STATE:** To authenticate a reader, the tag MUST "remember" the challenge it sends to the reader. This challenge represents state that must be kept by the tag between rounds 2 and 3. However, this brings up the possibility of the reader's reply never arriving, i.e., what happens if the protocol does not complete? The tag winds up in a state of "tilt" and requires additional logic to recover. All this translates into needing more resources on the tag.

Finally, the protocol makes an important assumption that a given tag is never authenticated (interrogated) more than once within the same interval. This has some bearing on the choice of the interval. A relatively short interval (e.g., a second) makes the assumption realistic for many settings. However, it translates into heavy computational burden for the server, i.e., frequent computation of ephemeral tables. On the other hand, a longer interval (e.g., an hour) results in much lower server burden, albeit, it may over-stretch our assumption, since a tag may need to be interrogated more than once per interval. One solution is to sacrifice some degree of untraceability in favor of increased functionality, i.e., allow a tag to iterate over the same time value (accept $T_r = T_t$) a fixed number of times, say k. This would entail storing an additional counter on the tag; once the counter for the same T_t reaches k, the tag refuses to accept $T_r = T_t$ and starts responding with random values as in Step 2.2 in the protocol. The resulting protocol would be k-**traceable** – an adversary would be able to track a tag over at most k sessions, with the same T_r value. (Note that the adversary can track actively, by interrogating the tag, or passively, by eavesdropping on interactions between the tag and valid readers.)

2.4 YA-TRAP: Adding Tag Authentication

Adding tag authentication to YA-TRIP is easy, requiring a few minor protocol changes. First, we amend the initial reader→tag message to include a random challenge R_r. Then, we include a MAC of both (reader and tag) challenges in the tag's reply message. Later, once the tag is identified by the server, it can be authenticated by verifying the MAC. The identification step is the same as in YA-TRIP. The resulting protocol (YA-TRAP) is shown in Figure 2.

Once the server identifies the tag (via $LOOKUP$), the extra cost of authenticating it is negligible amounting to one HMAC operation. The additional cost for the tag in YA-TRAP consists of one PRNG invocation and one HMAC to compute H_{auth}.

Introducing H_{auth} into the protocol serves another useful purpose. In the event that the tag has been previously de-synchronized (incapacitated) by a rogue reader and its T_t value has been set far into the future, H_{auth} alone can be used as a fall-back in order to identify and authenticate the tag. However, this would require the server to perform $O(n)$ operations – for each tag $0 \le j < n$, compute $HMAC_{K_j}(R_t, R_r)$ and compare with H_{auth}. This side-benefit of H_{auth} is useful in mitigating DoS attacks. On the other hand, it puts a much heavier load on the server which is arguably unimportant in the *batch mode*. Whereas, if used in *real time* mode, an adversary who is observing (and timing) tag-reader interaction might be able to discern a tag that has been previously desynchronized. Consider the environment where a successful reader-tag interaction results in some observable event, e.g., a door or a turnstile opens. Now, the adversary can measure the delay between the tag→ reader message (step 3 in Figure 2) and the observable event (which takes place after step 6). In the context of a previously desynchronized tag, this delay would be appreciably longer than that with a normal (synchronized) tag. Short of artificially padding the delay for all tags to be the same as for a desynchronized tag (which is clearly undesirable), there does not appear to be a workable solution.

We point out that the step from YA-TRIP to YA-TRAP is identical to that in the work of Juels [17] where the same idea was used in a somewhat different context.

[1] Tag $\longleftarrow$ Reader: T_r, R_r
[2] Tag:
   – [2.1] $\delta = T_r - T_t$
   – [2.2] if $(\delta \le 0)$ or $(T_r > T_{max})$
   –   [2.2.1] $H_{id} = PRNG_i^j$
   – [2.3] else
   –   [2.3.1] $T_t = T_r$
   –   [2.3.2] $H_{id} = HMAC_{K_i}(T_t)$
   – [2.4] $R_t = PRNG_i^{j+1}$
   – [2.5] $H_{auth} = HMAC_{K_i}(R_t, R_r)$
[3] Tag $\longrightarrow$ Reader: H_{id}, R_t, H_{auth}
   –   THEN, LATER:
[4] Reader $\longrightarrow$ Server: T_r, H_{id}, R_r, R_t, H_{auth}
[5] Server:
   – [5.1] $s = LOOKUP(HASH\_TABLE_{T_r}, H_{id})$
   – [5.2] if $(s == -1)$
   –   [5.2.1] MSG=TAG-ID-ERROR
   – [5.3] else if $(HMAC_{K_s}(R_t, R_r) \ne H_{auth})$
   –   [5.3.1] MSG=TAG-AUTH-ERROR
   – [5.4] else MSG=TAG-VALID
[6] Server $\longrightarrow$ Reader: MSG

Fig. 2. YA-TRAP: Tag Authentication

2.5   YA-TRAP*: Adding DoS Resistance

Both YA-TRIP and YA-TRAP are susceptible to DoS attacks whereby a rogue reader can easily incapacitate a tag by feeding it a "futuristic" (or even maximum) T_r value. Although it is not one of our initial goals (our emphasis is on efficient identification and authentication), we recognize that DoS resistance is an important issue in practice. Therefore, we now show how to extend YA-TRAP to mitigate Denial-of-Service (DoS) attacks aimed at incapacitating tags.

DoS attacks on YA-TRIP/YA-TRAP are possible because a tag has no means to distinguish a realistic (more-or-less current) time-stamp T_r from one that is too futuristic. Since adding a clock to a tag is not an option, we need to rely on external means of establishing timeliness.

Our approach to timeliness requires a reader to present an epoch token each time it queries a tag, as part of the initial reader→tag message. The epoch token allows a tag to ascertain that the reader-supplied T_r is not too far into the future. This token changes over time, but its frequency of change (epoch) is generally much slower than the unit of T_r or T_t time-stamps. For example, T_t and T_r are measured in minutes, whereas, the epoch token might change daily. The main idea is that a current epoch token can be used to derive past epoch tokens but cannot be used to derive future epoch tokens. A malicious or compromised reader might possess the current token but will not obtain future tokens. Also, since the epoch token changes slower than the time-stamp, multiple genuine interactions between one or more readers and the same tag might use the same epoch token but different (increasing) T_r values. We envisage the trusted server serving as the distribution point for epoch tokens. Upon (or near) each epoch, the server delivers (or securely broadcasts) the appropriate epoch token to all genuine readers.

The choice of the epoch duration directly influences the degree of vulnerability to DoS attacks. If the epoch is too long (e.g., a month), a rogue reader would be able to put tags out of commission for at most a month. (Note that the current epoch token is not secret; see below.) In contrast, if the epoch is very short (e.g., a minute), a tag might be out of service for at most a minute, however, the frequency of update becomes problematic since each reader would need to obtain the current epoch token from the trusted server or some other trusted repository.

The protocol (YA-TRAP*) is illustrated in Figure 3. DoS resistance in YA-TRAP* is obtained by introducing a much abused and over-used cryptographic primitive – a hash chain. A hash chain of length z is generated by starting with an initial value (say, X) and repeatedly hashing it z times to produce a root $H^z(X)$. The trusted (and, in batch mode, off-line) server is assumed to have initialized and generated the hash chain.

In addition to values mentioned in Section 1.4, each tag is initialized with a root of the hash chain $ET_0 = H^z(X)$ of length $z = T_{max}/INT$ where T_{max} is as defined in Section 1.4 and INT is the epoch duration, e.g., one day.

At any given time, a tag holds its last time-stamp of use T_t and the its last epoch token of use ET_t. (Note that "last" does not mean current or even recent; a tag may rest undisturbed for any period of time). When a reader queries a tag (in step 1), it includes ET_r, the current epoch token. The tag calculates the offset of ET_r as ν in step 2.2. Assuming a genuine reader, this offset represents the number of epochs between the last time the tag was successfully queried and ET_r. If T_r is deemed to be plausible in the first two OR clauses of step 2.3, the tag computes ν successive iterations of the hash function $H()$ over its prior epoch token ET_t and checks if the result matches ET_r. In case of a match, the tag concludes that T_t is not only plausible but is at most INT time units (e.g., one day) into the future. Otherwise, the tag assumes that it is being queried by a rogue reader and replies with two random values: $PRNG_i^j$ and $PRNG_i^{j+1}$, indistinguishable from $H_{id} = HMAC_{K_i}(T_t)$ and $HMAC_{K_i}(R_t, R_r)$, respectively.

We note that, even if $H^\nu(ET_t)$ matches ET_r, the tag cannot determine whether T_r and ET_r are **current**. The tag can only conclude that T_r is strictly greater than T_t and T_r corresponds to the same epoch as ET_r. We claim that this feature has no bearing on the security of YA-TRAP*. Since the tag has no clock, it cannot possibly distinguish between current and past-but-plausible values or T_r and ET_r. It can, however, establish with certainty that it has never replied to the same T_r before and that the epoch corresponding to ET_r is at most current (i.e., not future).

Another detail is that the purpose of Step 2.3.2 in Figure 3 is to inhibit the adversary's (whether a passive eavesdropper or a malicious reader) ability to differentiate between valid and invalid reader input, from the tag's point of view. However, it is NOT the purpose of Step 2.3.2 to obscure the value of ν (see Section 2.6 below).

---

[1] Tag $\longleftarrow$ Reader: T_r, R_r, ET_r

[2] Tag:
- [2.1] $\delta = T_r - T_t$
- [2.2] $\nu = \lfloor T_r/INT \rfloor - \lfloor T_t/INT \rfloor$
- [2.3] if $(\delta \leq 0)$ or $(T_r > T_{max})$ or $(H^\nu(ET_t) \neq ET_r)$
  - [2.3.1] $H_{id} = PRNG_i^j$;
  - [2.3.2] $R_t = PRNG_i^{j+1}$
  - [2.3.3] $H_{auth} = PRNG_i^{j+2}$
- [2.4] else
  - [2.4.1] $T_t = T_r$
  - [2.4.2] $ET_t = ET_r$
  - [2.4.3] $H_{id} = HMAC_{K_i}(T_t)$
  - [2.4.4] $R_t = PRNG_i^{j+1}$
  - [2.4.5] $H_{auth} = HMAC_{K_i}(R_t, R_r)$

Steps [3-6] are the same as in YA-TRAP

Fig. 3. YA-TRAP*: DoS Resistance

Remaining DoS Attacks: DoS resistance in YA-TRAP* is limited by the magnitude of the system-wide INT parameter. Once revealed by the server and distributed to the genuine readers, the current epoch token ET_r is not secret; it can be easily snooped on by the adversary. Therefore, the adversary can still incapacitate tags (however many it has access to) for at most the duration of INT if it queries each victim tag with the current epoch token and the maximum possible T_r value within the current epoch. We consider this kind of a limited DoS attack to be a relatively small price to pay.

2.6   Discussion and Extensions

Forward Security: None of the aforementioned protocols is forward-secure [15,14]. Forward security would require periodic key evolvement. If the tag's key (K_i) evolves in a one-way fashion (e.g., via as suitable hash function), then, an adversary who compromises a tag at time T cannot identify/link prior occurrences of the same tag. We view forward security as a feature orthogonal to our main design goals. However, it is relatively easy to add forward security to all three protocols; we sketch this out in the context of YA-TRAP* (refer to Figure 3):

- Introduce an additional operation for the tag:
  - [2.4.6] $K_i^\nu = H^\nu(K_i)$
- Change the way the server computes ephemeral tables:
  - Recall that, for each time-stamp T_c, the server pre-computes a table, where each entry corresponds to a unique tag i. Instead of computing each table entry as: $H_{K_i}(T_c)$, the server computes it as: $H_{K_i^\nu}(T_c)$ where $\nu = \lfloor T_c/INT \rfloor$

As a result of this simple modification, the tag's key is evolved one per epoch determined by INT and forward security is trivially achieved. The extra cost is due to the ν hash operations on the tag in step 2.4.6. If a tag i is compromised during epoch j, its key K_i^j is j-th evolution of the original key K_i^0. Due to one-way key evolvement, knowledge of K_i^j makes The adversary is faced with the following decision problem: given K_i^j, distinguish $HMAC_{K_i^s}(R_t, R_r)$ from a random value.

Timing Attacks: We claim that YA-TRIP and YA-TRAP are immune to crude timing attacks that aim to determine the tag's state (whether it is desynchronized) or its T_t value. From the timing perspective, Steps 2.2 and 2.3 in Figures 1 and 2) are indistinguishable since $PRNG$ and $HMAC$ are assumed to execute in the same time. However, YA-TRAP* is clearly vulnerable to timing attacks. Note that the execution the last OR clause in step 2.3 in Figure 3 is dependent upon the offset of T_r which can be freely selected by the adversary. Consequently, the adversary can mount a timing attack aimed at determining the epoch corresponding to the tag's last time-stamp of use (T_t). This is because the number of repeated hash operations in step 2.3 is based on $\nu = \lfloor T_r/INT \rfloor - \lfloor T_t/INT \rfloor$. One obvious countermeasure is to artificially "pad" the number of iterated hashes or introduce a random delay in tag's reply to the reader. However, we consider such countermeasures to be counterproductive as they increase protocol execution time which is undesirable, especially in batch mode.

As pointed out by Juels and Weis [10], YA-TRAP+ proposed by Burmester, et al. [4] (as well as our YA-TRAP) is susceptible to timing attacks whereby the adversary can distinguish between these two cases: (1) normal, synchronized tag and (2) desynchronized tag, based on timing on the server side. This is possible because (1) requires the server to perform a quick table lookup, whereas, (2) requires it to perform a brute-force search. This attack is only applicable in real-time mode since server operation in batch mode is not subject to being timed by the adversary.

2.7   Efficiency Considerations

We now consider the respective costs of the three protocols described above.

YA-TRIP is very efficient for tags. When an acceptable T_r is received, the computational burden on the tag is limited to a single keyed hash computation (e.g., an HMAC). Otherwise, a tag is required to generate a pseudo-random value (via $PRNG$), which, as discussed earlier, also amounts to a single keyed hash. Again, we stress that the two cases are indistinguishable with respect to their runtime. The reader is not involved computationally in YA-TRIP, YA-TRAP or YA-TRAP*, since it neither generates nor checks any values.

YA-TRAP requires a tag to perform two extra keyed hash operations (for a total of three): one to produce R_t in step 2.4 and the other – to compute H_{auth} in step 2.5.

In YA-TRAP*, a tag also performs three keyed hash operations (in either step 2.3 or 2.4) and, in addition, needs to compute ν hashes over ET_t. However, we stress that, in normal operation, ν is typically either zero or one. (Note that, if $\nu = 0$, the notation $H^0(ET_t)$ resolves to ET_t).

In all three protocols, although the computational load on the server is relatively heavy, most of the work is not done in real time. The real-time (on demand) computation amounts to a simple table look-up. The server can precompute ephemeral tables at any time. The amount of pre-computation depends on available storage, among other factors.

The efficiency with respect to server load can be illustrated by comparison. One simple and secure approach to untraceable tag identification and authentication entails the reader sending a random challenge R_r to the tag and the tag replying with keyed hash (or encryption) of the reader's challenge R_r and the tag's own nonce/challenge R_t, e.g., $H_{id-auth} = HMAC_{K_i}(R_r, R_t)$. . The reader then forwards the reply – comprised of $H_{id-auth}$, R_r and R_t – to the server. In order to identify the tag, the server needs to perform $O(n)$ on-line keyed hashes (or encryption operations), where n is the total number of tags. Although, on the average, the server only needs to perform $n/2$ operations to identify the tag, the work is essentially wasted, i.e., it is of no use for any other protocol sessions. Whereas, in our case, one ephemeral table can be used in the context of numerous (as many as n) protocol sessions.

The same issues arise when comparing YA-TRIP with the work of Molnar, et al. [2]. Although the MSW protocol from [2] is much more efficient than the naïve scheme we compared with above, it requires the tag to store $O(log n)$ keys and perform $O(log n)$ pseudo-random function (PRF) operations (each roughly equivalent to our keyed hash). In contrast, YA-TRIP only requires a single key on the tag and a single PRF.

As far as cost considerations, our requirement for (small) non-volatile RAM on the tag elevate the cost above that of cheapest tag types, i.e., less than 10 cents per tag. In this sense, YA-TRIP is more expensive than the one of the MSW protocols which does not require any non-volatile RAM (it only needs a physical random number generator). The other protocol presented in [2] requires tags to have non-volatile storage for a counter.

2.8   Security Analysis?

No formal security analysis of YA-TRIP, YA-TRAP and YA-TRAP* is included in this paper. However, we note that the security analysis in [6] is directly applicable to YA-TRIP. With respect to YA-TRAP, its extra feature of tag authentication is orthogonal to tag identification in YA-TRIP. In fact, if we strip tag identification from YA-TRAP, it becomes a trivial two message one-way authentication protocol whereby a tag simply replies to a challenge from the reader (R_r) with $HMAC_{K_i}(R_t, R_r)$ which is further randomized with tag's own nonce R_t. The security of this kind of authentication has been considered in the literature.

Security of YA-TRAP* is less clear. It offers limited DoS-resistance by checking the validity of the proffered epoch token (ET_r). As pointed out above (at the end of Section 2.5), YA-TRAP* still permits some limited DoS attacks and the degree to which such attacks are possible is based on INT – the duration of the authorization epoch. We consider this to be a reasonable trade-off between security and functionality.

Some recent work by Juels and Weiss [10] examined the properties of YA-TRIP as it originally appeared in [1]. They conclude that, in YA-TRIP, the adversary can easily "mark" a victim tag by feeding it an arbitrary future time-stamp (T_r) and later recognize/identify the same tag seeing whether it fails in an interaction with a genuine reader. This "attack" makes two assumptions: (1) that the success or failure of tag-reader interaction is observable by the adversary and (2) that the desynchronized tag(s) is/are unique. While the second assumption is perhaps realistic, the first one is not, at least in many practical settings. The first assumption is unrealistic in, for example, warehouse or inventory settings or wherever the interaction concludes without some publicly visible effect (such as a door opening). We also note that, even if both assumptions hold, the claimed attack has limited effect in the context of YA-TRAP* due to the DoS-resistance feature[6].

3 Related Work

There is a wealth of literature on various aspects of RFID security and privacy; see [11] for a comprehensive list. We consider only related work that seems relevant for comparison with our approach, i.e., protocols that emphasize efficient server computation, involve minimal 2-round reader-tag interaction, and aim to reduce tag requirements and computation. (Of course, this rules out some other notable and useful results.)

The first notable result is the set of MSW protocols by Molnar, et al. [2] which we use in section 2.7 above in comparing the efficiency of our protocols. The approach taken is to use hierarchical tree-based keying to allow for gradual and efficient tag identification/authentication. Tree-based keying involves a tree of degree k and depth $t = \log_k(n)$ where n is the total number of tags. Each tag holds $t = \log_k(n)$ distinct keys and, upon being challenged by a reader, responds with t MACs each based on a different key. The server can then identify/authenticate a tag with $O(\log_k(n))$ complexity. YA-TRIP and YA-TRAP are more efficient for tags in terms of computation and storage since the number of on-tag cryptographic operations (1 and 2, respectively) and tag storage

---

[6] We say "limited" since the attacker can still mark and recognize a tag, but, only within a single epoch.

requirements (1 key in each) are independent of the total number of tags. YA-TRAP* is less efficient: 3 cryptographic operations plus ν hashes to validate the epoch token. However, in normal operation, ν is either zero or one. (It is zero since a tag might be successfully and legitimately queried many times within one epoch.) MSW protocols appear more efficient on the server side since $t << n$. Nonetheless, if $O(n)$ sensors are queried with the same T_r value, the total server cost of MSW is $O(n \cdot \log_k(n))$. In contrast, our server cost is always $O(n)$ regardless of the number of tags queried. MSW protocols also have a security "feature" whereby an adversary who compromises one tag, is able to track/identify other tags that belong to the same families (tree branches) as the compromised tag. This vulnerability of MSW protocols has been explored by Avoine, et al. [9]. The same concern does not arise in our protocols since no two tags share any secrets. Finally, we note that MSW protocols are not easy to amend in order to support forward security.

Based in part on the early (and preliminary) version of this work [1], Burmester, et al. [4] came up with a secure universally-composable framework for RFID protocols. One of their sample protocols (called YA-TRAP+) is almost identical to YA-TRAP and, although they were developed independently and (most likely) concurrently, [4] was published earlier. As we mention above, in real-time mode, YA-TRAP+ and YA-TRAP are susceptible to some timing attacks. However, we note that, due to limited DoS-resistance, YA-TRAP* is not vulnerable to timing attacks, assuming that the server pre-computes all tables for each value of T_r within the current epoch[7].

Another proposal by Avoine and Oechslin (AO) [3] is similar in spirit, but very different in technical details, from the protocols in this paper. The AO approach involves offers built-in forward security (via one-way key evolvement for each tag query). It is based on a previously proposed OSK (Ohkubo-Suzuki-Kinoshita) protocol [5] coupled with Hellman's time/memory trade-off technique [8]. Because the tag's key evolves for each query, an active attacker can incapacitate any tag by repeatedly querying it; albeit, the number of queries might be large, as determined by the length of the hash chain, e.g., 2^{10}. Also, the AO and OSK protocols do not offer tag authentication; like YA-TRIP they offer only *tag identification*. It is simple to extend AO/OSK protocols to incorporate tag authentication and DoS-resistance along the lines of our approach in YA-TRAP and YA-TRAP*. Juels and Weis [10] show some potential vulnerabilities of the AO/OSK protocols.

Acknowledgements

Many thanks to Stephan Engberg, David Molnar, Ari Juels, Xiaowei Yang and Einar Mykletun for helpful input on early versions of this paper. We are also grateful to the PET'07 anonymous referees for their insightful comments.

---

[7] This would entail server maintaining up to INT distinct hash tables and looking up the H_{id} value over all of them. If hash tables are looked up in random order, the overall lookup time will be similarly randomized. Thus, timing attacks would not apply.

References

1. Tsudik, G.: Yet Another Trivial RFID Authentication Protocol, IEEE PerCom (Work-in-Progress Session) (March 2006)
2. Molnar, D., Soppera, A., Wagner, D.: A Scalable, Delegatable Pseudonym Protocol Enabling Ownership Transfer of RFID Tags. In: Preneel, B., Tavares, S. (eds.) SAC 2005. LNCS, vol. 3897, pp. 276–290. Springer, Heidelberg (2006)
3. Avoine, G., Oechslin, P.: A Scalable and Provably Secure Hash-Based RFID Protocol, PerSec Workshop (March 2005)
4. Burmester, M., de Medeiros, B., Van Le, T.: Provably Secure Ubiquitous Systems: Universally Composable RFID Authentication Protocols, IEEE/Createnet Securecomm (September 2006)
5. Ohkubo, M., Suzuki, K., Kinoshita, S.: Efficient hash-chain based RFID privacy protection scheme. In: UBICOMP Workshop on Privacy: Current Status and Future Directions (2004)
6. Herzberg, A., Krawczyk, H., Tsudik, G.: On Traveling Incognito. In: IEEE Workshop on Mobile Systems and Applications (December 1994)
7. Ateniese, G., Herzberg, A., Krawczyk, H., Tsudik, G.: On Traveling Incognito. Computer Networks 31(8), 871–884 (1999)
8. Hellman, M.: A cryptanalytic time-memory tradeoff. IEEE Transactions on Information Theory 26, 401–406 (1980)
9. Avoine, G., Dysli, E., Oechslin, P.: Reducing Time Complexity in RFID Systems. In: Preneel, B., Tavares, S. (eds.) SAC 2005. LNCS, vol. 3897, Springer, Heidelberg (2006)
10. Juels, A., Weis, S.: Defining Strong Privacy for RFID, IACR eprint (April 2006)
11. Avoine, G.: Security and Privacy in RFID Systems: Bibliography (February 2007), http://lasecwww.epfl.ch/~gavoine/rfid/
12. Steiner, J., Neuman, B., Schiller, J.: Kerberos: An Authentication Service for Open Network Systems. In: USENIX Winter 1988 Technical Conference, pp. 191–202 (1988)
13. Redl, S., Weber, M., Oliphant, M.: GSM and Personal Communications Handbook, Artech House (May 1998) ISBN 13: 978-0890069578
14. Krawczyk, H.: Simple forward-secure signatures from any signature scheme. In: ACM Conference on Computer and Communications Security, pp. 108–115. ACM Press, New York (2000)
15. Anderson, R.: Two remarks on public-key cryptology, Invited Talk. In: ACM Conference on Computer and Communications Security, ACM Press, New York (1997)
16. Tan, C., Sheng, B., Li, Q.: Serverless Search and Authentication Protocols for RFID. In: IEEE PerCom'2007, IEEE Computer Society Press, Los Alamitos (2007)
17. Juels, A., Syverson, P., Bailey, D.: High-Power Proxies for Enhancing RFID Privacy and Utility. In: Danezis, G., Martin, D. (eds.) PET 2005. LNCS, vol. 3856, Springer, Heidelberg (2006)
18. Weis, S., Sarma, S., Rivest, R., Engels, D.: Security and Privacy Aspects of Low-Cost Radio Frequency Identification Systems. In: Security in Pervasive Computing Conference (SPC'03) (March 2003)
19. Juels, A.: Yoking-Proofs for RFID Tags. In: Workshop on Pervasive Computing and Communication Security (PerSec) (2004)

Louis, Lester and Pierre:
Three Protocols for Location Privacy

Ge Zhong, Ian Goldberg, and Urs Hengartner

David R. Cheriton School of Computer Science
University of Waterloo
Waterloo, ON, Canada N2L 3G1
{gzhong,iang,uhengart}@cs.uwaterloo.ca

Abstract. Location privacy is of utmost concern for location-based services. It is the property that a person's location is revealed to other entities, such as a service provider or the person's friends, only if this release is strictly necessary and authorized by the person. We study how to achieve location privacy for a service that alerts people of nearby friends. Here, location privacy guarantees that users of the service can learn a friend's location if and only if the friend is actually nearby. We introduce three protocols—Louis, Lester and Pierre—that provide location privacy for such a service. The key advantage of our protocols is that they are distributed and do not require a separate service provider that is aware of people's locations. The evaluation of our sample implementation demonstrates that the protocols are sufficiently fast to be practical.

1 Introduction

The ubiquity of cellphones has led to the introduction of location-based services, which let cellphone users benefit from services that are tailored to their current location. For example, individuals can learn about interesting nearby places or get directions to a target location. Location privacy is of utmost concern for such location-based services, since knowing a person's location can leak information about her activities or her interests. Therefore, a person's location should be revealed to other entities only if this release is strictly necessary and authorized.

The potential of location-based services, together with rising interest in social-networking applications, has led to the introduction of buddy-tracking applications. For example, Boost Mobile, a US cellphone service targeted at young people, offers the Loopt Service [14], which alerts users of nearby friends. The drawback of the Loopt Service is that it is bound to a particular cellphone network and wireless technology. MIT's iFIND project [15] works around this problem by introducing a distributed buddy-tracking application, where a person's WiFi device determines its location and shares this information with the person's friends. While it is possible to exploit this approach for alerting people of nearby friends, its disadvantage is that the friends always learn each other's location, regardless whether they are actually nearby; that is, the approach may

N. Borisov and P. Golle (Eds.): PET 2007, LNCS 4776, pp. 62–76, 2007.

reveal more information than desired. What we really want is a distributed buddy-tracking application where users (and their devices) can learn information about their friends' locations if and only if their friends are actually nearby. In the rest of this paper, we call this problem the *nearby-friend problem*.

We present three protocols—Louis, Lester and Pierre[1]—for solving the nearby-friend problem. The Louis protocol requires a semi-trusted third party that does not learn any location information. The Lester protocol does not need a third party, but has the drawback that a user might be able to learn a friend's location even if the friend is in an area that is no longer considered nearby by the friend. However, this can happen only if the user is willing to invest additional work. The Pierre protocol does not have this disadvantage at the cost of not being able to tell the user the precise distance to a nearby friend.

Our protocols can run on wireless devices with limited communication and computation capabilities. The Louis protocol requires four communication steps, whereas the Lester and Pierre protocols require only two steps. Furthermore, the evaluation of our sample implementation shows that the cost of running our protocols is comparable to the cost of setting up a TLS [7] connection.

The rest of this paper is organized as follows. In section 2, we discuss previous approaches to solve the nearby-friend problem. Our protocols exploit homomorphic encryption, which we review in section 3. We present the Louis, Lester and Pierre protocols in sections 4, 5, and 6, respectively, and compare their features in section 7.

2 Related Work

Location cloaking has been a popular approach for providing location privacy [5,9,10,16]. Here, an individual's device or a third party cloaks the individual's location before giving it to the provider of a location-based service. Cheng et al. [5] study location cloaking for a service that alerts people of nearby friends. For each individual, the service provider knows only that the individual is within a particular region, but not where exactly. The authors develop a metric for describing the quality of an answer received from the service. This metric allows an individual to trade off privacy for better answer quality. A drawback of this approach is that the service provider learns some location information. Our protocols do not require such a third party. (In the Louis protocol, the third party does not learn any location information.) Furthermore, if a friend is nearby, our protocols will always return a positive answer and there is no doubt about the quality of the answer.

The nearby-friend problem is an instance of a secure multiparty computation problem, where multiple parties jointly compute the output of a function without learning each other's inputs. We next examine two previous approaches based on secure multiparty computation that are applicable to solving the nearby-friend problem.

---

[1] Our protocols are named after three former residents of 24 Sussex Drive, Ottawa.

Køien and Oleshchuk [12] present a secure two-party protocol for the point-inclusion problem. The protocol allows Alice to learn whether a point chosen by Bob is in a polygon determined by Alice, without Bob revealing the point to Alice and without Alice revealing the polygon to Bob. We could exploit this protocol for letting Alice know whether Bob is nearby. Namely, Alice determines the circle around her current location that corresponds to the area that she considers nearby and approximates the circle with a polygon; Bob picks the point that corresponds to his current location. However, Køien and Oleshchuk's protocol has a flaw: Alice can learn Bob's location by choosing a degenerate polygon. For example, if there are only two different edges in the polygon and all the other edges are identical to one of them, Alice will usually be able to solve a system of linear equations to determine Bob's location. Bob cannot detect degenerate polygons, assuming the underlying encryption scheme is semantically secure, so this protocol is not adequate for solving the nearby-friend problem.

Atallah and Du [1] also study the point-inclusion problem. Their protocol lets both Alice and Bob learn whether Bob's point is in Alice's polygon. The protocol is based on solving the secure two-party scalar product problem and the secure two-party vector dominance problem [1]. With the help of a semi-trusted third party, the first problem can be solved in three communication steps [8]. The solution of the second problem is based on solving Yao's millionaire problem [22]. The most efficient constant-round protocol for solving this problem requires six communication steps [3]. With a semi-trusted third party, the problem can be solved in three communication steps [4]. Our Louis protocol, which needs a semi-trusted third party, lets Alice know in four communication steps whether Bob is nearby and requires one additional step to inform Bob of this result. The Lester and Pierre protocols each require two communication steps to let Alice learn whether Bob is nearby. To let Bob know whether Alice is nearby, these protocols also require one additional step. In summary, to achieve the same result as Atallah and Du's protocol, our protocols require fewer communication steps and the Lester and Pierre protocols do not need a third party at all.

3   Homomorphic Encryption

Our protocols use the techniques of public-key cryptography, but we require the cryptosystems used to have a special algebraic property: that they are *additive homomorphic*. An additive homomorphic cryptosystem is one in which, given $\mathcal{E}(m_1)$ and $\mathcal{E}(m_2)$, one can efficiently compute $\mathcal{E}(m_1 + m_2)$. Our protocols use two of these systems, which we review here.

3.1   Paillier

The first of these systems is the Paillier cryptosystem [18]. Like the RSA cryptosystem, a user Alice selects random primes p and q and constructs $n = pq$; plaintext messages are elements of $\mathbb{Z}_n$. Unlike RSA, however, ciphertexts are elements of $\mathbb{Z}_{n^2}$. Alice picks a random $g \in \mathbb{Z}_{n^2}^*$ and verifies that

$\mu = (L(g^\lambda \bmod n^2))^{-1} \bmod n$ exists, where $\lambda = \text{lcm}(p - 1, q - 1)$ and $L(x) = (x - 1)/n$. Alice's public key is then (n, g) and her private key is (λ, μ).

To encrypt a message m, another user Bob picks a random $r \in \mathbb{Z}_n^*$ and computes the ciphertext $c = \mathcal{E}(m) = g^m \cdot r^n \bmod n^2$. To decrypt this message, Alice computes $\mathcal{D}(c) = L(c^\lambda \bmod n^2) \cdot \mu \bmod n$, which always equals m.

Given $\mathcal{E}(m_1) = g^{m_1} \cdot r_1^n \bmod n^2$ and $\mathcal{E}(m_2) = g^{m_2} \cdot r_2^n \bmod n^2$, Bob can easily compute $\mathcal{E}(m_1 + m_2) = \mathcal{E}(m_1) \cdot \mathcal{E}(m_2) \bmod n^2 = g^{m_1 + m_2} \cdot (r_1 r_2)^n \bmod n^2$.

Note that if Bob does not trust Alice enough to generate her Paillier modulus correctly, he can insist she prove its validity (that is, that it is the product of exactly two nearly equal primes) [13].

3.2 CGS97

Cramer, Genarro and Schoenmakers [6] present the CGS97 scheme. This is a variant on El Gamal, where we have (public) large primes p and q such that $q | p - 1$. Plaintexts are elements of $\mathbb{Z}_q$ and ciphertexts are elements of $\mathbb{Z}_p \times \mathbb{Z}_p$. Alice's private key is a random element $a \in \mathbb{Z}_q$ and her public key is $A = g^a \bmod p$.

To encrypt a message m, Bob picks a random $r \in \mathbb{Z}_q$ and computes $(c_1, c_2) = \mathcal{E}(m) = (g^r \bmod p, A^{r+m} \bmod p)$. To decrypt this message, Alice finds $A^m = c_2 \cdot c_1^{-a} \bmod p$ and computes m as the discrete log of that value with the base of A, mod p. Note that this can only be done if M, the number of possible plaintext messages, is small. In that event, the Pollard lambda, or "kangaroo", method [19] can find m in time $O(\sqrt{M})$.

Given $\mathcal{E}(m_1) = (g^{r_1} \bmod p, A^{r_1+m_1} \bmod p)$ and $\mathcal{E}(m_2) = (g^{r_2} \bmod p, A^{r_2+m_2} \bmod p)$, Bob can easily compute $\mathcal{E}(m_1 + m_2) = (g^{r_1+r_2} \bmod p, A^{r_1+r_2+m_1+m_2} \bmod p)$ by pointwise multiplication mod p.

4   The Louis Protocol

There are three participants in the Louis protocol: Alice, Bob and Trent. Alice and Bob are friends and Alice wants to know whether Bob is nearby. Alice considers Bob nearby if he is within a circle of some radius r centered around Alice. Alice informs Bob of r and Bob can refuse to participate in the protocol if he considers it to be too large. Trent acts as a third party and helps Alice and Bob decide whether they are nearby. Unlike other protocols for implementing location-based services that exploit third parties [5,9,10,14], the Louis protocol does not allow Trent to learn any location information about either Alice or Bob.

Our protocol consists of two phases. In the first phase, Alice and Bob jointly solve the nearby-friend problem and Alice learns whether Bob is nearby. If this is the case, Alice and Bob inform each other of their locations in the (optional) second phase of the protocol. Alice and Bob cannot learn each other's locations if they are not nearby.

Alice and Bob can misbehave and input fake locations into the protocol. However, the detection of misbehaviour by one of them will likely affect their

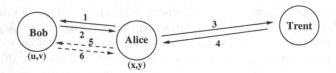

Fig. 1. System model of the Louis protocol. The dashed arrows indicate the optional second phase.

friendship, so they are less likely to misbehave. We discuss the detection of misbehaviour by Alice or Bob, and of cheating by the third party Trent in section 4.3.

4.1   Protocol Description

We assume that a location can be mapped to two-dimensional coordinates and that the mapping is known to Alice and Bob. Let Alice's location be (x, y) and Bob's be (u, v). By the definition above, they are nearby if $\sqrt{(x - u)^2 + (y - v)^2} < r$. Equivalently, we can check the sign of $d = (x - u)^2 + (y - v)^2 - r^2$. In particular, Bob is near Alice if $d < 0$.

Figure 1 presents the two communication channels used in our system model. The first is between Alice and Bob, and the second is between Alice and Trent. Alice also acts as a relay of the communication between Bob and Trent. The benefit of this approach is to hide Bob's identity from Trent, thus improving privacy. We assume that the two secure communication channels are set up before our protocol begins.

The protocol consists of two phases. The first phase lets Alice determine whether Bob is nearby. If this is the case, the (optional) second phase lets Alice and Bob learn each other's locations. In our protocol, $\mathcal{E}_A(\cdot)$ is the Paillier additive homomorphic encryption function using Alice's public key, $\mathcal{E}_T(\cdot)$ is a (non-homomorphic) public-key encryption function using Trent's public key, $\mathcal{H}(\cdot)$ is a cryptographic hash function, $sig_A(m)$ is Alice's signature on message m, and similarly with $sig_T(m)$.

1. **First phase:** Alice determines her location (x, y) and her desired radius r, and picks a random salt s_A.
   Alice→Bob: $\mathcal{E}_A(x^2 + y^2)$, $\mathcal{E}_A(2x)$, $\mathcal{E}_A(2y)$, r, $\mathcal{H}(x \parallel y \parallel s_A)$
2. Bob checks the value of r. If he thinks r is too large, he aborts the protocol. Otherwise, he determines his location (u, v), picks a random value k and computes
$$\mathcal{E}_A(d + k) = \frac{\mathcal{E}_A(x^2 + y^2) \cdot \mathcal{E}_A(u^2 + v^2) \cdot \mathcal{E}_A(k)}{(\mathcal{E}_A(2x))^u \cdot (\mathcal{E}_A(2y))^v \cdot \mathcal{E}_A(r^2)},$$
   Bob also chooses a random salt s_B.
   Bob→Alice: $\mathcal{E}_A(d + k)$, $\mathcal{E}_T(k)$, $\mathcal{H}(u \parallel v \parallel s_B)$, $\mathcal{H}(k)$.
3. Alice decrypts $\mathcal{E}_A(d + k)$.
   Alice→Trent: $d + k$, $\mathcal{E}_T(k)$, $sig_A(d + k)$, $sig_A(\mathcal{E}_T(k))$

Table 1. Runtime of the Louis protocol

	Alice	Bob	Trent
TLS connection time	516 ± 2 ms	255 ± 4 ms	256 ± 2 ms
Computation time	635 ± 4 ms	175 ± 4 ms	41 ± 0.6 ms

4. Trent decrypts $\mathcal{E}_T(k)$ and verifies Alice's signatures. Next, he computes d. If $d < 0$, Trent sets $answer = $'YES' else $answer = $'NO'.
   Trent→Alice: $answer$, $sig_T(answer \parallel sig_A(d+k) \parallel sig_A(\mathcal{E}_T(k)))$.
5. Alice verifies Trent's signature. Next, if $answer ==$ 'YES', she knows that Bob is nearby. Alice terminates the protocol if Bob is not nearby or if only the first phase of the protocol is run. Otherwise:

Second phase: Alice reveals her location to Bob:
Alice→Bob: $answer$, $d+k$, $sig_A(d+k)$, $sig_A(\mathcal{E}_T(k))$, $sig_T(answer \parallel sig_A(d+k) \parallel sig_A(\mathcal{E}_T(k)))$, x, y, s_A.

6. Bob verifies all signatures. He then computes $\mathcal{H}(x \parallel y \parallel s_A)$ and compares the hash value with the one provided by Alice in step 1. He also uses (x, y) to compute $d + k$ and compares it to the value received. If the values do not match, Bob aborts the protocol. Otherwise Bob reveals his location to Alice:
   Bob→Alice: u, v, s_B, k.
7. Alice computes $\mathcal{H}(u \parallel v \parallel s_B)$ and $\mathcal{H}(k)$ and compares the values with the hash values provided by Bob in step 2. Alice also computes $d + k$ based on (x, y), (u, v), and k and verifies whether it equals the decrypted value of $\mathcal{E}_A(d + k)$.

Note that our protocol checks whether $d < 0$. In the Paillier cryptosystem, d will be an element of $\mathbb{Z}_n$, so to check this condition, we ensure that n is sufficiently large, and we say $d < 0$ if $n/2 < d < n$.

4.2 Measurements

We implemented our protocols using the OpenSSL [17] and NTL [21] libraries. We chose RSA for the non-homomorphic encryption and signature functions. The key sizes of all the cryptographic functions are 2048 bits. Our hash function is SHA-256, and the cipher stack in TLS is AES256 in CBC mode with ephemeral Diffie-Hellman key exchange. (The ephemeral keys can be used in the Lester and Pierre protocols, below.) We evaluated these protocols on a 3.0 GHz Pentium 4 desktop. We ran the protocol one hundred times and measured TLS connection-setup time and overall computation time for each protocol participant. Table 1 shows our results.

With 2048-bit keys, it takes about a quarter second to set up a TLS connection. Alice initiates two TLS connections, which takes about half a second. Trent's computation time is very small. The major burden is on Alice, who takes about 0.6 s; Bob's computation time is less than one third of Alice's. In short, if a mobile device can set up a TLS connection, it should be able to finish the Louis protocol in comparable time or shorter.

4.3 Analysis

The Louis protocol can directly detect scenarios where Alice and Bob reveal other locations than the ones they committed to. We next explain how Alice and Bob can discover other kinds of misbehaviour.

Alice detects misbehaviour by Bob or Trent. If Alice detects suspicious behaviour, such as not spotting nearby Bob though she was told that he is nearby, and if only the first phase of the protocol has been run, Alice asks Bob to execute the second phase. If Bob refuses, Alice will suspect that Bob misbehaved. Otherwise, Alice proceeds as follows:

If Alice is told by Trent that Bob is nearby, but then fails to spot Bob at his released, nearby location, Alice will realize Bob's misbehaviour. If the released location is not nearby, Alice asks Bob to reveal the random values that he used in his calculations and repeats the calculations. If the results are not identical to the ones released by Bob, Bob must have misbehaved. Otherwise, there was cheating by Trent.

If Alice is told by Trent that Bob is not nearby, but then spots him in her vicinity, she proceeds in a similar way. Namely, if the location released by Bob is not nearby, Bob must have misbehaved. If it is nearby, Alice repeats Bob's calculations, as explained above, to detect cheating by Trent.

Finally, if step 7 in the protocol fails, Alice also repeats Bob's calculations to discover who misbehaved.

Bob detects misbehaviour by Alice or Trent. If the second phase of the protocol is not run, Bob does not learn any location information about Alice, which makes it impossible for him to detect misbehaviour. However, Bob can refuse to answer multiple queries from Alice if they arrive within a very short time. These queries could be part of a probing attack, where Alice knows a set of likely locations for Bob and uses each of them for invoking the protocol.

If the second phase of the protocol is run and Bob detects suspicious behaviour, Bob uses mechanisms similar to Alice's to discover misbehaviour.

Alice or Bob collude with Trent. Our protocol cannot detect collusion, where Trent tells the value of d to one of the parties. However, Alice and Bob can jointly choose the third party, which reduces the risk of collusion.

5 The Lester Protocol

The Louis protocol allows Alice and Bob to learn each other's locations if and only if they are nearby, but it requires the participation of Trent. In our second protocol, Lester, we do away with the need for Trent. However, this comes at some small costs. First, the information disclosure is now only one-way; that is, Alice learns about Bob's location, but not vice versa. Alice and Bob could of course run the protocol a second time, with the roles reversed, to mutually exchange information. (Note that this requires only one extra message, since the resulting two messages from Bob to Alice can be combined.) Second, Alice learns less exact information about Bob; she only learns the distance between them, although this may actually be a benefit, depending on the context.

5.1 Protocol Description

This protocol uses the CGS97 cryptosystem of section 3.2. Recall that this cryptosystem has an unusual property: the amount of work Alice must do in order to decrypt a message depends on the number of possible messages. We use this property to our advantage in this protocol.

The Lester protocol is very simple. Let a and b be Alice and Bob's private keys, and $A = g^a$ and $B = g^b$ be their public keys. Note that these keys may be ephemeral; if Alice and Bob are communicating via TLS [7], for example, they can use the key pairs from an ephemeral Diffie-Hellman key exchange. Alice and Bob can each calculate $C = A^b = B^a$. Alice sends Bob $\mathcal{E}_A(x^2 + y^2)$, $\mathcal{E}_A(2x)$, $\mathcal{E}_A(2y)$. Bob picks a *workfactor* t (see below) and a random salt s of length t, and sends to Alice $t, \mathcal{E}_A(b \cdot (D \cdot 2^t + s))$, where $D = (x - u)^2 + (y - v)^2$ is the square of the distance between Alice and Bob. Alice receives this message, and can calculate $A^{b \cdot (D \cdot 2^t + s)} = C^{D \cdot 2^t + s}$.

If Alice wants to learn whether Bob is closer than some threshold distance r away, she uses the kangaroo method [19] to determine $D \cdot 2^t + s$ if it is in the range $[0, r^2 \cdot 2^t]$. This can be done in time $O(r \cdot 2^{t/2})$ and space $O(t \log r)$. Other methods to calculate discrete logarithms, such as baby step-giant-step [20], can solve this problem with the same runtime, but with exponentially larger space requirements. If this step is successful, shifting the result by t bits yields D. The effect of Bob including a factor of b in his response to Alice is that Alice's discrete logarithm calculation is to the base of the ephemeral C rather than A. This prevents Alice from doing a certain amount of reusable precomputation derived from a predetermined base.

Bob should choose t so that he is comfortable with the amount of work Alice would have to do in order to discover the distance between them. This will likely depend on things Bob knows about his friend Alice, such as the computational capacity of Alice's cellphone.

5.2 Measurements

The runtime of the Lester protocol is dominated by Alice's computation of the discrete log of $C^{D \cdot 2^t + s}$ to the base of C. In Figure 2, we plot this time against the workfactor value t, chosen by Bob. For fixed r, we expect this runtime to scale as $2^{t/2}$ and the log plot shows that this is indeed the case. This gives Bob a fair amount of control over the amount of work Alice will need to do to find the distance between them: in our setup, if $t = 20$, Alice needs only about a quarter of a second, and if $t = 40$, Alice needs a few minutes of computation time. If this is not enough, Bob could choose even larger values, and the exponential nature of the runtime means he can make Alice work a very long time with only a small increase in t.

We measured Bob's computation time, on the other hand, to be 175 ± 2 ms, comparable to that of the Louis protocol, and this value is independent of t.

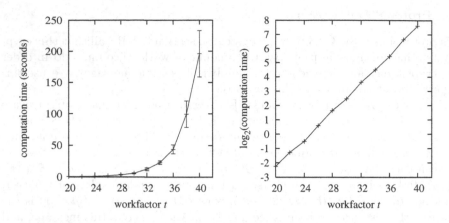

Fig. 2. Alice's computation time in the Lester protocol

5.3 Analysis

This protocol has no way to detect if Alice or Bob use incorrect locations as their input. This could allow Alice to confirm a guess of Bob's location simply by entering that guess as her own location and seeing if the protocol successfully finds Bob to be very nearby. Alice could also check specific ranges of large values of D. For example, if locations are measured in metres, she could check whether Bob is between 10000 and 11000 m away for about the same cost as checking whether he is between 0 and 4600 m away. Of course, the former ring represents a much more widely spread out geographical area, and knowing only that Bob is in that ring probably gives less useful information to Alice. An exception is when Alice knows a few places that Bob is likely to be: his home, his work, etc.; she can then confirm those guesses with minor difficulty. Note that Bob has a little bit of extra power: not only can he choose a large t if he suspects Alice is probing for his exact location, but he can also effectively refuse to participate in the protocol, without letting Alice know. He does this by returning an *unconditional negative*; that is, an encryption of a random value instead of the correct response. This makes it extremely probable that Alice's discrete log computation will fail. If Bob wants to be extra careful, he should be sure to avoid revealing he has done this to side channels, such as timing differences [11]. Conversely, he could return an *unconditional positive* by returning an encryption of a small number rather than the result of his calculation. If Alice cares, she can prevent the latter by adding a random value k to her $x^2 + y^2$ and dividing Bob's response by $C^{k \cdot 2^t}$. Of course, as in the Louis protocol, Alice is likely to notice if Bob claims to be nearby but is not.

Another downside of this protocol is that Bob only has very coarse control over the threshold distance; he can choose how much work Alice would have to do in order to discover that he was, say, 500 metres away, but with only twice as much work, Alice could discover that Bob was 1000 metres away. A minor modification to the Lester protocol, however, can make Alice's work be quadratic

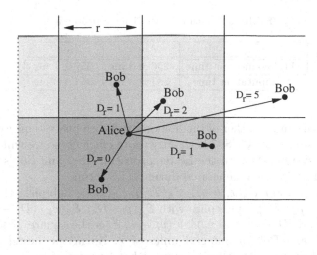

Fig. 3. Grid distances in the Pierre protocol. The x and y distances between Alice and Bob are measured in grid cells (integral units of r), and $D_r = (\Delta x_r)^2 + (\Delta y_r)^2$. Alice can determine whether Bob is in the dark grey, medium grey, or light grey area, but no more specific information than that.

in the threshold distance instead of linear. Instead of the CGS97 cryptosystem, the Boneh-Goh-Nissim cryptosystem [2] can be used. This protocol has the same properties (additive homomorphic; decryption takes $O(\sqrt{M})$ time) as CGS97, but also allows calculations of encryptions of *quadratic* functions, in addition to linear ones. With this system, Bob could compute $\mathcal{E}_A(D^2 \cdot 2^t + s)$ for a random salt s between 0 and $(2D + 1)2^t - 1$, and Alice's work to find the distance to Bob will be $O(r^2 \cdot 2^{t/2})$.

6   The Pierre Protocol

Our third protocol, Pierre, solves the above problems with the Lester protocol and gives Bob more confidence in his privacy. On the other hand, if Alice and Bob are nearby, the Pierre protocol will inform Alice of that fact, but will give her much less information about Bob's exact location.

6.1   Protocol Description

In this protocol, Alice picks a *resolution distance* r, roughly analogous to the threshold distance r in the previous protocols. Alice and Bob then express their coordinates in (integral) units of r; that is, if Alice's true position is (x, y), then for the purposes of this protocol, she will use coordinates $(x_r, y_r) = (\lfloor \frac{x}{r} \rfloor, \lfloor \frac{y}{r} \rfloor)$, and similarly for Bob. This has the effect of dividing the plane into a grid, and Alice and Bob's location calculations only depend on the grid cells they are in; see Figure 3.

Table 2. Runtime of the Pierre protocol

	Alice	Bob
TLS connection time	256 ± 3 ms	257 ± 1 ms
Computation time	384 ± 4 ms	354 ± 3 ms

This protocol can use either of the homomorphic cryptosystems we have mentioned. It turns out that CGS97 is slightly more efficient, so we will use the notation of that system. As with the Lester protocol, Alice and Bob's public keys can be the ephemeral ones generated during TLS setup.

Alice sends to Bob $r, \mathcal{E}_A(x_r^2 + y_r^2), \mathcal{E}_A(2x_r), \mathcal{E}_A(2y_r)$. Bob picks three random elements ρ_0, ρ_1, ρ_2 of $\mathbb{Z}_p^*$ and replies with $\mathcal{E}_A(\rho_0 \cdot D_r), \mathcal{E}_A(\rho_1 \cdot (D_r - 1)), \mathcal{E}_A(\rho_2 \cdot (D_r - 2))$, where $D_r = (x_r - u_r)^2 + (y_r - v_r)^2$ is the square of the distance between Alice and Bob, in integral units of r. As in the Lester protocol, if Bob is uncomfortable with Alice's query, either because of her choice of r, her frequency of querying, or some other reason, Bob can reply with encryptions of three random values, ensuring Alice will not think he is nearby.

Note that $\rho_0 \cdot D_r = 0$ if Alice and Bob are in the same grid cell and is a random element of $\mathbb{Z}_p^*$ otherwise. Similarly, $\rho_1 \cdot (D_r - 1) = 0$ if Alice and Bob are in adjacent grid cells and random otherwise, and $\rho_2 \cdot (D_r - 2) = 0$ if Alice and Bob are in diagonally touching grid cells and random otherwise.

In CGS97, it is easy for Alice to check whether a received ciphertext (c_1, c_2) is an encryption of 0: this is the case exactly when $c_2 = c_1{}^a \bmod p$, where a is Alice's private key. Therefore, with this protocol, Alice can tell when Bob is in the same, adjacent, or diagonally touching grid cell (and learns which is the case), but she learns no more specific information than that.

6.2   Measurements

We measured the computation time of the Pierre protocol using 2048-bit keys for both TLS and CGS97; the results are shown in Table 2. For comparison, we also show the time to set up an TLS connection between Alice and Bob. The computation times shown are for the worst-case situation; that is, Alice and Bob are not nearby.

We can see that the computational cost of the Pierre protocol is only slightly more expensive than setting up TLS; this suggests that the protocol would be reasonable to run on mobile devices.

6.3   Analysis

As with the other protocols, we cannot prevent Alice from using an incorrect location in order to try to confirm a guess of Bob's location. However, in the Lester protocol, as mentioned above, Alice can try to verify a number of guesses with a single query to Bob. This is not the case in the Pierre protocol; each protocol run tells Alice only whether Bob is near the location she entered, and she can extract no other information from Bob's reply.

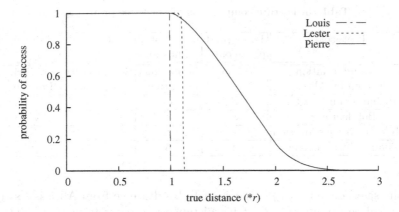

Fig. 4. Success probabilities of the three protocols, as a function of the actual distance between Alice and Bob (as a multiple of r)

Like the Lester protocol, the Pierre protocol can gain a minor benefit from using the Boneh-Goh-Nissim cryptosystem. Bob can combine two of his responses and reply with, for example, $\mathcal{E}_A(\rho_1 \cdot D_r \cdot (D_r - 1)), \mathcal{E}_A(\rho_2 \cdot (D_r - 2))$. If the first ciphertext decrypts to 0, then Alice knows that D_r is either 0 or 1, but not which. This gains Bob a small amount of privacy, and at the same time slightly decreases the size of his reply, even taking into account that Boneh-Goh-Nissim is elliptic curve based.

A more dramatic benefit could be gained by using a *ring homomorphic* encryption system; that is, a system in which, given $\mathcal{E}(x)$ and $\mathcal{E}(y)$, one can efficiently compute both $\mathcal{E}(x + y)$ and $\mathcal{E}(x \cdot y)$. With such a system, Bob could reply with the single ciphertext $\mathcal{E}_A(\mu \cdot D_r \cdot (D_r - 1) \cdot (D_r - 2))$. Bob could also include more factors of $(D_r - i)$ inside the encryption while reducing r and be able to more accurately approximate a circle around Alice by using more grid cells of a smaller size. Unfortunately, no secure ring homomorphic cryptosystem is yet known to exist.

7   Comparison of the Protocols

In each of our three protocols we say Alice *succeeds* if she discovers Bob is nearby. In some of the protocols, if Alice succeeds, she also learns extra information about Bob's location. We have set up each of our three protocols so that if Alice and Bob are within a distance r of each other, Alice will succeed. In the Louis protocol, the inverse is also true: if Alice and Bob are slightly more than distance r apart, Alice will not succeed. This behaviour does not match realistic use models, however; it is unlikely that Alice will want to learn if Bob is 199 m away, but not if Bob is 201 m away. In our other two protocols, the probability that Alice succeeds does not fall to 0 as soon as Bob is slightly further than r away; rather, it gradually drops to 0 as Bob gets further, reaching 0 at some

Table 3. Feature comparisons of our three protocols

Protocol	Louis (first phase only)	Louis (both phases)	Lester	Pierre
Extra information learned by Alice	none	Bob's exact location	Bob's exact distance	Bob's grid cell distance
Requires third party	✓	✓		
Bob learns r	✓	✓		✓
Bob learns Alice's location		✓		
Communication steps	4	6	2	2

outer threshold distance r_{out}. That is, if Bob's distance from Alice is less than r, Alice will certainly succeed; if his distance is greater than r_{out}, Alice will certainly not succeed, and between those values, Alice's probability of success gradually decreases. This seems to fit better with what Alice is likely to want.

In Figure 4 we plot Alice's success probability against Bob's distance from her (in units of r), for each of the three protocols. As you can see, all three protocols succeed with probability 1 when the distance is less than r. The success probability of the Louis protocol drops immediately to 0 at that point, while the other protocols fall to 0 more gradually. The success probability of the Lester protocol starts dropping slowly as the distance increases past r, but then has a rapid decrease to 0 soon after; this is due to the fact that the kangaroo method for finding discrete logarithms has a small chance of succeeding, even if the logarithm in question is outside the expected exponent range. The success probability of the Pierre protocol, on the other hand, decreases to 0 gradually as the distance increases from r to $r_{out} = 2\sqrt{2}r$; this last value is the maximum distance by which Alice and Bob can be separated and still be in diagonally touching cells.

In Table 3 we summarize the properties of our three protocols. For each, we indicate what additional information Alice learns about Bob's location in the event that the protocol succeeds, and whether the protocol requires the participation of a third party. We also indicate whether Bob learns Alice's choice of r, whether Bob learns any information about Alice's location, and the number of communication steps.

8   Conclusion

We have presented three protocols to solve the nearby-friend problem without requiring a third party that learns location information. Compared to previous work, our protocols require fewer rounds of computation. Moreover, we have demonstrated their feasibility with a sample implementation and its evaluation.

Alerting people of nearby friends is only one of many possible location-based services. A topic of further investigation is what other services can be built with the techniques exploited in this paper.

Acknowledgments

We thank the anonymous reviewers for their comments. This work is supported by the Natural Sciences and Engineering Research Council of Canada.

References

1. Atallah, M.J., Du, W.: Secure Multi-party Computational Geometry. In: Dehne, F., Sack, J.-R., Tamassia, R. (eds.) WADS 2001. LNCS, vol. 2125, pp. 165–179. Springer, Heidelberg (2001)
2. Boneh, D., Goh, E.-J., Nissim, K.: Evaluating 2-DNF Formulas on Ciphertexts. In: Kilian, J. (ed.) TCC 2005. LNCS, vol. 3378, pp. 325–341. Springer, Heidelberg (2005)
3. Brandt, F.: Efficient Cryptographic Protocol Design based on Distributed El Gamal Encryption. In: Won, D.H., Kim, S. (eds.) ICISC 2005. LNCS, vol. 3935, pp. 32–47. Springer, Heidelberg (2006)
4. Cachin, C.: Efficient Private Bidding and Auctions with an Oblivious Third Party. In: Proceedings of 6th ACM Conference on Computer and Communications Security, pp. 120–127. ACM Press, New York (1999)
5. Cheng, R., Zhang, Y., Bertino, E., Prabhakar, S.: Preserving User Location Privacy in Mobile Data Management Infrastructures. In: Danezis, G., Golle, P. (eds.) PET 2006. LNCS, vol. 4258, pp. 393–412. Springer, Heidelberg (2006)
6. Cramer, R., Gennaro, R., Schoenmakers, B.: A Secure and Optimally Efficient Multi-Authority Election Scheme. In: Fumy, W. (ed.) EUROCRYPT 1997. LNCS, vol. 1233, pp. 103–118. Springer, Heidelberg (1997)
7. Dierks, T., Rescorla, E.: The Transport Layer Security (TLS) Protocol Version 1.1. RFC 4346 (April 2006), http://www.ietf.org/rfc/rfc4346.txt
8. Du, W., Zhan, Z.: A Practical Approach to Solve Secure Multi-party Computation Protocols. In: Proceedings of 2002 Workshop on New Security Paradigms Workshop, pp. 127–135 (September 2002)
9. Gedik, B., Liu, L.: Location Privacy in Mobile Systems: A Personalized Anonymization Model. In: ICDCS 2005. Proceedings of 25th International Conference on Distributed Computing Systems (June 2005)
10. Gruteser, M., Grunwald, D.: Anonymous Usage of Location-Based Services Through Spatial and Temporal Cloaking. In: MobiSys 2003. Proceedings of First International Conference on Mobile Systems, Applications, and Services (May 2003)
11. Kocher, P.: Timing Attacks on Implementations of Diffie-Hellman, RSA, DSS, and Other Systems. In: Koblitz, N. (ed.) CRYPTO 1996. LNCS, vol. 1109, pp. 104–113. Springer, Heidelberg (1996)
12. Køien, G.M., Oleshchuk, V.A.: Location Privacy for Cellular Systems; Analysis and Solutions. In: Danezis, G., Martin, D. (eds.) PET 2005. LNCS, vol. 3856, pp. 40–58. Springer, Heidelberg (2006)
13. Liskov, M., Silverman, R.: A Statistical Limited-Knowledge Proof for Secure RSA Keys. IEEE P1363 working group (1998)
14. Loopt, Inc.: loopt - Live In It. (Accessed February 2007), http://www.loopt.com/
15. MIT SENSEable City Lab: iFind (Accessed February 2007), http://ifind.mit.edu/

16. Mokbel, M.F., Chow, C.-Y., Aref, W.G.: The New Casper: Query Processing for Location Services without Compromising Privacy. In: Proceedings of the 32nd International Conference on Very Large Data Bases (VLDB 2006), September 2006, pp. 763–774 (2006)
17. The OpenSSL Project. OpenSSL: The Open Source toolkit for SSL/TLS (Accessed February 2007), http://www.openssl.org/
18. Paillier, P.: Public-Key Cryptosystems Based on Composite Degree Residuosity Classes. In: Stern, J. (ed.) EUROCRYPT 1999. LNCS, vol. 1592, pp. 223–238. Springer, Heidelberg (1999)
19. Pollard, J.M.: Monte Carlo Methods for Index Computation (mod p). Mathematics of Computation 32(143), 918–924 (1978)
20. Shanks, D.: Class number, a theory of factorization, and genera. Proceedings of Symposia in Pure Mathematics 20, 415–440 (1971)
21. Shoup, V.: NTL: A Library for doing Number Theory (Accessed February 2007) http://www.shoup.net/ntl/
22. Yao, A.C.: Protocols for Secure Computations. In: Proceedings of 23rd IEEE Symposium on Foundations of Computer Science, pp. 160–164. IEEE Computer Society Press, Los Alamitos (1982)

Efficient Oblivious Augmented Maps: Location-Based Services with a Payment Broker

Markulf Kohlweiss[1], Sebastian Faust[1], Lothar Fritsch[2], Bartek Gedrojc[3], and Bart Preneel[1]

[1] K.U. Leuven ESAT/COSIC, Kasteelpark Arenberg 10
3001 Leuven, Belgium
[2] Johann Wolfgang Goethe-Universität
60054 Frankfurt am Main, Germany
[3] TU Delf ICT, Mekelweg 4
2628 CD Delft, The Nederlands

Abstract. Secure processing of location data in location-based services (LBS) can be implemented with cryptographic protocols. We propose a protocol based on oblivious transfer and homomorphic encryption. Its properties are the avoidance of personal information on the services side, and a fair revenue distribution scheme. We discuss this in contrast to other LBS solutions that seek to anonymize information as well as possible towards the services. For this purpose, we introduce a proxy party. The proxy interacts with multiple services and collects money from subscribing users. Later on, the proxy distributes the collected payment to the services based on the number of subscriptions to each service. Neither the proxy nor the services learn the exact relation between users and the services they are subscribed to.

1 Introduction

Does my electronic map need to know where I am – or that I am looking at it? Electronic maps can be augmented with information provided by location-based services (LBS). This way subscribed users can find what they need fast. With LBSs, location privacy is at stake. To reach good privacy, it is advisable to limit access to identity information and access to location information. Even the regular observation of service usage patterns might reveal private information.

Today LBSs are provided in one of two ways. Either all the service specific data is made available to the user who computes the result locally—this is the case for car navigation systems; or the service is provided remotely. The latter is the dominant approach for providing LBSs in mobile communication networks. Such LBSs can be seen as a by-product of the GSM system (Global System for Mobile Communications), as the location of subscribers is already used for mobility management [16]. Given these constraints, we aim at achieving privacy for mobile subscribers who want to use LBSs. We presume that the location will be gathered from a mobile network, while the service will be provided by external service providers.

N. Borisov and P. Golle (Eds.): PET 2007, LNCS 4776, pp. 77–94, 2007.

Our approach uses cryptographic protocols to ensure privacy: Oblivious transfer and homomorphic encryption. By developing a framework where the user's location and subscription are processed in the encrypted domain, we achieve privacy for certain classes of LBSs in a new way. Unlike classic approaches using Mixes or anonymous credentials [18], our approach achieves the following strong privacy properties: First, the mobile operator learns nothing in addition to what he already knows except for the set of users that are at all interested in using LBSs. Thus, no usage profiles can be collected. Second, the service providers only learn the number of subscribers to their service. Thus, service providers do not learn the users' location.

Our protocol offers the additional privacy property of service unobservability. Even the service providers do not know whether a user is accessing their service or not. By introducing a privacy trustee we are able to preserve service unobservability in case of service/operator collaboration.

The privacy provided is optimal: the operator needs to know the set of LBSs users such that he can localize and charge them, and services are payed by the operator depending on the number of subscribers they were able to attract.

Efficiency consideration. Despite the strong security requirements, our protocol scales well: The initialization is independent of the number of users. Subscriptions are linear both in effort and in size in the number of services. This is unavoidable, as all services need to be involved to guarantee service unobservability. The mobile user as the party with the most restricted resources has to receive and decrypt only a single message.

Related Work. Various privacy enhancing technologies (PET) have been proposed for LBSs. Most of these techniques focus on providing pseudonymity and anonymity for LBSs. Federath et al. [12] proposed the use of a trusted fixed station and Mixes [8] for hiding the relation of real world identities to location data in GSM networks. While our protocol can be adapted to such a privacy enhanced GSM network by letting the fixed station localize the user (and take over some of the responsibilities of the mobile operator), we explicitly focus on the less privacy friendly but more practical setting where a third party knows the user's location.

Researchers started to develop LBS specific PETs called mix-zones (see [4] and [15]). Mix-zones allow users to switch pseudonyms associated to their location in an unobservable way. Kölsch et al. [18] use pseudonymization techniques in the following realistic setting. A network operator (or a party connected to multiple operators) knows the user's location, while the LBSs are provided by independent service providers that know the user only under short lived pseudonyms. Basically, as location information is inherently attached to a person's life, reidentification is often easy [14]. Location needs to be hidden, not anonymized.

Structure of the paper. Section 2 considers cryptographic tools. We describe the properties and high level implementation of our privacy protecting LBS scheme in Sec. 3. The detailed construction is given in Sec. 4. We analyze the efficiency and security of our solution in Sec. 5 and finally conclude in Sec 6.

2 Tools

Zero-Knowledge Proofs of Knowledge. A *zero-knowledge* proof is an interactive proof in which the verifier learns nothing besides the fact that the statement proven is true. Zero-knowledge proofs-of-knowledge protocols exist for proving various statements about discrete logarithms in groups of known and hidden order [3,5,7,24]. These techniques allow to prove statements about cryptographic primitives that operate in these groups, for instance that two commitments contain the same value, or that a value was verifiably encrypted. Given a statement $\mathsf{Alg}(x) = y$ and $\mathsf{Alg}'(x') = y'$ about two algorithms, with secret input x, x' and public output y, y', it is possible to prove AND and OR relations of these statements. Such protocols can be made non-interactive by applying a cryptographic trick called the Fiat-Shamir heuristic [13]. We write in a short form notation, e.g., for AND

$$\pi = PK\{(x, x') : \mathsf{Alg}(x) = y \land \mathsf{Alg}'(x') = y'\}.$$

Homomorphic Encryption. Homomorphic encryption is a form of malleable encryption. Given two ciphertexts, it is possible to create a third ciphertext, with a plain text that is related to the first two. For (additive) homomorphic encryptions, the encrypted plain texts fulfill the following relations:

$$\mathsf{Enc}_h(m_1) \oplus \mathsf{Enc}_h(m_2) = \mathsf{Enc}_h(m_1 + m_2), \qquad c \otimes \mathsf{Enc}_h(m) = \mathsf{Enc}_h(c \cdot m).$$

We speak of additive homomorphic encryption because $+$ corresponds to the addition operation of a ring. We write $c \otimes \mathsf{Enc}_h(m)$ to denote the c times homomorphic addition of $\mathsf{Enc}_h(m)$. Note that for Damgård-Jurik Encryption [11] $c \otimes \mathsf{Enc}_h(m)$ corresponds to $\mathsf{Enc}_h(m)^c$ and can be implemented efficiently.

Damgård-Jurik Encryption. The Damgård-Jurik cryptosystem is a generalization and adaptation of the Pallier cryptosystem [22] based on the decisional composite residuosity assumption. It allows for the encryption of arbitrary long messages without the need to generate new keys. It preserves the homomorphic property of Pallier. They also describe the zero-knowledge proofs and threshold decryption techniques required by our protocol.

Threshold encryption. In a distributed decryption protocol a private key is shared among a group of parties, where only a qualified subset of the parties is allowed to decrypt a ciphertext c, whereas fewer parties learn nothing on the secret nor on the decryption of c. In our scheme we use the special case of a distributed 3-out-of-3 threshold encryption scheme, which could be implemented, e.g., with the threshold protocol presented in [11].

Oblivious Transfer. Oblivious transfer (OT) was first introduced by Rabin [23]. The primitive captures the notion of a protocol by which a sender sends some information to the receiver, but remains oblivious as to what is sent.

Adaptive OT from Blind Signatures. For LBSs, we are not so much interested in single executions of OT, but want to query the same database multiple times at different indices (for different users and changing locations). Adaptive OT protocols were proposed in [10,19,20]. Camenisch et al. [6] recognized that the schemes in [10,20] are based on a common principle to construct adaptive OT from unique blind signature schemes (UBSS). The first UBSS is described by Chaum in [9].

We briefly sketch the basic idea of adaptive OT schemes based on UBSS. First, all messages $m_1, \ldots, m_n$ are symmetrically encrypted using the hashed signature of the index i, $1 \leq i \leq n$, as the key. Thus $C_i = \mathsf{Enc}_s(m_i; H(\mathsf{Sign}(i; sk)))$. H is a symmetric hash function, Enc_s is a secure symmetric cipher, Sign is the signature algorithm corresponding to the UBSS, and sk is the signing key of the sender that will be used for creating the blind signature. The ciphertexts $C_1, \ldots, C_n$ are transferred to the receiver. To obtain message $m_{\hat{\imath}}$, the receiver runs a blind signature protocol with the sender on message $\hat{\imath}$ to obtain the symmetric key (signature on $\hat{\imath}$).

OT using Homomorphic Encryption. It is a known property of additive homomorphic encryption that given an encryption $Q = \mathsf{Enc}_h(1)$ it is possible to compute an encryption of a message m as $m \otimes Q = \mathsf{Enc}_h(m \cdot 1) = \mathsf{Enc}_h(m)$. However, if $Q = \mathsf{Enc}_h(0)$, the same operation does not change anything, i.e., $m \otimes \mathsf{Enc}_h(0) = \mathsf{Enc}_h(0)$ [21].

Given the semantic security of the encryption, the party trying to encode the message cannot distinguish the two cases above. Based on this observation an OT can be constructed by using a vector $\boldsymbol{Q} = (Q_1, \ldots, Q_\ell)$. To request message $m_{\hat{\jmath}}$, $Q_{\hat{\jmath}} = \mathsf{Enc}_h(1)$ and $Q_j = \mathsf{Enc}_h(0)$ for $j \neq \hat{\jmath}$. Zero-knowledge proofs can be used to prove the correct construction of Q. The communication complexity of the protocol can be reduced by computing $E = \bigoplus_{j=1}^{\ell} m_j \otimes Q_j$, and transferring only E to the recipient.

3   Privacy Protected LBS Scheme: Security Definition and Solution Sketch

3.1   Definition

Parties. Our protocol involves a user $\mathcal{U}$ who accesses LBSs over her mobile device. Her goal is to obtain location specific information on topics of her interest. This information is collected and served by service providers $\mathcal{L}_1, \ldots, \mathcal{L}_\ell$. A third party that knows the user's location and stands in a financial relationship with the user acts as a proxy $\mathcal{P}$ between users and services — this could be the mobile operator of the user or an organization associated with it. The proxy is responsible for the security of the location information and assists in the payment transaction. We assume that the number of users connected over a proxy is much higher than the number of services. Finally, we assume the existence of an independent party without any commercial interests: a privacy protection organization $\mathcal{T}$ that can be offline for most of the time. We refer to all parties except users as organizations.

Security and Privacy Requirements. A secure and privacy friendly LBS protocol should protect the assets and interests of all involved parties. The assets that need to be protected are: the user's location, the user's subscription, the topic specific databases of the $\mathcal{L}_j$, and the payment. We consider the following requirements:

- *Location privacy:* The protocol does not reveal the user's location to the service.
- *Service usage privacy:* Even when the proxy and the LBSs collude, the secrecy of the user's subscription remains protected. This includes message privacy; i.e., only the users can decrypt the messages of services.
- *Database secrecy:* The user and the proxy get no information about the topic specific database of $\mathcal{L}_j$. A user gets only the information for the locations she requested. This property must hold even if the proxy and the proxy collude.
- *Fairness:* It is guaranteed that either the user receives the expected data for the requested location and the LBS receives his expected payment, or the cheating party can be uniquely identified. In order to preserve service usage privacy, the user reveals the cheating party only to the trustee $\mathcal{T}$.

Protocol phases. In the *Setup* phase the involved parties generate their keys. During the *Service Update* phase, each service $\mathcal{L}_j$ encrypts its topic specific database and transfers it to the proxy. In the *Subscription* phase a user $\mathcal{U}$ creates an encrypted subscription for a service, sends it to the proxy, and is charged the subscription fee. In the *Data Retrieval* phase the proxy runs a protocol with every service $\mathcal{L}_j$ and obtains an encrypted result. The proxy combines them into a single encrypted result for the user such that she only receives the data of the subscribed service. The fair allocation of the money collected in the subscription phase takes place in the *Settlement* phase under the supervision of the trustee $\mathcal{T}$.

Remarks. The database of a service $\mathcal{L}_j$ is represented as a one-dimensional vector with one element for each location. We assume that the number of locations n is the same for all services. Further, we assume that services only update the whole database at once. In the current version of our protocol a user is only subscribed to a single service. Service usage privacy is guaranteed with respect to the total number of users that subscribed during a subscription period. A subscription period is defined as the time between two settlement phases. Finally, we assume that parties communicate over secure channels and that $\mathcal{P}$, $\mathcal{L}_j$, and $\mathcal{T}$, are able to authenticate communication, and to sign messages using their identity.

3.2 High-Level Approach and First Sketch

We follow a constructive approach in the description of our protocol. We use building blocks from Sec. 2, put them into place, and describe their function in our construction. Some of the security requirements can be fulfilled by the functionality provided by individual building blocks; others require a complex interplay between building blocks. As a consequence the mapping from building blocks to the sub-protocols of our solution is not one-to-one. We will sketch the sub protocols (cf. Fig. 1) as they get assembled from their building blocks.

Our main building blocks are two variants of OT and a threshold encryption scheme. Homomorphic encryption and zero-knowledge protocols serve as sub - building blocks in the previous schemes, but are also used to glue them together in a secure way. The two OT protocols are specifically selected for their good performance under repetition of input data. The blind signature based OT scheme (cf. Sec. 2) is optimized for the case that the input database remains fixed, while the index varies. The homomorphic encryption based OT is efficient in the opposite case; it is efficient for fixed indices.

During the protocol execution, a single proxy interacts with a multitude of users and multiple services. The first building block we put into place is a blind signature based OT protocol. It is executed with the proxy acting as the requester and one of the services as the sender. It allows the proxy to retrieve location specific information $m_{\hat{i},j}$ for a user at location $\hat{i}$ without service L_j learning the user's location. This guarantees *location privacy*. The proxy executes this sub-protocol with all offered services. This assures *service privacy* at the service side. In this way the proxy obtains an information vector $m_{\hat{i},1}, \ldots, m_{\hat{i},\ell}$.

Our second building block is a homomorphic encryption based OT protocol (cf. Sec. 2). It is run with the proxy acting as the sender (using the aforementioned vector as input) and the user acting as the requester (using the index of the service $L_{\hat{j}}$ she subscribed to as input). The protocol allows the user to learn $m_{\hat{i},\hat{j}}$ without the proxy learning the user's subscription; we achieve full *service privacy*.

Note how the choice of OT protocols is crucial for the performance of our protocol. In the first OT, the same database is queried by the proxy for all users (and different locations as they move about). The database needs to be encrypted and transferred to the proxy only once (cf. Fig. 1.2). For the second OT between user and proxy, the subscribed service is invariant for the duration of a subscription period and it is sufficient to send the first (and expensive) message of the homomorphic OT only once (cf. Fig 1.3 ①). Consequently we split off these operations as sub-protocols which have the semantic of a service update and a user's subscription.

This gives us a first instantiation of the first 4 protocol phases. The outline of the protocol is depicted in Fig. 1. Note that some of the sub protocols are not yet implemented. For ease of presentation we use a simplified notation. The detailed protocol description is given in Section 4.

Setup. (cf. Fig. 1.1: ① KeygenU, ② KeygenL) Every user generates a key-pair for a homomorphic encryption scheme ①. These keys are used for the OT based on homomorphic encryption. Every service generates a key-pair (skB, pkB) that is used for OT based on blind signatures ②.

Service Update. (cf. Fig. 1.2: ② EncryptData) The database of the LBS L_j consists of the n elements $m_{(1,j)}, \ldots, m_{(n,j)}$ ①. Each of the elements is encrypted with its own symmetric key $H(k_i)$ that is computed by hashing the signature

$k_i = \mathsf{Sign}(i; skB)$ of the index ②. The encrypted database $DB_j = (C_1, \ldots, C_n)$, with $C_i = \mathsf{Enc}_s(m_i, H(k_i))$ is sent to the proxy ③.

Subscription. (cf. Fig. 1.3: ① Subscribe) A user's subscription ① consists of ℓ elements $S_{(U,1)}, \ldots, S_{(U,\hat{j})}, \ldots, S_{(U,\ell)}$, one for each service ②. Each element contains a ciphertext Q of the homomorphic encryption scheme. Q decrypts to 1 for the service $\mathcal{L}_{\hat{j}}$ the user subscribes to and to 0 otherwise. To ensure the security of the OT the user proves in zero-knowledge that all $S_{(U,j)}$ are correctly constructed.

Data Retrieval. (cf. Fig. 1.4: ① Request, ② Combine, ④ Decrypt) In the data retrieval phase a user obtains location-specific data from her subscribed service. The proxy is involved since he is aware of the user's location and stores the encrypted databases of the services. Recall that these databases are encrypted using hashed signatures as keys. The proxy acts on the user's behalf and can request decryption of individual items without revealing the location of the user. To guarantee service usage privacy the proxy has to repeat the following steps for every service $\mathcal{L}_j$ ①:

The proxy blinds the location $\hat{i}$ and sends the blinded value $\mathsf{Blind}(\hat{i}; b, pkB)$ to the service. The service replies with the blinded signature $\langle k_{\hat{i}} \rangle_{blind}$. The proxy computes $m_{i,j} = \mathsf{Dec}_s(C_{\hat{i}}; H(\mathsf{Unblind}(\langle k_{\hat{i}} \rangle_{blind}; b, pkB)))$. This completes the first OT. The proxy collects $m_{\hat{i},1}, \ldots, m_{\hat{i},\ell}$ and continues with the second OT (the user's first message is taken from her subscription). The proxy takes the Q corresponding to $S_{(U,j)}$ and computes $E_j = m_{\hat{i},j} \otimes Q$ for all $1 \leq j \leq \ell$. This corresponds to an encryption of $m_{\hat{i},\hat{j}}$ for $\mathcal{L}_{\hat{j}}$ and an encryption of 0 otherwise.

As a last step the proxy combines the E_j by homomorphically adding all the encryptions (not knowing which of them contain the message) ②. This way all encryptions of 0 cancel out. The result is transferred to the user ③. She decrypts E to obtain $m_{i,\hat{j}}$ ④.

The two main flaws of this construction are (1) the fact that the proxy learns the $m_{i,j}$ vector for the locations of all users. This is a compromise of *database secrecy* and (2) the lack of a fair payment infrastructure.

3.3 First Revision: Database Secrecy

We address the lack of *database secrecy* by intertwining the first OT with the second. To this end we let the proxy pass on $S_{(U,j)}$ to $\mathcal{L}_j$. Now (after agreeing on who sends which bit range) both $\mathcal{L}_j$ and the proxy can act as senders in the second OT without learning each others inputs. This is made possible by the properties of homomorphic encryption, which lets everyone manipulate encrypted data. Informally, the last message of the first OT will be transferred as part of the encrypted payload of the second OT. This guarantees that only the user with her secret decryption key can obtain the results of both protocols.

More concretely the following changes have to be made in the subscription and data retrieval phases.

Subscribe. The $S_{(U,j)}$ are now also sent to the services ②.

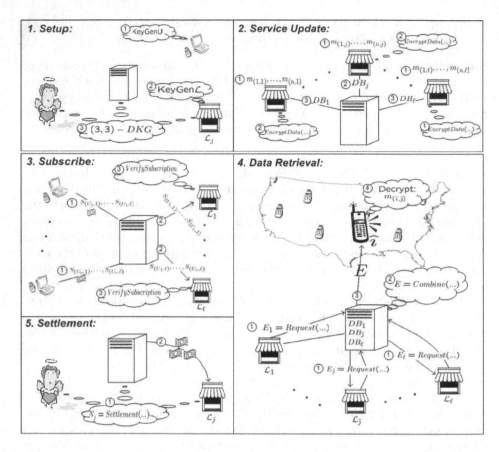

Fig. 1. Setup and Service Update, Subscription, Data Transfer, and the Settlement phase: Subscription $S_{(U,j)}$, encrypted database DB_j, service result E_j, combined result E, location-specific message $m_{(\hat{i},\hat{j})}$, number of subscriptions N_j, location $\hat{i}$, and the subscribed service $\hat{j}$

Data Retrieval. During Request ① the proxy blinds the location $\hat{i}$ and sends the blinded value $\mathsf{Blind}(\hat{i}; b, pkB)$ to the service. To ensure that only the user (and not the proxy) can decrypt $C_{\hat{i}}$, the service encrypts the blinded signature $\langle k_{\hat{i}} \rangle_{blind}$. This is done with an additive homomorphic encryption scheme. Remember that during subscription the user (through the proxy) provided the service $\mathcal{L}_{\hat{j}}$ with an encryption $Q = \mathsf{Enc}_h(1)$. The service computes $E_{\hat{j}} = \langle k_{\hat{i}} \rangle_{blind} \otimes Q = \mathsf{Enc}_h(\langle k_{\hat{i}} \rangle_{blind} \cdot 1) = \mathsf{Enc}_h(\langle k_{\hat{i}} \rangle_{blind})$. The result is sent to the proxy who uses a similar approach to add b and $C_{\hat{i}}$ to $E_{\hat{j}}$. These requests are done for all services, including those the user did not subscribe to. The latter however received $Q = \mathsf{Enc}_h(0)$ during Subscribe and all the operations result in $E_j = \mathsf{Enc}_h(0)$, for $j \neq \hat{j}$.

As a last step the proxy computes the homomorphic sum of all encryptions—not knowing which of them contain the unblinding information, the encrypted message, and the blinded signature ②. This way all encryptions of 0 cancel out. The result is transferred to the user ③. She decrypts E, obtains $b\|C_{\hat{\imath}}\|\langle k_{\hat{\imath}}\rangle_{blind}$, and computes $m_{\hat{\imath}\hat{\jmath}} = \mathsf{Dec}_s(C_{\hat{\imath}}; H(\mathsf{Unblind}(\langle k_{\hat{\imath}}\rangle_{blind}; b, pkB)))$ ④.

3.4 Second Revision: Payment Infrastructure

The core idea for the payment infrastructure is to bind the request of the second OT (the subscription) to a vote. Now revenues can be fairly distributed between services by anonymously counting the number of times users voted for (subscribed to) a service. We use ballot counting techniques based on homomorphic encryption and threshold decryption. We make the following changes to the setup and subscription phase, and we provide an implementation for the settlement phase.

Setup. (cf. Fig. 1.1: ③ PaymentSetup) Each LBS $\mathcal{L}_j$ runs a distributed key generation protocol together with the proxy and the privacy trustee ③. This results in a key pair with a secret key shared according to a $(3, 3)$-threshold scheme. The shared key is needed in the settlement phase to jointly compute the payment result.

Subscription. (cf. Fig. 1.3: ① Subscribe, ③ VerifySubscription) A user's subscription ① consists of ℓ elements $S_{(U,1)}, \ldots, S_{(U,\hat{\jmath})}, \ldots, S_{(U,\ell)}$, one for each service ②. Each element contains two ciphertexts Q and P of the homomorphic encryption scheme, where the first is encrypted with the user's public key and the latter with the payment key. Both Q and P decrypt to 1 for the service $\mathcal{L}_{\hat{\jmath}}$ the user subscribes to, and to 0 otherwise. To ensure the security of the OT and the payment, $\mathcal{U}$ proves in zero-knowledge that Q and P are constructed correctly. The service providers check these proofs before providing the service ③.

Settlement. (cf. Fig. 1.5: ① Settlement) The technique used in the Settlement phase is similar to a technique used in electronic voting protocols. The non-interactive zero-knowledge proof sent by the user in the subscription ensures that P and Q encrypt the same value (either 1 or 0). The homomorphic property of the ciphertexts allows to anonymously sum up the content of all different P values. The trustee $\mathcal{T}$ ensures that only the homomorphic sums (and not individual subscriptions) are decrypted in a 3-out-of-3 threshold decryption ①. Based on the result the proxy divides the subscription money received from the users during subscription in a fair way ②.

4 Our Multi-party Proxy LBS Scheme

Notation. We write cryptographic primitives as $\mathsf{Alg}(x; k)$, where x denotes the processed inputs of the algorithm and k denotes keys, randomness, or public parameters. When it is clear from the context k is omitted. We use the $\mathsf{Alg}(\mathcal{E}_1(x_1; k_1), \mathcal{E}_2(x_2; k_2))$ to denote an interactive algorithm between entities $\mathcal{E}_1$ and $\mathcal{E}_2$ with the respective inputs and keys.

Length Parameters. Let κ be a security parameter that determines the key sizes of the underlying cryptographic schemes. We use $l_N \in \Theta(\kappa)$ to denote the length of the RSA modulus N used for Damgård-Jurik encryption. The length of a ciphertext for a plaintext of length N^s is N^{s+1}. For simplicity we use ciphertexts of length $l_N(s+1)$, to encode plaintexts of length $(l_N - 1)s$. We use l_H to denote the length of the plaintext for the homomorphic encryption scheme. Let l_B, l_b, and l_D be the length of a blinded signature, the blinding factor, and an encrypted database entry respectively. We require $l_B + l_b + l_D \leq l_H$.

Setup. PaymentSetup($\mathcal{L}_j(1^\kappa), \mathcal{P}(1^\kappa), \mathcal{T}(1^\kappa)$) is executed for each service $\mathcal{L}_j$. The privacy trustee $\mathcal{T}$, the proxy $\mathcal{P}$ and the LBS $\mathcal{L}_j$ run a distributed key generation protocol to generate a public payment key pkS_j. The secret key skS_j is shared according to a $(3,3)$-threshold encryption scheme such that only the three parties together can reconstruct the key. This results in three secret shares $skS_{(\mathcal{L}_j,j)}$, $skS_{(\mathcal{P},j)}$, and $skS_{(\mathcal{T},j)}$, which are included in the secret key of $\mathcal{P}$, $\mathcal{L}_j$, and $\mathcal{T}$ respectively.

LBS Key Generation. Every service $\mathcal{L}_j$ runs KeygenL(1^κ) to generate the keypair $(pk_{\mathcal{L}_j}, sk_{\mathcal{L}_j})$ that contains amongst others a key pair (pkB_j, skB_j) for a unique blind signature protocol.

Proxy Key Generation. For our construction the proxy does not need to generate keys on his own. The public key $pk_{\mathcal{P}}$ of $\mathcal{P}$ results from adding the public payment keys of the services. Hence $pk_{\mathcal{P}}$ contains $pkS_1, \ldots, pkS_\ell$. His secret key $sk_{\mathcal{P}}$ contains the corresponding secret shares $skS_{(\mathcal{P},1)}, \ldots, skS_{(\mathcal{P},\ell)}$.

User Key Generation. KeygenU(1^κ) generates a key pair $(pk_{\mathcal{U}}, sk_{\mathcal{U}})$ for an additive homomorphic Damgård-Jurik cryptosystem [11] used for homomorphic OT [21].

Service update. Each LBS $\mathcal{L}_j$ encrypts its location specific information using algorithm EncryptData($m_{(1,j,v)}, \ldots, m_{(n,j,v)}, v; sk_{\mathcal{L}_j}$). The value v denotes the version number of the data update. Note that $m_{(i,j,v)}$ contains i,j, and v and is signed by $\mathcal{L}_j$ to allow for checks of authenticity. A service $\mathcal{L}_j$ uses his secret key skB_j to compute $DB_{(j,v)} = (C_{(1,j,v)}, \ldots, C_{(n,j,v)}, v)$:

$$k_{(i,j,v)} = \mathsf{Sign}(i\|v; skB_j)$$
$$C_{(i,j,v)} = \mathsf{Enc}_s(m_{(i,j,v)}; H(k_{(i,j,v)})).$$

The cryptographic hash function H is used for computing the symmetric key. Note that in Sign the values i and v need to be interpreted as fixed length bit strings. The resulting database $DB_{(j,v)}$ is sent to the proxy.

Subscription. User $\mathcal{U}$ must subscribe to a service $\mathcal{L}_j$ to receive location related information from him. This is done by running the protocol Subscribe($\mathcal{P}(sk_{\mathcal{P}}, pk_{\mathcal{U}})$, $\mathcal{U}(\hat{j}; sk_{\mathcal{U}}, pk_{\mathcal{P}})$) together with the proxy. The proxy's public key is parsed as $pk_{\mathcal{P}} = (pkS_1, \ldots, pkS_\ell)$ and the user proceeds as follows:

1. $\mathcal{U}$ uses her public key $pk_{\mathcal{U}}$ to compute subscription elements $S_{(\mathcal{U},j)}, 1 \leq j \leq \ell$:

$$S_{(\mathcal{U},j)} = (Q_{(\mathcal{U},j)}, P_{(\mathcal{U},j)}, \pi_j) \text{ where}$$

$$Q_{(\mathcal{U},j)} = \begin{cases} \mathsf{Enc}_h(1; pk_{\mathcal{U}}) & \text{if } j = \hat{j} \\ \mathsf{Enc}_h(0; pk_{\mathcal{U}}) & \text{otherwise} \end{cases}, \quad P_{(\mathcal{U},j)} = \begin{cases} \mathsf{Enc}_h(1; pkS_j) & \text{if } j = \hat{j} \\ \mathsf{Enc}_h(0; pkS_j) & \text{otherwise} \end{cases}$$

$$\pi_j = SPK\{(r_1, r_2):$$
$$(Q_{(\mathcal{U},j)} = \mathsf{Enc}_h(1; r_1, pk_{\mathcal{U}}) \wedge P_{(\mathcal{U},j)} = \mathsf{Enc}_h(1; r_2, pkS_j)) \vee$$
$$(Q_{(\mathcal{U},j)} = \mathsf{Enc}_h(0; r_1, pk_{\mathcal{U}}) \wedge P_{(\mathcal{U},j)} = \mathsf{Enc}_h(0; r_2, pkS_j))\}$$

   The $Q_{(\mathcal{U},j)}$ are used to request the location specific information from the LBS $\mathcal{L}_j$ and the $P_{(\mathcal{U},j)}$ are used for the oblivious payment.
2. The resulting $S_{(\mathcal{U},1)}, \dots, S_{(\mathcal{U},\ell)}$ are sent to the proxy together with the payment for the subscription, e.g., by using a credit card.
3. Additionally, the user proves in zero-knowledge that the homomorphic sum of the values $Q_{(\mathcal{U},j)}$ is an encryption of 1. This can be done using standard techniques from [11]. See also Sec. 2.
4. If the verification of the the last proof and of the individual π_j proofs succeeds, the proxy adds a time stamp to each $S_{(\mathcal{U},j)}$ and signs it.

The proxy passes each subscription $S_{(\mathcal{U},j)}$ on to the respective service $\mathcal{L}_j$. He keeps a counter of the number of user subscriptions in this subscription period. Optionally the proxy may also retain all $S_{(\mathcal{U},j)}$.

Verify Subscription. Service $\mathcal{L}_j$ runs $\mathsf{VerifySubscription}(S_{(\mathcal{U},j)}, j; pk_{\mathcal{U}}, pk_{\mathcal{P}})$ to verify that $S_{(\mathcal{U},j)}$ is correct, i.e., that the content of the queries $Q_{(\mathcal{U},j)}$ and $P_{(\mathcal{U},j)}$ are equal and encryptions of 0 or 1, and that the proxy cannot deny that the user has subscribed. The first is done by verifying the proofs of knowledge, the latter by verifying the proxy's time stamp and signature.

If the algorithm succeeds, $S_{(\mathcal{U},j)}$ is added to a list of subscriptions S_j. The $P_{(\mathcal{U},j)}$ of S_j will later on be added up using the homomorphic property of the underlying encryption scheme Enc_h. If one of the verifications done by the services $\mathcal{L}_j, 1 \leq j \leq \ell$ fails, they refuse to provide the information and the proxy has to refund the payment for the subscription to the user.

Data retrieval. The proxy runs $\mathsf{Request}(\mathcal{P}(DB_{(j,\hat{v})}, \hat{\imath}; sk_{\mathcal{P}}, pk_{\mathcal{L}_j}), \mathcal{L}_j(S_{(\mathcal{U},j)}; sk_{\mathcal{L}_j}, pk_{\mathcal{U}}, pk_{\mathcal{P}}))$ with $\mathcal{L}_j$ to request location specific information for user $\mathcal{U}$.

The input of the algorithm is the database $DB_{(j,\hat{v})}$ with most up-to-date version $\hat{v}$ and the current location of the user $\hat{\imath}$. The proxy's output is either an encryption of $m_{(\hat{\imath},j,\hat{v})}$ based on the location of the user or an encryption of 0 if $\mathcal{U}$ is not subscribed to $\mathcal{L}_j$.

1. The proxy chooses a random b and computes

$$\langle \hat{\imath} \| \hat{v} \rangle_{blind} = \mathsf{Blind}(\hat{\imath} \| \hat{v}; pkB_j, b).$$

   The random blinding factor b hides the location $\hat{\imath}$ of the user in $\langle \hat{\imath} \| \hat{v} \rangle_{blind}$.

2. The proxy sends $\langle \hat{\imath} \| \hat{v} \rangle_{blind}$ to $\mathcal{L}_j$, $1 \leq j \leq \ell$, which computes

$$E_j = \langle k_{(\hat{\imath},j,\hat{v})} \rangle_{blind} \otimes Q_{(\mathcal{U},j)}, \quad \text{where } \langle k_{\hat{\imath},j,\hat{v}} \rangle_{blind} = \mathsf{Sign}(\langle \hat{\imath} \| \hat{v} \rangle_{blind}; skB_j)$$

3. Every service $\mathcal{L}_j$ sends E_j back to the proxy.
4. The proxy enriches E_j with $C_{(\hat{\imath},j,\hat{v})}$ and b. This is done by computing $E_j :=$ $E_j \oplus ((C_{(\hat{\imath},j,\hat{v})} \| b) \ll l_B) \otimes Q_{(\mathcal{U},j)}$. Where $\ll$ denotes shifting to the left. This only changes the content of E_j if $Q_{(\mathcal{U},j)}$ is an encryption of 1.

Combining. After running Request with every $\mathcal{L}_j$ and receiving the corresponding E_j, the proxy runs $\mathsf{Combine}(E_1, \ldots, E_l, sk_{\mathcal{P}}, pk_{\mathcal{U}})$ to compute $E = \bigoplus_{j=1}^{\ell} E_j$.

Decrypting. The user decrypts E using $\mathsf{Decrypt}(E; sk_{\mathcal{U}}, pk_{\mathcal{L}_j})$:

$$\begin{aligned} C_{(\hat{\imath},\hat{\jmath},\hat{v})} \| b \| \langle k_{(\hat{\imath},\hat{\jmath},\hat{v})} \rangle_{blind} &= \mathsf{Dec}_h(E; sk_{\mathcal{U}}) \\ k_{(\hat{\imath},\hat{\jmath},\hat{v})} &= \mathsf{Unblind}(\langle k_{(\hat{\imath},\hat{\jmath},\hat{v})} \rangle_{blind}; b, pkB_{\hat{\jmath}}) \\ m_{(\hat{\imath},\hat{\jmath},\hat{v})} &= \mathsf{Dec}_s(C_{(\hat{\imath},\hat{\jmath},\hat{v})}; H(k_{(\hat{\imath},\hat{\jmath},\hat{v})})) \end{aligned}$$

Settlement. The proxy $\mathcal{P}$ can share the money collected during subscription fairly by counting the number of users that subscribed to service $\mathcal{L}_j$ in a given subscription period. However, this has to be done without revealing the user's service usage. First, $\mathcal{L}_j$ transfers S_j to the proxy and the privacy trustee. $\mathcal{P}$ and $\mathcal{T}$ check the signature and the time stamp of each $S_{(\mathcal{U},j)}$ to make sure that $\mathcal{L}_j$ does not add self generated subscriptions. Moreover, the proxy checks if $|S_j|$ corresponds to his subscription counter. This is needed to guarantee that services do not try to shrink the anonymity set of users. As the trustee is not online all the time he can only check the plausibility of the value. However, privacy savvy users can submit their encrypted subscriptions (or its hash) to the privacy trustee, which checks if their descriptions are considered during settlement.

The computation of $\mathcal{L}_j$'s fraction of the money is jointly done by the proxy, the privacy trustee and the service $\mathcal{L}_j$. First, they compute $\bigoplus_{\mathcal{U}} P_{(\mathcal{U},j)}$. The result is an encryption of the number of users having subscribed to service $\mathcal{L}_j$. Since $\bigoplus_{\mathcal{U}} P_{(\mathcal{U},j)}$ is encrypted with pkS_j, all three parties have to participate in a distributed $(3,3)$-threshold decryption. The output of $\mathsf{Settlement}(\mathcal{L}_j(S_j; sk_{\mathcal{L}_j}, pk_{\mathcal{P}}),$ $\mathcal{P}(sk_{\mathcal{P}}, pk_{\mathcal{L}_j}), \mathcal{T}(sk_{S_j,T}))$ is the total number of users subscribed to service $\mathcal{L}_j$. As long as not all parties collude, the service usage privacy of the users is guaranteed. See Section 5.2 for details.

5   Security and Efficiency

5.1   Efficiency Analysis

For our efficiency analysis we focus on two main factors. The first is the limitation in computation and communication resources on small mobile devices. The other factor is scalability for the organizations with respect to location resolution, i.e. number n of map cells, number of services ℓ, and number of users. The costs for the setup of the payment and the service and proxy key generation are independent of the number of users and map cells. They are executed by unrestricted parties, and are thus ignored in the analysis. A similar argument holds for the settlement. We consider only public-key operations and use the length parameters from Section 4.

User. The costs incurred by the user are key generation, subscription, and decryption. *Computation:* Key generation involves the generation of a single RSA key. The decryption requires a single Damgård-Jurik decryption. The most relevant cost for the user is the generation of the subscriptions with 12 exponentiations. However, this cost is incurred only once per subscription period. In principle, the computed values can even be reused for multiple periods. *Communication:* A Damgård-Jurik ciphertext size is about $l_H + l_N$, where l_N is the size of the RSA modulus. The overhead in addition to the message length l_D is $l_B + l_b + l_N$. If we use RSA blind signatures, this is three times the size of an RSA modulus. The size of a subscription is about $12\ell(l_H + l_N)$. For small devices and slow communication channels, we suggest to do the key generation and subscription over the user's PC, and synchronize $sk_\mathcal{U}$ to the user's mobile device, or create the keys on the device, and move only $pk_\mathcal{U}$ to the PC for added security.

Organizations. The scalability of our service is nearly optimal. Key setup and database encryption are independent of the number of users. Database encryption is linear in the number of locations. Subscriptions are linear in the number of services—optimal as all services need to be involved to guarantee service privacy. Practically data transfer is independent of the number of locations and again only depends on the number of services.[1]

Computation: The most prominent cost incurred by the service is database encryption requiring one signature operation per location. *Communication:* The most dominant cost for $\mathcal{L}_j$ and $\mathcal{P}$ is the transmission of the encrypted database $DB_{(j,v)}$ which has length $n \cdot l_D$. Moreover, this costs incur whenever any of the m_i should be updated. This is a consequence of our strong database security definition. For a wide range of services it appears reasonable to relax this requirements. Updated encryptions C_i are computed like in EncryptData but only for a subset $U \subset \{1, \ldots, n\}$ of updated locations.

5.2 Security Analysis

Our main goal is to implement LBSs without revealing additional information about the user's location and her service usage profiles. An adversary involved in our protocol should learn nothing except what he already could have learned by being involved in a scenario without LBSs. For the proxy this implies that he is allowed to know the user's location but should not learn anything about the user's service usage profiles. For service providers this implies that both the

---

[1] De facto the dependence is logarithmic as locations are included in the message; 4 billion different locations can be encoded using 32 bits.

user's location and the user's service usage profiles have to be concealed. Note that in a scenario that includes payment mechanisms we have to diminish slightly from this strong security notion of no additional knowledge since a service can infer the number of subscribed users from the received amount of money.

As a further trust assumption we state that the proxy helps to solve fairness conflicts between users and service providers. This trust assumption is supported by the rationality of the proxy: his core competence is setting up the mobile infrastructure such that services and users can communicate in a fair way. Cheating or not cooperating in resolving fairness disputes decreases his reputation, thus decreasing his profit. Only in cases where accusing the cheater would endanger the users service privacy, we make use of the privacy trustee as an additional off-line trusted party. The assumption of a trusted third party to resolve fairness problems is common in the literature of fair exchange protocols. [1,2] have shown that the problem of fairly exchanging data requires at least an off-line trusted party.

Location privacy. For the location privacy note first that in our protocol services only get in contact with location related information in the data retrieval phase. However, there the OT based on blind signatures protects location related information from being revealed unintentionally. The security of the OT scheme is based on the signature's blindness property. This property guarantees that for any malicious service $\hat{\mathcal{L}}_j$ the view of $\hat{\mathcal{L}}_j$ for a messages $M_0 = i\|v$ and for a message $M_1 = i'\|v'$ is computationally indistinguishable. As the user's location $\hat{i}$ is hidden in $\langle\hat{i}\|\hat{v}\rangle_{blind}$, the location privacy can be reduced to the blindness property of the used blind signature scheme.

Service usage privacy is more challenging. Unfortunately, achieving service usage privacy First, the relationship user/service plays a role in different protocol stages; i.e. it is present during data retrieval and in the payment processes. Second, we consider a stronger, but realistic, adversary model and allow for a corrupted proxy, who possibly collaborates with any service. This implies that the service usage privacy cannot rely on the help of the proxy. We proceed by analyzing the relevant phases.

In the subscription phase, the user's subscription together with the proof of knowledge could reveal the user's service usage. In case of the first the crucial information is protected by the semantic security of the underlying homomorphic encryption scheme. The semantic security guarantees that two different subscriptions are indistinguishable. The zero-knowledge property of π_j ensures that no further information is revealed.

During the settlement, privacy is protected by using a joint decryption technique, i.e. a ciphertext can only be decrypted if the three parties, the $\mathcal{P}$, $\mathcal{L}_j$, and $\mathcal{T}$ work together. Hence, even if $\mathcal{P}$ and $\mathcal{L}_j$ are corrupted, there is no way for the adversary to force the decryption of a single subscription that would reveal the user/service relationship. This is only true as long as it is not possible to present faked subscriptions to the privacy trustee, which later on get accepted. This would reduce the size of the anonymity set $|S_j|$. The faked subscription attack reduces to $n - 1$-attack [8], against which a full protection is impossible.

However, to make it more difficult for an adversary, it could be mandatory for users to always submit a subscription (or hash of it) to the trustee. This technique leads to a lower bound for the size of the anonymity set $|S_j|$. To some extent the sensitivity to these attacks can be reduced by using authenticated channels such that subscriptions can be assigned to real users[2].

Although one cannot assume the honesty of the proxy in general, it often seems more realistic to limit the adversaries' power to corrupt only services. This is further supported by our assumption of the proxy's rationality. In the case of the proxy's honesty, we have a stronger protection against the faking attack: first, because the proxy and the trustee verify the correctness of the signature and the time stamp and second, because the proxy checks for the equality of $|S_j|$ and his subscription counter. Both techniques help to protect against attempts in shrinking the anonymity set.

Database secrecy. In contrast to location and service usage privacy the database secrecy protects the interest of the LBS. It guarantees that a user gets no more than the requested information even if she collaborates with the proxy. The database secrecy of our scheme, relies on two aspects: First, the service encrypts his database before he sends it to the proxy. Second, as a result of the data retrieval phase the user only gets to know the requested data. This is due to the so called 'Database security' [20] of the underlying secure OT protocol.

Fairness. Our system is said to be fair if both the interests of the user and of the service are equally protected. With respect to our protocol this means that neither the user gets access to content without paying nor the service is able to cheat and receive a non-authorized payment without providing the information.

The fairness of our protocol significantly relies on the rationality and the consequential semi-honesty of the proxy. Furthermore we require a trade off between service privacy and fairness to protect against active attacks by services.

User fairness. From the user's perspective fairness is accomplished when the user receives the appropriate location information for her payment.

The proxy sends a request to each service. The service responds with a signed value E_j that is either an encryption of 0 (if the user did not subscribe to $\mathcal{L}_j$) or an encryption of the requested data. Should a service fail to provide any value E_j, the proxy forces it to pay a fee corresponding to the price of a service subscription and passes that money on to the affected user.

Now the proxy computes the user's final value E by combining all responses. The user decrypts E and checks whether it corresponds with her requested data. To facilitate this, the messages $m_{(\hat{i},\hat{j},\hat{v})}$ contain $\hat{i},\hat{j}$, and $\hat{v}$ and is signed by $\mathcal{L}_j$. If a message is incorrect, the user can file a complaint.[3]

---

[2] A powerful adversary will always find ways to forge subscriptions, even if it is just by convincing real users with money.

[3] Note that a complaining user acts as a decryption oracle. Together with the homomorphic property this can lead to the decryption of arbitrary messages. Consequently, user should not complain about random looking messages to an untrusted party.

In this case the user has three choices: she can either choose full privacy and give up her money; she can file the complaint with the privacy trustee; or she can complain directly with the proxy. Complaints contain a proof of correct decryption of a signed E. The recipient of the complaint verifies the proof and pays the money back. $\mathcal{T}$ will ask the proxy for the money given to users during conflict resolution in return for a list of bad services. These services will receive reduced payment or be sanctioned otherwise. Should the proxy refuse to pay the money to the trustee this can only be resolved legally.

Our protocol does not protect against denial of service attacks in which malicious services send random ciphertexts instead of $\langle k_{(\hat{i},j,\hat{v})}\rangle_{blind} \otimes Q_j$. However, this can be detected if users are willing to give up their privacy towards the proxy. We again rely on an optimistic strategy and the punishment of attackers upon detection. It is an open problem to propose an efficient data retrieval protocol based on zero-knowledge protocols that solves this problem.

Service fairness means that service providers receive fair payment. In particular, a service provider must receive money for every user he serves.

This is ensured by the checks done in VerifySubscription. The algorithm checks that $Q_{(\mathcal{U},j)}$ and $P_{(\mathcal{U},j)}$ encode the same value $v \in \{0,1\}$. We refer to $P_{(\mathcal{U},j)}$ as the vote. Obviously if $v = 0$, no service is provided. Consider the case of $v = 1$: if (1) all votes are considered and (2) the votes are counted correctly, $P_{(\mathcal{U},j)}$ increases the subscription counter of $\mathcal{L}_j$ by 1. The first is ensured by the time stamp and signature of the proxy. The second property relies on the security of the homomorphic encryption scheme and the security of the distributed decryption against active adversaries.

6   Conclusion

We introduced the first privacy-preserving LBS framework based on cryptographic techniques, namely, on oblivious transfer and homomorphic encryption. The privacy of the user is protected by hiding the user's location from the services and by not revealing information on the user/service relationship. Additionally, we presented a system for subscription management including a fair yet anonymous payment scheme.

We have given strong intuitions on the different security properties of our scheme, however, it remains an open challenge to prove them in a formal context.

References

1. Asokan, N., Schunter, M., Waidner, M.: Optimistic protocols for fair exchange. In: CCS 1997. Proceedings of the 4th ACM conference on Computer and communications security, pp. 7–17. ACM Press, New York, NY, USA (1997)
2. Asokan, N., Shoup, V., Waidner, M.: Asynchronous protocols for optimistic fair exchange. sp 00, 0086 (1998)

3. Bangerter, E., Camenisch, J., Maurer, U.M.: Efficient proofs of knowledge of discrete logarithms and representations in groups with hidden order. In: Hutter and Ullmann [17], pp. 154–171
4. Beresford, A.R., Stajano, F.: Location Privacy in Pervasive Computing. IEEE Pervasive Computing 2(1), 46–55 (2003)
5. Brands, S.: Rapid demonstration of linear relations connected by boolean operators. In: Fumy, W. (ed.) EUROCRYPT 1997. LNCS, vol. 1233, pp. 318–333. Springer, Heidelberg (1997)
6. Camenisch, J., Neven, G., Shelat, A.: Adaptive oblivious transfer from blind signatures (unpublished manuscript through personal communication) (2006)
7. Camenisch, J., Stadler, M.: Proof systems for general statements about discrete logarithms. Technical Report TR 260, Institute for Theoretical Computer Science, ETH Zürich (March 1997)
8. Chaum, D.: Untraceable electronic mail, return addresses, and digital pseudonyms. Communications of the ACM 24(2), 84–90 (1981)
9. Chaum, D.: Blind signatures for untraceable payments. In: CRYPTO, pp. 199–203 (1982)
10. Chu, C.-K., Tzeng, W.-G.: Efficient k-out-of-n oblivious transfer schemes with adaptive and non-adaptive queries. In: Vaudenay, S. (ed.) PKC 2005. LNCS, vol. 3386, pp. 172–183. Springer, Heidelberg (2005)
11. Damgård, I., Jurik, M.: A generalisation, a simplification and some applications of paillier's probabilistic public-key system. In: Kim, K.-c. (ed.) PKC 2001. LNCS, vol. 1992, pp. 119–136. Springer, Heidelberg (2001)
12. Federrath, H., Jerichow, A., Kesdogan, D., Pfitzmann, A.: Security in Public Mobile Communication Networks. In: IFIP TC 6 International Workshop on Personal Wireless Communications, pp. 105–116 (1995)
13. Fiat, A., Shamir, A.: How to prove yourself: Practical solutions to identification and signature problems. In: Odlyzko, A.M. (ed.) CRYPTO 1986. LNCS, vol. 263, pp. 186–194. Springer, Heidelberg (1987)
14. Fritsch, L.: Profiling and location based services. In: Hildebrandt, M., Gutwirth, S. (eds.) FIDIS D7.5: Profiling the European Citizen, Cross- disciplinary perspectives (2007)
15. Gruteser, M., Grunwald, D.: Anonymous usage of location-based services through spatial and temporal cloaking. In: MobiSys'03. Proceedings of First International Conference on Mobile Systems, Applications, and Services, pp. 31–42 (2003)
16. GSM Association: Location Based Services. Permanent reference document. Technical report, SE.23 (2003)
17. Hutter, D., Ullmann, M. (eds.): SPC 2005. LNCS, vol. 3450. Springer, Heidelberg (2005)
18. Kölsch, T., Fritsch, L., Kohlweiss, M., Kesdogan, D.: Privacy for profitable location based services. In: Hutter and Ullmann [17], pp. 164–178
19. Naor, M., Pinkas, B.: Oblivious transfer with adaptive queries. In: Wiener, M.J. (ed.) CRYPTO 1999. LNCS, vol. 1666, pp. 573–590. Springer, Heidelberg (1999)
20. Ogata, W., Kurosawa, K.: Oblivious keyword search. Journal of Complexity 20(2-3), 356–371 (2004)

21. Ostrovsky, R., Skeith I I I, W.: Private searching on streaming data. In: Shoup, V. (ed.) CRYPTO 2005. LNCS, vol. 3621, pp. 223–240. Springer, Heidelberg (2005)
22. Paillier, P.: Public-key cryptosystem based on composite degree residuosity classes. In: Stern, J. (ed.) EUROCRYPT 1999. LNCS, vol. 1592, pp. 223–228. Springer, Heidelberg (1999)
23. Rabin, M.O.: How to exchange secrets by oblivious transfer. Technical Report TR-81, Harvard Aiken Computation Laboratory (1981)
24. Schnorr, C.P.: Efficient signature generation for smart cards. Journal of Cryptology 4(3), 239–252 (1991)

Pairing-Based Onion Routing

Aniket Kate, Greg Zaverucha, and Ian Goldberg

David R. Cheriton School of Computer Science
University of Waterloo
Waterloo, ON, Canada N2L 3G1
{akate,gzaveruc,iang}@cs.uwaterloo.ca

Abstract. This paper presents a novel use of pairing-based cryptography to improve circuit construction in onion routing anonymity networks. Instead of iteratively and interactively constructing circuits with a telescoping method, our approach builds a circuit with a single pass. The cornerstone of the improved protocol is a new pairing-based privacy-preserving non-interactive key exchange. Compared to previous single-pass designs, our algorithm provides practical forward secrecy and leads to a reduction in the required amount of authenticated directory information. In addition, it requires significantly less computation and communication than the telescoping mechanism used by Tor. These properties suggest that pairing-based onion routing is a practical way to allow anonymity networks to scale gracefully.

1 Introduction

The concept of onion routing [27] plays a key role in many efforts to provide anonymous communication. In the world of cryptographic protocols, bilinear pairings [9] have also had comparable impact. Their meeting is not surprising. This paper applies pairing-based cryptographic techniques—namely non-interactive key agreement—to the problem of session key establishment in anonymity networks based on onion routing. We show that this approach offers better performance, evidenced by reduced computational cost and fewer network communications. This improved performance is of particular interest to low-latency anonymity networks, as it increases responsiveness and network capacity. While using fewer resources for cryptography, we are careful to simultaneously meet the security goals provided by existing methods.

1.1 Our Contributions

This paper makes four primary contributions in the field of anonymous communication.

1. We define a privacy-preserving key agreement protocol using bilinear pairings in an identity-based infrastructure. We then adapt it to achieve unilateral (one-way) anonymity with non-interactive key agreement.

N. Borisov and P. Golle (Eds.): PET 2007, LNCS 4776, pp. 95–112, 2007.

2. We use our protocol to build onion routing circuits for anonymity networks like Tor [7]. Our protocol constructs a circuit in a single pass and also provides a practical way to achieve forward secrecy.
3. The performance of our circuit construction protocol surpasses that of Tor, requiring significantly less computation and fewer network communications.
4. Our protocol does not require the public keys of onion routers to be authenticated. This reduces the load on directory servers and improves the scalability of anonymity networks.

The anonymous authentication scheme we present extends the non-interactive key agreement scheme of Sakai, Ohgishi, and Kasahara [29]. Previous work related to pairing-based key exchange, as well as to anonymity networks, is covered in Section 2. We describe the cryptographic protocols in Section 3, and an onion routing system built with a Boneh-Franklin identity-based infrastructure in Section 4. Some of the more practical issues in such a system are discussed in Section 5. Finally, we compare our computational and communications costs to those of Tor in Section 6, and Section 7 concludes.

2 Related Work

Over the years, a large number of anonymity networks have been proposed and some have been implemented. Common to many of them is *onion routing*, a technique whereby a message is wrapped in multiple layers of encryption, forming an *onion*. As the message is delivered via a number of intermediate *onion routers* (ORs), or *nodes*, each node decrypts one of the layers, and forwards the message to the next node. This idea goes back to Chaum [3] and has been used to build both low- and high-latency communication networks. Formalizations and security discussions of onion routing can be found in [2,19,22,32].

A common realization of an onion routing system is to arrange a collection of nodes that will relay traffic for users of the system. Some examples are [5,7,10,27,28] (the related work section of [7] contains a thorough list). To date, the largest onion routing system is Tor, which has approximately 1000 onion routers and hundreds of thousands of users [33]. These numbers (and their growth) underscore the demand for anonymity online.

To use a network of onion routers, users randomly choose a path through the network and construct a *circuit*—a sequence of nodes which will route traffic. After the circuit is constructed, each of the nodes in the circuit shares a symmetric key with the user, which will be used to encrypt the layers of future onions. In the original Onion Routing project [14,27,32] (which was superseded by Tor) circuit construction was done as follows. The user created an onion where each layer contained the symmetric key for one node and the location of the next node, all encrypted with the original node's public key. Each node decrypts a layer, keeps the symmetric key and forwards the rest of the onion along to the next node. The main drawback of this approach is that it does not provide forward secrecy (as defined in [7]). Suppose a circuit is constructed from the user to the sequence of nodes $A \Leftrightarrow B \Leftrightarrow C$, and that A is malicious. If A records the traffic, and at a later time compromises B (at which point he learns the next hop is C), then compromises C, the complete route is known, and A learns who the user has communicated with.

A possible fix for this problem is to frequently change the public keys of each node. This limits the amount of time A has to compromise B and C, but requires that the users of the system frequently contact the directory server to retrieve authentic keys. Later systems constructed circuits incrementally and interactively (this process is sometimes called *telescoping*). The idea is to use the node's public key only to initiate a communication during which a temporary session key is established via the Diffie-Hellman key exchange. Tor constructs circuits in this way, using the Tor authentication protocol (TAP). TAP is described and proven secure in previous work of the last author [13].

Trade-offs exist between the two methods of constructing circuits. Forward secrecy is the main advantage of telescoping, but telescoping also handles nodes that are not accepting connections; if the third node is down during the construction of a circuit, for example, the first two remain, and the user only needs to choose an alternate third. Information about the status and availability of nodes is therefore less important. The drawback of telescoping is the cost; establishing a circuit of length ℓ requires $O(\ell^2)$ network communications, and $O(\ell^2)$ symmetric encryptions/decryptions.

Øverlier and Syverson [24] improve the efficiency of telescoping-based circuit construction using a half-certified Diffie-Hellman key exchange [21, Sec. 12.6]. They further define an efficient single-pass circuit construction and a few variants. The proposed variants offer different levels of forward secrecy, which is traded off against computation and communication. For example, their eventual forward secret variants use frequent rotation of nodes' public keys, presenting the same issues as the first generation onion routing; their immediate forward secrecy variant uses the same amount of communication as the current Tor ($O(\ell^2)$), but less computation.

Privacy-preserving authentication schemes can be one- or two-way (also referred to as unilateral or bilateral). After one-way authentication between Anonymous and Bob, Anonymous has confirmed Bob's identity and Bob learns nothing about Anonymous, except perhaps that he or she is a valid user of a particular system. In a two-way scheme, both users can confirm they are both valid users without learning who the other is.

The work of Okamoto and Okamoto [23] presents schemes for anonymous authentication and key agreement. In Rahman et. al. [26], an anonymous authentication protocol is presented as part of an anonymous communication system for mobile ad-hoc networks. The protocols in both papers are complex, and limited motivation is given for design choices. Further, both papers neglect to discuss the security of their proposed protocols. The protocols we present in Section 3.2 are a great deal simpler than previous protocols. This allows them to be more easily understood, and simplifies the discussion of their security, which appears in Section 3.3.

Previous protocols (as well as ours) owe a lot to the non-interactive key exchange protocol of Sakai, Ohgishi and Kasahara [29]. In the next section, we will review their scheme after covering relevant background material.

3   Pairing-Based Key Agreement with User Anonymity

In one of the pioneering works of pairing-based cryptography, Sakai et al. suggested an identity-based, non-interactive key agreement scheme using bilinear pairings [29]. In this section, we extend this key agreement scheme. We replace the identities of the participants by pseudonyms and our new scheme provides unconditional anonymity to participating users.

3.1   Preliminaries

We briefly review bilinear pairings and the original non-interactive key agreement scheme of Sakai et al. For a detailed presentation of pairings and cryptographic applications thereof see Blake et al. [9] and references therein.

Bilinear Pairings. Consider two additive cyclic groups $\mathbb{G}$ and $\hat{\mathbb{G}}$ and a multiplicative cyclic group $\mathbb{G}_T$, all of the same prime order n. A bilinear map e is a map $e : \mathbb{G} \times \hat{\mathbb{G}} \to \mathbb{G}_T$ with following properties.

1. **Bilinearity:** For all $P \in \mathbb{G}$, $Q \in \hat{\mathbb{G}}$ and $a, b \in \mathbb{Z}_n$, $e(aP, bQ) = e(P, Q)^{ab}$.
2. **Non-degeneracy:** The map does not send all pairs in $\mathbb{G} \times \hat{\mathbb{G}}$ to unity in $\mathbb{G}_T$.
3. **Computability:** There is an efficient algorithm to compute $e(P, Q)$ for any $P \in \mathbb{G}$ and $Q \in \hat{\mathbb{G}}$.

Our protocols, like many pairing-based cryptographic protocols, use a special form of bilinear map called a *symmetric pairing* which has $\mathbb{G} = \hat{\mathbb{G}}$. For such pairings $e(P, Q) = e(Q, P)$ for any $P, Q \in \mathbb{G}$. The modified Weil pairing over elliptic curve groups [34] is an example of a symmetric bilinear pairing. In the rest of the paper, unless otherwise specified, all bilinear pairings are symmetric.

The Bilinear Diffie-Hellman Assumption. The *Bilinear Diffie-Hellman* (BDH) problem is to compute $e(P, P)^{abc} \in \mathbb{G}_T$ given a generator P of $\mathbb{G}$ and elements aP, bP, cP for $a, b, c \in \mathbb{Z}_n^*$. An equivalent formulation of the problem, due to the bilinearity of the map, is to compute $e(A, B)^c$ given a generator P of $\mathbb{G}$, and elements A, B and cP.

If there is no efficient algorithm to solve the BDH problem for $\langle \mathbb{G}, \mathbb{G}_T, e \rangle$, they are considered to satisfy the *BDH assumption*.

Boneh-Franklin Setup and Non-Interactive Key Agreement. In a Boneh-Franklin Identity-Based Encryption (BF-IBE) setup [1], a trusted authority, called a private key generator (PKG), generates private keys (d_i) for clients using their well-known identities (ID_i) and a master secret s. A client with identity ID_i receives the private key $d_i = sH(\text{ID}_i) \in \mathbb{G}$, where $H : \{0,1\}^* \to \mathbb{G}^*$ is a full-domain cryptographic hash function and $\mathbb{G}^*$ denotes the set of all elements in $\mathbb{G}$ except the identity.

Sakai et al. observed that, with such a setup, any two clients of the same PKG can compute a shared key using only the identity of the other participant and their own private keys. Only the two clients and the PKG can compute this key. For two clients with identities ID_A and ID_B, the shared key is given by $K_{AB} = e(Q_A, Q_B)^s = e(Q_A, d_B) = e(d_A, Q_B)$ where $Q_A = H(\text{ID}_A)$ and $Q_B = H(\text{ID}_B)$.

Dupont and Enge proved this protocol is secure in the random oracle model assuming the BDH problem in $\langle \mathbb{G}, \mathbb{G}_T, e \rangle$ is hard [8].

3.2 Anonymous Key Agreement

We observe that by replacing the identity hashes with pseudonyms generated by users, a key agreement protocol with unconditional anonymity is possible. In our protocol, a participant can confirm that the other participant is a client of the same PKG, but can not determine his identity. Each client can randomly generate many possible pseudonyms and the corresponding private keys.

Suppose Alice, with (identity, private key) pair (ID_A, d_A), is seeking anonymity. She generates a random number r_A and creates the pseudonym and corresponding private key $(P_A = r_A Q_A = r_A H(\text{ID}_A), r_A d_A = s P_A)$. In a key agreement protocol, she sends the pseudonym P_A instead of her actual identity to another participating client, who may or may not be anonymous. For two participants (say Alice and Bob) with pseudonyms P_A and P_B, the shared session key is given as

$$ K_{AB} = e(P_A, P_B)^s = e(Q_A, Q_B)^{r_A r_B s} $$

where r_A and r_B are random numbers generated respectively by Alice and Bob. If Bob does not wish to be anonymous, he can just use $r_B = 1$ instead of a random value, resulting in $P_B = Q_B$. If persistent pseudonymity is desired instead of anonymity, the random values can easily be reused.

Two participants can perform a session key agreement by exchanging pseudonyms. Further, two participants can also perform an authenticated key agreement by modifying any secure symmetric-key based mutual authentication protocol and simply replacing their identities by their pseudonyms.

One-Way Anonymous Key Agreement. Anonymous communication generally requires anonymity for just one of the participants; the other participant often works as a service provider and the anonymous participant needs to confirm her identity. In the key agreement protocol, the service provider uses her actual identity rather than a pseudonym. Further, in this one-way anonymity setting two participants can agree on a session key in a non-interactive manner. A non-interactive scheme to achieve this is defined next.

Suppose Alice and Bob are clients of a PKG. As before, Alice has identity ID_A and private key $d_A = s Q_A = s H(\text{ID}_A)$. Alice wishes to remain anonymous to Bob, but she knows Bob's identity ID_B.

1. Alice computes $Q_B = H(\text{ID}_B)$. She chooses a random integer $r_A \in \mathbb{Z}_n^*$, generates the corresponding pseudonym $P_A = r_A Q_A$ and private key $r_A d_A = s P_A$, and computes the session key $K_{AB} = e(sP_A, Q_B) = e(Q_A, Q_B)^{sr_A}$. She sends her pseudonym P_A to Bob.
2. Bob, using P_A and his private key d_B, computes the session key $K_{AB} = e(P_A, d_B) = e(Q_A, Q_B)^{sr_A}$.

Note that in step 1, Alice can also include a message for Bob symmetrically encrypted with the session key; we will use this in Section 4. Note also that in practice, the session key is often derived from K_{AB}, and not K_{AB} itself.

Key Authentication and Confirmation. In most one-way anonymous communication situations, it is also required to authenticate the non-anonymous service provider. With the non-interactive protocols of this section, the key is implicitly authenticated; Alice is assured that only Bob can compute the key. If Alice must be sure Bob has in fact computed the key, explicit key confirmation can be achieved by incorporating any symmetric-key based challenge-response protocol.

3.3 Security and Anonymity

In this section, we discuss the security and anonymity of our key agreement schemes in the random oracle model. We make following claims:

Unconditional Anonymity: It is impossible for the other participant in a protocol run, the PKG or any third party to learn the identity of an anonymous participant in a protocol run.

No Impersonation: It is infeasible for a malicious client of the PKG to impersonate another (non-anonymous) client in a protocol run. In the case of persistent pseudonymity, it is not feasible for a malicious entity to communicate using a different entity's pseudonym.

Session Key Secrecy: It is infeasible for anyone other than the two participants or the PKG to determine a session key generated during a protocol run.

Next, we present informal proofs for each of our claims. For complete security proofs, we refer the reader to the full version of this paper [15].

Unconditional Anonymity. For an anonymous client with identity ID_C, the pseudonym $P_C = r_C Q_C \in \mathbb{G}$ is the only parameter exchanged during the protocol that is derived from her identity. Because $\mathbb{G}$ is a cyclic group of prime order, multiplying by the random r_C perfectly blinds the underlying identity. The anonymity set is restricted to the clients of a PKG, unless a random pair $(U, d_U) \in \mathbb{G}$ is made public. In the latter case, anyone can generate a pseudonym and participate in the protocol using (U, d_U).

No Impersonation. Suppose an adversarial client with ID_{adv}, d_{adv} wishes to impersonate a non-anonymous participant (say, Bob with ID_B) while communicating with an anonymous client with pseudonym P_A. The adversary would need to compute $K_{AB} = e(P_A, Q_B)^s$ given P_A, Q_B, Q_{Adv} and sQ_{Adv}. But this is just the BDH problem, so under the BDH assumption on $\langle \mathbb{G}, \mathbb{G}_T, e \rangle$, impersonation of other clients is infeasible.

Similarly, if the adversary wishes to communicate with Bob using the persistent pseudonym P_A of some other pseudonymous entity, it must compute $K_{AB} = e(P_A, Q_B)^s$ given P_A, Q_B, Q_{Adv} and sQ_{Adv}. Again, the adversary must solve the BDH problem.

Session Key Secrecy. Dupont and Enge [8] prove the security of the key agreement scheme of Sakai et al. in the random oracle model. According to this proof, an attacker cannot compute the shared key if the BDH assumption holds on $\langle \mathbb{G}, \mathbb{G}_T, e \rangle$, and H is modelled by a random oracle. Our protocol simply modifies that of Sakai et al. to use $P_i = H'(\texttt{ID}_i)$ instead of $Q_i = H(\texttt{ID}_i)$, where $H'(x) = r_i \cdot H(x)$ for a random value r_i, so the proof of security in [8] is easily modified to suit our protocol.

3.4   Distributed PKG

The PKG in the BF-IBE framework, with the master key, has the power to decrypt all messages encrypted for clients. As our schemes use the same setup as BF-IBE, the PKG can compute a session key from the publicly available pseudonyms and the master key s. Due to this, compromise of the PKG is a single point of failure for security.

Boneh and Franklin suggest the use of a distributed PKG instead a single PKG to mitigate this problem. Their distributed PKG uses t out of m threshold cryptography [31], which involves distributing the master key information among m PKGs, such that any t of them, but no fewer, can compute the master key or generate a private key for a client. Their key distribution scheme uses a dealer who actually decides the master key and thus becomes a candidate for attack and can be a single point of failure. Instead, we suggest the use of a distributed key generation protocol such as that of Pedersen [25] or Gennaro et al. [12]. In these protocols, a master key is generated in a completely distributed way with each of m PKGs contributing a random share. The distributed design is additionally more robust; at any given time only t of the m PKGs must be online in order for a client to retrieve his private key.

3.5   Applications of Our Anonymity Schemes

Our anonymous key agreement schemes can be used to perform anonymous communication in any setting having a BF-IBE setup. In recent years, numerous BF-IBE based solutions have been suggested for various practical situations, such as ad-hoc networks. [4,16,30] Our anonymous key agreement schemes can be used in all of these setups without any extra effort. In this paper, we focus on a new pairing-based onion routing protocol which achieves forward secrecy and constructs circuits without telescoping. We describe this protocol in the next section.

4 Pairing-Based Onion Routing

Low-latency onion routing requires one-way anonymous key agreement and forward secrecy. In this section, we describe a new pairing-based onion routing protocol using the non-interactive key agreement scheme defined in Section 3.2.

Our onion routing protocol has a significant advantage over the original onion routing protocol [14] as well as the protocol used in Tor [7]; it provides a practical way to achieve forward secrecy without building circuits by telescoping. Though this is possible with the original onion routing protocol, that method involves regularly communicating authenticated copies of ORs' public keys to the system users; forward secrecy is achieved by periodically rotating these keys. This does not scale well; every time the public keys are changed *all* users must contact a directory server to retrieve the new authenticated keys. However, our onion routing protocol uses ORs' identities, which users can obtain or derive without repeatedly contacting a central server, thus providing practical forward secrecy without telescoping.

4.1 Design Goals and Threat Model

As our protocol only differs from existing onion routing protocols in the circuit construction phase, our threat model is that of Tor. For example, adversaries have complete control over some part (but not all) of the network, as well as control over some of the nodes themselves.

We aim at frustrating attackers from linking multiple communications to or from a single user. Like Tor, we do not try to develop a system secure against a global observer, which can in theory follow end-to-end traffic. Further, it should not be feasible for any node to determine the identity of any node in a circuit other than its two adjacent nodes. Finally, we require forward secrecy: after some amount of time, the session keys used to protect node identities and the contents of messages are irrecoverable, even if all participants in the network are subsequently compromised.

4.2 Pairing-Based Onion Routing Protocol

An onion routing protocol involves a service provider, a set of onion routers, and users. In our protocol, a user does not build the circuit incrementally via telescoping, but rather in a single pass. The user chooses ℓ ORs from the available pool and generates separate pseudonyms for communicating with each of them. The user computes the corresponding session keys and uses them to construct a message with ℓ nested layers of encryption. This process uses the protocol given in Section 3.2 ℓ times.

The service provider works as the PKG for the ORs and provides private keys for their identities.

Forward Secrecy. There are two time-scale parameters in our protocol: the *master key validity period* (MKVP) and the *private key validity period* (PKVP).

Both of these values relate to the forward secrecy of the system. The PKVP specifies how much exposure time a circuit has against compromises of the ORs that use it. That is, until the PKVP elapses, the ORs have enough information to collectively decrypt circuit construction onions sent during that PKVP. After each PKVP, ORs discard their current private keys and obtain new keys from the PKGs. This period can be short, perhaps on the order of an hour.

The MKVP specifies the circuit's exposure time against compromises of the (distributed) PKG which reveal the master secret s. Because changing s involves the participation of all of the ORs as well as the PKGs, we suggest the MKVP be somewhat longer than the PKVP, perhaps on the order of a day. Remember that in the t of m distributed PKG, if at least $m - t + 1$ PKG members are honest and not compromised, no one will ever learn the value of a master secret.

Protocol Description. As discussed above, we propose the use of a distributed PKG, but for simplicity, our discussion will consider the PKG to be a single entity. Using a distributed PKG affects only the setup and key generation steps.

Setup: Given the security requirements, the PKG generates a digital signature key pair (for any secure digital signature scheme). It also generates a prime n, two groups $\mathbb{G}$ (written additively) and $\mathbb{G}_T$ (written multiplicatively) of order n and a bilinear map $e : \mathbb{G} \times \mathbb{G} \to \mathbb{G}_T$. Finally, the PKG chooses a full-domain cryptographic hash function $H : \{0,1\}^* \to \mathbb{G}^*$. The PKG publishes all of these values except its private signature key.

Key Generation: For each MKVP, the PKG generates a random master key $s \in \mathbb{Z}_n^*$ and a random $U \in \mathbb{G}$, and calculates sU. The PKG publishes a signed copy of (v_m, U, sU), where v_m is a timestamp for the MKVP in question. This U is a common value to be shared by all users of the system.

For every valid OR with identity $\mathtt{ID}_i$, and for every PKVP v that overlaps with the MKVP, the PKG generates the private key $d_{vi} = sH(v\|\mathtt{ID}_i)$. The PKG distributes these private keys, as well as a copy of the signed (v_m, U, sU), to the appropriate ORs over a secure authenticated forward-secret channel. If an OR becomes compromised, the PKG can revoke it by simply no longer calculating its values of d_{vi}.

Note that this key distribution can be *batched*; that is, the PKG can precompute the master keys and private keys in advance (say a week at a time), and deliver them to the ORs in batches of any size from one PKVP at a time on up. This batching reduces the amount of time the PKG has to be online, and does not sacrifice forward secrecy. On the other hand, large batches will delay the time until a revocation becomes effective.

User Setup: Once every MKVP v_m, each user must obtain a new signed tuple (v_m, U, sU) from any OR or from a public website. Once every PKVP v, the user computes the following pairing for each OR i and stores the results locally:

$$\gamma_{vi} = e(sU, Q_{vi}) = e(U, Q_{vi})^s \text{ where } Q_{vi} = H(v\|\mathtt{ID}_i)$$

Circuit Construction: During a PKVP v, a user U chooses a set of ORs (say $A, B, \ldots, N$) and constructs a circuit $U \Leftrightarrow A \Leftrightarrow B \Leftrightarrow \cdots \Leftrightarrow N$ with the following steps.

1. For each OR i in the circuit, the user generates a random integer $r_i \in \mathbb{Z}_n^*$ and computes the pseudonym $P_{Ui} = r_i U$ and the value $\gamma_{vi}{}^{r_i} = e(U, Q_{vi})^{sr_i}$. From $\gamma_{vi}{}^{r_i}$ two session keys are derived: a forward session key K_{Ui} and a backward session key K_{iU}. Finally, the following onion is built and sent to A, the first OR in the circuit:

$$r_A U, \{B, r_B U, \{\cdots \{N, r_N U, \{\emptyset\}_{K_{UN}}\} \cdots\}_{K_{UB}}\}_{K_{UA}}$$

   Here $\{\cdots\}_{K_{Ui}}$ is symmetric-key encryption and $\emptyset$ is an empty message which informs N that it is the exit node.

2. After receiving the onion, the OR with identity ID_i uses the received $r_i U$ and its currently valid private key d_{vi} to compute $e(r_i U, d_{vi}) = e(U, Q_i)^{r_i s} = \gamma_{vi}{}^{r_i}$. It derives the forward session key K_{Ui} and the backward session key K_{iU}. It decrypts the outermost onion layer $\{\cdots\}_{K_{Ui}}$ to obtain the user's next pseudonym, the nested ciphertext, and the identity of the next node in the circuit. The OR then forwards the pseudonym and ciphertext to the next node. To avoid replay attacks, it also stores pseudonyms (see Section 5). The process ends when an OR (N in this case) gets $\emptyset$.

3. The exit node N sends a confirmation message encrypted with the backward session key $\{Confirm\}_{K_{NU}}$ to the previous OR in the circuit. Each OR encrypts the confirmation with its backward session key and sends it to the previous node, until the ciphertext reaches the user. The user decrypts the ciphertext layers to verify the confirmation.

4. If the user does not receive the confirmation in a specified time, she selects a different set of ORs and repeats the protocol.

The circuit construction is further illustrated in Figure 1, where a user builds a three-node circuit.

Anonymous Communication: After the circuit is constructed, communication proceeds in the same manner as Tor. The user sends onions through the circuit with each layer encrypted with the forward keys K_{Ui}, and each hop decrypts one layer. Replies are encrypted at each hop with the backward key K_{iU}, and the user decrypts the received onion.

Note that as an optimization, one or more messages can be bundled inside the original circuit construction onion, in place of $\emptyset$.

4.3   Security Analysis

Camenisch and Lysyanskaya [2] formally define the requirements of a secure onion routing construction in the universal composability (UC) framework in terms of onion-correctness, onion-integrity and onion-security. We observe that our circuit construction trivially achieves onion-correctness and onion-integrity.

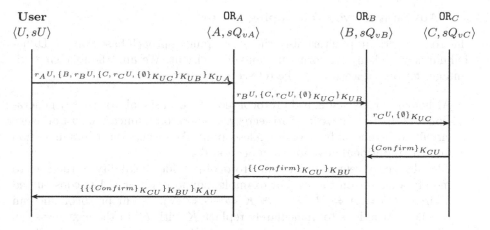

Fig. 1. A user builds a circuit with three ORs

They also define a secure (in the UC framework) onion routing circuit construction using any IND-CCA-2 public key encryption scheme. As an encryption in our circuit construction $(rU_i, \{\cdots\}_{K_{Ui}})$ is a generalization of the `BasicIdent` scheme $(rU_i, \{\cdots\} \oplus \{K_{Ui}\})$ from BF-IBE [1], it is IND-CPA secure. Along similar lines to [1], we can use a technique due to Fujisaki-Okamoto [11] to convert our scheme to an IND-CCA-2 construction: $(rU_i, \{\sigma\}_{K_{Ui}}, \{\cdots\}_{H'(\sigma)})$ for a random binary string σ and a cryptographic hash H'. Therefore, a combination of this IND-CCA-2 encryption and the Camenisch-Lysyanskaya circuit construction is secure in the UC framework. But such a circuit construction is less efficient than ours, and we consider proving onion-security for our circuit construction defined in Section 4.2 to be important future work.

4.4 Advantages over First-Generation Onion Routing

As discussed earlier, it is possible to achieve forward secrecy in first-generation onion routing by periodically replacing the public-private key pairs of the ORs. Following the change, the service provider publishes signed copies of the new OR public keys after getting authentic copies from the ORs. However, this requires all users to regularly obtain fresh authenticated public key information for all ORs.

In contrast, with our system, each user only needs to obtain the single authenticated value (v_m, U, sU), and only once every MKVP. The user can then calculate the required γ_{vi} values on her own until the end of that period, thus reducing the load on the service provider. This load is further reduced by having the service provider never communicate directly with users at all, but only with the ORs.

As a consequence, our pairing-based onion routing is a more practical solution for low-latency anonymous communication.

4.5   Advantages over Telescoping in Tor

The Tor network, in practice, uses the telescoping approach based on the Diffie-Hellman key exchange to form an anonymity circuit. We find the following advantages for our protocol over the telescoping approach.

- Although our above-defined protocol requires occasional private key generation for ORs to achieve forward secrecy, it saves communication cost at every circuit construction by avoiding telescoping. We discuss our communication and computational advantages in Section 6.4.
- The absence of telescoping in our protocol provides flexibility to the user to modify a circuit on the fly. For example, suppose a user U has constructed a circuit $(U \Leftrightarrow A \Leftrightarrow B \Leftrightarrow \cdots \Leftrightarrow K \Leftrightarrow \cdots \Leftrightarrow N)$. In our protocol, she can bundle instructions to immediately replace K with K' in the next message, while keeping the remaining circuit intact. Her circuit would then be $(U \Leftrightarrow A \Leftrightarrow B \Leftrightarrow \cdots \Leftrightarrow K' \Leftrightarrow \cdots \Leftrightarrow N)$.

4.6   Issues with the Proposed Scheme

The certifying authorities in the Tor system need to be less trusted than the PKG in our scheme. With a short PKVP and MKVP (compared to the key replacement period in Tor), our PKGs (any t of them) need to be online with greater reliability. Further, if fewer than t are available, the whole system is paralysed after the current batch.

It is also possible for t malicious PKGs to passively listen to all of the traffic as they can compute private keys for all ORs. A geographically and politically distributed implementation of m PKGs certainly reduces this possibility.

To passively decrypt an OR's messages, an adversary of the Tor system must know the OR's private key, as well as the current Diffie-Hellman key (established for each circuit). In our scheme, as it is non-interactive, an adversary who knows only the OR's private key can decrypt all of the messages for that OR. This may be an acceptable trade-off, considering the advantages gained from the non-interactive protocol.

5   Systems Issues

In this section, we describe how components of an onion routing system such as Tor would behave in a pairing-based setting. To implement pairings, we must choose groups where pairings are known, and are efficiently computable. Once these groups are fixed we can estimate the computational cost required to construct a circuit. The next section will compare the cost of our scheme to the cost of setting up a circuit in Tor.

PKG. As discussed in Section 3.4, the PKG should be distributed across servers run by independent parties. To provide robustness, a "t of m" secret sharing scheme may be employed; this would mean that an OR need only contact t of

m "pieces" of the PKG to learn its complete private key. Naturally, private key information must always be communicated over a secure channel. We note that end users of the system will have no reason to contact the PKG; the PKG only communicates with ORs, and sends one private key (an element of $\mathbb{G}$) per PKVP to each. The load on the PKG should therefore be quite manageable. For added protection from attack, the PKG could even situate itself as a "hidden service" [7, §5], so that only known ORs could even connect to it, and no one would know where many of the pieces were located.

Channel Security. The security and forward secrecy depends on the channel between the PKG and the OR used to compute the private key. With a non-distributed PKG, an attacker can compromise an OR's private key by compromising this channel. The distributed PKG provides robustness here as well, since the attacker must subvert t secure channels to reconstruct the private key from the shares.

Onion Router Identities. Users calculate γ_{vi} based on each router's identity ID_i. This identity can be as simple as a port number and a hostname or IP address. In that case, the BF-IBE setup ensures that if a user knows how to contact an OR, she automatically knows its public key.

The value γ_{vi} is also based on the current PKVP v. To avoid requiring tight synchronization between the clocks of ORs and users, ORs should keep their private keys d_{vi} around for a short time after the official end of the PKVP, but must securely discard them after that.

Replay Prevention. To avoid attacks where adversaries replay old circuit construction onions, ORs should store the pseudonyms they receive for the duration of a PKVP and drop onions which re-use a pseudonym. After circuit construction, replay attacks can be prevented with existing methods (see [6] for an example).

Directory Servers. Directory servers can be used to provide signed information about the list of available ORs to the users of the system. The directory servers in Tor, for example, provide a list of the ORs along with their public keys, status, capabilities and policies. In our pairing-based setting, of course, the public keys are unnecessary.

6 Performance

In this section, we consider the cost of creating a circuit from a user through ℓ onion routers. We estimate the computational cost, and count the number of AES-encrypted network communications. We compare the performance of our system to that of Tor.

6.1 Security Levels and Parameter Sizes

Before comparing the costs of the cryptography in both schemes we determine the parameter sizes required to provide the same level of security currently provided by Tor.

Tor uses public key parameters to provide security at the 80-bit level [13]. The discrete log problem is in a 1024-bit field, and the RSA problem is also at the 1024-bit level. The symmetric parameters provide significantly more security, by using AES with a 128-bit key.

We must choose appropriate groups $\mathbb{G}$ and $\mathbb{G}_T$ over which our pairing will be defined, in order to offer similar strength. The current favourite choice is the group of torsion points of an elliptic curve group over a finite field, with either the Weil or Tate pairing. To achieve an 80-bit security level, the elliptic curve discrete log problem an attacker faces must be in a group of at least 160 bits. Due to the reduction of Menezes, Okamoto and Vanstone [20], we must also ensure that discrete logs are intractable in the target group, $\mathbb{G}_T$. In our case, $\mathbb{G}_T = \mathbb{F}_{p^k}$, where k is the embedding degree of our curve taken over $\mathbb{F}_p$. We must then choose our curve E, a prime p, and embedding degree k such that $E(\mathbb{F}_p)$ has a cyclic subgroup of prime order $n \approx 2^{160}$, and p^k is around 2^{1024}. This can be achieved in a variety of ways, but two common choices are $k = 2, p \approx 2^{512}$ and $k = 6, p \approx 2^{171}$. Pairing implementations with both sets of parameters are available in the PBC library [18]. Efficiency studies suggest that $k = 2$ and the Tate pairing can offer better performance at this security level [17], so we make that choice.

6.2   Cost of Building a Circuit with Tor

Tor builds circuits by telescoping. A user Uriel chooses a Tor node (say Alice), and establishes a secure channel using an encrypted Diffie-Hellman exchange. She then picks a second node, Bob, and over this secure channel, establishes a new secure channel to Bob with another (end-to-end) encrypted Diffie-Hellman exchange. She proceeds in this manner until the circuit is of some desired length ℓ. For details, see the Tor specification [6]. Note that Uriel cannot use the same Diffie-Hellman parameters with different nodes, lest those nodes be able to determine that the same user was communicating with each of them.

Each Diffie-Hellman exchange requires Uriel to perform two modular exponentiations with 1024-bit moduli and 320-bit exponents. Likewise, each server also performs two of these exponentiations. Uriel RSA encrypts the Diffie-Hellman parameter she sends the server, and the server decrypts it. The AES and hashing operations involved have negligible costs compared to these.

Uriel's circuit construction to Alice takes two messages: one from Uriel to Alice, and one from Alice to Uriel. When Uriel extends this circuit to Bob (via Alice), there are four additional messages: Uriel to Alice, Alice to Bob, Bob to Alice, and Alice to Uriel. Continuing in this way, we see that the total number of messages required for Tor to construct a circuit of length ℓ is $\ell(\ell + 1)$. Note that each of these messages needs to be encrypted and decrypted at each hop.

6.3   Cost of Building a Circuit with Paring-Based Onion Routing

In order to create a circuit of length ℓ with our scheme, the user Uriel must choose ℓ random elements r_i of $\mathbb{Z}_n^*$. As above, Uriel should not reuse these values. She

Table 1. Comparison of costs of setting up a circuit of length ℓ. The values in the Tor column are based on the Tor specification [6]. PB-OR is our pairing-based onion routing scheme.

Operation	Time	Tor		PB-OR	
		client	each server	client	each server
Pairing	2.9 ms	0	0	0	1
RSA decryption	2.7 ms	0	1	0	0
Modular exponentiation	1.5 ms	2ℓ	2	0	0
Multiplication in $\mathbb{G}$	1.0 ms	0	0	ℓ	0
Exponentiation in $\mathbb{G}_T$	0.2 ms	0	0	ℓ	0
RSA encryption	0.1 ms	ℓ	0	0	0
Total time (ms)		3.1ℓ	5.7	1.2ℓ	2.9
Total AES-encrypted messages		$\ell(\ell+1)$		2ℓ	

then computes $r_S U$ and $\gamma_S{}^{rs}$, and derives the forward and backward keys K_{US} and K_{SU} from $\gamma_S{}^{rs}$, for each server S in the circuit. Each server computes $e(r_S U, d_S) = \gamma_S{}^{rs}$ for its current private key d_S and derives K_{US} and K_{SU}.

Uriel creates one message, as in Figure 1, and sends it to the first server in the chain. This server decrypts a layer and sends the result to the second server in the chain, and so on, for a total of ℓ hop-by-hop encrypted messages. At the end of the chain, the last server replies with a confirmation message that travels back through the chain, producing ℓ more messages, for a total of 2ℓ.

6.4 Comparison and Discussion

We summarize the results of the previous two sections in Table 1. We count the number of "bignum" operations for each of the client and the servers, both for Tor and for our pairing-based onion routing protocol. We ignore the comparatively negligible computational costs of AES operations and hashing.

For each bignum operation, we include a benchmark timing. These timings were gathered on a 3.0 GHz Pentium D desktop using the PBC pairing-based cryptography library [18]. We can see that the total computation time to construct a circuit of length ℓ using our method is 61% less on the client side and 49% less on the server side as compared to using Tor. In addition, our method uses only a linear number of AES-encrypted messages, while Tor uses a quadratic number.

7   Conclusion

We have presented a new pairing-based approach for circuit construction in onion routing anonymity networks. We first extended the protocol of Sakai et al. [29] to allow for one-way or two-way anonymous or pseudonymous key agreement. We then used this extension to produce a new circuit construction protocol for onion routing networks. Our new pairing-based protocol creates circuits in a single pass, and also provides forward secrecy.

This protocol uses significantly less computation and communication than the corresponding protocol in Tor, and reduces the load on the network support infrastructure. These improvements can be used to enhance the scalability of low-latency anonymity networks.

Acknowledgements. We would like to thank the Natural Sciences and Engineering Research Council of Canada for supporting this research with a Discovery Grant (Kate, Goldberg) and a PGS-D postgraduate scholarship (Zaverucha). We thank the anonymous reviewers for their constructive feedback, which improved the quality of this paper. We would also like to thank Sk. Md. Mizanur Rahman for providing us with an advance copy of the proceedings version of [26].

References

1. Boneh, D., Franklin, M.: Identity-Based Encryption from the Weil Pairing. In: Kilian, J. (ed.) CRYPTO 2001. LNCS, vol. 2139, pp. 213–229. Springer, Heidelberg (2001)
2. Camenisch, J., Lysyanskaya, A.: A Formal Treatment of Onion Routing. In: Shoup, V. (ed.) CRYPTO 2005. LNCS, vol. 3621, pp. 169–187. Springer, Heidelberg (2005)
3. Chaum, D.: Untraceable Electronic Mail, Return Addresses, and Digital Pseudonyms. Communications of the ACM 4(2), 84–88 (1981)
4. Chien, H., Lin, R.: Identity-based Key Agreement Protocol for Mobile Ad-hoc Networks Using Bilinear Pairing. In: SUTC'06. IEEE International Conference on Sensor Networks, Ubiquitous, and Trustworthy Computing, pp. 520–529. IEEE Computer Society Press, Los Alamitos (2006)
5. Dai, W.: PipeNet 1.1. Post to Cypherpunks mailing list (November 1998)
6. Dingledine, R., Mathewson, N.: The Tor Protocol Specification (accessed February 2007), http://tor.eff.org/svn/trunk/doc/spec/tor-spec.txt
7. Dingledine, R., Mathewson, N., Syverson, P.: Tor: The Second-Generation Onion Router. In: Proceedings of the 13th USENIX Security Symposium (August 2004)
8. Dupont, R., Enge, A.: Provably secure non-interactive key distribution based on pairings. Discrete Applied Mathematics 154(2), 270–276 (2006)
9. Blake, I. (ed.): Advances in Elliptic Curve Cryptography. London Mathematical Society Lecture Note Series, vol. 317. Cambridge University Press, Cambridge (2005)
10. Freedman, M.J., Morris, R.: Tarzan: A Peer-to-Peer Anonymizing Network Layer. In: CCS 2002. Proceedings of the 9th ACM Conference on Computer and Communications Security, ACM Press, Washington, DC (2002)
11. Fujisaki, E., Okamoto, T.: Secure integration of asymmetric and symmetric encryption schemes. In: Kilian, J. (ed.) CRYPTO 2001. LNCS, vol. 2139, pp. 537–554. Springer, Heidelberg (2001)
12. Gennaro, R., Jarecki, S., Krawczyk, H., Rabin, T.: Secure Distributed Key Generation for Discrete-Log Based Cryptosystems. Journal of Cryptology 20(1), 51–83 (2007)
13. Goldberg, I.: On the Security of the Tor Authentication Protocol. In: Danezis, G., Golle, P. (eds.) PET 2006. LNCS, vol. 4258, pp. 316–331. Springer, Heidelberg (2006)

14. Goldschlag, D., Reed, M., Syverson, P.: Hiding Routing Information. In: Anderson, R. (ed.) Information Hiding. LNCS, vol. 1174, pp. 137–150. Springer, Heidelberg (1996)

15. Kate, A., Zaverucha, G.M., Goldberg, I.: Pairing-Based Onion Routing. Technical Report CACR, 2007-08, Centre for Applied Cryptographic Research (2007), Available at
http://www.cacr.math.uwaterloo.ca/techreports/2007/cacr2007-08.pdf

16. Khalili, A., Katz, J., Arbaugh, W.: Toward Secure Key Distribution in Truly Ad-Hoc Networks. In: IEEE Workshop on Security and Assurance in Ad-Hoc Networks 2003, pp. 342–346. IEEE Computer Society Press, Los Alamitos (2003)

17. Koblitz, N., Menezes, A.: Pairing-Based Cryptography at High Security Levels. In: Smart, N.P. (ed.) Cryptography and Coding. LNCS, vol. 3796, pp. 13–36. Springer, Heidelberg (2005)

18. Lynn, B.: PBC Library – The Pairing-Based Cryptography Library (accessed February 2007), http://crypto.stanford.edu/pbc/

19. Mauw, S., Verschuren, J., de Vink, E.: A Formalization of Anonymity and Onion Routing. In: Samarati, P., Ryan, P.Y A, Gollmann, D., Molva, R. (eds.) ESORICS 2004. LNCS, vol. 3193, pp. 109–124. Springer, Heidelberg (2004)

20. Menezes, A., Okamoto, T., Vanstone, S.: Reducing Elliptic Curve Logarithms to Logarithms in a Finite Field. In: STOC 1991. Proc. of the twenty-third annual ACM Symposium on Theory of Computing, pp. 80–89. ACM Press, New York (1991)

21. Menezes, A., Van Oorschot, P., Vanstone, S.: Handbook of Applied Cryptography, 1st edn. CRC Press, Boca Raton, USA (1997)

22. Möller, B.: Provably Secure Public-Key Encryption for Length-Preserving Chaumian Mixes. In: Joye, M. (ed.) CT-RSA 2003. LNCS, vol. 2612, Springer, Heidelberg (2003)

23. Okamoto, E., Okamoto, T.: Cryptosystems Based on Elliptic Curve Pairing. In: Torra, V., Narukawa, Y., Miyamoto, S. (eds.) MDAI 2005. LNCS (LNAI), vol. 3558, pp. 13–23. Springer, Heidelberg (2005)

24. Øverlier, L., Syverson, P.: Improving efficiency and simplicity of Tor circuit establishment and hidden services. In: Borisov, N., Golle, P. (eds.) PET 2007. LNCS, vol. 4776, pp. 134–152. Springer, Heidelberg (2007)

25. Pedersen, T.: A Threshold Cryptosystem without a Trusted Party. In: Davies, D.W. (ed.) EUROCRYPT 1991. LNCS, vol. 547, pp. 522–526. Springer, Heidelberg (1991)

26. Rahman, S., Inomata, A., Okamoto, T., Mambo, M., Okamoto, E.: Anonymous Secure Communication in Wireless Mobile Ad-hoc Networks. In: ICUCT 2006. LNCS, vol. 4412, pp. 140–149. Springer, Heidelberg (2006)

27. Reed, M., Syverson, P., Goldschlag, D.: Anonymous Connections and Onion Routing. IEEE Journal on Selected Areas in Communications 16(4), 482–494 (1998)

28. Rennhard, M., Plattner, B.: Introducing MorphMix: Peer-to-Peer based Anonymous Internet Usage with Collusion Detection. In: WPES 2002. Proceedings of the Workshop on Privacy in the Electronic Society, Washington, DC, USA (November 2002)

29. Sakai, R., Ohgishi, K., Kasahara, M.: Cryptosystems based on pairing. In: SCIS 2000. Symposium on Cryptography and Information Security (2000)

30. Seth, A., Keshav, S.: Practical Security for Disconnected Nodes. In: IEEE ICNP Workshop on Secure Network Protocols, 2005 (NPSec), pp. 31–36. IEEE Computer Society Press, Los Alamitos (2005)

31. Shamir, A.: How to Share a Secret. Commun. ACM 22(11), 612–613 (1979)
32. Syverson, P., Tsudik, G., Reed, M., Landwehr, C.: Towards an Analysis of Onion Routing Security. In: Federrath, H. (ed.) Designing Privacy Enhancing Technologies. LNCS, vol. 2009, pp. 96–114. Springer, Heidelberg (2001)
33. The Tor Project. Tor: anonymity online (accessed February 2007), http://tor.eff.org/
34. Verheul, E.: Evidence that XTR Is More Secure than Supersingular Elliptic Curve Cryptosystems. In: Pfitzmann, B. (ed.) EUROCRYPT 2001. LNCS, vol. 2045, pp. 195–210. Springer, Heidelberg (2001)

Nymble: Anonymous IP-Address Blocking*

Peter C. Johnson[1], Apu Kapadia[1,2], Patrick P. Tsang[1], and Sean W. Smith[1]

[1] Department of Computer Science
Dartmouth College
Hanover, NH 03755, USA
[2] Institute for Security Technology Studies
Dartmouth College
Hanover, NH 03755, USA
{pete,akapadia,patrick,sws}@cs.dartmouth.edu

Abstract. Anonymizing networks such as Tor allow users to access Internet services privately using a series of routers to hide the client's IP address from the server. Tor's success, however, has been limited by users employing this anonymity for abusive purposes, such as defacing Wikipedia. Website administrators rely on IP-address blocking for disabling access to misbehaving users, but this is not practical if the abuser routes through Tor. As a result, administrators block *all* Tor exit nodes, denying anonymous access to honest and dishonest users alike. To address this problem, we present a system in which (1) honest users remain anonymous and their requests unlinkable; (2) a server can complain about a particular anonymous user and gain the ability to blacklist the user for future connections; (3) this blacklisted user's accesses before the complaint remain anonymous; and (4) users are aware of their blacklist status before accessing a service. As a result of these properties, our system is agnostic to different servers' definitions of misbehavior.

1   Introduction

Anonymizing networks such as Crowds [25] and Tor [15] route traffic through independent nodes in separate administrative domains to hide the originating IP address. Unfortunately, misuse has limited the acceptance of deployed anonymizing networks. The anonymity provided by such networks prevents website administrators from blacklisting individual malicious users' IP addresses; to thwart further abuse, they blacklist the *entire* anonymizing network. Such measures eliminate malicious activity through anonymizing networks at the cost of denying anonymous access to honest users. In other words, a few "bad apples" can spoil the fun for all. (This has happened repeatedly with Tor.[1])

Some approaches for blacklisting abusive users are based on pseudonyms [11, 13, 14, 19]. In these systems, of which Nym [17] seems most relevant, users are required to

---

* This research was supported in part by the NSF, under grant CNS-0524695, and the Bureau of Justice Assistance, under grant 2005-DD-BX-1091. The views and conclusions do not necessarily reflect the views of the sponsors.
[1] The *Abuse FAQ for Tor Server Operators* lists several such examples at http://tor.eff.org/faq-abuse.html.en

log into websites using an assigned pseudonym, thus assuring a level of accountability. Unfortunately, this approach results in *pseudonymity* for *all* users—ideally, honest users should enjoy full anonymity, and misbehaving users should be blocked.

To this end, we present a secure system in which users acquire an ordered collection of *nymbles*, a special type of pseudonym, to connect to websites. Without additional data, these nymbles are computationally hard to link, and hence using the stream of nymbles simulates anonymous access to services. Websites, however, can blacklist users by obtaining a *trapdoor* for a particular nymble, allowing them to link future nymbles from the same user—those used before the complaint remain unlinkable. Servers can therefore blacklist anonymous users without knowledge of their IP addresses while allowing honest users to connect anonymously. Our system ensures that users are aware of their blacklist status before they present a nymble, and disconnect immediately if they are blacklisted. Furthermore, websites avoid the problem of having to prove misbehavior: they are free to establish their own independent blacklisting policies. Although our work applies to anonymizing networks in general, we consider Tor for purposes of exposition. In fact, any number of anonymizing networks can rely on the same nymble system, blacklisting anonymous users regardless of their anonymizing network(s) of choice.

Our research makes the following contributions:

- **Blacklisting anonymous users.** We provide a means by which servers can blacklist users of an anonymizing network without deanonymizing them. Honest users enjoy anonymous access and are unaffected by the misbehavior of other users.
- **Practical performance.** A system such as ours, relying on a server to issue nymbles, will be adopted only if performance is acceptable. Our protocol minimizes storage requirements and the use of expensive asymmetric cryptographic operations.
- **Prototype implementation.** With the goal of contributing a workable system, we have built a prototype implementation. We provide performance statistics to show that our system is indeed a viable approach for selectively blocking users of large-scale anonymizing networks such as Tor.

Many in the community worry that "deanonymization" will become a vehicle for suppressing individuals' rights. This project moves in the other direction, by allowing websites to block users without knowing their identities, hopefully increasing mainstream acceptance of anonymizing technologies such as Tor.

2   Related Work

Anonymous credential systems such as Camenisch and Lysyanskaya's [7, 8] use group signatures for anonymous authentication, wherein individual users are anonymous among a group of registered users. Non-revocable group signatures such as Ring signatures [26] provide no accountability and thus do not satisfy our needs to protect servers from misbehaving users. Basic group signatures [1, 2, 3, 12] allow revocation of anonymity by no one except the *group manager*. As only the group manager can revoke a user's anonymity, servers have no way of linking signatures to previous ones and must query the group manager for every signature; this lack of scalability makes it unsuitable for our goals. *Traceable signatures* [18, 30] allow the group manager to release a trapdoor that allows *all* signatures generated by a particular user to be traced; such an approach does not provide the *backward anonymity* that we desire, where a user's accesses before the complaint remain anonymous. Specifically, if the server is interested in blocking only future accesses of bad users, then such reduction of user anonymity is unnecessarily drastic. When a user makes an anonymous connection the connection should *remain* anonymous. And misbehaving users should be blocked from making further connections after a complaint.

In some systems, misbehavior can be defined precisely. For instance, double-spending of an "e-coin" is considered misbehavior in anonymous electronic cash systems [4, 10]. Likewise, compact e-cash [6], k-times anonymous authentication [28] and periodic n-times anonymous authentication [5] deem a user to be misbehaving if she authenticates "too many" times. In these cases, convincing evidence of misbehavior is easily collected and fair judgment of misbehavior can be ensured. While such approaches can encourage certain kinds of fair behavior in anonymizing networks (e.g., e-coins can be used to control bandwidth consumption of anonymous users), it is difficult to map more complex notions of misbehavior onto "double spending" or related approaches. It may be difficult to precisely define what it means to "deface a webpage" and for Wikipedia to *prove* to a trusted party that a particular webpage was defaced. How can the user be sure these "proofs" are accurate and fairly judged? Can we avoid the problem of judging misbehavior entirely? In this paper we answer affirmatively by proposing a system that does not require proof of misbehavior. Websites may complain about users for any reason; our system ensures users are informed of complaints against them, thus "making everybody happy"—except, of course, the misbehaving users, who remain anonymous but are denied access.

Syverson et al. [27] provide a solution to a closely-related problem. To facilitate anonymous and unlinkable transactions, users are issued a blind signature for access to a service. This blind signature can be renewed with another blind signature (for the subsequent connection) each time the user has been served. If a user misbehaves, a server can terminate its service to that user by not renewing that user's blind signature. As a result, misbehavior must be detected *during* the user's connection. In contrast, our system targets scenarios in which misbehavior is detected *after* the user has disconnected.

A preliminary *work-in-progress* version of this paper (suggesting the use of trusted hardware) was presented at the Second Workshop on Advances in Trusted Computing [29].

3 System Overview

Resource-based blocking. Our system provides servers with a means to block misbehaving users of an anonymizing network. Blocking a particular *user*, however, is a formidable task since that user can acquire several identities—the *Sybil* attack is well known [16] in this regard. Our system, therefore, focuses on blocking *resources* that are (usually) controlled by a single user. In this paper, we focus on IP addresses as the resource, but our scheme generalizes to other resources such as identity certificates, trusted hardware, and so on. Our system ensures that *nymbles* are bound to a particular resource, and servers can block nymbles for that resource. We note that if two users can prove access to the

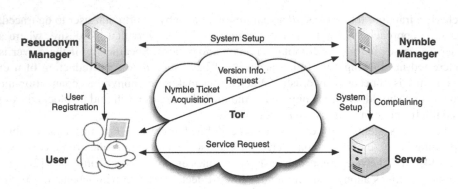

Fig. 1. System Architecture

same resource (e.g., if an IP address is reassigned to another user), they will obtain the same stream of nymbles. Since we focus on IP address blocking, in the remainder of the paper, the reader should be aware that blocking "a user" really means blocking that user's IP address (although, as mentioned before, other resources may be used). We will address the practical issues related with IP-address blocking in Section 7.

Pseudonym Manager. The user must first contact the *Pseudonym Manager (PM)* and demonstrate control over a resource; for IP-address blocking, a user is required to connect to the PM directly (i.e., not through a known anonymizing network), as shown in Figure 1. We assume the PM has knowledge about Tor routers, for example, and can ensure that users are communicating with it directly.[2] Pseudonyms are deterministically chosen based on the controlled resource, ensuring that the same pseudonym is always issued for the same resource.

Note that the user *does not* disclose what server he or she intends to connect to, and therefore the user's connections are anonymous to the PM. The PM's duties are limited to mapping IP addresses (or other resources) to pseudonyms.

Nymble Manager. After obtaining a pseudonym from the PM, the user connects to the *Nymble Manager (NM)* through the anonymizing network, and requests nymbles for access to a particular server (such as Wikipedia). Nymbles are generated using the user's pseudonym and the server's identity. The user's connections, therefore, are pseudonymous to the NM (as long as the PM and the NM do not collude) since the NM knows only the pseudonym-server pair, and the PM knows only the IP address-pseudonym pair. Note that due to the pseudonym assignment by the PM, nymbles are bound to the user's IP address and the server's identity. To improve the collusion resistance of our system, the PM's duties can be split between n different PMs, which behave like Mixes [9]. As long as at least one of the Mix nodes is honest, the user's connections will be pseudonymous to the NM and anonymous to the PM (or PMs). For the purposes of clarity, we assume a single PM.

---

[2] Note that if a user connects through an unknown anonymizing network or proxy, the security of our system is no worse than that provided by real IP-address blocking, where the user could have used an anonymizing network unknown to the server.

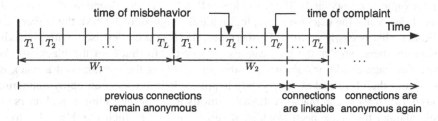

Fig. 2. The life cycle of a misbehaving user in our system

To provide the requisite cryptographic protection and security properties, the NM encapsulates nymbles within *nymble tickets*, and trapdoors within *linking tokens*. Therefore, we will speak of linking tokens being used to link future nymble tickets. The importance of these constructs will become apparent as we proceed.

As illustrated in Figure 2, in our system, time is divided into linkability windows of duration $\mathcal{W}$, each of which is split into smaller time periods of duration $\mathcal{T}$, where the number of time periods in a linkability window $L = \frac{\mathcal{W}}{\mathcal{T}}$ is an integer. We will refer to time periods and linkability windows chronologically as $T_1, T_2, \ldots, T_L$ and $W_1, W_2,$ $\ldots$ respectively. While a user's access *within* a time period is tied to a single nymble ticket, the use of different nymble tickets *across* time periods grants the user anonymity between time periods—smaller time periods provide users with enough nymble tickets to simulate anonymous access. For example, $\mathcal{T}$ could be set to 5 minutes, and $\mathcal{W}$ to 1 day. The linkability window serves two purposes—it allows for *dynamism* since IP addresses can get reassigned to different well-behaved users, making it undesirable to blacklist an IP address indefinitely, and it ensures *forgiveness* of misbehavior after a certain period of time. We will discuss the choice of these parameters in Section 7.

Blacklisting a user. If a user misbehaves, the website may link any future connection from this user within the current linkability window (e.g., the same day). Consider Figure 2 as an example: A user misbehaves in a connection to a website during time period T_ℓ within linkability window W_2. The website detects the misbehavior and complains in time period $T_{\ell'}$ by presenting to the NM the nymble ticket associated with the misbehaving user and obtaining a linking token therefrom. The website is then able to link future connections by the user in time periods $T_{\ell'+1}, T_{\ell'+2}, \ldots, T_L$ of linkability window W_2. Therefore, users are blacklisted for the rest of the day (the linkability window) once the website has complained about that user. Note that the user's connections in $T_{\ell+1}, \ldots, T_{\ell'}$ remain unlinkable. This property ensures that a user's previous accesses remain anonymous, and allows our system to avoid judging misbehavior. We now describe how users are notified of their blacklisting status.

Notifying the user of blacklist status. Users who make use of Tor expect their connections to be anonymous. If a server obtains a linking token for that user, however, it can link that user's subsequent connections (we emphasize that the user's previous connections remain anonymous). It is of utmost importance, then, that users be notified of their blacklisting status before they present a nymble ticket to a server. In our system, the user can download the server's blacklist and verify whether she is on the blacklist. If so, the user disconnects immediately (the server learns that "some blacklisted user" attempted a connection). Since the blacklist is cryptographically signed by the NM, the authenticity of the blacklist is easily verified. Furthermore, the NM provides users with "blacklist version numbers" so that the user can also verify the freshness of the blacklists. We ensure that race conditions are not possible in verifying the freshness of a blacklist. Our system therefore makes "everybody happy"—honest users can enjoy anonymity through Tor, servers can blacklist the anonymous users of their choice, and users can check whether they have been blacklisted before presenting their nymble ticket to the server. If blacklisted, the user does not present the nymble ticket, and disconnects.

4   The Nymble Authentication Module

In this section we present the *Nymble Authentication Module* (Nymble-Auth), our cryptographic construction that centers on the services provided by the *Nymble Manager (NM)*. Nymble-Auth allows users to authenticate to servers in a manner that both preserves the privacy of honest users and protects servers from misbehaving users. Nymble-Auth thus serves as the fundamental building block in our NYMBLE system. For simplicity, in this section we assume that users contact the NM directly. In the next section, we describe the entire NYMBLE system, which also includes the *Pseudonym Manager (PM)*.

4.1   The Model

Syntax. Nymble-Auth uses a semi-trusted third party, the *Nymble Manager (NM)*, to issue *nymble tickets* to users to authenticate themselves to servers. More specifically, Nymble-Auth consists of three entities: the NM, a set of *users*, and a set of *servers*, and a tuple of (possibly probabilistic) polynomial-time algorithms: Setup, NymbleTktGen, LinkingTknExt, ServerVerify, NMVerify and Link.

   To initialize Nymble-Auth, the NM invokes Setup to initialize the system. Upon receiving a request from a user, the NM executes NymbleTktGen to generate a nymble ticket for that user. The user can obtain service at a server by presenting a valid nymble ticket for that server. Upon request from a server, the NM executes LinkingTknExt to extract a *linking token* from a valid nymble ticket of some user for linking future nymble tickets of the same user. The NM and the servers may run NMVerify and ServerVerify respectively to check the validity of a nymble ticket. Finally, servers may run Link to test if a user's nymble ticket is linked to a linking token.

Security Notions. Roughly speaking, a secure Nymble-Auth must satisfy the following security properties (we will formalize these properties in Appendix A.1):

1. *Nymble tickets are Unforgeable.* As a result, they can be obtained only from the NM. Valid nymble tickets serve as legitimate authenticators issued by the NM for users to authenticate to servers.
2. *Nymble tickets are Uncircumventably Forward-Linkable.* Once a linking token is issued for a user/server/linkability-window tuple, all future nymble tickets for that tuple are linkable. This property allows for blacklisting misbehaving users.

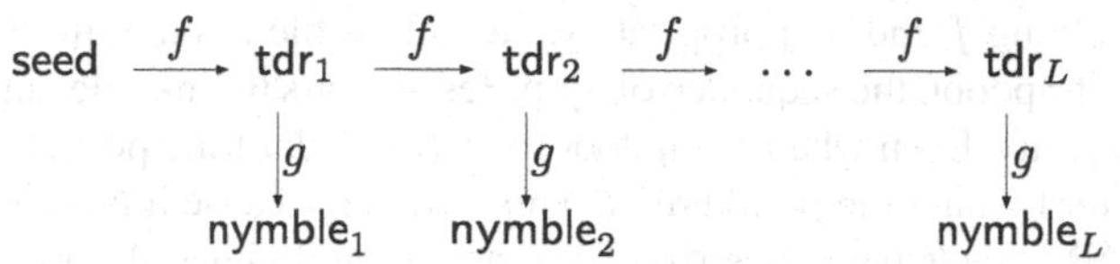

$$\text{seed} \xrightarrow{\;f\;} \text{tdr}_1 \xrightarrow{\;f\;} \text{tdr}_2 \xrightarrow{\;f\;} \ldots \xrightarrow{\;f\;} \text{tdr}_L$$

$$\Big\downarrow g \qquad\quad \Big\downarrow g \qquad\qquad\qquad\quad \Big\downarrow g$$

$$\text{nymble}_1 \qquad \text{nymble}_2 \qquad\qquad\qquad \text{nymble}_L$$

Fig. 3. Evolution of trapdoors and nymbles

3. *Nymble tickets are Backward Anonymous.* Without a linking token, nymble tickets are all anonymous and thus unlinkable. Given a linking token for a user/server/ linkability-window tuple, previous nymble tickets are still anonymous, and so are nymble tickets of the same user for other servers and other linkability windows. This property ensures that all accesses by a user before the time of complaint remain anonymous.

Communication Channels and Time Synchronization. There are different security requirements for the communication channels between the entities in various protocols. A channel may be confidential and/or authenticated at one or both ends. Such a channel may be realized using SSL/TLS over HTTP under a PKI such as X.509. We call a channel secure if it is both confidential and mutually-authenticated. A channel may also be anonymous, in which case the communication happens through Tor. We emphasize that while the NM, the PM, and the servers must set up PKI key-pairs, our system does *not* require users to have PKI key-pairs.

All entities are assumed to share a synchronized clock. The requirement of the granularity of the clock depends on the application in question. We will have more discussion on how we ensure time synchronization and its consequences in Section 6.

4.2 Our Construction

Overview. At its core, Nymble-Auth leverages a hash-chain-like structure for establishing the relationship between nymbles and trapdoors. The same structure was used by Ohkubo et al. [24] for securing RFID tags by ensuring both indistinguishability and forward security of the tags. Although the primitive we use in this paper shares similarities with that in [24], our construction possesses different security requirements that must be satisfied to secure our system as a whole. In particular, the hash structure in Ohkubo et al. [24] satisfies *Indistinguishability* and *Forward Security*, both of which are captured by our security notion of *Backward Anonymity*. We formalize the *Unforgeability* requirement for Nymble-Auth, which assumes a different trust model from that in [24]. Finally, we also introduce a unique security requirement called *Uncircumventable Forward Linkability*.

As shown in Figure 3, trapdoors evolve throughout a linkability window using a *trapdoor-evolution function f*. Specifically, the trapdoor for the next time period can be computed by applying f to the trapdoor for the current time period. A nymble is evaluated by applying the *nymble-evaluation function g* to its corresponding trapdoor. We will instantiate both f and g with collision-resistant cryptographic hash functions in our construction. In essence, it is easy to compute future nymbles starting from a particular trapdoor by applying f and g appropriately, but infeasible to compute nymbles otherwise. Without a trapdoor, the sequence of nymbles appears unlinkable, and honest users can enjoy anonymity. Even when a trapdoor for a particular time period is obtained, all the nymbles prior to that time period remain unlinkable because it is infeasible to invert f and g. The NM *seeds* the sequence of trapdoors (and hence the nymbles) with its secret, the user's ID, the server's ID and the linkability window's ID of the requested connection. Seeds are therefore specific to source-destination-window combinations. As a consequence, a trapdoor is useful only for a particular website to link a particular user (or more specifically an IP address) during a particular linkability window.

Parameters. Let $\lambda \in \mathbb{N}$ be a sufficiently large security parameter. Let f and g be secure cryptographic hash functions, H be a secure keyed hash, HMAC be a secure keyed-hash message authentication code (HMAC), and Enc be a secure symmetric encryption, such that their security parameters are polynomial in λ. Let $|S|$ denote the number of servers.

Protocol Details. Now we detail each protocol in Nymble-Auth.

- $(nmsk, (hmk_{NS_1}, \ldots, hmk_{NS_{|S|}})) \leftarrow \mathsf{Setup}(1^\lambda)$.
  To set up the system, the NM picks, all uniformly at random from their respective key-spaces,
    1. a key khk_N for keyed hash function H,
    2. a key sek_N for secure symmetric encryption Enc, and
    3. $|S| + 1$ keys hmk_N and $hmk_{NS_1}, hmk_{NS_2}, \ldots, hmk_{NS_{|S|}}$ for HMAC,
  and sets its secret key $nmsk$ as $(khk_N, sek_N, hmk_N, hmk_{NS_1}, \ldots, hmk_{NS_{|S|}})$. The NM stores $nmsk$ privately and, for each server S_j, sends hmk_{NS_j} to S_j through a secure channel. Each S_j then stores its secret key ssk_j as (hmk_{NS_j}) privately.
- $\mathtt{nymbleTKT} \leftarrow \mathsf{NymbleTktGen}_{nmsk}(\mathtt{id}, j, k, \ell)$.
  To generate a nymble ticket that allows a user with identity $\mathtt{id}$ to authenticate to server S_j during time period T_ℓ of linkability window W_k, the NM computes the following using its secret key $nmsk$:
    1. $\mathtt{seed} \leftarrow H_{khk_N}(\mathtt{id}, j, k)$, the seed for trapdoor evolution,
    2. $\mathtt{tdr} \leftarrow f^{(\ell)}(\mathtt{seed})$, the trapdoor for T_ℓ,
    3. $\mathtt{nymble} \leftarrow g(\mathtt{tdr})$, the nymble for the same time period,
    4. $\overline{\mathtt{tdr}||\mathtt{id}} \leftarrow \mathsf{Enc.encrypt}_{sek_N}(\mathtt{tdr}||\mathtt{id})$, a ciphertext that only the NM can decrypt,
    5. $\mathtt{mac}^N \leftarrow \mathsf{HMAC}_{hmk_N}(j||k||\ell||\mathtt{nymble}||\overline{\mathtt{tdr}||\mathtt{id}})$, the HMAC for the NM,
    6. $\mathtt{mac}^{NS} \leftarrow \mathsf{HMAC}_{hmk_{NS_j}}(j||k||\ell||\mathtt{nymble}||\overline{\mathtt{tdr}||\mathtt{id}}||\mathtt{mac}^N)$, the HMAC for S_j.
  Finally the NM returns $\mathtt{nymbleTKT}$ as $\langle j, k, \ell, \mathtt{nymble}, \overline{\mathtt{tdr}||\mathtt{id}}, \mathtt{mac}^N, \mathtt{mac}^{NS} \rangle$.
- $\mathtt{valid/invalid} \leftarrow \mathsf{ServerVerify}_{ssk_j}(k, \ell, \mathtt{nymbleTKT})$.
  To verify if a nymble ticket $\mathtt{nymbleTKT} = \langle j', k', \ell', \mathtt{nymble}, \overline{\mathtt{tdr}||\mathtt{id}}, \mathtt{mac}^N, \mathtt{mac}^{NS} \rangle$ is valid for authenticating to server S_j at time period T_ℓ during linkability window W_k, S_j does the following using its key ssk_j:
    1. return $\mathtt{invalid}$ if $(j, k, \ell) \neq (j', k', \ell')$, or
      $\mathsf{HMAC}_{hmk_{NS_j}}(j'||k'||\ell'||\mathtt{nymble}||\overline{\mathtt{tdr}||\mathtt{id}}||\mathtt{mac}^N) \neq \mathtt{mac}^{NS}$,
    2. return $\mathtt{valid}$ otherwise.

- valid/invalid ← NMVerify$_{nmsk}(j, k, \ell, \text{nymbleTKT})$.
  To verify if a nymble ticket nymbleTKT = $\langle j', k', \ell', \text{nymble}, \overline{\text{tdr}||\text{id}}, \text{mac}^N, \cdot \rangle$ is valid for authenticating to server S_j at time period T_ℓ during linkability window W_k, the NM does the following using its key $nmsk$:
  1. return invalid if $(j, k, \ell) \neq (j', k', \ell')$, or
     $\text{HMAC}_{hmk_N}(j'||k'||\ell'||\text{nymble}||\overline{\text{tdr}}||\text{id}) \neq \text{mac}^N$,
  2. return valid otherwise.

- linkingTKN/⊥ ← LinkingTknExt$_{nmsk}(j, k, \ell^*, \text{nymbleTKT})$.
  To extract the linking token from a nymble ticket nymbleTKT = $\langle \cdot, \cdot, \ell, \cdot, \overline{\text{tdr}||\text{id}}, \cdot, \cdot \rangle$ for server S_j's use at time period T_{ℓ^*} during linkability window W_k, the NM does the following using his secret key $nmsk$:
  1. return ⊥ if $\ell^* < \ell$ or NMVerify$_{nmsk}(j, k, \ell, \text{nymbleTKT}) = \text{invalid}$,
  2. compute $\text{tdr}||\text{id} \leftarrow \text{Enc.decrypt}_{sek_N}(\overline{\text{tdr}||\text{id}})$,
  3. pick tdr* uniformly at random from the range of f if a linking token has already been issued for the (id, j, k)-tuple, otherwise compute tdr* as $f^{(\ell^*-\ell)}$ (tdr) and record that a linking token has been issued for the (id, j, k)-tuple,[3]
  4. return linkingTKN as $\langle j, k, \ell^*, \text{tdr}^* \rangle$.

- linked/not-linked ← Link(nymbleTKT, linkingTKN).
  To test if a nymble ticket nymbleTKT = $\langle j, k, \ell, \text{nymble}, \cdot, \cdot, \cdot \rangle$ is linked by the linking token linkingTKN = $\langle j', k', \ell', \text{tdr}' \rangle$, anyone can do the following:
  1. return not-linked if $(j, k) \neq (j', k')$ or $\ell < \ell'$, or if $g(f^{(\ell-\ell')}(\text{tdr})) \neq \text{nymble}$,
  2. return linked otherwise.

Security Analysis. We formalize the notions of *Correctness*, *Unforgeability*, *Backward Anonymity* and *Uncircumventable Forward Linkability* in Appendix A.1. We now state the following theorem about the security of Nymble-Auth, and sketch its proof in Appendix A.2.

Theorem 1. *Our* Nymble-Auth *construction is secure in the Random Oracle Model.*

5   The NYMBLE System

We now describe the full construction of our system, focusing on the various interactions between the Pseudonym Manager (PM), the Nymble Manager (NM), the servers and the users.

Parameters. In addition to those in the Nymble-Auth module, parameters in the NYMBLE system include the description of an additional secure cryptographic hash function h and a secure signature scheme Sig with security parameters polynomial in λ. Also, T denotes the duration of one time period and L denotes the number of time periods in one linkability window. Let t_0 be the system start time.

---

[3] In Section 5.5, we will show how state about issued trapdoors is offloaded to servers.

5.1 System Setup

In this procedure, the NM and the PM set up the NYMBLE system together. The PM picks a key khk_P for keyed hash function H uniformly at random from the key-space. The NM, on the other hand, does the following:

1. execute Setup of Nymble-Auth on some sufficiently large security parameter λ, after which the NM gets its secret key $nmsk$ and each server S_j gets its own secret key ssk_j as described in the previous section,
2. generate a private/public-key-pair (x, y) for Sig using its key generation algorithm,
3. pick an HMAC key hmk_{NP} for HMAC uniformly at random from the key-space and share it with the PM over a secure channel, and
4. give each server S_j an empty blacklist $\text{BL}_j = \langle j, 1, \langle \perp \rangle, \perp, \sigma \rangle$ through a secure channel, where σ is the signature generated as $\text{Sig.sign}_x(j||1||1)$. Why the blacklist is formatted this way will become clear soon.

At the end of this procedure, the PM stores (khk_P, hmk_{PN}) privately, while the NM stores $(nmsk, x, hmk_{PN})$ privately and publishes the signature public key y. Also, each server S_j stores ssk_j privately.

5.2 User Registration

In this procedure, user Alice interacts with the PM in order to register herself to the NYMBLE system for linkability window k. Alice obtains a pseudonym from the PM upon a successful termination of such an interaction. The communication channel between them is confidential and PM-authenticated.

To register, Alice authenticates herself as a user with identity id to the PM by demonstrating her control over some resource(s) as discussed, after which the PM computes $\text{pnym} \leftarrow H_{khk_P}(\text{id}, k)$ and $\text{mac}^{PN} \leftarrow \text{HMAC}_{hmk_{NP}}(\text{pnym}, k)$, and returns $\langle \text{pnym}, \text{mac}^{PN} \rangle$ to Alice, who stores it privately.

5.3 Acquisition of Nymble Tickets

In order for Alice to authenticate to any server S_j during any linkability window W_k, she must present a nymble ticket to the server. The following describes how she can obtain a credential from the NM containing such tickets. The communication channel is anonymous (e.g., through Tor), confidential and NM-authenticated.

Alice sends her $\langle \text{pnym}, \text{mac}^{PN} \rangle$ to the NM, after which the NM:

1. asserts that $\text{mac}^{PN} = \text{HMAC}_{hmk_{NP}}(\text{pnym}, k)$,
2. computes $\text{nymbleTKT}_\ell \leftarrow \text{NymbleTktGen}_{nmsk}(\text{pnym}, j, k, \ell)$, for $\ell = 1$ to L, and
3. returns cred as $\langle \text{seed}, \text{nymbleTKT}_1, \text{nymbleTKT}_2, \ldots, \text{nymbleTKT}_L \rangle$, where $\text{seed} = H_{khk_N}(\text{pnym}, j, k)$ is the seed used within NymbleTktGen.

Alice may acquire credentials for different servers and different linkability windows at any time. She stores these credentials locally before she needs them.

Efficiency. This protocol has a timing complexity of $O(L)$.[4] All the computations are quick symmetric operations—there are two cryptographic hashes, two HMACs and one symmetric encryption per loop-iteration A credential is of size $O(L)$.

5.4 Request for Services

At a high level, a user Alice presents to server Bob the nymble ticket for the current time period. As nymble tickets are unlinkable until servers complain against them (and thereby blacklisting the corresponding user or IP address), Alice must check whether she is on Bob's blacklist, and verify its integrity and freshness. If Alice decides to proceed, she presents her nymble ticket to Bob, and Bob verifies that the nymble ticket is not on his blacklist. Bob also retains the ticket in case he wants to later complain against the current access. For example, Wikipedia might detect a fraudulent posting several hours after it has been made. The nymble ticket associated with that request can be used to blacklist future accesses by that user.

Each server in the system maintains two data structures, the blacklist BL and the linking-list LL, to handle blacklisting-related mechanisms to be described below. BL is in the form of $\langle j, k, \langle \text{entry}_1, \dots, \text{entry}_v \rangle, \text{digest}, \sigma \rangle$, where each entry $\text{entry}_m = \langle m, \text{nymbleTKT}_m, T_m \rangle$. LL is a list of $\langle t_m, \text{tdr}_m, \text{nymble}_m \rangle$ entries.

The following describes in detail the protocol, during which Alice wants to access the service provided by server Bob (S_j) at time period T_ℓ during linkability window W_k. She will need to make use of seed and nymbleTKT_ℓ in cred, which is the credential she obtained from the NM earlier for accessing Bob's service within window W_k. The communication channel between Alice and the NM is NM-authenticated and anonymous (through Tor), while that between Alice and Bob is secure, server-authenticated and anonymous (through Tor).

1. *(Blacklist Request.)* Upon receiving Alice's request, Bob returns to Alice his current blacklist BL, where $\text{BL} = \langle \cdot, \cdot, \langle \text{entry}_1, \dots, \text{entry}_v \rangle, \cdot, \sigma \rangle$, each $\text{entry}_m = \langle m, \text{nymbleTKT}_m, T_m \rangle$ and each $\text{nymbleTKT}_m = \langle \cdot, \cdot, \cdot, \text{nymble}_m, \cdot, \cdot, \cdot \rangle$.[5] As described earlier, each entry corresponds to a blacklisted user, where nymbleTKT_m was the nymble ticket used by that user in time period T_m.

2. *(Version-number Request.)* Upon receiving Alice's request, the NM returns v_j, the current version number of Bob's blacklist recorded by the NM.

3. *(Blacklist Inspection.)* Alice terminates immediately as failure if:

   - $\text{Sig.Verify}_y(j\|k\|v_j\|h(\dots h(h(\text{entry}_1)\|\text{entry}_2)\dots\|\text{entry}_v), \sigma) = \text{invalid}$,[6] i.e., the blacklist is not authentic or not intact, or

---

[4] A naïve implementation would involve a two-level for-loop with $O(L^2)$ complexity at the NM. However, such a loop can be trivially collapsed into single-level, with $O(L)$ complexity instead.

[5] If Bob doesn't want to use the NYMBLE system for this request, he may skip the rest of the protocol and start serving (or denying) Alice immediately.

[6] By remembering an older digest if Alice has accessed Bob earlier within the same window, Alice can instead compute only part of the recursive hash above.

- $g(f^{(T_m)}(\texttt{seed})) = \texttt{nymble}_m$ for some $m \in \{1, \ldots, v\}$,[7] i.e., Alice has been blacklisted.

Otherwise she sends $\texttt{nymbleTKT}_\ell = \langle \cdot, \cdot, \cdot, \texttt{nymble}, \cdot, \cdot, \cdot \rangle$ to Bob.

4. *(Ticket Inspection.)* Bob returns failure if:
   - $\mathsf{ServerVerify}_{ssk_j}(k, \ell, \texttt{nymbleTKT}) = \texttt{invalid}$, i.e., the ticket is invalid, or
   - $\texttt{nymble}$ appears in his linking-list LL, i.e. the connecting user has already been blacklisted.

   Otherwise Bob grants Alice's request for service and starts serving Alice. Bob records $\texttt{nymbleTKT}_\ell$ along with appropriate access log for potentially complaining about that connection in the future.

Efficiency. Recall that v is the size of Bob's blacklist. Blacklist integrity checking is of $O(v)$ in time. Again, all cryptographic operations in each loop-iteration are symmetric and there is only one digital verification at the end, independent of v. Checking if being linked has a time complexity of $O(vL)$ at the user in the worst case, but all computations involved are simple hashes. Also, one could trade off space to make it $O(v)$ instead. Time complexity of nymble matching at the server is linear in the size of the Linking-list using linear search. But efficient data structures exist which can make these steps logarithmic or even constant (e.g., using hash tables).

5.5 Complaining

By presenting to the NM the nymble ticket associated with an access in which Bob thinks the user misbehaved, Bob obtains a linking token that will allow him to link all future nymble tickets for that user.[8] The following enumerates the protocol, during which server Bob (S_j) complains about $\texttt{nymbleTKT}$. The communication between Bob and the NM is conducted over a secure channel. Let the time of complaint be at time period T_ℓ during linkability window W_k, where $\ell < L$, i.e. the complaint is not during the last period of a linkability-window.

1. *(Complaining.)* Bob sends to the NM the nymble ticket $\texttt{nymbleTKT} = \langle \cdot, \cdot, \ell', \cdot, \cdot, \cdot, \cdot \rangle$ he wants to complain about and $\langle \texttt{digest}, \sigma \rangle$ from his current blacklist BL.
2. *(Complaint Validation.)* The NM rejects a complaint if
   - $\mathsf{NMVerify}_{nmsk}(j, k, \ell', \texttt{nymbleTKT}) = \texttt{invalid}$, i.e., the ticket is invalid, or
   - $\mathsf{Sig.verify}_y(j\|k\|v_j\|\texttt{digest}, \sigma) = \texttt{invalid}$, where v_j is the version number of Bob's blacklist recorded by NM, i.e. the (digest of) Bob's blacklist is not authentic, intact or fresh.

   The NM proceeds otherwise.
3. *(Linking-token Issuing.)* The NM computes the following:
   - $\texttt{linkingTKN} \leftarrow \mathsf{LinkingTknExt}_{nmsk}(j, k, \ell + 1, \texttt{nymbleTKT})$,

---

[7] This step may be sped up by trading off space by storing the original nymble tickets issued in the user's credential, making this step a simple lookup.

[8] Here "future" means starting from the next time period, rather than the same period immediately after the complaint. This prevents race conditions such as when a user has inspected that she is not blacklisted by Bob and is about to present her nymble ticket, but in the meantime Bob obtains a linking-token for the current time period.

- entry$'$ $\leftarrow$ $(v_j + 1, \text{nymbleTKT}, \ell)$, digest$'$ $\leftarrow$ $h(\text{digest}||\text{entry}')$ and then $\sigma' \leftarrow \text{Sig.sign}_x(j||k||v_j + 1||\text{digest}')$.

The NM increments v_j by 1 and returns $\langle\text{linkingTKN}, \text{entry}', \text{digest}', \sigma'\rangle$ to Bob.

4. *(List Update.)* Bob updates his blacklist BL and linking-list LL as follows:
   - In BL, Bob increments v by 1, inserts entry$'$ as the last entry, and updates σ to σ' and digest to digest$'$.
   - In LL, Bob appends a new entry $\langle\ell+1, \text{tdr}, \text{nymble}\rangle$, where tdr is the trapdoor in linkingTKN and nymble $\leftarrow g(\text{tdr})$.

Efficiency. The NM's timing complexity is $O(L + v)$. The $O(L)$ is due to a call to LinkingTknExt, which involves only hashing or HMAC operations. Verifying if a linking token has already been issued for the user involves $O(v)$ symmetric decryption operations. Signing one digital signature is the only asymmetric cryptographic operation.

5.6 Update

Misbehavior is forgiven every time the system enters a new linkability window. Users who misbehaved previously can then connect to websites anonymously until they misbehave and are complained against again. The nymble tickets, linking tokens, and pseudonyms that are specific to one linkability window become useless when the system enters a new window. Consequently, servers empty their blacklists and linking-lists while NM resets all version numbers to zero at the end of every linkability window. Moreover, the NM also issues empty blacklists to the servers in the same way as in the System Setup procedure.

At the end of each time period $T_{\ell'}$ that is not the last one in a linkability window, each server updates its linking-list LL by replacing every entry $\langle\ell, \text{tdr}_\ell, \text{nymble}_\ell\rangle$ such that $\ell = \ell'$ with the entry $\langle\ell + 1, f(\text{tdr}_\ell), g(f(\text{tdr}_\ell))\rangle$. Only hashing is required to accomplish this and the number of hash operations involved is two times the size of LL.

6 Evaluation

We chose to implement our system using PHP because of its popularity for interactive web sites (including MediaWiki, the software behind Wikipedia). PHP contains both built-in cryptographic primitives (e.g., SHA-1 hashing) as well as an interface to the OpenSSL cryptographic library; we used both as appropriate to maximize performance. Additionally, we chose to use a relational database to store blacklists and blacklist versions because the interface is convenient in PHP and database servers are generally available in the environments in which we envision the Nymble system being used.

We picked SHA-256 [21] for collision-resistant hash functions f, g and h; HMAC-SHA-1 [23] with 160-bit keys for both keyed hash function H and keyed-hash message authentication code HMAC; AES-256 in OFB mode with block size of 32 bytes [22] for symmetric encryption Enc; and 1024-bit RSA [20] for digital signature Sig. We chose RSA over DSA for digital signatures because of its higher signature verification speed—in our system, signature verification occurs more often than signing.

Our implementation consists of separate modules to be deployed to the Pseudonym Manager, the Nymble Manager, and servers, as well as common modules for database access and cryptographic operations. Orthogonal to the correctness of the system, we felt deployability was also an important goal, and to that end we attempted to minimize modifications required to "Nymble-protect" existing applications.

Applications wishing to use our system include a single PHP file defining two functions: `nymbletkt_is_required(ip)` and `nymbletkt_is_valid (nymbletkt)`. The former determines whether an operation from a particular IP address requires a nymble ticket; the second determines whether the supplied nymble ticket is valid for the current time period. Hence the only modifications necessary are to supply a nymble ticket input field if it is required and to verify the nymble ticket when it is submitted.

To test the system, a single machine acted as Pseudonym Manager, Nymble Manager, and server, running PHP 5.1.6, PostgreSQL 8.1, and Apache 2.0.55, atop a default install of Ubuntu 6.10 and Linux 2.6.17 with SMP enabled. The machine itself was an Intel Core 2 Duo 6300 (2 cores at 1.86 GHz each) and 1 GB memory. Clients of various hardware configurations accessed the server via the local network.

Table 1 shows the speed of operations important to both end-users and server administrators evaluating the Nymble system. Experiments were run 50 times and the results averaged. The *all-ticket credentials* generated were for 1-day linkability windows with 5-minute time periods, thus consisting of 288 nymble tickets. We also measured performance with *single-ticket credentials* containing the ticket for only the time period in which access to a service was requested. Single-ticket credentials are much more efficient to generate, but the NM learns all the time periods (as opposed to only the first time period) when connections are made by the pseudonymous users. The nymble ticket verification step is the added overhead required during a single user action, visible to both the server and the client. The linking token generation is the operation carried out by NM when a server complains. Every time period, each server must iterate every entry in its blacklist; our measurement reflects the time required for a single server to iterate 100 entries.

We believe the all-ticket credential generation time of 224ms is reasonable for a network like Tor, especially since nymble tickets will be needed only for restricted actions such as edits on Wikipedia—latest data indicate that about two edits per second to Wikipedia's English pages.[9] We expect much fewer edits to be made via Tor. If all-ticket credential generation proves to be a bottleneck, the NM can issue single-ticket credentials to drastically reduce the load. We expect the measured time of 1.1ms for generating single-ticket credentials to be more than sufficient.

We have implemented a Firefox extension that automatically obtains a pseudonym from the PM, obtains a credential for a server when needed, verifies the server's blacklist, chooses the correct nymble ticket for the current time period, and inserts it into an HTML form every time the user wishes to traverse a protected page. We assume that the NM is the arbiter of time, and the user and servers can obtain the current time period and linkability window from the NM. For example, when a user obtains the current version number for a particular website's blacklist, the user also learns the current time period.

---

[9] http://stats.wikimedia.org/EN/PlotsPngDatabaseEdits.htm

Table 1. Timing measurements

Operation	Executed by	Time
All-ticket credential generation (288 `nymbleTKTs`)	NM	224 ms
Single-ticket credential generation (1 `nymbleTKT`)	NM	1.1 ms
Nymble ticket verification (Verify)	Server	1 ms
Linking token generation (LinkingTknExt)	NM	15 ms
Blacklist update	Server	8 ms

Finally, we emphasize the NYMBLE system also scales well in terms of space complexities. Credentials that users store are of size $20 + 148L$ bytes each, or 42KB when $L = 288$. The blacklist has a size of $168 + 152v$ bytes, where v is the number of users blacklisted by the server during the current linkability window. Most importantly, the amount of data the NM has to maintain is minimal, namely only one 32-bit integer per registered server for storing the server's current version number.

7   Discussion

IP-address blocking. As described in Section 3, users demonstrate control over an IP address by connecting to the PM directly. Since this connection is made without Tor, some users may object to the temporary loss of anonymity. It is important to provide users with an accurate portrayal of the associated risks (and benefits) before using our system.

There are some inherent limitations to using IP addresses as the scarce resource. If a user can obtain multiple IP addresses she can circumvent nymble-based blocking and continue to misbehave. We point out, however, that this problem exists in the absence of anonymizing networks as well, and the user would be able to circumvent regular IP-address based blocking using multiple IP addresses. Some servers alleviate this problem with subnet-based IP blocking, and while it is possible to modify our system to support subnet-blocking, new privacy challenges emerge; a more thorough description of subnet-blocking is left for future work. Another limitation is that a user Alice may acquire nymbles for a particular IP address and then use them at a later time (to misbehave) within the linkability window even after she has relinquished control over that IP address. This type of attack allows Alice a little more flexibility—with regular IP-based blocking, Alice would have to perform misbehaviors while in control of the various IP addresses.

Some other resource may be used to acquire pseudonyms, but we believe IP-address blocking is still the most pragmatic approach in today's Internet. Our approach closely mimics IP-address blocking that many servers on the Internet rely on routinely. Some may be concerned that users can misbehave through Tor *after* their IP address has been blocked, effectively allowing them to misbehave twice before being blocked (once using regular IP-address blocking, and once using Nymble). We argue, however, that servers concerned about this problem could require Nymble-based authentication from *all* users, whether or not they connect through an anonymizing network.

Time periods and linkability windows. Since nymbles are associated with time periods, it is desirable to keep the duration $\mathcal{T}$ of time periods small. On the other hand, larger values of $\mathcal{T}$ can be used to limit the rate of anonymous connections by a user. Since users remain blacklisted for the remainder of the linkability window after a complaint, it is desirable to keep the duration of the linkability window $\mathcal{L}$ long enough to curtail the malicious user's activities, but not so long as to punish that user (or honest users to whom the IP address may get reassigned) indefinitely. In our example we suggested $\mathcal{T} = 5$ min and $\mathcal{L} = 1$ day, but further experimentation is needed to determine reasonable values for these parameters.

Server-specific linkability windows. An enhancement would be to provide support to vary $\mathcal{T}$ and $\mathcal{L}$ for different servers. As described, our system does not support varying linkability windows, but does support varying time periods. This is because the PM is not aware of the server to which the user wishes to connect, yet it must issue pseudonyms specific to a linkability window. In our system, therefore, the linkability window must be fixed across all servers. Supporting varying time periods is easy, and the NM can be modified to issue the appropriate set of nymble tickets based on the servers' parameters.

8   Conclusion

We present a system that allows websites to selectively block users of anonymizing networks such as Tor. Using our system, websites can blacklist users *without* knowing their IP addresses. Users not on the blacklist enjoy anonymity, while blacklisted users are blocked from making future accesses. Furthermore, blacklisted users' previous connections remain anonymous. Since websites are free to blacklist anonymous users of their choice, and since users are notified of their blacklisting status, our system avoids the complications associated with judging "misbehavior." We believe that these properties will enhance the acceptability of anonymizing networks such as Tor by enabling websites to selectively block certain users instead of blocking the entire network, all while allowing the remaining (honest) users to stay anonymous.

Acknowledgments

This paper greatly benefited from discussions with Sergey Bratus, Alexander Iliev, and Anna Shubina. We also thank Roger Dingledine, Paul Syverson, Parisa Tabriz, Seung Yi, and the anonymous reviewers for their helpful comments.

References

1. Ateniese, G., Camenisch, J., Joye, M., Tsudik, G.: A practical and provably secure coalition-resistant group signature scheme. In: Bellare, M. (ed.) CRYPTO 2000. LNCS, vol. 1880, pp. 255–270. Springer, Heidelberg (2000)
2. Bellare, M., Micciancio, D., Warinschi, B.: Foundations of group signatures: Formal definitions, simplified requirements, and a construction based on general assumptions. In: Biham, E. (ed.) Advances in Cryptology – EUROCRPYT 2003. LNCS, vol. 2656, pp. 614–629. Springer, Heidelberg (2003)

3. Bellare, M., Shi, H., Zhang, C.: Foundations of group signatures: The case of dynamic groups. In: Menezes, A.J. (ed.) CT-RSA 2005. LNCS, vol. 3376, pp. 136–153. Springer, Heidelberg (2005)

4. Brands, S.: Untraceable off-line cash in wallets with observers (extended abstract). In: Stinson, D.R. (ed.) CRYPTO 1993. LNCS, vol. 773, pp. 302–318. Springer, Heidelberg (1994)

5. Camenisch, J., Hohenberger, S., Kohlweiss, M., Lysyanskaya, A., Meyerovich, M.: How to win the clonewars: efficient periodic n-times anonymous authentication. In: Juels, A., Wright, R.N., De Capitani di Vimercati, S. (eds.) ACM Conference on Computer and Communications Security, pp. 201–210. ACM Press, New York (2006)

6. Camenisch, J., Hohenberger, S., Lysyanskaya, A.: Compact e-cash. In: Cramer, R.J.F. (ed.) EUROCRYPT 2005. LNCS, vol. 3494, pp. 302–321. Springer, Heidelberg (2005)

7. Camenisch, J., Lysyanskaya, A.: An efficient system for non-transferable anonymous credentials with optional anonymity revocation. In: Pfitzmann, B. (ed.) EUROCRYPT 2001. LNCS, vol. 2045, pp. 93–118. Springer, Heidelberg (2001)

8. Camenisch, J., Lysyanskaya, A.: Signature schemes and anonymous credentials from bilinear maps. In: Franklin, M. (ed.) CRYPTO 2004. LNCS, vol. 3152, pp. 56–72. Springer, Heidelberg (2004)

9. Chaum, D.: Untraceable electronic mail, return addresses, and digital pseudonyms. Communications of the ACM 4(2) (1981)

10. Chaum, D.: Blind signatures for untraceable payments. In: CRYPTO, pp. 199–203 (1982)

11. Chaum, D.: Showing credentials without identification transfeering signatures between unconditionally unlinkable pseudonyms. In: Seberry, J., Pieprzyk, J.P. (eds.) AUSCRYPT 1990. LNCS, vol. 453, pp. 246–264. Springer, Heidelberg (1990)

12. Chaum, D., van Heyst, E.: Group signatures. In: Davies, D.W. (ed.) EUROCRYPT 1991. LNCS, vol. 547, pp. 257–265. Springer, Heidelberg (1991)

13. Chen, L.: Access with pseudonyms. In: Dawson, E.P., Golić, J.D. (eds.) Cryptography: Policy and Algorithms. LNCS, vol. 1029, pp. 232–243. Springer, Heidelberg (1996)

14. Damgård, I.: Payment systems and credential mechanisms with provable security against abuse by individuals. In: Goldwasser, S. (ed.) CRYPTO 1988. LNCS, vol. 403, pp. 328–335. Springer, Heidelberg (1990)

15. Dingledine, R., Mathewson, N., Syverson, P.: Tor: The Second-Generation Onion Router. In: Usenix Security Symposium, pp. 303–320 (2004)

16. Douceur, J.R.: The sybil attack. In: Druschel, P., Kaashoek, M.F., Rowstron, A. (eds.) IPTPS 2002. LNCS, vol. 2429, pp. 251–260. Springer, Heidelberg (2002)

17. Holt, J.E., Seamons, K.E.: Nym: Practical pseudonymity for anonymous networks. Internet Security Research Lab Technical Report 2006-4, Brigham Young University (June 2006)

18. Kiayias, A., Tsiounis, Y., Yung, M.: Traceable signatures. In: Cachin, C., Camenisch, J.L. (eds.) EUROCRYPT 2004. LNCS, vol. 3027, pp. 571–589. Springer, Heidelberg (2004)

19. Lysyanskaya, A., Rivest, R.L., Sahai, A., Wolf, S.: Pseudonym systems. In: Heys, H.M., Adams, C.M. (eds.) SAC 1999. LNCS, vol. 1758, pp. 184–199. Springer, Heidelberg (2000)

20. NIST. FIPS 186-2: Digital signature standard (DSS). Technical report, National Institute of Standards and Technology (NIST) (2000),
http://csrc.nist.gov/publications/fips/fips186-2/
fips186-2-change1.pdf

21. NIST. FIPS 180-2: Secure hash standard (SHS). Technical report, National Institute of Standards and Technology (NIST) (2001), http://csrc.nist.gov/publications/
fips/fips180-2/fips180-2withchangenotice.pdf

22. NIST. FIPS 197: Announcing the advanced encryption standard (AES). Technical report, National Institute of Standards and Technology (NIST) (2001), http://csrc.nist.gov/publications/fips/fips197/fips-197.pdf
23. NIST. FIPS 198: The keyed-hash message authentication code (HMAC). Technical report, National Institute of Standards and Technology (NIST) (2002), http://csrc.nist.gov/publications/fips/fips198/fips-198a.pdf
24. Ohkubo, M., Suzuki, K., Kinoshita, S.: Cryptographic approach to "privacy-friendly" tags. In: RFID Privacy Workshop, MIT, MA, USA (November 2003)
25. Reiter, M.K., Rubin, A.D.: Crowds: Anonymity for Web Transactions. ACM Transactions on Information and System Security 1(1), 66–92 (1998)
26. Rivest, R.L., Shamir, A., Tauman, Y.: How to leak a secret. In: Boyd, C. (ed.) ASIACRYPT 2001. LNCS, vol. 2248, pp. 552–565. Springer, Heidelberg (2001)
27. Syverson, P.F., Stubblebine, S.G., Goldschlag, D.M.: Unlinkable serial transactions. In: Hirschfeld, R. (ed.) FC 1997. LNCS, vol. 1318, pp. 39–56. Springer, Heidelberg (1997)
28. Teranishi, I., Furukawa, J., Sako, K.: k-times anonymous authentication (extended abstract). In: Lee, P.J. (ed.) ASIACRYPT 2004. LNCS, vol. 3329, pp. 308–322. Springer, Heidelberg (2004)
29. Tsang, P.P., Kapadia, A., Smith, S.W.: Anonymous IP-address blocking in tor with trusted computing (work-in-progress). In: The Second Workshop on Advances in Trusted Computing (WATC '06 Fall) (November 2006)
30. von Ahn, L., Bortz, A., Hopper, N.J., O'Neill, K.: Selectively traceable anonymity. In: Danezis, G., Golle, P. (eds.) PET 2006. LNCS, vol. 4258, pp. 208–222. Springer, Heidelberg (2006)

A   Security Model, Proofs and Analysis

A.1   Security Model for Nymble-Auth

Correctness means the system functions as intended when all entities are honest. Unforgeability guarantees that valid nymble tickets can only be obtained from NM. Backward Anonymity makes sure nymble tickets are anonymous without an associated trapdoor and remain anonymous even with an associated trapdoor as long as that trapdoor is meant for a time period later than the nymble tickets. Finally, Uncircumventable Forward Linkability says that valid nymble tickets are always linked to an associated trapdoor meant for a time prior to those nymble tickets.

Definition 1 (Correctness). A Nymble-Auth construction is *correct* if it has *Verification Correctness* and *Linking Correctness*, defined as follows:

- *(Verification Correctness.)* If all entities in the system are honest (i.e. they execute the algorithms according to the system specification), then ServerVerify returns 1 (indicating valid) on any nymbleTKT output by NymbleTktGen, with overwhelming probability.
- *(Linking Correctness.)* If all entities in the system are honest, then Link returns linked on any linkingTKN generated by LinkingTknExt(i, j, k, ℓ) and any nymbleTKT generated by NymbleTktGen(i', j', k', ℓ') if and only if $(i, j, k) = (i', j', k')$ and $j \leq j'$, with overwhelming probability.   □

We describe three oracles before defining various security games. The existence of the oracles models the adversary's capability in the real world of learning as much information about the nymbles and trapdoors as possible by probing the system. They are:

- $\mathcal{O}_{TKT}(i, j, k, \ell)$, or the *Ticket Oracle*. It returns nymbleTKT$_{i,j,k,\ell}$, the nymble ticket as output by the NymbleTktGen algorithm on input (i, j, k, ℓ),
- $\mathcal{O}_{TKN}($nymbleTKT$, \ell)$, or the *Token Oracle*. It returns the linking token linkingTKN$_{i,j,k,\ell}$ as output by the LinkingTknExt algorithm on input (nymbleTKT$, \ell)$, and
- $\mathcal{O}_K(j)$, or the *Server Corruption Oracle*. It returns k_{NS_j}, the symmetric key of server S_i as output by the Setup algorithm.

Definition 2 (Unforgeability). A Nymble-Auth construction is *Unforgeable* if no *Probabilistic Poly-Time (PPT)* adversary $\mathcal{A}$ can win the following game against the Challenger $\mathcal{C}$ with non-negligible probability:

1. *(Setup Phase.)* $\mathcal{C}$ executes Setup(1^λ) on a sufficiently large λ, keeps *nmsk* secret and gives *nmpk* to $\mathcal{A}$.
2. *(Probing Phase.)* $\mathcal{A}$ may arbitrarily and adaptively query three oracles $\mathcal{O}_{TKN}$ (nymbleTKT$, \ell)$, $\mathcal{O}_{TKT}(i, j, k, \ell)$ and $\mathcal{O}_K(j)$.
3. *(End Game Phase.)* $\mathcal{A}$ returns $\langle j^*, k^*\ell^*,$ nymbleTKT$^*\rangle$. $\mathcal{A}$ wins the game if nymbleTKT* is not an output of a previous $\mathcal{O}_{TKT}(\cdot, \cdot, \cdot, \cdot)$ query, $\mathcal{A}$ did not query $\mathcal{O}_K(j^*)$ and Verify$_{k_{NS_{j^*}}}(j^*, k^*, \ell^*,$ nymbleTKT$^*) = 1$. □

That is, $\mathcal{A}$ should not be able to forge a valid nymbleTKT without the NM's secret parameters.

Definition 3 (Backward Anonymity). A Nymble-Auth construction has *Backward Anonymity* if no PPT adversary $\mathcal{A}$ can win the following game against the Challenger $\mathcal{C}$ with probability non-negligibly greater than 1/2:

1. *(Setup Phase.)* $\mathcal{C}$ executes Setup on a sufficiently large security parameter, keeps *nmsk* secret, and gives *nmpk* to $\mathcal{A}$.
2. *(Probing Phase I.)* $\mathcal{A}$ may arbitrarily and adaptively query the three oracles $\mathcal{O}_{TKT}(\cdot, \cdot, \cdot, \cdot)$, $\mathcal{O}_{TKN}(\cdot, \cdot)$ and $\mathcal{O}_K(\cdot)$.
3. *(Challenge Phase.)* $\mathcal{A}$ decides on positive integers $i_0^*, i_1^*, j^*, k^*, \ell^*$ such that the following conditions hold:
    - For all queries $\mathcal{O}_{TKT}(i, j, k, \ell)$, for each $b \in \{0, 1\}$ we have that $(i, j, k, \ell) \neq (i_b^*, j^*, k^*, \ell^*)$, i.e., $\mathcal{A}$ has not already obtained any of the challenge nymbleTKTs from $\mathcal{O}_{TKT}$.
    - For all queries $\mathcal{O}_{TKN}(\cdot, \ell)$, $\ell > \ell^*$, i.e. all trapdoors obtained are of time periods greater than the challenge nymble tickets.
    - For each $b \in \{0, 1\}$, for all queries $\mathcal{O}_{TKT}(i_1, j_1, k_1, \ell_1)$ where $(i_1, j_1, k_1) = (i_b^*, j^*, k^*)$ and queries $\mathcal{O}_{TKN}($nymbleTKT$, \ell)$ where nymbleTKT is the output of some query $\mathcal{O}_{TKT}(i_2, j_2, k_2, \ell_2)$ such that $(i_2, j_2, k_2) = (i_b^*, j^*, k^*)$, $\ell_1 < \ell$, i.e. the adversary is not allowed to query for a linking token and a nymble

ticket such that the trapdoor within the linking token can be used to link the nymble ticket.[10]

Then C flips a fair coin $b^* \in_R \{0,1\}$ and returns A with

$$\langle \texttt{nymbleTKT}_{i_{b^*},j^*,k^*\ell^*}, \texttt{nymbleTKT}_{i_{\widetilde{b^*}},j^*,k^*,\ell^*} \rangle,$$

where $\widetilde{b^*}$ is the negation of b^*.

4. *(Probing Phase II.)* A may arbitrarily and adaptively query the three oracles, except that the conditions above must still hold.
5. *(End Game Phase.)* A returns guess $\hat{b} \in \{0,1\}$ on b^*. A wins if $\hat{b} = b^*$.   □

That is, A should not be able to link nymbleTKTs without the appropriate linkingTKN.

Definition 4 (Uncircumventable Forward Linkability). A Nymble-Auth construction has *Uncircumventable Forward Linkability* if no PPT adversary can win the following game she plays against the Challenger C with non-negligible probability:

1. *(Setup Phase.)* C executes Setup on a sufficiently large security parameter, keeps *nmsk* secret and gives *nmpk* to A.
2. *(Probing Phase.)* A may arbitrarily and adaptively query the three oracles $\mathcal{O}_{TKN}(i,j,k,\ell)$, $\mathcal{O}_{TKT}(i,j,k,\ell)$ and $\mathcal{O}_K(j)$, where $i,j,k,\ell \geq 1$.
3. *(End Game Phase.)* A returns $\langle j^*, k^*, \ell_0^*, \ell_1^*, \texttt{nymbleTKT}_0^*, \texttt{nymbleTKT}_1^*, \ell^* \rangle$. A wins the game if $\mathsf{Verify}(j^*, k^*, \ell_b^*, \texttt{nymbleTKT}_b^*) = 1$ for $b \in \{0,1\}$, $\ell_0^* \leq \ell^* \leq \ell_1^*$, A did not query $\mathcal{O}_K(\cdot)$ on j^* and

$$\mathsf{Link}(\texttt{nymble}_1^*, \mathsf{TrapdoorExt}(\texttt{nymble}_0^*, \ell^*)) = 0.$$

□

That is, A cannot obtain two nymbleTKTs for any server such that they are unlinkable, but should have otherwise been linkable, with the appropriate linkingTKN.

A.2 Security Proofs for Nymble-Auth

Proof (Theorem 1). (Sketch.) We prove the theorem by showing our Nymble-Auth construction is correct, unforgeable, backward anonymous and uncircumventably forward linkable. Due to page limitation, we gives only proof sketches here.

CORRECTNESS. Correctness of Nymble-Auth is straightforward. Namely, verification correctness is implied by the correctness of the HMAC HMAC. Linking correctness is implied by the determinism and collision-resistance of hash functions f, g.

UNFORGEABILITY. Our Nymble-Auth construction has unforgeability due to the security of HMAC, which guarantees that without the knowledge of the associated key, no PPT adversary can produce a valid MAC on any input string, even if the adversary learns arbitrary input-output HMAC pairs. As a result, any PPT in our construction is

---

[10] This restriction is justified because we will use Nymble-Auth in such a way that a user will never present a nymble ticket again to a server once the server has acquired a linking token for that user.

allowed to query the oracle for arbitrary nymble tickets and yet is unable to produce a new one with a correct MAC on it.

BACKWARD ANONYMITY. Our Nymble-Auth construction has backward anonymity due to the security of the symmetric encryption Enc and the collision-resistance of the hash functions f and g. The only pieces within a nymble ticket that are correlated to user identities are the nymble and the encrypted trapdoor. The security of Enc guarantees that ciphertexts leak no information about their underlying plaintexts to any PPT adversary, so that the encrypted trapdoor is computationally uncorrelated to the underlying trapdoor and thus the identity of the user to which the nymble ticket belongs. The nymble is the output of $g(\cdot)$ on its associated trapdoor, which is in turn the output after a series of application of $f(\cdot)$ on a seed dependent on the user identity. Under the Random Oracle Model, hash function outputs are random (but consistent), therefore the nymbles are distinguishable from random strings in the view of an adversary who does not have any trapdoor for the user-server-window tuple to which nymbles in the challenge nymble tickets are associated.

Knowing one or more associated trapdoors does not help the adversary in winning the game as the trapdoors are also indistinguishable from random values. This is the case because all except the first linking token returned by $\mathcal{O}_{TKN}$ contain a true random value as the trapdoor. The first linking token contains a genuine trapdoor, but it is indistinguishable from a random value because $f(\cdot)$ and $g(\cdot)$ are random oracles and the adversary is not allowed to query $\mathcal{O}_{TKT}$ for a nymble ticket and query $\mathcal{O}_{TKN}$ for a linking token such that the time period of the nymble ticket is greater than or equal to the time period of the linking token.

UNCIRCUMVENTABLE FORWARD LINKABILITY. Our Nymble-Auth construction has Uncircumventable Forward Linkability as a consequence of unforgeability and linking correctness. Specifically, assume there exists an PPT adversary who can break uncircumventable forward linkability; then the two nymble tickets she output at the End Game phase must be such that they are query outputs of the nymble ticket oracle, because otherwise the adversary would have broken the unforgeability of Nymble-Auth, which leads to a contradiction. Now since the two output nymble tickets are generated according to specification, the linking algorithm will return linked on any trapdoor extracted from the nymble ticket earlier in time period, which again leads to a contradiction.   □

Improving Efficiency and Simplicity of Tor Circuit Establishment and Hidden Services

Lasse Øverlier[1,2] and Paul Syverson[3]

[1] Norwegian Defence Research Establishment, P.B. 25, 2027 Kjeller, Norway
lasse.overlier@ffi.no
http://www.ffi.no/
[2] Gjøvik University College, P.B. 191, 2802 Gjøvik, Norway
lasse@hig.no
http://www.hig.no/
[3] Center for High Assurance Computer Systems
Naval Research Laboratory Code 5540, Washington, DC 20375
syverson@itd.nrl.navy.mil
http://chacs.nrl.navy.mil, http://www.onion-router.net

Abstract. In this paper we demonstrate how to reduce the overhead and delay of circuit establishment in the Tor anonymizing network by using predistributed Diffie-Hellman values. We eliminate the use of RSA encryption and decryption from circuit setup, and we reduce the number of DH exponentiations vs. the current Tor circuit setup protocol while maintaining immediate forward secrecy. We also describe savings that can be obtained by precomputing during idle cycles values that can be determined before the protocol starts. We introduce the distinction of eventual vs. immediate forward secrecy and present protocols that illustrate the distinction. These protocols are even more efficient in communication and computation than the one we primarily propose, but they provide only eventual forward secrecy. We describe how to reduce the overhead and the complexity of hidden server connections by using our DH-values to implement valet nodes and eliminate the need for rendezvous points as they exist today. We also discuss the security of the new elements and an analysis of efficiency improvements.

1 Introduction

Since its public deployment in October 2003, the Tor [7] anonymizing network has been a huge success. It currently consists of around 900 server nodes (onion routers) scattered throughout all inhabited continents. With a weekly estimated 200.000+ users, and no down-time since launch, it is also the largest distributed anonymizing network in use. There are other anonymizing networks: JAP [2] and Freenet [5] are the most well-known implementations. In addition there exist several commercial services offering anonymity through anonymizing proxies, e.g., Relakks [21] and Anonymizer [1].

In this paper we describe new protocols for establishing circuits through Tor and for accessing hidden services over Tor that are substantially more efficient

N. Borisov and P. Golle (Eds.): PET 2007, LNCS 4776, pp. 134–152, 2007.

than those currently deployed. All the Tor modifications described in the paper were motivated by our intent to simplify and reduce the overhead of using hidden services. However, as with the introduction of entry guards motivated by our previous analysis of hidden services [17], we discovered that much of our work applies to Tor circuits in general, not just those for accessing hidden services. For clarity of exposition, we have thus separated our presentation into protocol changes that apply to all Tor circuits and protocol changes that apply only to hidden services.

Our generally applicable protocols provide (1) reduced overhead and greater efficiency for the Tor network overall, (2) improved overhead and efficiency for Tor client machines, (3) examples to refine and explicate the concept of forward secrecy, and (4) most significantly, reduced load on individual server nodes. The basic idea of onion routing was to make low-latency anonymous communication feasible by adopting a circuit approach and limiting expensive public-key crypto use to circuit setup. This has been largely successful and, for most circuits over Tor, symmetric-key crypto has always dominated CPU consumption. Still, as the network grew past 100 nodes in Spring 2005 it became necessary to modify Tor to handle the public-key overhead by shifting the default rotation interval for used-circuits from one minute to ten minutes. Because Tor is a volunteer network, many of those who would like to contribute a node can only offer either unused spare machines—which are often older, slower, and have less memory— or machines that have other jobs to do, thus that can only spare computational resources for Tor if the overhead is not too great. Therefore, our techniques effectively lower the barrier to becoming a Tor node in significant ways and so encourage the network to grow.

In addition to the reduced computational requirements for circuit establishment, we describe reductions in message flows, both for basic circuit establishment and to establish circuits for communication with hidden services, where we use the new circuit construction and the valet nodes [18] extension to hidden services to make the design simpler. The currently implemented hidden service design [7] is complex and involves the building of four circuits collectively comprised of as many as twelve Tor server nodes—not including the service lookup, the client or the hidden service node. The latency of connecting to hidden services and interacting with them and the network load resulting from this complexity may have contributed to the relatively low number of hidden services deployed to date. There is also the effect simply that perceived complexity can imply reduced expectation of security and performance. However, the lower priority placed on maintaining and improving hidden services by the Tor developers, (not in general but simply relative to other aspects of Tor) no doubt also plays a role, as does the less immediate need for hidden services for the typical Tor user. Our protocol eliminates the rendezvous server as it is used today, and we reduce the number of involved nodes from twelve to six and the number of circuits from four to two in the best case scenario. In the worst case, there are three circuits comprised of nine nodes.

In section 2 we give a short overview of the history of onion routing and circuit telescoping. In section 3 we present new methods of setting up anonymous tunnels, both as a proposal for reducing Tor overhead and to explicate forward secrecy, and in section 4 we look at some new methods of performing hidden service connections. Section 5 discusses anonymity, security, and efficiency of the new designs, and section 6 concludes.

2   Background

Onion routing is an approach to low-latency anonymous communication on public networks. The first two generations of onion routing used data structures comprised of layers of public-key encryptions to establish circuits and to distribute session keys to nodes along the circuit. The session keys were used, also in a layered fashion, to encrypt and decrypt the data traveling back and forth between the circuit initiator and responder. In the current generation of onion routing, Tor, circuits are established by Diffie-Hellman (DH) key exchange with each node in the circuit, each exchange being tunneled through the already established circuit and encrypted with established session keys. This technique has been called "telescoping" since its introduction in the Freedom Network [3]. Using DH provides (perfect)[1] forward secrecy (FS), meaning that, because keys are formed from exchanged messages rather than sent in encrypted form, once the session is over and the keys discarded, an adversary who stored all previous communication cannot decrypt it by somehow later obtaining a private key used to encrypt a session key.

Interestingly the original onion routing system designers considered but abandoned in the spring of 1996 [11] the option of using public Diffie-Hellman values to achieve efficiency gains in computation. Our intended design was to include the public DH-values from the originator inside the layers of circuit building onions, which were used in the first few generations of onion routing designs, and then to combine these with public DH keys (that we assume are DH-values used for generating keys). This is very similar to one of the protocols described below. Our focus was not on FS but simply to be more computationally efficient. We were certainly aware of FS and intentionally chose a protocol for securing links between onion routers that provided it, but we only pursued it with respect to outside attackers rather than against compromised network nodes as well. The idea of using DH for basic circuit building was simply another dropped design idea until work began on the Tor design, when it was picked up for the forward secrecy it provided and for freedom from the need to store onions against replay. The first description [10,19] and implementation of onion routing uses RSA public keys for distributing circuit session keys and DH-established link encryption between the server nodes. The current version of onion routing, Tor, uses both a DH key exchange and an RSA encryption/decryption for each step on the

---

[1] Forward secrecy was called 'perfect forward secrecy' when it was introduced and often still is. We will follow the convention common in cryptologic literature of referring to it simply as 'forward secrecy'.

anonymizing tunnel setup. The computational advantages of using DH that we contemplated in 1996 have lain dormant until now.

Hidden services [7,17] have also been a part of onion routing since 1997 [11] and in their current form have been deployed on the public Tor network since 2004. They offer resistance to distributed DoS and other types of location oriented attacks. Hidden services are hidden by the network in the sense that their network locations cannot be found through access to the service, and this hiding makes the services suitable for censorship resistance, such as for dissidents or journalists publishing information accessible from anywhere. These location hidden services have been shown to have potential vulnerabilities [16,17] some of which have been addressed. Improvements to availability and QoS have been added [18], although these have also made the protocol even more complex.

In this paper we present various DH-based protocols for more efficient establishment of circuits in an onion routing network and present both efficiency improvements and simplifications to the existing hidden services protocol (in addition to those from our more efficient circuit setup protocols).

3   Circuit-Building Protocol Description

We assume that the functionality of the existing Tor protocol is known to the reader. Description of Tor circuit setup can be found in [6,7].

3.1   Overview

The central idea of all our protocols is to have certified ephemeral key exchange values at every server node inside the anonymizing network that the client uses to generate session keys for use with the nodes. These keys are used for symmetric encryption inside the created circuits. In this way it is similar to the originally contemplated use of DH in onion routing a decade ago. In all the protocols we describe we save computational overhead because there are now about half as many exponentiations per circuit established when compared to the existing Tor circuit building protocol. We present four protocols. The first provides the building blocks on which the others are based. We then consider issues of forward secrecy and message replay. We illustrate these via a succession of protocols in which communications efficiency and to some extent computational efficiency is in each following protocol traded off for improvements in forward secrecy or replay prevention, culminating in a protocol with the computational improvements we have already noted but that provides immediate forward secrecy. These ideas will be explained below.

3.2   Protocol Description

Our new protocols use an ElGamal key agreement [8], which is also widely known as a half-certified Diffie-Hellman key exchange [15], to initialize the keys along the circuit. Construction of DH keys is computationally expensive, so it should happen as infrequently as possible. But new DH keys enable forward secrecy when both parameters are discarded, so it should happen as often as possible. But rotation can also require an update of the public (or user) accessible information, so it should happen as infrequently as possible. Our presentation of the various protocols below is in part designed to explore these apparently conflicting needs and to illustrate ways to either make appropriate tradeoffs or to satisfy both needs at once.

Unlike the current Tor network, no RSA key is used to encrypt client-server or server-server communication. RSA keys are used only for the node to sign public information about itself. Thus, server initialization and publishing of node information is completed as in the current Tor implementation. (1) Every server node has a permanent server key pair $PS_{pub/priv}$ as before. The private key is used for signing server information, including the public key and all information published in the directory service. (2) The server creates DH parameters $DH_{x,pub/priv}$ that are to be used in forming circuits. The public values of are made part of the information published in the directory service together with the public server key. These public values need to be updated regularly. Following current practice for the onion keys (circuit-building RSA keys) in the Tor network, the default is to have a single server DH key good for one week, with the previous week's key being retained and usable to avoid synchronization problems at the time of switching to a new key. (We could add a list of public-key-exchange values valid in different periods of time, e.g. one new DH value every day, to the published and signed list of information about this node. This would permit the servers to have multiple values with different periods of validity to support both circuit setup and to be used with valet nodes in the hidden service design. On the other hand, this would clearly increase the directory overhead of Tor at a time when directory size is seen as a main cost of running Tor and when Tor developers are looking for ways to reduce the directory size and frequency of updates.)

3.3   Setting Up the Circuit

There are two main uses of circuit constructions within Tor. (1) Setting up a standard circuit, for example to reach an exit-node in order to retrieve information from outside the anonymizing network. (2) Setting up a circuit to a hidden service using special setup paths that protect the location of the accessed server as well as the location of the client. The latter will be described in section 4.

We have in our examples described the plain Diffie-Hellman based ElGamal key exchange protocol. An implementation could use an ECC (Elliptic Curve Cryptography) version to reduce overhead in communication and computing time when deriving the session keys. Besides technical questions, the many patents in this area would need to be investigated before recommending an ECC version for Tor use. We will not discuss here the cryptographic differences or advantages between these key exchange methods.

Plain circuit setup, using circuit setup onions. The client, C, wants to communicate through nodes X and Y to node Z, and from there to exit the network to server S, just as in current Tor communication.

First the client wants to share an ephemeral encryption key with node X. Every accessible node has signed and published their global DH-parameters, $DH_{x,pub}$, as described above.[2] A discussion of the various methods to use for distributing DH-parameters and public keys will not be addressed in this paper: see [7,18] for this. Now, when the client wants to establish a communication channel, it creates its own ephemeral DH value pair for use with each node, e.g., $DH_{cx,priv/pub}$, for communication between C and X. It then sends the public part to node X together with the additional information encrypted with the newly constructed key.[3]

As noted above, this is essentially a half-certified ElGamal key agreement. Now one can use the client's contact with the first server node to tunnel information to the second, and to the third, and so on.

The first protocol uses this new key exchange to set up each extension of the tunnel quite similarly to the current handshake of Tor, except that we use the public Diffie-Hellman value for identifying the server node. The connection between the server node and its public DH value is established via the signature on node information that the client must verify. (Alternatively it could be possible to use pairing-based cryptography to set up an identity-based Diffie-Hellman scheme for circuit building obviating the need for signed certificates [13]. However, amongst other limitations, existing pairing-based schemes require a trusted server to generate and distribute private keys to all the server nodes. A threshold system can be used to reduce trust in a single entity for generating and distributing these keys with a concomitant increase in overhead. We therefore think it unlikely that any existing pairing-based scheme will be both practical and adequately trustable for deployment on the public Tor network. Nonetheless, the potential advantages of an identity-based scheme are clear. Thus it is a worthwhile research question to explore applying these schemes to onion routing networks and similar systems. An identity-based scheme may also be useful for similar but distinct existing applications or in other contexts.)

The setup packet to X contains

$$DH_{cx,pub}, \{CREATE, ID_{cx}, data\}_{K_{cx}}$$

and the reply is similar to the current Tor key establishment "CREATED" messages, except that it can be encrypted with the common key K_{xc} because the

---

[2] This value is calculated from their private DH-parameter, $DH_{x,pub} = g^{DH_{x,priv}}$, signed and retrieved by C.

[3] E.g. in plain Diffie-Hellman the key K_{cx} is found by using $(DH_{cx,pub})^{DH_{x,priv}} = (DH_{x,pub})^{DH_{cx,priv}}$ as key material. Note that this key material is for use only in one circuit. If C were to build another circuit through X during the lifetime of $DH_{x,pub}$, it would use $DH_{x,pub}$, but would generate a new $DH_{cx,pub}$. Note also that $K_{cx} \neq (DH_{cx,pub})^{DH_{x,priv}}$: as is usual cryptographic practice, a key derivation function (kdf) is needed to produce K_{cx} from $(DH_{cx,pub})^{DH_{x,priv}}$, and a different kdf is used for K_{cx} (for communication from C to X) than the kdf used for K_{xc} (for communication from X to C).

key is established at both client and node once this setup message is processed.[4] The same alteration to original Tor applies for the extension from X to Y when sent from the client. The result will look something like

$$\{ID_{cx}, EXTEND, DH_{cy,pub}, \{CREATE, ID_{cy}, data\}_{K_{cy}}\}_{K_{cx}} \qquad (1)$$

with a reply that uses the new keys K_{xc} and K_{yc}[5]. Similar extension is done from Y to Z. We have only described the changes to the protocol. There exist checksums and key verification parameters in the current Tor protocol that will fit easily in the same way in the new protocol. Notice that if we use $DH_{cx,pub/priv} = DH_{cy,pub/priv} \neq DH_{cz,pub/priv}$ or $DH_{cx,pub/priv} \neq DH_{cy,pub/priv} = DH_{cz,pub/priv}$ we save one DH initialization and will still have FS as long as the private value is discarded after circuit use. The main reason for not having Z's value equal to X's value is that X and Z should not be able to use the value as an index to trivially tell if they are a part of the same circuit.

This first protocol will serve as the basic building block for those that follow, which are all variants on it.

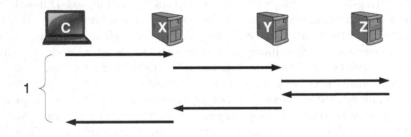

Fig. 1. Circuit setup, second protocol

The second protocol creates the complete circuit by sending a single packet to the first server node, X, propagating its way through Y to Z, as shown in Fig. 1. The initial packet sent from C will look something like

$$DH_{cx,pub}, \{cmd, ID_{cx}, Y, DH_{cy,pub}, \{cmd, ID_{cy}, Z, DH_{cz,pub},$$
$$\{cmd, ID_{cz}, data\}_{K_{cz}}\}_{K_{cy}}\}_{K_{cx}} \qquad (2)$$

The client (and intermediate nodes) will replace (actually "shift left") the data and add as much padding as they have removed in order to maintain constant data length when stripping off headers. The *data* in Expression 2 can be parameters to the command for the last node of the circuit, e.g. connect to an external service or a simple "SETUP_COMPLETE" to let the last node know that it should send back a "SETUP_OK". The *data* field will always be followed by

---

[4] Note that since the client contributes only a fresh, ephemeral, and unauthenticated value in this exchange, any concern about Key Compromise Impersonation attacks simply do not apply to our protocols [4].

[5] Recall $K_{yc} \neq K_{cy}$, but they are both derived from equal key exchange material.

termination information and random data adequate to keep a constant length. This is the same technique to hide correlation between onion size and relative position in a circuit used in the two generations of onion routing that preceded Tor [10,20].

This general approach of (1) using just DH in exactly this way and (2) abandoning RSA for circuit establishment was seriously considered [11] by the developers of onion routing when moving from the generation 0 to the generation 1 system design, but ultimately RSA encryption in circuit setup has been used in the code for all three generations of onion routing that have been deployed.

Preventing replay in circuit setup. If someone were to obtain the onion in Expression 2, he could replay it and cause the exact same circuit to be built with the exact same keys. He could not read any traffic without breaking three private and/or session keys. And, he could only replay it for the lifetime of onion routers' public DH keys. If any of them were to expire and the corresponding private keys be discarded, the nodes would not be able to process the circuit. But during that period, he could build the circuit repeatedly and possibly conduct traffic attacks based on doing so. That is not possible in the current Tor circuit-building protocol because each server contributes an ephemeral DH key to the session keys each time a circuit is built. We now explore how to add this replay preventability.

Following the structure of the first protocol above, we can have the "CREATED" message contain a random value generated by X. This can then be combined with the session-key seed to form a new session key. (In current Tor, the key material generated by the DH exponentiations would not be used directly to encrypt messages. Rather a hash of that material with two different known values is used for two different key derivation functions that produce keys for encryption in each direction in the circuit. Similar kdfs are used to produce keys for integrity checks, etc. [6]. As in most publications, our protocol description glosses over this detail.)

This addition to the handshake can similarly be added to the "CREATED" messages from Y and Z, resulting in a re-keying of the circuit even as it is being built. Thus, while the original message from the client to X might be replayed, subsequent messages through X will be encrypted under a different variant of K_{cx}.

The third protocol adds this ephemeral feature to the above protocol designs while reducing the total number of messages and still without requiring any additional exponentiations over the first protocol.

If we were to simply add this node-generated randomness to the second protocol above, it would be possible to rekey the circuit with a single flow up and single flow down the circuit. The full circuit establishment could not be replayed because of this rekeying. But, it would not prevent replay of the onion and of the resulting path laying all the way through the circuit. An attacker could still replay the onion to do traffic analysis of the circuit establishment as long as the servers' DH keys remained usable.

The current Tor protocol contains a "CREATE_FAST" option for the handshake between the client and the first node. The link between them is already encrypted using TLS (in a DH mode that insures that link encryptions have forward secrecy). Thus, against a link eavesdropper, there is no advantage to using a DH key exchange in the Tor handshake. Therefore both the client and first node simply send each other symmetric key seeds which are combined using XOR to form the Tor session key between them [6].[6]

We can use this technique, but extend it slightly to still reduce the number of ping-pong exchanges used to establish a circuit. The first message from the client is encrypted only with the TLS encryption of the link. It contains an extend instruction and a random value from the client to be combined with a random value contributed by the first node, X, to form their session key. Ignoring the TLS encryption, it is very similar to the message in Expression 1 with one extra field and one less layer of encryption.

$$EXTEND, random\_value_{c_x}, DH_{cy,pub}, \{CREATE, ID_{cy}, data\}_{K_{cy}}$$

X forwards this (minus the fields $random\_value_{c_x}$ and $EXTEND$) to Y. Y responds with

$$\{ID_{cy}, CREATED, random\_value_{y_c}, data\}_{K_{yc}}$$

to which X attaches a random value and returns to the client

$$ID_{cx}, EXTENDED, random\_value_{x_c},$$
$$\{ID_{cy}, CREATED, random\_value_{y_c}, data\}_{K_{yc}}$$

The client then produces K'_{cx} and K'_{xc} from the parameters $random\_value_{c_x}$ and $random\_value_{x_c}$, and the keys K'_{cy} and K'_{yc} are created from K_{cy} and $random\_value_{y_c}$. These keys are used by C as session keys to communicate with X and Y respectively for the remainder of the session. Using the session keys the client sends an "EXTEND" message to Y, for extending to Z, just as in the first protocol. The entire sequence of exchanges is depicted in Fig. 2.

We achieve a savings of two messages compared to the current circuit construction by creating an onion from the client to Y as shown in Fig. 2, and then do an extend from Y to Z as above. The initial handshake with X is now bundled in the onion sent to Y. And, even if an attacker obtained the onion despite the TLS encryption on the client-X link, he could replay it for at most two hops (and only during the time $DH_{y,pub}$ is valid). He cannot rebuild the entire circuit to the final node because Y will not decrypt the extension request

---

[6] One might even go further and question the need for any encryption at all beyond the TLS link encryption for communication between the client and the first node. This would also allow the removal of one ping-pong exchange of handshake messages while otherwise leaving the protocol intact. We will consider just such a reduction next, but without eliminating the exchange of keys. The overhead of keeping these keys is slight, especially if this does not require its own ping-pong of messages, and it provides consistency with other protocol features, hence flexibility. We will thus not pursue further in this paper completely removing the Tor session key between the client and the first node.

unless it is encrypted under the new key. Note also that this use of a two-hop onion will only allow X to identify its position in the circuit. The circuit will be indistinguishable by Y or Z from one built only by telescoping. This is not a factor in the typical case as most Tor circuits are built from clients not operating on a Tor network node.

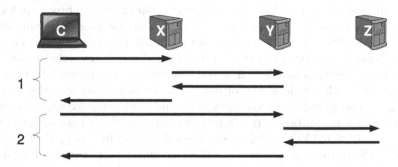

Fig. 2. Circuit setup, third protocol

Another option that will prevent replay while using a single onion to establish the circuit (as in the second protocol), is to use timestamps. If timestamps are added to each layer of the onion, then honest nodes will not process them once they have expired. To be resilient to clock skew, we probably need to have an expiry interval of c. a half hour or hour rather than a few minutes. This however raises the prospect that, e.g., the first node if compromised could replay the onion as much as desired for that hour for whatever traffic-analysis value that could have. Thus, we could have nodes store a checksum of a few bytes or so for all onions that pass through within an hour. It can be quite short given the small likelihood of collision, so neither storage nor lookup should be a problem even for slow nodes without much memory. And, even if our checksum length is so short that each node denies, e.g., ten valid circuits a day because of collisions, the load on the network from circuit setup messages is still greatly reduced, as is the expected setup time for establishing new circuits. Of course timestamps can be added to the third protocol so that even replays just to Y can occur for a shorter period.

Given that most clients are outside the known server node network, it will be trivial for first nodes to recognize themselves as such. In fact, given the use of entry guards in all Tor circuits [17], it is likely that all first nodes can identify themselves with high probability for most circuits. Nonetheless, Tor clients on Tor network nodes can avoid giving away even this little redundant information by always building circuits using telescoping, even from the first to second nodes. The use of onions (where recommended) saves one exchange of messages by bundling the handshakes of the first and second nodes into one flow up and one flow down the circuit. Note that the use of "CREATE_FAST" to form circuits from a client located on a Tor node using the current Tor protocol for similar reasons faces the same issues.

The *fourth protocol*[7] is useful in cases where forward secrecy is desired not only a week after a circuit is closed but as soon as the circuit is closed. This protocol provides *immediate FS*, whereas the others provide *eventual FS*. In the fourth protocol the number and sequence of message exchanges is the same as in the current Tor circuit establishment protocol (and the same as in the first protocol). The number of exponentiations is much fewer however: eleven vs. eighteen total per circuit, and six vs. nine for exponentiations that cannot be precomputed and must be done during the protocol run. The others can be done in advance during idle cycles. Another virtue of the protocol is that it is compatible with changes that are being contemplated by the Tor developers[8] to improve efficiency in what is stored in directories and how it is distributed. Adding immediate FS to the first protocol in the obvious way of having nodes send back an ephemeral DH public key (as opposed to a random value for modifying the existing session key as in the replay prevention of the third protocol) would not have either of these advantages. If "CREATE_FAST" can be used for the first hop, then the total exponentiations drops from eleven to seven, of which four must be done during the protocol run.

The first message from the client to X is similar to the first message of the first protocol, except that nothing is encrypted (other than by link TLS) because the client is not yet able to form any session key.

$$DH_{cx,pub}, CREATE, ID_{cx},$$

X responds with

$$DH_{xc,pub}, ID_{cx}, \{CREATED, data\}_{K_{xc}}$$

where, if r_c is the client's private ephemeral DH key and r_x is X's private ephemeral DH key, and since

$$(DH_{cx,pub})^{(DH_{x,priv}+r_x)} = g^{r_c \cdot (DH_{x,priv}+r_x)} = g^{DH_{x,priv} \cdot r_c} g^{r_x \cdot r_c} =$$
$$(DH_{x,pub})^{r_c} \cdot (DH_{xc,pub})^{r_c} = (DH_{x,pub} \cdot DH_{xc,pub})^{r_c}$$

both C and X can use this as key material for the directional keys K_{cx} and K_{xc}. The ephemeral key pair $DH_{xc,pub/priv}$ (with $DH_{xc,priv} = r_x$) is formed by X for answering *one* Tor circuit establishment request, and the private component is discarded as soon as it is used to form session keys. Note that the exponentiation necessary to form the DH key pair does not need to be done during the protocol run. Pairs can be formed and stored during idle cycles of the server. The only exponentiation that must be done by X during the protocol is the one creating key material $(DH_{cx,pub})^{(DH_{x,priv}+r_x)}$. The client also has only one exponentiation to do during the protocol (for each node in the circuit), namely $(DH_{x,pub} \cdot DH_{xc,pub})^{r_c}$ to form the same key material. The basic underlying point is one that is well known to apply to DH protocols in general; nonetheless the current version of Tor does not seem to take advantage of it.

---

[7] Thanks to Kim Philby for discussions on attempts to break the fourth protocol.
[8] Private communication.

Unlike the first protocol, authentication comes from X being the only one who could encrypt the response rather than being the only one who could decrypt the challenge. In both cases only X possesses $DH_{x,priv}$, and the client knows that $DH_{x,pub}$ is X's midterm DH key from the signed directory information the client has. Thus, the client knows that X is the only one who could form K_{cx} and K_{xc} besides the client, given normal assumptions. (What we have done here is effectively a half-authenticated variant of some existing protocols for authenticated DH key establishment that combine ephemeral and longer term DH parameters, much as our ElGamal key agreement above was a half-authenticated simplification of basic DH; although the exact relation between this protocol and existing ones is not as clear. We will discuss this more in section 5.)

The client next sends the same "EXTEND" message to X for extending to Y as in the first protocol, except that as immediately above, there is no encryption of the message portion arriving at Y, other than the link encryption between X and Y. Y responds just as X did above. The extension to Z is of the same form as the extension to Y.

4   Hidden Service Protocol Description

Using the new circuit protocol in existing hidden service designs. Hidden services can work almost as in the existing deployed design [7,17] only adapting to the new DH-based carrier in the circuits. It is also possible to incorporate so-called *valet nodes* [18], which protect the introduction points from being identified by the client or anyone contacting a directory (or the directories themselves). A server sets up circuit connections to some introduction points and there it listens for connections. Inside the contact information published or given to the client the server adds a valet node extension to the means for reaching introduction points, which is encrypted so that only the valet node knows where the introduction point is. This is completed as described in the just-cited paper [18].

New Hidden Services setup. One of the major problems with the existing hidden services protocol is that it has become too complex. Both the deployed hidden service design and the design using valet nodes require the building of four circuits collectively comprised of as many as twelve Tor server nodes— not including the service lookup, the client, or the hidden service node itself. Extending design ideas from the proposed addition of valet nodes to protect the introduction point [18], we here propose how to drastically reduce both complexity and latency when connecting to a hidden service.

Connection between a client and a hidden service requires the setup of two separate paths, each comprised of two mated Tor circuits. Why incur the large overhead cost and delay of the second pair of circuits and connection made through the rendezvous point? Rendezvous circuits provide at least three things in the deployed hidden service design. (1) Introduction points are not responsible for serving up the contents of the hidden server for which they are introduction points. (2) Hidden servers (and thus the network) do not have to maintain open circuits adequate to carry the maximum number of simultaneous connections they might have. (3) None of the nodes carrying traffic between the client and hidden server can recognize that they are carrying traffic for that hidden service. In particular, blocking of an introduction point is neither as significant nor therefore as desirable for an adversary wishing to deny service provided by the hidden server.

The introduction of the valet nodes and contact information changed this, as we now can have valet nodes protecting the introduction points. And contact information is structured and served such that it requires some effort for either valet nodes or introduction points to determine any hidden service for which they are valet or introduction nodes respectively, even if the hidden service is publicly listed. Since there are several of each, the value of determining this is also limited and thus less likely to be pursued. We propose herein to further change the introduction points into contact points where the service can either (1) remain connected to the client rather than opening a new connection (Fig. 3), or (2) set up a new connection to the node preceding the valet node, using this as a rendezvous point (Fig. 4).

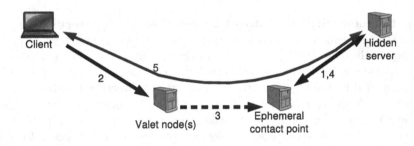

Fig. 3. New direct hidden service usage

The first scenario from Fig. 3 follows simple setup. First the service opens up connections to contact points (1) and tells them to listen for connections. Then it locates the valet nodes and produces the contact information which is somehow[9] received by the client. The client tunnels out to the valet node and transfers the valet ticket (2). The valet node unpacks the valet ticket, and extends the tunnel to the ephemeral contact point (3). After using the valet ticket information to authorize himself to the contact point, the contact point submits (4) client information to the hidden service and connects the two circuits (5) for the client and the hidden service talking directly. This is much faster but has some implications that we will discuss in section 5.

The second scenario shown in Fig. 4 is optional and could e.g. be used when connecting to a public hidden service. The first part of the service setup is the same, but the client now first constructs a tunnel to the last node in front

---

[9] Could be off-line distribution, or via a directory service, DHT, etc.

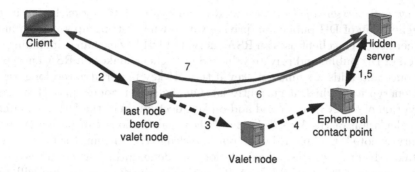

Fig. 4. New direct hidden service using new rendezvous point

of the valet node (2) and asks this node to listen for a potential connection request. This node will now act as a potential rendezvous point for connections back from the hidden service. Then the client extends to the valet node (3), informs the contact point (4) which authorizes and submits the information to the hidden service (5). The hidden service now determines whether to establish the connection through the valet node as in the first scenario, or to contact the new rendezvous point (6), and the client and the hidden service will have their new communication channel (7).

Note that, as described, the two scenarios need not be considered two entirely distinct protocols, but rather dynamic options. As observed earlier, the first scenario addresses all of the contributions of using rendezvous points except possibly for the overhead caused by the number of open circuits that a hidden server must maintain to remain reachable. The network overhead can potentially be reduced somewhat already by the suggested approach since circuits to the contact points may be shorter because the valet node is also chosen by the hidden server. As just observed the hidden service can dynamically choose whether to communicate with the client through the already opened circuits or to open a new circuit to the offered rendezvous point. If the server has adequate reserve contact circuit sockets and bandwidth, it can use the open circuits. If not, it can use a new circuit to the rendezvous point, thus addressing the open circuits issue, but doing so in a more efficient, dynamic way.

5   Discussion

5.1   Calculation Reduction

We are ignoring the TLS encryption overhead as this is expected to be almost like persistent connections and these will exist in all protocols in any case. We will also ignore the symmetric encryption and the signature verifications as they are the same in the two versions. The servers will have the additional production of public DH values for authentication during every rotation period, which safely can be ignored: we assume a default rotation of one per week.

The current version of Tor uses an RSA encrypted DH key exchange including generation of DH public and private values when setting up a new circuit to another node. The client uses an RSA encrypted DH key exchange including generation of DH public and private values. So the client makes an RSA-encryption only once and adds a symmetric key if the DH key material is too long for one RSA encryption (which it currently is). On the server node's part there is the decryption of the RSA data and add-on key, decryption of the DH key material, and calculation of the keys[10]. Some of these calculations can be made on idle circuits as noted in Table 1, but to our knowledge the current Tor protocol does not take advantage of this: all calculations are done during the circuit establishment protocol. The "CREATE_FAST" option in the current version will result in one less DH key exchange and one less RSA encryption/decryption.

Our new proposal. The second protocol uses two DH value generations on the client side (one for X and Y, and one for Z) but these can be made on idle cycles, and since the server nodes' DH values are known through the data from a directory service, the client can complete the DH-key generation and calculate the keys from this value. The client then encrypts the rest of the data with the correct keys immediately. The client avoids the need for RSA encryption for each node. In addition the nodes do not need to decrypt the RSA data. They generates the keys directly. In addition the nodes need not send the initial DH-value since the client uses its public DH values, as shown in Table 1. *The fourth protocol* also has two initial exponentiations for the client, but for these and for each of the circuit nodes the initial exponentiation can be done on idle cycles, and these should therefore not count in comparing resources. The client will also have to finalize all three temporary session keys by doing one exponentiation each, and so will each of the circuit nodes. The "CREATE_FAST" option to the fourth protocol will result in one less DH key exchange. Unlike for the second protocol, the client should use the same ephemeral public DH key for Y and Z, to save an exponentiation from this reduction. So there will be one initialization at the client, and none at X. As with the current Tor circuit protocol, "CREATE_FAST" should not be used if the circuit is initiated by a client at a directory-listed Tor node.

5.2   Location Hidden Service Effects

Using new DH circuits on the currently deployed hidden service design. As most circuits used by a client are premade to at least two hops out, there would be no noticeable change to the user experience from the existing hidden service design. But every circuit initialization will save the network the number of exponentiations reflected in Table 1. And as we still have three new circuits opened for every connection to a hidden service our new protocol reduces the number of exponentiations in the network significantly.

---

[10] The DH-key is used to generate multiple keys for both encryption and MACs.

Table 1. Number of exponentiations calculated during a single circuit setup. *These initializations can be preconstructed on idle cycles.*

Calculation type in a three node circuit	Current design	Current FAST	Second protocol	Fourth protocol	Fourth FAST
# of client RSA encryptions	3*	2*	0	0	0
# of nodes' RSA decryptions	3	2	0	0	0
# of client DH-initializations	3*	2*	2*	2*	1*
# of nodes' DH-initializations	3*	2*	0	3*	2*
# of client DH-finalizations	3	2	3	3	2
# of nodes' DH-finalizations	3	2	3	3	2

Using new circuits and valet nodes. If the new circuit setup were implemented on the valet nodes design an estimated reduction in calculations would be the same as in the existing functionality. Even if our protocol suggestion supports and makes implementation of valet nodes easier, we will only see the same amount of latency as in the original version. The only difference is that the valet node can be based on a half-finished DH exchange and therefore may also replace the RSA encryption of the valet token.

Using new circuits and direct communication. One of the primary objections to using the old introduction points as contact points for the hidden service, was that they might become liable for the content of the hidden service. The introduction of the valet nodes changed this because the introduction points no longer know which service they are assisting. But now the valet nodes could identify themselves as associated with a service, *if* they had access to the contact information for the hidden service. In addition, there could be many valet nodes per introduction point, so we estimate that the potential problem of being blocked by some valet node is not likely to be critical for the hidden service. When we are talking about really hidden services that have private contact information this is no issue at all.

By dynamically choosing whether to communicate through the contact and valet circuits or open a new circuit to the rendezvous point (node before the valet node in the valet circuit), the hidden server can more effectively manage the network costs of connections to hidden services. Note that the incentives of the hidden service align with those of the network in that it is incented to only open new rendezvous circuits when utilization of its contact circuits is relatively high. It would be interesting to investigate further whether the optimal choice of resources in terms of number of open circuits to contact points maintained vs. percentage of rendezvous circuits needed is the same for a given hidden server and the network it is on. Clearly different principals in the system also learn different things about the relative load on a hidden service from the dynamic choice of whether to create a rendezvous circuit (e.g., the valet, contact potential-rendezvous, and guard nodes). Whether there is any significant information discernible from that (and whether it would be discernible in the currently deployed hidden service design) is another interesting question worthy of further study.

5.3   Security

Forward Secrecy and Replay. Perhaps the largest security change from current Tor implied by all the protocols except the fourth is that the FS they offer is eventual rather than immediate. If DH keys for server nodes are used for a week and kept for two, as would be consistent with existing directory usage in Tor, then it can be as much as two weeks from the time a circuit is initiated until the session keys in it attain FS; although, it will typically be much shorter. This has two effects: first is the replayability of circuit setup for traffic analysis purposes and the vulnerability of circuits to an adversary that attacks nodes along a circuit during the lifetime of the DH keys to uncover traffic and data, up to potentially everything sent over a circuit. Only a protocol with eventual FS is vulnerable to replay once the circuit closes. However, as we showed via the third protocol, it is possible for an eventual-FS protocol to be vulnerable to an attack on servers or keys before the FS takes effect but still not be vulnerable to replay. An adversary willing to go to the effort of such traffic analysis as can be obtained from replay probably is determined enough to attack servers and keys as well. This is the reason that we recommend the fourth protocol as a new Tor circuit protocol rather than the third even if the third is resistant to replay. Nonetheless, for the vast majority of Tor traffic, both of these concerns are beyond a reasonable threat model.

Authentication and Protocol Security. The current Tor circuit protocol was designed to fit message constraints that "a single cell is too small to fit both a public key and a signature" [7]. It was thus forced to use a nonstandard design. For this reason, it was analyzed by the NRL protocol analyzer before it was deployed and found to be secure in the Dolev-Yao model [7]. In 2005, the Tor developers noticed and corrected that the cryptographic instantiation of the protocol failed to properly perform adequate checks and left circuit building subject to significant attacks. Analysis by Ian Goldberg [9] showed that the corrected protocol instantiation was secure in the random oracle model. What assurances do we have that the protocols we have presented are secure? At this point we have only indications, which we now discuss.

Using DH, we do not have the message size issues of the current Tor circuit protocol, but we have as yet performed neither formal analysis nor a cryptographic proof of the security for any of our protocols. Nonetheless, all but the fourth protocol are essentially ElGamal key exchange. This is a widely studied and understood simple protocol for providing implicit one-sided authentication. As such, these protocols are unlikely to have significant flaws. The fourth protocol combines long-term and ephemeral DH elements in a manner similar to many protocols, but again for only one-sided authentication so that it is simpler. It is in some ways like a simplification of the MQV protocol [14]. It has the overt structure of MQV to authenticate the server node to the client and obviously none of the structure authenticating the client to the server. Our protocol also does not make use of the specialized group exponentiation that MQV uses. Like ElGamal, MQV is also a well-studied protocol. Its original design was vulnerable to attacks against properties that are not needed for our purposes and were later corrected and led to its adoption as an IEEE standard[12]. Despite adoption as a standard, MQV has not been proven secure either formally or cryptographically. The only protocol in this group to have a security proof is the so-called Unified Model (UM) protocol [4]. Adapting the UM protocol in a straightforward way to our purposes would increase the number of exponentiations required vs. our fourth protocol. While similarities to UM and other protocols is encouraging, we intend to subject our protocols to more formal scrutiny in future work.

6   Conclusion

We have proposed a way to simplify circuit setup in the Tor anonymizing network. We have explained how to use predistributed Diffie-Hellman values for setting up session keys based on half-certified ElGamal key exchange. By using this new setup for a circuit the client saves three RSA encryptions, and each of the nodes in the circuit saves one RSA decryption in addition to the initialization of a DH value. In addition we noted how both the current Tor circuit building protocol and our new proposed protocols can benefit from precomputation of much of the information needed for the protocols. This is perhaps especially beneficial at the nodes rather than clients, where public-key overhead can be a bottleneck. One of our protocols offers less calculation overhead, and incorporates immediate forward secrecy. Others provided even more substantial savings in computation and in communication but only eventual FS. They also serve to illustrate the distinctions between eventual FS, replay-resistant eventual FS, and immediate FS.

We have also proposed two new hidden service protocols that uses valet nodes to protect the introduction point, and therefore can eliminate the circuits to external rendezvous points. As a result of this improvement the hidden service protocol can now make more direct, lower-overhead connections to hidden services without compromising on anonymity or security.

References

1. The Anonymizer. http://www.anonymizer.com/
2. Berthold, O., Federrath, H., Köpsell, S.: Web MIXes: A system for anonymous and unobservable Internet access. In: Federrath, H. (ed.) Designing Privacy Enhancing Technologies. LNCS, vol. 2009, pp. 115–129. Springer, Heidelberg (2001)
3. Boucher, P., Shostack, A., Goldberg, I.: Freedom systems 2.0 architecture. White paper, Zero Knowledge Systems, Inc. (December 2000)
4. Boyd, C., Mathuria, A.: Protocols for Authentication and Key Establishment. Springer, Heidelberg (2003)
5. Clarke, I., Sandberg, O., Wiley, B., Hong, T.W.: Freenet: A distributed anonymous information storage and retrieval system. In: Federrath, H. (ed.) Designing Privacy Enhancing Technologies. LNCS, vol. 2009, pp. 46–66. Springer, Heidelberg (2001)
6. Dingledine, R., Mathewson, N.: Tor protocol specification (February 2007), http://tor.eff.org/svn/trunk/doc/spec/tor-spec.txt

7. Dingledine, R., Mathewson, N., Syverson, P.: Tor: The second-generation onion router. In: Proceedings of the 13th USENIX Security Symposium (August 2004)
8. ElGamal, T.: A public key cryptosystem and a signature scheme based on discrete logarithms. IEEE Trans. on Information Theory 31(4), 469–472 (1985)
9. Goldberg, I.: On the security of the Tor authentication protocol. In: Danezis, G., Golle, P. (eds.) PET 2006. LNCS, vol. 4258, Springer, Heidelberg (2006)
10. Goldschlag, D.M., Reed, M.G., Syverson, P.F.: Hiding Routing Information. In: Anderson, R. (ed.) Information Hiding. LNCS, vol. 1174, pp. 137–150. Springer, Heidelberg (1996)
11. Onion Routing: Brief Selected History, http://www.onion-router.net/history.html
12. IEEE. P1363 standard specifications for public-key cryptography. IEEE Std 1363-2000 (January 2000)
13. Kate, A., Zaverucha, G., Goldberg, I.: Pairing-based onion routing. In: Borisov, N., Golle, P. (eds.) PET 2007. LNCS, vol. 4776, pp. 95–112. Springer, Heidelberg (2007)
14. Manezes, A.J., Qu, M., Vanstone, S.A.: Some new key agreement protocols providing implicit authentication. In: Workshop in Selected Areas of Cryptography (SAC'95), pp. 22–32 (1995)
15. Menezes, A.J., van Oorschot, P.C., Vanstone, S.A.: Handbook of Applied Cryptography. CRC Press, Boca Raton, USA (1997)
16. Murdoch, S.J.: Hot or not: Revealing hidden services by their clock skew. In: CCS 2006. Proceedings of the 13th ACM Conference on Computer and Communications Security, pp. 27–36. ACM Press, New York (2006)
17. Øverlier, L., Syverson, P.: Locating hidden servers. In: Proceedings of the 2006 IEEE Symposium on Security and Privacy, IEEE Computer Society Press, Los Alamitos (2006)
18. Øverlier, L., Syverson, P.: Valet services: Improving hidden servers with a personal touch. In: Danezis, G., Golle, P. (eds.) PET 2006. LNCS, vol. 4258, Springer, Heidelberg (2006)
19. Reed, M.G., Syverson, P.F., Goldschlag, D.M.: Proxies for Anonymous Routing. In: Proceedings of the 12th Annual Computer Security Applications Conference, pp. 95–104. IEEE Computer Society Press, Los Alamitos (1996)
20. Reed, M.G., Syverson, P.F., Goldschlag, D.M.: Anonymous connections and onion routing. IEEE Journal on Selected Areas in Communications 16(4), 482–494 (1998)
21. Relakks. http://www.relakks.com/

Identity Trail: Covert Surveillance Using DNS

Saikat Guha and Paul Francis

Cornell University, Ithaca NY 14853, USA
{saikat,francis}@cs.cornell.edu

Abstract. The Domain Name System (DNS) is the only globally deployed Internet service that provides user-friendly naming for Internet hosts. It was originally designed to return the same answer to any given query regardless of who may have issued the query, and thus all data in the DNS is assumed to be public. Such an assumption potentially conflicts with the privacy policies of private Internet hosts, particularly the increasing numbers of laptops and PDAs used by mobile users as their primary computing device. IP addresses of such devices in the DNS reveal the host's, and typically the user's, dynamic geographic location to anyone that is interested without the host's knowledge or explicit consent. This paper demonstrates, and measures the severity of an attack that allows anyone on the Internet to covertly monitor mobile devices to construct detailed user profiles including user identity, daily commute patterns, and travel itineraries. Users that wish to identify their private hosts using user-friendly names are locked into the DNS model, thus becoming unwitting victims to this attack; we identify a growing number of such dynamic DNS users (two million and climbing), and covertly trail over one hundred thousand of them. We report on a large scale study that demonstrates the feasibility and severity of such an attack in today's Internet. We further propose short-term and long-term defenses for the attack.

1 Introduction

The Domain Name System (DNS) is a core Internet infrastructure that maps user-friendly mnemonics to non-user-friendly IP addresses. The DNS resolves IP addresses for both *public services*[1] like Google, as well as *private services*[2] such as Alice's personal laptop. The DNS does not distinguish between the scope of the services it resolves.

As stated in RFC 4033 [1], the DNS was originally designed with the assumption that the DNS will return the same answer to any given query regardless of who may have issued the query, and that all data in the DNS is thus public. The DNS does not provide any authorization mechanism or other means of differentiating between inquirers. Indeed, DNS nameservers do not even know the IP address of the querying host. Network DoS attackers exploit this shortcoming to learn the IP address of the victim and overwhelm the victim's link

---

[1] Services available to everyone e.g. www.google.com
[2] Services available to a small group of people e.g. alice.dyndns.org

N. Borisov and P. Golle (Eds.): PET 2007, LNCS 4776, pp. 153–166, 2007.

to the Internet. This paper identifies a different attack whereby merely learning the IP address of the victim can result in a breach of privacy defined as contextual-integrity [2].

An IP address implicitly encodes a wealth of information about the host. The address identifies the host's ISP (university, corporation, residential broadband ISP etc.), and the geographical location of the host to within a nearby city [3]. This information is available in public WHOIS databases, reverse DNS entries [4], and commercial databases [5]. While leaking the geographic location of static Internet hosts (e.g. a corporate webserver) may not be a critical privacy concern, leaking the dynamic geographic location of private, and often mobile hosts (e.g. employee laptops) may comprise an unacceptable privacy breach. The DNS does not capture this difference between public and private hosts.

Private services that wish to use user-friendly names are consequently forced to make their existence and location visible to everyone on the Internet. Alice, for instance, may wish to run a private FTP server on her personal laptop that she can use to transfer files to and from her laptop whether she is at work or at home. Since the laptop may often acquire a different IP address each time she connects, Alice is forced to relearn her address each time. Alternatively, Alice can configure her laptop to update the DNS with its latest address such that she can use a stable user-friendly DNS name in her FTP client. By putting her address in the DNS for *her own personal use*, however, Alice unwittingly reveals her geographic location to *anyone* on the Internet.

DynDNS [6], No-IP [7], TZO [8], and many other online services [9,10,11] cater to individuals such as Alice that wish to register DNS names and dynamically update their IP address mapping. Update clients are available for a wide range of platforms including not only Windows, Linux and MacOS, but also cellphones, pocket PCs and embedded devices [12]. While commercial services like Akamai [13] provide IP address confidentiality of the origin service by redirecting all data through Akamai proxies, it is typically targeted at large public websites (Google, Microsoft etc.) and not small private services such as Alice's. Users such as Alice are entirely dependent on the dynamic DNS services mentioned earlier for user-friendly names, with services such as DynDNS boasting of a growing user-base of two million users [14].

As we report later, a majority of these dynamic DNS names are for mobile private hosts. Common services running on these hosts include private FTP and web servers, BitTorrent trackers, and web-cams. Even though each of the services may enforce access control policy at the service level, simply registering the host's address in the DNS leaks private information to anyone who cares to learn it. The service owner must therefore chose either user-friendly DNS naming or privacy.

This privacy issue was not considered one way or another in the design of the DNS. In a largely static Internet, the IP address does not divulge much private information and thus the issue has not been important in the past. In the present Internet, however, with mobile private hosts, the lack of confidentiality of private IP addresses published into the DNS is a privacy risk as mobile hosts, unlike static hosts, reveal the dynamic geographic location of the user. This is exacerbated by current trends where laptops are surpassing desktops in retail sales [15].

Overall this paper makes three contributions.

1. We identify an attack that allows an attacker to covertly monitor a victim's location at any given moment, and over time build a detailed profile of the victim including the victim's identity, daily commute patterns, and trip itineraries.
2. We demonstrate the feasibility of such an attack on the Internet today by performing surveillance on over a hundred thousand users without raising any alarms and report the depth of private information gleaned.
3. We propose short-term fixes to the DNS that can be deployed today to mitigate this attack, and discuss a long-term solution for secure name resolution for private services on the Internet.

The rest of the paper is organized as follows. Section 2 presents an overview on the DNS, dynamic DNS services and related work in DNS security. Section 3 presents our attack. Section 4 reports on a covert surveillance experiment of over a hundred thousand Internet users. Section 5 discusses short-term and long-term measures to defend against such an attack. Section 6 concludes the paper and outlines future work.

2   DNS Overview and Related Work

The DNS describes the architecture and infrastructure for name resolution on the Internet [16]. The namespace is hierarchical for user-friendliness and ease of administration. Each subtree of the namespace (called *zone* or *domain*) is managed by designated nameservers referred to as the *authoritative nameservers* for that domain. An authoritative nameserver responds with the IP address (or other information in the DNS) for a DNS name in its domain when queried. If the DNS name lies outside the nameserver's domain, the server can forward the query to another nameserver that may be able to answer authoritatively (called *recursive querying*), and forward the response back to the original inquirer. Alternatively, the server can simply return the address of the next server to query (called *non-recursive querying*). A server that performs recursive querying may cache the results of any queries that it forwards and respond to subsequent queries for the same DNS name from its cache thereby improving performance and reducing the load on the authoritative nameservers. Clients OS network stacks typically implement the minimum functionality necessary to send the query to a recursive nameserver; ISPs and public services provide recursive nameservers that customers can use for all queries.

The DNS does not enforce any access control policy before name resolution. In particular, the authoritative nameserver typically does not learn the identity of the host performing the name resolution. This is because a recursive DNS query contains the address of only the nameserver performing the recursive lookup, and not the address of the host on whose behalf the query is being performed. Furthermore, when a response is cached and a query answered from the cache, the authoritative nameserver does not learn that a lookup took place. Any host on the Internet can query for the IP address of another host through a recursive nameserver without revealing the original inquirer's identity to the authoritative nameserver.

Dynamic DNS services such as DynDNS administer multiple zones within which a user can create a DNS name (e.g. alice.dynalias.org, or bob.homeip.net). The user configures a background DynDNS client application to run on their laptop and update the laptop's IP address with the service every time the IP address changes. DNS name creation and dynamic updates of the associated IP address are performed over HTTP and protected with HTTP-based authentication methods. The nameservers for these dynamic DNS services, however, are typical DNS nameservers that cannot authenticate the source of a DNS query.

In addition to resolving the DNS name to an IP address, the DNS provides inverse resolution that maps an IP address to a canonical DNS name for that host. The canonical name for an IP address is assigned by the host's ISP. For example, the DNS name alice.dyndns.org may resolve to 192.0.2.1 in the address block allocated to Acme Inc. The reverse DNS resolution for the same IP, however, may return host-342.acme.org as the canonical name for the host. Anyone can find the ISP-assigned canonical name for the host that a DNS name points to.

Past work in securing DNS can be classified into two categories. The first category deals with protecting the DNS from outages and DoS attacks. CoDNS [17] and CoDoNS [18] use a peer-to-peer substrate for DNS queries in order to improve resiliency against failures and shield authoritative nameservers from flash crowds and DoS attacks, but otherwise allow anyone to resolve the DNS name for any host. The second category of past work deals with the integrity of DNS responses. DNSSEC [1] provides data and origin authentication of DNS data. ConfiDNS [19] provides better integrity of non-DNSSEC responses in CoDNS. Gabrilovich et al. [20] identify homograph attacks against the DNS where a user can be tricked to resolve a look-alike DNS name instead of the intended DNS name, and offer some potential solutions. None of these systems authenticate the source of the DNS query, and consequently cannot defend against the attack identified in this paper.

Proposed replacements for the DNS allow an individual to learn the victim's routing and addressing information without the victim's explicit consent. DOA [21] unconditionally resolves an endpoint identifier to a stack of addresses revealing the route to the destination. UIA [22] allows endpoint addresses to be resolved as long as the endpoint can be named; the ability to name another endpoint is transitive and is likely to be universal for global communication. Neither of the proposed approaches are designed to protect the confidentiality of a private host's address.

3   Identity Trail Attack

The attack intends to track a victim's location covertly. The 9-line attack code is listed in Fig. 1. The attack consists of logging a DNS lookup (line 6) and IP address to geolocation result (line 8) every hour. The geolocation uses a public service [5] that returns the city, province, and country of the host as well as the canonical hostname for the IP address. The attack assumes that the attacker knows the DNS name of the victim's laptop; while this is easy to arrange for a boss spying on their employee or a spouse spying on their significant other, to demonstrate the attack at scale we discuss in the next section how we learned the names of tens of thousands of potential victims. The attack uses only public services such as the DNS and IP geolocation as they were designed. The attack does not require superuser privileges, nor does it need to send any packets to the host being monitored. Finally, thousands of hosts can be monitored in parallel. The extent of private information that can be extracted using this attack is explored in the next section.

```
1: #!/bin/bash
2: HOST=victim.dynalias.net
3: GEO='http://www.ippages.com/simple/'
4: FLD='hostname,ip,city,state,country'
5: while sleep 3600; do
6:     IP=$(host $HOST | awk '{print $4}')
7:     date
8:     curl -s "$GEO?get=$FLD&ip=$IP"
9: done
```

Fig. 1. BASH shell script tracking the location of victim.dynalias.net every hour

4   Attack Validation

In order to determine the feasibility and severity of launching the described attack over the Internet today, we monitored the mobility of over a hundred thousand Internet users. The attack involved discovering names of potential victims and monitoring their IP address for extended periods of time without being detected. Finally, we analyzed the mobility patterns in the trace to profile our victims' daily commute patterns, business and personal trip itineraries and, in some cases, even the identities of the victim.

4.1   Discovering DNS Names

The attack presented in the previous section assumes that the attacker knows the DNS hostname for the victim's computer. While this can be easily arranged when the attacker knows the victim (later we report on how one of the authors of this paper was tracked), in order to broaden our investigation we targeted anonymous DynDNS users.

We discovered 36,011 potential victims through a variety of methods. In our first experiment, we targeted users of the DynDNS service by first performing Google and Yahoo! searches for all 65 DynDNS-controlled domains under which users can register DNS names. We found 4351 DNS names (far fewer than we expected) mentioned in web pages, mailing list archives, USENET posts, and other publicly searchable forums. In our second experiment, we performed a dictionary scan of four of the most popular DynDNS domains. Our dictionary consisted of 24,289 combinations of common first and last names and initials. The scan successfully resolved 31,660 DNS names with a success rate of up to 39% for the dyndns.org domain; the high success rate suggest similarities with [23] where the authors find that registered userids, in many cases, match first or last names of the user. The scan was performed from 40 hosts in 5 hours and rate-limited to a conservative aggregate of 5 packets per second distributed over 5 DynDNS nameservers[3] to avoid triggering potential DDoS responses. Only 9 of the hosts discovered in the dictionary scan were also returned by the online search engines suggesting almost all the names discovered by the dictionary scans are for private services. To verify this hypothesis, we performed a third experiment where we used Nmap [24] to scan a subset of 100 hosts discovered to determine the services provided. We discovered that 50% run HTTP servers, 21% run FTP servers, and 11% run the Windows File-and-Printer sharing service; the FTP and Windows services requires authentication while the default HTTP homepage is usually devoid of content and hyperlinks (possibly privacy by obscurity, where the actual content is located at a secret URL on the server).

Overall we make the following three observations from the above experiments. (1) The services discovered are intended for private use based on service authentication, lack of advertisement on public Internet forums, and lack of content on default landing pages. (2) An attacker can covertly discover a large number of potential victims without triggering alarms. (3) Poorly chosen DNS names registered by DynDNS users, in some cases, leak the name of the user for a mobile host.

4.2   Monitoring Hosts

In our first surveillance experiment, we monitored 18,720 hosts from July 20, 2006 to August 8, 2006 and found evidence of deliberate user mobility. The monitoring load was rate-limited to 1 packet per second and did not raise any alarms at DynDNS or at the source (to the best of our knowledge). Figure 2 is a screenshot of a summer road-trip taken by user M as tracked by our application. M's name resolves to a Seattle IP on 7/20. It subsequently resolves to Port Angeles WA on 7/21, and continues down a southern route along the west-coast through Otis OR, Smith River CA, Garberville CA, Los Angeles CA, Los Alamos CA, and Garden Grove CA at 1–2 day intervals. M then resolves to Las Vegas, NV for 3 days starting the night of 8/2. Finally, M appears to drive north through Montana back home to Saskatoon, Canada on 8/8, which

---

[3] Distributed Denial of Service.

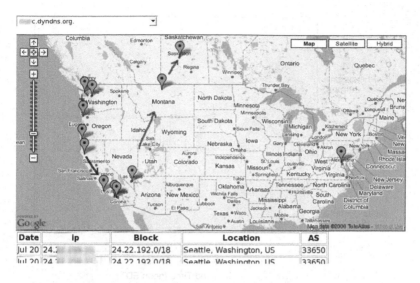

Date	ip	Block	Location	AS
Jul 20	24.2...	24.22.192.0/18	Seattle, Washington, US	33650
Jul 20	24.2...	24.22.192.0/18	Seattle, Washington, US	33650

Fig. 2. Tracking a user's summer road-trip through the DNS

is where he was resolved to on 11/7 as well. Based on reverse DNS lookups, M logs in through local broadband ISPs except on 7/29 when M logs in through a dial-up ISP whose proxy servers are located in Reston, Virginia; fundamental limitations of geolocalization pertaining to proxies are explained in [3]. M runs a local firewall configured to filter all inbound packets. Unfortunately, we were unable to disambiguate M's real identity enough to contact him for verification.

In another trace (not illustrated), user S is geolocated to San Mateo CA until 7/30. S is subsequently resolved to Hyderabad, India for the week commencing Monday 7/31 through Sunday 8/6. For a few hours on 7/30 and 8/6, S is geolocated to a Singapore address suggesting that S flew across the pacific on these dates. In yet another trace, user K is geolocated to Vancouver Canada until 7/26, and then to Ottawa Canada after that. In this case, we were able to identify K through the webpage (hosted on the mobile host) and contact him over email for positive confirmation of the correctness of our tracking. That said, we failed to contact the users for an overwhelming majority of the hostnames tracked due to the private nature of services run by them; in particular, as mentioned previously, FTP servers when present required non-anonymous user authentication, HTTP servers delivered blank default pages (except for user K for example) and so on.

Confirmation from user K above notwithstanding, we verified the correctness of our application in our second surveillance experiment where we tracked the authors of this paper and compared their traces to known real-world data. Figure 3 plots the mobility of one of the authors from August 18, 2006 to November 2, 2006. All the information in the figure was gathered by performing geolocalization and reverse DNS lookups for the IP address. Geolocation within the United States was correct to within 100 mi, and in Italy was correct to within

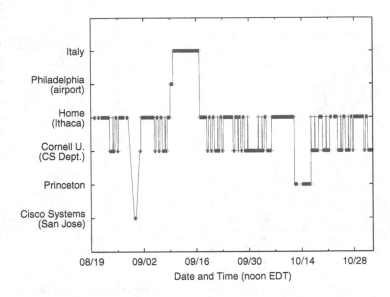

Fig. 3. Tracking a user's daily commute and travel through the DNS

250 mi. The daily commute patterns are usually correct to within one or two hours, but in some instances when the author did not turn the tracked laptop on for several hours after commuting, the trace is inaccurate. The trace, however, does accurately capture university holidays, work related trips and one airport layover. Based on the reverse DNS lookups suggesting the user's affiliation to the Cornell University Computer Science Department, the trip to Cisco Systems Inc. in San Jose, the overlap of the Italy trip with SIGCOMM 2006, a popular data communications conference in Italy during the same period, and the published proceedings of the conference, there was enough information to narrow down the identity of the person tracked to within two people in the Cornell CS department. Additional public information available on the department homepage yielded a unique match.

In our third surveillance experiment, we follow a random sampling of 118,000 DNS names for 77 days beginning August 14, 2006. Anonymized update records were obtained from logs kept by DynDNS. We filter out updates where consecutive IP addresses for a user belong to the same /24 subnet, or belong to the same ISP and are geolocated to the same city in order to discount many DHCP-related updates. Figure 4 plots the number of unique cities, provinces, countries and networks that mobile users were resolved to in rank order. To account for the geolocation errors observed in the previous experiment, we cluster geolocations within ±0.75° latitude and longitude of each other to a single location, which is plotted as a separate curve in the figure. As evident from the figure, the median number of updates across all users was 64; in the median case a user logged in from IP addresses geolocated to 15 cities, and 3 provinces over the course of our measurement. The number of users connected to more than one ISP was 15,055,

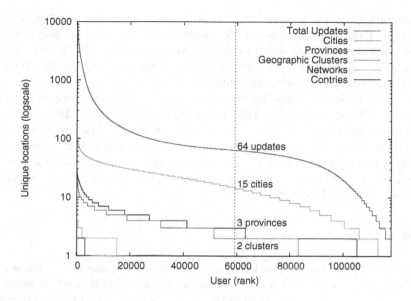

Fig. 4. Tracking the mobility of 118,000 users

while that geolocated to more than one country was 3,210. The median number of geographically distinct clusters a host was geolocated to was 2.

While the data above is indicative of user mobility, we are quick to point out the limitations of our measurement.

1. First, we do not exclude dynamic DNS entries potentially caused by botnets. In [25], the authors claim that botnet operators use Dynamic DNS services to relocate the "command and control" (C&C) server to dodge efforts by local authorities shutting down identified C&C servers. While such activities may explain the outliers in our sample (hosts that resolve to a hundred cities in only 77 days), we do not investigate such outliers any further.
2. Second, we use a proprietary commercial service for geolocation. The accuracy of such services is biased towards country-level and province-level geolocation more than city-level geolocation based on anecdotal evidence, although city-level geolocation is typically accurate to a within a nearby city. Recent systems such as Constraint-based geolocation [26] and Octant [27] have been proposed to improve geolocalization accuracy, however, the coverage provided by these services was not sufficient for our dataset.
3. Third, a host switching between different network providers in one city may be geolocated to different nearby cities based on the providers' access routes. Conversely, a mobile host accessing the network from different nearby cities through the same provider may be geolocated to a common nearby city.
4. Fourth, a physically static host behind an ISP that uses the same address space for a geographically diverse region, particularly in combination with traditional NATs [28], may be geolocated to different cities in that region.

Clustering geolocations based on proximity helps mitigate the effect of these artifacts, but does not completely eliminate them. Nevertheless, based on our (rather noisy) geolocation data, we believe that between 70% (based on clustering) to 91% (based on actual geolocations) of the users in our DynDNS-log dataset logged in from at least two different locations[4].

Overall we make the following four observations. (1) A majority of users updating their IP address on DynDNS are mobile users. (2) The IP address can accurately track a user to within a few hundred miles. (3) The extent of private information leaked over time is potentially significant enough to reconstruct trip itineraries, daily commute patterns, and in some cases, narrow down the identity of the user. (4) This entire surveillance operation can be performed covertly by any attacker on the Internet.

5   Solutions

Fundamentally, the Internet lacks an access-controlled name resolution service for private hosts. The DNS has been shoehorned to fill this need, however, as illustrated by the attack described in this paper, it is ill suited for this purpose. Particularly, the DNS lacks access control policy enforcement for name resolution. At present, any attacker on the Internet can track the mobility of any DNS-named host at any given time. In the short-term, there is no substitute for DNS for naming private endhosts, however, nameservers can use heuristics to limit the scope of the attack without requiring any client modifications. In the long-term, however, the core issue of name resolution policy of private services must be tackled.

5.1   Short-Term Defense

The DNS does not provide any mechanism for a host to specify access control policies for its own name. One fix would be to encourage users to pick obscure DNS names and restrict their dissemination to trusted parties. While this approach would hinder our dictionary attack, somewhat counterintuitive is that the obscurity provided by this approach is nullified when combined with DNSSEC. The DNSSEC [1] standard currently *requires* that the entire list of zone names be revealed to all in order to provide signed proof of non-existence of names that do not exist. An attacker can therefore simply enumerate all the names in a DNSSEC secured zone to discover potential victims[5].

A different fix would be for the authoritative nameserver to restrict host lookup to a white-list of recursive nameservers authorized for that host. The white-list may be set statically by the user, dynamically by the update application, or heuristically by the nameserver based on query patterns. Deploying a white-list does not require changes to the DNS protocol or client applications.

---

[4] Where "location" includes different providers (residential ISP, public wi-fi, office etc.) in the same city, as well as different cities.

[5] NSEC3 [29], a proposed extension to DNSSEC, addresses this issue.

This approach relies on access control of ISPs' recursive nameservers, which is typically enabled in response to recent attacks [30]. The approach protects against attackers on networks far from the victim, but not from attackers on the same network as the victim since both would have access to a common ISP recursive nameserver, which would be on the white-list.

Another way to add access control to the DNS protocol itself is to encrypt responses at the nameserver so only authorized users may decrypt them. Users of a private service could configure shared secrets or public keys with the authoritative nameserver. The nameserver could then encrypt the IP address using symmetric or asymmetric encryption [31,32] based on the attack model. The key management required for such a solution that properly takes into account the distributed caching and recursion inherent in DNS as well as complex endhost privacy policies, however, is likely to be a challenge.

A flawed approach is to require application-level proxies for private services. For example, a private service could subscribe to, and advertise the address of, a public proxying service which would proxy application data between the endpoints. Akamai [13] offers such a commercial HTTP and FTP proxy service. The cost of providing such a service is significant as the service proxies application data unlike the DNS, which only participates in initial name resolution. As a result, the proxy service must be well-provisioned and massively replicated. While a commercial model for using such a proxy service exists for large commercial services (e.g. Google, Microsoft, CNN etc.) it is not obvious whether one exists for smaller private services (e.g. Alice's private FTP service). Furthermore, operating at the application-level in the middle of the network, such data proxies constrain innovation at the network edges as the middle must be upgraded to support each new application — a consequence of violating the end-to-end underpinnings of the Internet [33]. A better approach combines the *off-path*[6] aspect of DNS with the privacy preserving aspect of proxying, as described below.

5.2 Long-Term Defense

Modifying the name resolution process to identify the inquirer and to directly involve the access control policies of the private host provides access-controlled and scalable name resolution in the long run. Consider a name resolution architecture where Alice's laptop registers its IP address with a *registrar*. The registrar plays the role similar to that played by an authoritative nameservers in the DNS. In order to communicate with Alice, Bob contacts Alice's registrar. Instead of returning Alice's IP address to Bob, however, Alice's registrar *proxies* Bob's query to Alice's IP address and proxies Alice's responses to Bob[7]. The registrar conceals Alice's IP address from Bob. Alice can conduct an identification protocol over this proxied path, and reveal her IP address to Bob if he is granted

---

[6] A service not along the application data path, but rather off to the side such that application data packets do not have to pass through it.

[7] Similar to SIP [34], except endhosts do *not* depend on the registrars to perform authentication. Registrars simply provide a proxied communication channel that conceals the IP addresses involved.

access. While this proxy-based end-to-end name resolution architecture doesn't allow for in-network caching, it has been shown that caching the heavy-tail of DNS queries [35] for private hosts is of little value in the first place [36].

Proxy-based end-to-end secure name resolution complements emerging Internet architectures for private hosts. In [37], we propose an Internet architecture where endpoints negotiate protocol stacks, configuration parameters and coordinate the opening of NAT/firewall ports given a third party to proxy and mediate connection-setup messages; the registrar used for access-controlled name resolution can provide this proxy service for private hosts.

More research is needed, however, to better understand the privacy-performance trade-off for the DNS as well as for end-to-end secure name-resolution in the context of public and private services. For public services, it may be the case that there is no need to replace the DNS with the more heavy-weight approach as policy usually allows anyone to learn the IP address. For private services, on the other hand, it may be the case that the need for secure name resolution outweighs the latency added by the proxy mechanism.

6 Conclusions and Future Work

This paper presents an attack on mobile users that dynamically register their IP address in the DNS. The attack allows any attacker on the Internet to covertly glean private information about the user including daily commute patterns and itineraries for trips. The paper demonstrates the ease with which hundreds of thousands of vulnerable users can be monitored without their knowledge. This information could easily be logged for later use should the attacker later learn or infer the identity of the user. The root cause of the attack lies in the lack of access control for DNS name resolution combined with an increasing number of mobile Internet users. This paper suggests a short-term patch to existing DNS services that restricts the scope of the attacker, and a more long-term solution that involves end-to-end secure name resolution for private services on the Internet. The proposed solutions are preliminary in that we do not have a lot of field experience with them. One goal of this paper is to draw the attention of the community to attacks on the DNS that stem from design assumptions in the original Internet architecture that are no longer valid.

Because this attack exploits the public nature of IP addresses for private hosts, this paper additionally suggests that it is appropriate to ask whether the DNS with its focus on public services should be supplemented with a secure name resolution service for private hosts.

We certainly do not answer this question—indeed we have not fully implemented the end-to-end name resolution architecture, much less experimented with it on a broad scale and studied its security provisions. We do believe, however, that secure name resolution for private services deserves debate within the research community.

Acknowledgemnts

The authors would like to acknowledge the support of Jeremy Hitchcock and the DynDNS team for this study. We would also like to thank the anonymous reviewers for their helpful suggestions, including the one about interactions with the DNSSEC enumeration vulnerability.

References

1. Arends, R., Austein, R., Larson, M., Massey, D., Rose, S.: RFC 4033: DNS Security Introduction and Requirements (March 2005)
2. Nissenbaum, H.: Privacy as Contextual Integrity. Washington Law Review 79(1), 119–158 (2004)
3. Padmanabhan, V.N., Subramanian, L.: An investigation of geographic mapping techniques for Internet hosts. In: Proceedings of the SIGCOMM 2001, San Diego, CA (August 2001)
4. Spring, N., Mahajan, R., Anderson, T.: Quantifying the Causes of Path Inflation. In: Proceedings of the SIGCOMM 2003, Karlsruhe, Germany (August 2003)
5. The Privacy Ecosystem: IPPages – IP Address properties of your Internet Connection
6. Dynamic Network Services, Inc.: DynDNS – A free DNS service for those with dynamic IP addresses
7. Vitalwerks Internet Solutions, LLC.: No-IP – Dynamic DNS, Static DNS for Your Dynamic IP
8. Tzolkin Corporation: TZO.com – Dynamic DNS Services for your Dynamic or Static IP Address
9. Deerfield dot com: DNS2GO – Dynamic DNS Services for your IP Address
10. CanWeb Internet Services Ltd.: DynIP – Dynamic DNS Service
11. GravityFree: DtDNS – Your Complete DNS Solution
12. Dynamic Network Services, Inc.: DynDNS: Third Party Clients – keep IP address current, use with all DNS services
13. Akamai Technologies, Inc.: Akamai: How it works
14. Dynamic Network Services, Inc.: Private communications (2006)
15. Kanellos, M.: Notebooks pass desktops in U.S. retail, ZDNet News (February 2006)
16. Mockapetris, P., Dunlap, K.: Development of the Domain Name System. In: Proceedings of the SIGCOMM 1988, Stanford, CA (August 1988)
17. Park, K., Pai, V.S., Peterson, L., Wang, Z.: CoDNS: Improving DNS performance and reliability via cooperative lookups. In: Proceedings of the Sixth Symposium on Operating Systems Design and Implementation (OSDI 2004), San Francisco, CA (December 2004)
18. Ramasubramanian, V., Sirer, E.G.: CoDoNS: The Design and Implementation of a Next Generation Name Service for the Internet. In: Proceedings of SIGCOMM 2004, Portland, OR (August 2004)
19. Poole, L., Pai, V.S.: ConfiDNS: Leveraging Scale and History to Improve DNS Security. In: Proceedings of WORLDS 2006, Seattle, WA (November 2006)
20. Gabrilovich, E., Gontmakher, A.: The Homograph Attack. Communications of the ACM 45(2), 128 (2002)
21. Walfish, M., Stribling, J., Krohn, M., Balakrishnan, H., Morris, R., Shenker, S.: Middleboxes No Longer Considered Harmful. In: Proceedings of the OSDI 2004, San Francisco, CA (December 2004)

22. Ford, B., Strauss, J., Lesniewski-Laas, C., Rhea, S., Kaashoek, F., Morris, R.: Persistent Personal Names for Globally Connected Mobile Devices. In: Proceedings of the OSDI 2006, Seattle, WA (November 2004)
23. Perkowitz, M., Doorenbos, R.B., Etzioni, O., Weld, D.S.: Learning to Understand Information on the Internet: An Example-Based Approach. Journal of Intelligent Information Systems 8(2), 133–153 (2004)
24. Gordon Lyon: Nmap Security Scanner
25. Dagon, D., Gu, G., Zou, C., Grizzard, J., Dwivedi, S., Lee, W., Lipton, R.: A Taxonomy of Botnets. In: Proceedings of CAIDA DNS-OARC Workshop, San Jose, CA (July 2005)
26. Gueye, B., Ziviani, A., Crovella, M., Fdida, S.: Constraint-based geolocation of internet hosts. IEEE/ACM Transactions on Networking 14(6), 1219–1232 (2006)
27. Wong, B., Stoyanov, I., Sirer, E.G.: Octant: A Comprehensive Framework for the Geolocalization of Internet Hosts. In: Proceedings of the NSDI 2007, Cambridge, MA (May 2007)
28. Srisuresh, P., Egevang, K.: RFC 3022: Traditional IP Network Address Translator (Traditional NAT) (January 2001)
29. Laurie, B., Sisson, G., Arends, R., Blacka, D.: Internet draft: DNSSEC Hashed Authenticated Denial of Existence Work in progress. draft-ietf-dnsext-nsec3-11.txt (July 2007)
30. US-CERT: The Continuing Denial of Service Threat Posed by DNS Recursion (v2.0)
31. Bellare, M., Desai, A., Jokipii, E., Rogaway, P.: A Concrete Security Treatment of Symmetric Encryption. FOCS 00, 394 (1997)
32. Boneh, D., Gentry, C., Waters, B.: Collusion Resistant Broadcast Encryption With Short Ciphertexts and Private Keys. In: Shoup, V. (ed.) CRYPTO 2005. LNCS, vol. 3621, Springer, Heidelberg (2005)
33. Saltzer, J.H., Reed, D., Clark, D.D.: End-to-end arguments in system design. ACM Transactions on Computer Systems 2(4), 277–288 (1984)
34. Rosenberg, J., Schulzrinne, H., Camarillo, G., Johnston, A., Peterson, J., Sparks, R., Handley, M., Schooler, E.: RFC 3261: SIP Session Initiation Protocol (June 2002)
35. Jung, J., Sit, E., Balakrishnan, H., Morris, R.: DNS Performance and Effectiveness of Caching. In: Proceedings of SIGCOMM Internet Measurement Workshop, San Francisco, CA (November 2001)
36. Breslau, L., Cao, P., Fan, L., Phillips, G., Shenker, S.: Web Caching and Zipf-like Distributions: Evidence and Implications. In: Proceedings of INFOCOM 1999, New York, pp. 126–134 (March 1999)
37. Guha, S., Francis, P.: An End-Middle-End Approach to Connection Establishment. In: Proceedings of SIGCOMM 2007, Kyoto, Japan (August 2007)

Sampled Traffic Analysis by Internet-Exchange-Level Adversaries

Steven J. Murdoch and Piotr Zieliński

University of Cambridge, Computer Laboratory
http://www.cl.cam.ac.uk/users/{sjm217, pz215}

Abstract. Existing low-latency anonymity networks are vulnerable to traffic analysis, so location diversity of nodes is essential to defend against attacks. Previous work has shown that simply ensuring geographical diversity of nodes does not resist, and in some cases exacerbates, the risk of traffic analysis by ISPs. Ensuring high autonomous-system (AS) diversity can resist this weakness. However, ISPs commonly connect to many other ISPs in a single location, known as an Internet eXchange (IX). This paper shows that IXes are a single point where traffic analysis can be performed. We examine to what extent this is true, through a case study of Tor nodes in the UK. Also, some IXes sample packets flowing through them for performance analysis reasons, and this data could be exploited to de-anonymize traffic. We then develop and evaluate Bayesian traffic analysis techniques capable of processing this sampled data.

1 Introduction

Anonymity networks may be split into two categories: high latency (e.g. Mixminion [1] and Mixmaster [2]) and low latency (e.g. Tor [3], JAP [4] and Freedom [5]). High latency networks may delay messages for several days [6] but are designed to resist very powerful attackers which are assumed to be capable of monitoring all communication links, so called *global passive adversaries*. However, the long potential delay makes these systems inappropriate for popular activities such as web-browsing, where low-latency is required. Although, in low-latency anonymity networks, communications are encrypted to maintain bitwise-unlinkability, timing patterns are hardly distorted, allowing an attacker to deploy traffic analysis to de-anonymize users [7,8,9]. While techniques to resist traffic analysis have been proposed, such as link padding [10], their cost is high and they have not been incorporated into deployed networks.

Instead, these systems have relied on the assumption that the global passive adversary is unrealistic, or at least those who are the target of such adversaries have larger problems than anonymous Internet access. But even excluding the global passive adversary, the possibility of partial adversaries remains reasonable. These attackers have the ability to monitor a portion of Internet traffic but not the entirety. Distributed low-latency anonymity systems, such as Tor, aim to resist this type of adversary by distributing nodes, in the hope that connections through the network will pass through enough administrative domains to prevent a single entity from tracking users.

N. Borisov and P. Golle (Eds.): PET 2007, LNCS 4776, pp. 167–183, 2007.

This raises the question of how to select paths through the anonymity network to maximize traffic analysis resistance. Section 2 discusses different topology models of the Internet and their impact on path selection. We suggest that existing models, based on *Autonomous System* (AS) diversity, do not properly take account of the fact that while, at the AS level abstraction, a path may have good administrative domain diversity, physically it could repeatedly pass through the same *Internet eXchange* (IX). Section 3 establishes, based on Internet topology measurements, to what extent the Tor anonymity network is vulnerable to traffic analysis at IXes.

Section 4 describes how IXes are particularly relevant since, to assist load management, they record traffic data from the packets being sent through them. As aggregate statistics are required and the cost of recording full traffic would be prohibitive, only sampled data is stored. Hence, the quality of data is substantially poorer than was envisaged during the design and evaluation of previous traffic analysis techniques. Section 5 shows that, despite low sampling rates, this data is adequate for de-anonymizing users of low-latency anonymity networks. Finally, Section 6 discusses further avenues of research under investigation.

2   Location Diversity in Anonymity Networks

Tor has been long suspected, and later confirmed [11,12], to be vulnerable to an attacker who could observe both the entry and exit point of a connection through an anonymity network. As no intentional latency is introduced, timing patterns propagate through the network and may be used to correlate input and output traffic, allowing an attacker to track connection endpoints.

Delaying messages, as done with email anonymity systems, would improve resistance to these attacks, at least for a small number of messages. However, the additional latency here (hours to days) would, if applied to web browsing, deter most users and so decrease anonymity for the remainder [13]. In addition to the scarce bandwidth in a volunteer network, full link-padding would also introduce catastrophic denial of service vulnerabilities, because all parties would need to stop communicating and re-negotiate flow levels when one party left. Hence, the only remaining defense against traffic analysis is to ensure that the adversary considered in the system threat model is not capable of simultaneously monitoring enough points in the network to break users' anonymity.

While this approach would be of no help against a global passive adversary, more realistic attackers' traffic monitoring capabilities are likely to be limited to particular jurisdiction(s), whether they derive from legal or extra-legal powers. This intuitively leads to the idea that paths through anonymity networks should be selected to go through as many different countries as possible. The hope here is that an attacker attempting to track connections might have the ability to monitor traffic in some countries, but not all those on the path.

Unfortunately, Feamster and Dingledine [14] showed this approach could actually hurt anonymity because international connections were likely to go through one of a very small number of *tier-1* Internet Service Providers (ISP) – those who

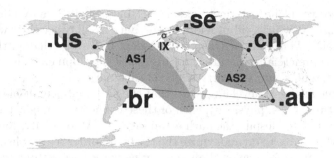

Fig. 1. Multiple-country path through a hypothetical anonymity network at geographical and AS level abstractions. Here, despite the path traveling through 3 countries between Brazil (.br) and the US (.us), there are two tier-1 ISPs which see all links. For example, the hop through China (.cn) is vulnerable since the incoming and outgoing links are observed by AS2. At first glance, the Swedish (.se) hop seems secure, as the incoming link is seen by AS2 and the outgoing by AS1. However, the Swedish ISP connects to AS1 and AS2 at LINX (IX), opening up the risk of observation there.

offer transit to the full Internet. Thus, connections to and from a far-flung Tor node are likely to both pass through a single tier-1 ISP, negating the anonymity benefit against an ISP level adversary. So, while – at the abstraction level of direct connections – a multi-country path may appear to have location diversity, by taking into account the ISPs that the data passes through between Tor nodes, weak points become clear, as shown in Fig. 1.

Instead, Feamster and Dingledine propose, when selecting paths, the relationship between ISPs carrying data between pairs of Tor nodes is taken into account. They did this by collecting Border Gateway Protocol (BGP) data, which controls how packets are routed between entities on the Internet, known as Autonomous Systems (AS) and roughly correspond to ISPs. From this data, assumptions about commercial relationships between ISPs, and heuristics about routing patterns, it is possible to estimate the ASes which will be on each path.

Optimizing path selection to maximize AS diversity reduces the likelihood that there will be one ISP who can observe the connection though the anonymity network at enough points to de-anonymize the user. However, although this level of abstraction is a substantial improvement over the naïve model of direct node connection, it does not fully take in account all potential monitoring points. This will be illustrated in the following section.

3   Impact of Internet Exchanges on Physical Topology

In the previous section, we discussed the advantages of selecting paths through anonymity networks such that there was no single AS which could monitor all hops between anonymity network nodes. This may be achieved by selecting nodes on ASes with high-degree i.e. those which are connected to multiple other ASes. ISPs owning such ASes might purchase cable connections to many other ISPs, but doing so would be extremely expensive. Instead, ISPs may connect their network to an IX, which will provide connectivity to all other ISPs with a presence at that IX. This approach is more prevalent in Europe than in the US, due to differing commercial structures and historical development; also because of language differences, intra-country traffic is substantial.

Thus, while at the AS level it appears that the path makes multiple transitions between distinct ASes, physically, each of these connections might pass through the same IX. Hence, despite the path attaining high AS diversity, there remains one entity who is able to de-anonymize the traffic. In order to establish how much of a problem this is for deployed anonymity networks, we set out to determine how successful an IX level adversary would be, compared to an AS level one, in de-anonymizing Tor users.

The techniques of Feamster and Dingledine [14] rely on building a map of AS paths from BGP data, but this is not helpful for our purposes as the IXes do not appear at this level. From the perspective of a router in an IX, packets travel directly to the destination AS. Furthermore, their approach depends on information about ISP relationships and routing policies which are a carefully guarded secret and so must be guessed. However, it is common practice to allocate each router in an IX an IP address from a single subnet.

Hence, while the AS path of a connection will not reveal whether it is going through an IX, a `traceroute` [15] is likely to. Unlike finding AS paths, collecting `traceroute` data requires access to the system at both ends of the path. As Tor does not currently implement a mechanism for performing `traceroutes`, the operator of the node must do so manually. To limit the effort to a feasible level, here we take the UK as a case study.

3.1   Experimental Results

Based on geo-location databases and manual investigation, we identified Tor nodes hosted in the UK and contacted the operators to request that they run a script to collect data to validate our hypothesis. One of our constraints was that no custom binary applications could be used, as the recipient could not easily confirm they were benign. Instead, we simply invoked the OS provided `traceroute` (or on Windows, `tracert`). These are not designed with speed or parallelism in mind, so to keep the runtime reasonable (2–24 hours, depending on timeouts) on the slower Windows test machines we only traced 140 destinations, and on *nix machines, tested 595 destinations. These destinations consisted of the same 15 websites and 11 US consumer ISPs tested in [14] and the remainder were randomly selected Tor nodes.

We received 19 (14 *nix, 5 Windows) responses from the 33 operators we were able to contact. This totaled 9 025 paths with an average path length of 14 hops (excluding failed responses). For each hop we established whether it was in one of the subnets of LINX (London InterNet eXchange), AMS-IX (AMSterdam Internet eXchange) or DE-CIX (the German Internet exchange, in Frankfurt). Also, using the Team Cymru Database [16], we established the BGP origin AS for each IP address. Note that although we are arranging data by AS, this path

Table 1. Number of paths passing through ASes and IXes

AS name (ASN)	Paths	%	IX name (subnet)	Paths	%
Level 3 (3356)	1 961	22%	LINX (195.66.224.0/22)	2 392	27%
NTL (5089)	1 445	16%	DE-CIX (80.81.192.0/22)	231	3%
Zen (13037)	1 258	14%	AMS-IX (195.69.144.0/22)	202	2%
JANET (786)	1 224	14%			
Datahop (6908)	996	11%			
Tiscali (3257)	953	11%			
Sprint (1239)	935	10%			
Cogent (174)	871	10%			
Telewest (5462)	698	8%			
Telia (1299)	697	8%			

is not the same as the BGP path discussed in [14]. Importantly, while IXes may have an AS, they do not broadcast routes, and so do not appear in BGP paths, whereas `traceroute` establishes the IP address of the border routers, from which the IX can be inferred.

The results are summarized in Table 1. As can be seen, Level 3, a large tier-1 ISP appears at least once on 22% of paths and other tier-1 ISPs, such as Tiscali, Sprint, Cogent and Telia also appear. Since our tests were all from UK Tor nodes, mainly run by volunteers, consumer ISPs also feature, such as NTL, Zen and Telewest, as does the UK academic network operator, JANET. Finally, Datahop, who provide connectivity between 10 data-centers in London, are present on 11% of paths. This broadly matches the results of [14], in that a small number of ISPs are present many paths.

However, if we now examine whether an IX is on the path, we find a new class of observation points. Despite being invisible at the BGP level, LINX is present on 27% of paths. There are 22 distinct ASes in the previous hop to LINX and 109 following the LINX hop, so AS-diverse paths will not substantially impact LINX crossings. Hence, exploiting the IX as an observation point is an effective attack against both existing and proposed anonymity network routing schemes. The connectivity graph of selected ASes, based on our data, is shown in Fig. 2.

4   Traffic Analysis from Sampled Data

The previous section has shown how an adversary positioned at an IX would be capable of monitoring a substantial quantity of traffic through the Tor network. A powerful adversary would be in a position to install expensive hardware to mount conventional traffic analysis attacks but such an adversary would likely be able to deploy other, more effective, attacks. However, the network infrastructure provided by an IX may already have the traffic analysis capabilities that a more modest attacker could use.

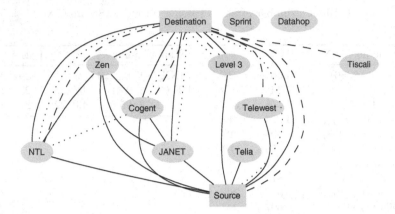

Fig. 2. AS connectivity via IX graph. Only ASes in Table 1 are shown and all sources and destinations are collapsed to single nodes. Links between ASes which pass through LINX are shown as solid lines, AMS-IX is shown by dotted lines and DE-CIX by dashed lines. Paths which go through none of these IXes are omitted. From this we can see that, in our data, connections through Sprint and Datahop go from source to destination without passing through any of the IXes we have selected.

To aid network management, high-end switches and routers have monitoring features which, although not designed for this purpose, may still be effective in tracing users of anonymity networks. This section will evaluate the suitability of network monitoring data for traffic analysis.

4.1   Traffic Monitoring in High-Speed Networks

On low-bandwidth small-office or business networks, full packet analysis tools such as `tcpdump` [17] are adequate to monitor traffic for debugging or to measure load. However, on links found on high-speed networks, the capacity required to store all packets rapidly becomes infeasible. For example, at time of writing, both LINX and AMS-IX carry approximately 150 Gb/s, which exceeds the theoretical maximum capacity of the high-speed PCIe bus, 64 Gb/s (32 lanes at 2 Gb/s each). Despite these difficulties, there is high demand for monitoring of such high-speed links, to detect problems such as routing loops, balance load across network infrastructure and anticipate future demands on capacity.

These applications do not rely on packet content, and for privacy reasons it may be desirable not to record this at all. Thus, medium to high-end networking equipment is commonly equipped with the ability to record aggregate data on the traffic passing through it. One such mechanism is *NetFlow* [18], developed by Cisco Systems but supported by other equipment manufacturers. NetFlow equipped infrastructure records unidirectional *flows* as defined by a tuple (source IP, destination IP, source port, destination port, IP protocol, interface, class of service). For each of these, the device will record information such as the number of packets, total byte count and bitwise-or of TCP flags.

A disadvantage of this approach is that it requires the network hardware to inspect every packet flowing through it. This can incur substantial load at higher network speeds, so to counter this difficulty *sampled NetFlow* only inspects a proportion q of packets. While sampling reduces CPU load, the network hardware must still store state for every flow it considers to be live, which could potentially be very large. An alternative, as adopted by *sFlow* [19], is to move the aggregation out of the network device by immediately exporting sampled packet headers. This approach also gives access to additional fields in packet headers, such as the sequence number, which could be useful for traffic analysis. However, to ensure generality, we will concentrate on information available in sampled NetFlow style data, which could be constructed from sFlow logs if needed (the converse is not true).

Not only is high-speed traffic monitoring possible with standard networking equipment, but it is common practice to do so. Two examples which are particularly relevant to this paper are that AMS-IX record data for traffic management monitoring [20] and LINX (who record 1 in 2 048 packets [21]) additionally are considering using sFlow data for detecting email spam [22]. The same data could also assist tracking users of an anonymity network because Section 3.1 showed that a significant number of Tor flows pass through an IX. In the following section we will examine how successful this type of traffic analysis would be.

4.2 Traffic Analysis Assumptions

There are two basic types of traffic analysis. The first treats the anonymity network as a "black-box" and only inspects traffic entering and leaving the network. The second approach additionally examines flows within the network, and so improves the accuracy of the attack. In this paper, we will concentrate on the former category. As this does not make any assumptions about the structure of the network, it is the more general approach. However, the techniques we present here could also be applied to the latter category of attacks, as intra-network Tor traffic will also often cross a small number of Internet exchanges.

We assume that the attacked flow passes through an attacker controlled IX on both its path into and out of the anonymity network. This would be the case if, for example, both the customer and site are hosted on ISPs whose backbone connection was through an IX under surveillance. Also, we assume that packet sampling is independently and identically distributed over the flow. Although some models of network hardware implement periodic sampling, rather than random, this assumption will remain true because Tor traffic makes up an insignificant proportion of overall traffic.

The attacker observes a single flow going into the network and wishes to establish which of several outgoing flows it corresponds to. This could be, for example, finding which website a known criminal is uploading stolen data to. Alternatively, the attacker might wish to discover who has uploaded a particular video to a news website – now there is one outgoing flow and many incoming candidates. In both cases, the attacker will have a number of candidates in mind who are also generating traffic at the same time, and for our simulation we assume that these produce around $1\,000$ flows per hour. We also assume that the adversary can distinguish Tor traffic from other traffic, which may trivially done by IP address and port number, based on information in the Tor directory.

5 Mathematical Analysis

5.1 Model

Our model consists of n client-server flows. Each flow $p = p_1, \ldots, p_m$ is a collection of packets sent at times $t_1, \ldots, t_m$. We model the times as a Poisson process with a start time s, duration l, and rate r (average packets per second). These three parameters are chosen independently at random for each flow.

Neither s, l, r nor the flow p are directly observable. The attacker sees a down-sampled version of p, in which each packet is retained independently with a fixed probability q, called a sampling rate (typically about $1/2\,000$). Each flow is sampled at the input and at the output, resulting in two vectors of times: x and y. Given a flow p, the sampling processes $p \to x$ and $p \to y$ are independent:

$$s, l, r \xrightarrow{\text{Poisson}} p \qquad x \xleftarrow{\text{sampling}} p \xrightarrow{\text{sampling}} y \qquad (1)$$

In an n-flow system, the attacker sees all n output vectors $y_1, \ldots, y_n$, and one input vector x, which corresponds to some y_k. The task of the attacker is to compute the probability $P(T_k)$ that x corresponds to y_k, for each k.

To simplify the model, we assume that no packet from p appears simultaneously in both x and y. Since x and y are independently sampled from p, a given packet from p appears in both x and y with the probability of $q^2 = 2.5 \cdot 10^{-7}$, that is, once every $1/q^2 = 4 \cdot 10^6$ packets ($\approx 2\,\text{GB}$). Seeing the same packet on the input and the output is thus very unlikely, which prevents packet-matching attacks [9] and makes independent random delays of individual packets practically unobservable in the sampled data. For simplicity, we therefore assume instantaneous packet transmission. Section 5.5 shows that introducing a moderate delay to the system does not change the effectiveness of our attack.

The assumption of no common packets in x and y allows us to simplify (1) by observing that x and y are now *independent* Poisson processes with rate rq.

$$x \xleftarrow{\text{Poisson}} s, l, rq \xrightarrow{\text{Poisson}} y \qquad (2)$$

This simplification eliminates the original (unobservable) flow p from the model.

5.2 Basic Solution

Let T_k denote the event in which input x and output y_k belong to the same flow. In our model, the exact probabilities $P(T_k)$ can be uniquely determined from Bayes' formula:

$$P(T_k | y_{1..n}, x) = \frac{P(y_{1..n} | T_k, x) P(T_k | x)}{\sum_i P(y_{1..n} | T_i, x) P(T_i | x)}. \qquad (3)$$

Probabilities $P(T_k|\boldsymbol{x})$ express our prior information about the target, possibly based on the sampled input flow $\boldsymbol{x}$ (but not output flow $\boldsymbol{y}$). For example, we might know that a particular server k is just more popular than others, or that it is the only one to regularly receive high-volume traffic and $\boldsymbol{x}$ looks to be high-volume. For simplicity, in the rest of the analysis, we treat all servers equally; any prior information can be easily taken into account using (3).

The probabilities $P(\boldsymbol{y}_{1..n}|\boldsymbol{x}, T_k)$ in (3) can be computed as follows:

$$P(\boldsymbol{y}_{1..n}|\boldsymbol{x}, T_k) = P(\boldsymbol{y}_k|\boldsymbol{x}, T_k) \prod_{i \neq k} P(\boldsymbol{y}_i) = \frac{P(\boldsymbol{y}_k|\boldsymbol{x}, T_k)}{P(\boldsymbol{y}_k)} \prod_i P(\boldsymbol{y}_i). \qquad (4)$$

Here, we used the fact that output flows $\boldsymbol{y}_i$ are independent, and that $P(\boldsymbol{y}_i|T_k) = P(\boldsymbol{y}_i)$: the information about input-output connection T_k is only relevant for statements that involve both inputs and outputs (such as $P(\boldsymbol{y}_k, \boldsymbol{x}|T_k)$).

Since we are only interested in relative probabilities for different k's, we can ignore all factors independent of k, such as $P(\boldsymbol{x}|T_k) = P(\boldsymbol{x})$ or $\prod_i P(\boldsymbol{y}_i)$, as they would cancel out in (3) anyway:

$$P(T_k|\boldsymbol{y}_{1..n}, \boldsymbol{x}) \overset{(3)}{\sim} P(\boldsymbol{y}_{1..n}|\boldsymbol{x}, T_k) \overset{(4)}{\sim} \frac{P(\boldsymbol{y}_k|\boldsymbol{x}, T_k)}{P(\boldsymbol{y}_k)} = \frac{P(\boldsymbol{y}_k, \boldsymbol{x}|T_k)}{P(\boldsymbol{x}|T_k)P(\boldsymbol{y}_k)} \sim \frac{P(\boldsymbol{x}, \boldsymbol{y}_k|T_k)}{P(\boldsymbol{y}_k)}. \qquad (5)$$

We therefore need to compute $P(\boldsymbol{y}_k)$ and $P(\boldsymbol{x}, \boldsymbol{y}_k|T_k)$. We are dealing with a single flow $\boldsymbol{x} \leftarrow \boldsymbol{p} \rightarrow \boldsymbol{y}_k$, so – to avoid notational clutter – we will drop the explicit index k and assumption T_k from our formulae. In the new notation, we have $P(\boldsymbol{y})$ and $P(\boldsymbol{x}, \boldsymbol{y})$, which can be computed from appropriate conditional probabilities by integrating out the unknown parameters s, l, r:

$$P(\boldsymbol{y}) = \int_{s,l,r} P(\boldsymbol{y}|s,l,r)P(s,l,r). \qquad (6)$$

$$P(\boldsymbol{x}, \boldsymbol{y}) = \int_{s,l,r} P(\boldsymbol{x}, \boldsymbol{y}|s,l,r)P(s,l,r) = \int_{s,l,r} P(\boldsymbol{x}|s,l,r)P(\boldsymbol{y}|s,l,r)P(s,l,r). \quad (7)$$

The last equality holds because $\boldsymbol{x}$ and $\boldsymbol{y}$, generated by model (2), are independent given s, l, r. The distribution $P(s, l, r)$ expresses our prior knowledge about flow starting times, durations, and rates.

We divide the interval $[s, s + l]$ into infinitesimally small windows of size dt. Since $\boldsymbol{y}$ is a Poisson process (2), the probability of observing a single packet in one such window is $rq\,dt$. The probability of no packets in $[s, s+l]$ is e^{-rql}. Thus,

$$P(\boldsymbol{y}|s,l,r) = \begin{cases} e^{-rql}(rq\,dt)^{n_{\boldsymbol{y}}} & \text{if all times in } \boldsymbol{y} \in [s, s+l], \\ 0 & \text{otherwise.} \end{cases} \qquad (8)$$

Here, $n_{\boldsymbol{y}}$ is the number of packets in $\boldsymbol{y}$. The same formula (with $n_{\boldsymbol{x}}$) holds for $P(\boldsymbol{x}|s,l,r)$. Since $P(\boldsymbol{x}, \boldsymbol{y}|s,l,r) = P(\boldsymbol{x}|s,l,r)P(\boldsymbol{y}|s,l,r)$, we also have

$$P(\boldsymbol{x}, \boldsymbol{y}|s,l,r) = \begin{cases} e^{-2rql}(rq\,dt)^{n_{\boldsymbol{x}}+n_{\boldsymbol{y}}} & \text{if all times in } \boldsymbol{x}, \boldsymbol{y} \in [s, s+l], \\ 0 & \text{otherwise.} \end{cases} \qquad (9)$$

5.3 Long-Lived Flows

We first consider a simplified model, in which all flows start at the same known time s and have the same known duration l (basically, $[s, s+l]$ is our observation window). The only factor distinguishing the flows is their (unknown) rate r. From (8), we get:

$$P(\boldsymbol{y}) = \int_r P(\boldsymbol{y}|r)P(r) = \int_r e^{-rql}(rq\,dt)^{n_y}P(r). \tag{10}$$

where $P(r)$ is our prior information about the rate r. Since r is a positive parameter, we express our complete lack of prior knowledge by using the scale-invariant Jeffrey's ignorance prior $P(r) \sim r^{-1}\,dr$ [23]. This basically says that $\log r$ is distributed uniformly: the probability of $r \in [a, b]$ is proportional to $\log(b/a)$. For example, $r \in [1, 10]$ and $r \in [10, 100]$ have the same probability.

$$P(\boldsymbol{y}) \overset{(10)}{=} \int_r (rq\,dt)^{n_y} e^{-rql}P(r) = (q\,dt)^{n_y}\int_{r=0}^{\infty} r^{n_y-1}e^{-rql}\,dr = \frac{dt^{n_y}}{l^{n_y}}\Gamma(n_y). \tag{11}$$

We used $\int_0^\infty z^{a-1}e^{-bz}\,dz = \Gamma(a)/b^a$; for integer n we have $\Gamma(n) = (n-1)!$.
Similarly, from (9),

$$P(\boldsymbol{x}, \boldsymbol{y}) = \int_r (rq\,dt)^{n_x+n_y}e^{-2rql}P(r) = \frac{dt^{n_x+n_y}}{(2l)^{n_x+n_y}}\Gamma(n_x+n_y). \tag{12}$$

We can now use (5) to compute the final probability:

$$P(T_k|\boldsymbol{y}_{1..n}, \boldsymbol{x}) \sim \frac{P(\boldsymbol{x}, \boldsymbol{y}_k|T_k)}{P(\boldsymbol{y}_k)} = \frac{dt^{n_x}}{(2l)^{n_x}}\cdot\frac{\Gamma(n_x+n_{y_k})}{2^{n_{y_k}}\Gamma(n_{y_k})} \sim \frac{\Gamma(n_x+n_{y_k})}{2^{n_{y_k}}\Gamma(n_{y_k})}. \tag{13}$$

Interpretation. Fig. 3(a) shows a normalized plot of (13) for $n_x = 5$ as a function of n_y. The maximum probability is assigned to $n_y \approx n_x$, when the numbers of observed packets on the input and on the output are similar. This confirms our intuition and also yields quantitative probabilities for different n_y's, which can be used for combining evidence from multiple observations.

The exact maximum occurs for $n_y > n_x$ because the prior $P(r) \sim r^{-1}\,dr$ causes $P(r \in [4, 5]) > P(r \in [5, 6])$ (because $\frac{5}{4} > \frac{6}{5}$). This makes small n_y's more probable to be produced by chance than larger ones, decreasing their match probability. Using Stirling's approximation of $n!$, we get (see appendix):

$$P(T_k|\boldsymbol{y}_{1..n}, \boldsymbol{x}) \sim \frac{(n_x+n_y-1)^{n_x+n_y-\frac{1}{2}}}{2^{n_y}(n_y-1)^{n_y-\frac{1}{2}}}, \tag{14}$$

which very closely matches the original, as shown in Fig. 3(a). The maximum of (14), obtained by comparing its derivative to zero, is $n_y \approx n_x + \frac{1}{2}$.

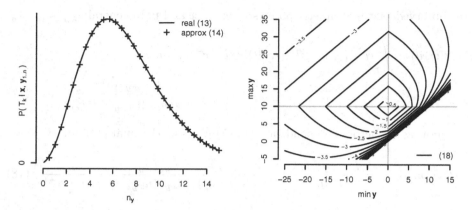

(a) $P(T_k|\boldsymbol{x}, \boldsymbol{y}_{1..n})$ given by (13) for fixed $n_{\boldsymbol{x}} = 5$ and $n_{\boldsymbol{y}}$ ranging from 0 to 15.

(b) $\log P(T_k|\boldsymbol{x}, \boldsymbol{y}_{1..n})$ given by (18) for $n_{\boldsymbol{x}} = n_{\boldsymbol{y}} = 5$, $\min \boldsymbol{x} = 0$, $\max \boldsymbol{x} = 10$, and variable $\min \boldsymbol{y}$ and $\max \boldsymbol{y}$.

Fig. 3. Relative probabilities based on (a) observed packet counts and (b) lengths

5.4   General Flows

Now, we consider the general case, in which flows have different (unknown) durations l and starting times s. From (8), we can compute $P(\boldsymbol{y}|l, r)$ by integrating s out. For a given duration l, the possible starting times s belong to the interval $[\max \boldsymbol{y} - l, \min \boldsymbol{y}]$. If $l_{\boldsymbol{y}} = \max \boldsymbol{y} - \min \boldsymbol{y}$ is the observed length of $\boldsymbol{y}$, then this interval of possible values of s has the length $(l - l_{\boldsymbol{y}})_0 = \max\{l - l_{\boldsymbol{y}}, 0\}$. Assuming lack of prior knowledge about s (uniform prior $P(s) \sim \mathrm{d}s$), we have

$$P(\boldsymbol{y}|l, r) = \int_s P(\boldsymbol{y}|s, l, r)P(s) \overset{(8)}{\sim} (l - l_{\boldsymbol{y}})_0 e^{-rql}(rq\,\mathrm{d}t)^{n_{\boldsymbol{y}}}. \tag{15}$$

Using Jeffrey's priors $P(l) \sim l^{-1}\,\mathrm{d}l$ and $P(r) \sim r^{-1}\,\mathrm{d}r$, we get:

$$P(\boldsymbol{y}) = \int_{l,r} P(\boldsymbol{y}|l, r)P(l, r) = \int_{l,r} (l - l_{\boldsymbol{y}})_0 e^{-rql}(rq\,\mathrm{d}t)^{n_{\boldsymbol{y}}} l^{-1} r^{-1}\,\mathrm{d}r\,\mathrm{d}l =$$

$$(q\,\mathrm{d}t)^{n_{\boldsymbol{y}}} \int_l (l - l_{\boldsymbol{y}})_0 l^{-1} \int_r e^{-rql} r^{n_{\boldsymbol{y}}-1}\,\mathrm{d}r\,\mathrm{d}l =$$

$$(q\,\mathrm{d}t)^{n_{\boldsymbol{y}}} \int_l (l - l_{\boldsymbol{y}})_0 l^{-1} \Gamma(n_{\boldsymbol{y}})(ql)^{-n_{\boldsymbol{y}}}\,\mathrm{d}l =$$

$$\mathrm{d}t^{n_{\boldsymbol{y}}} \Gamma(n_{\boldsymbol{y}}) \int_{l=l_{\boldsymbol{y}}}^{\infty} (l - l_{\boldsymbol{y}}) l^{-n_{\boldsymbol{y}}-1}\,\mathrm{d}l = \mathrm{d}t^{n_{\boldsymbol{y}}} \Gamma(n_{\boldsymbol{y}}) \frac{l_{\boldsymbol{y}}^{-n_{\boldsymbol{y}}+1}}{n_{\boldsymbol{y}}(n_{\boldsymbol{y}} - 1)}. \tag{16}$$

We can compute $P(\boldsymbol{x}, \boldsymbol{y})$ in a similar way. Let $n_{\boldsymbol{x}\boldsymbol{y}} = n_{\boldsymbol{x}} + n_{\boldsymbol{y}}$ be the total number of packets in $\boldsymbol{x}$ and $\boldsymbol{y}$, and $l_{\boldsymbol{x}\boldsymbol{y}} = \max\{\max \boldsymbol{x}, \max \boldsymbol{y}\} - \min\{\min \boldsymbol{x}, \min \boldsymbol{y}\}$

the observed length of superimposed sequences $\boldsymbol{x}$ and $\boldsymbol{y}$. In general, $l_{\boldsymbol{xy}} \neq l_{\boldsymbol{x}} + l_{\boldsymbol{y}}$.

$$P(\boldsymbol{x}, \boldsymbol{y}) = \int_{l,r} (l - l_{\boldsymbol{xy}})_0 e^{-2rql} (rq\,dt)^{n_{\boldsymbol{xy}}} l^{-1} r^{-1}\,dr\,dl =$$

$$\frac{\Gamma(n_{\boldsymbol{xy}})\,dt^{n_{\boldsymbol{xy}}}}{2^{n_{\boldsymbol{xy}}}(n_{\boldsymbol{xy}})(n_{\boldsymbol{xy}} - 1)l_{\boldsymbol{xy}}^{n_{\boldsymbol{xy}}-1}}. \quad (17)$$

Ignoring all factors independent of k, (5) gives us the final probability

$$P(T_k|\boldsymbol{x}, \boldsymbol{y}_{1..n}) = \frac{P(\boldsymbol{x}, \boldsymbol{y}_k|T_k)}{P(\boldsymbol{y}_k)} \sim \frac{\Gamma(n_{\boldsymbol{xy}_k})}{2^{n_{\boldsymbol{xy}_k}}\Gamma(n_{\boldsymbol{y}_k})} \cdot \frac{n_{\boldsymbol{y}_k}(n_{\boldsymbol{y}_k} - 1)}{n_{\boldsymbol{xy}_k}(n_{\boldsymbol{xy}_k} - 1)} \cdot \frac{l_{\boldsymbol{y}_k}^{n_{\boldsymbol{y}_k}-1}}{l_{\boldsymbol{xy}_k}^{n_{\boldsymbol{xy}_k}-1}}. \quad (18)$$

Interpretation. Formula (18) consists of three factors: (i) the rate formula (13), (ii) a rate-dependent correction $n_{\boldsymbol{y}}(n_{\boldsymbol{y}} - 1)/(n_{\boldsymbol{xy}}(n_{\boldsymbol{xy}} - 1))$, and (iii) the length-dependent factor $l_{\boldsymbol{y}}^{n_{\boldsymbol{y}}-1}/l_{\boldsymbol{xy}}^{n_{\boldsymbol{xy}}-1}$, which is of the most interest to us here.

Consider matching an input flow with the observed starting time $\min \boldsymbol{x} = 0$, ending time $\max \boldsymbol{x} = 10$, and $n_{\boldsymbol{x}} = 5$ observed packets, against output flows $\boldsymbol{y}$ with the same number of observed packets $n_{\boldsymbol{y}} = 5$. For various starting and ending times $\min \boldsymbol{y}$ and $\max \boldsymbol{y}$, Fig. 3(b) presents the matching likelihood assigned by (18) (since $n_{\boldsymbol{x}}$ and $n_{\boldsymbol{y}}$ are constant, so are the first two factors).

As expected, the maximum is attained when the observed starting and ending times of both flows coincide: $\min \boldsymbol{x} = \min \boldsymbol{y} = 0$ and $\max \boldsymbol{x} = \max \boldsymbol{y} = 10$. Each contour line consists of two parallel straight lines joined by two curves. The two straight lines correspond to the observed input flow period completely containing the observed output flow period, and vice versa.

Optimality. The derivation of (18) is strictly Bayesian, so – given the model assumptions – the result is exact and uses all relevant information. Note that, despite the timings of all packets being available through $\boldsymbol{x}$ and $\boldsymbol{y}$, formula (18) uses only the total packet counts ($n_{\boldsymbol{y}}$, $n_{\boldsymbol{xy}}$) and the observed lengths ($l_{\boldsymbol{y}}$, $l_{\boldsymbol{xy}}$). This shows that the exact timings of individual packets (used by timing-based attacks) are irrelevant for the inference in our model.

5.5 Evaluation

To evaluate the effectiveness of our method in attacking an individual Tor node, we first collected real traffic distributions of observed flow rates and durations (Fig. 4). Then, we performed a number of simulations of a 120 min execution of a node. Flow durations (1–30 min) and rates (0.1–50 packets/s) were drawn from the log-uniform ($P(z) \sim z^{-1}\,dz$) prior, consistent with Fig. 4. Starting times were selected uniformly from the interval $[0, 120\,\text{min} - l]$.

Our scoring method was "1" if the highest probability was assigned to the correct target, and "0" otherwise (if $i > 1$ targets shared the top probability, then the score was $1/i$ instead of 1). For each simulation, we applied the attack independently to each input, and then averaged the results.

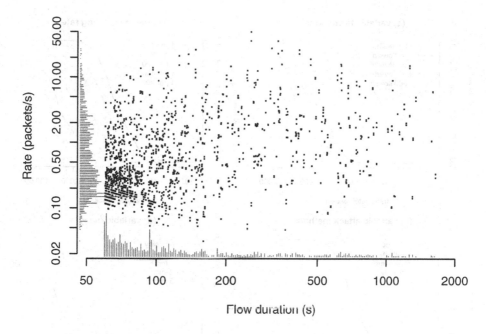

Fig. 4. Distribution of observed rates and flow durations on a single Tor node. Only flows that completed the three-way TCP handshake, at least 1 minute long, and consist of at least 5 packets are shown. Flows are closed after being idle for 1 minute.

We varied the following parameters: the number of flows per hour (50–1 000), the sampling rate q (1/100–1/2 000), the mean network latency (0–10 min), and the attack method. Our parameter ranges are consistent with their real values: our Tor node transmitted 479 flows/h on average, the average Tor network latency was 0.5 s, and the current typical sampling rate is 1/2 048, but may increase in the future. The results of our simulations are summarized in Fig. 5.

Average number of flows. Fig. 5(a) confirms that more flows provide more protection. For a typical number of 500 flows/h, the attack had a 50% chance of success when the target sends $\approx 20\,000$ packets, that is ≈ 10 MB of data. With 50 flows/h, the same success rate required only 7 000 packets (3.5 MB).

Sampling rate. Fig. 5(b) suggests that the effectiveness of the attack depends only on the number of sampled packets, so doubling the sampling rate is equivalent to doubling the number of transmitted packets. For the technically feasible sampling rate of 1/100, a success rate of 50% required only 1 000 transmitted packets (500 kB).

Attack methods. We compared the following attacks: (i) *rate attack*, which applies (13), taking into account the observed number of packets and ignoring packet times; (ii) *rate+overlap attack*, which additionally ignores outputs with observed packet timings disjoint with the input; (iii) *length attack*, which selects the output y with the highest ratio l_y/l_{xy}; (iv) *full attack*, which uses (18).

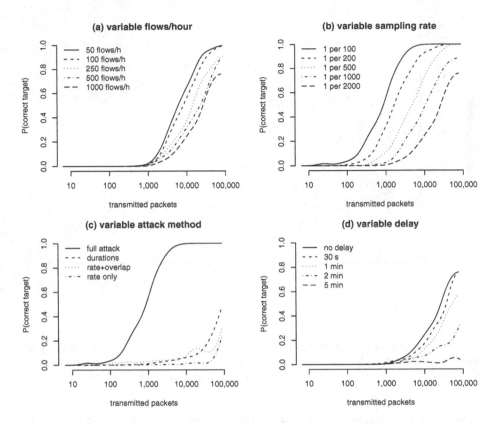

Fig. 5. Simulation results: the probability of choosing the correct target, as a function of the number of transmitted packets, for varying numbers of flows/hour (default 1 000), sampling rate (1/2 000, except (c)), attack method (full attack), and delay (0)

Fig. 5(c) shows the effectiveness of these four methods in a system with a sampling rate of 1/100. The combined rate and length information (18) resulted in a 50% success rate for ≈ 1 000 packets (10 sampled). In comparison, taking only one factor (rate or length) into account, required 100 times more packets to achieve the same accuracy.

Delays. Fig. 5(d) shows the effects of introducing an exponentially distributed random delay to the system. The effectiveness of our attack stayed approximately the same for delays up to 30 s, and then started to deteriorate, reaching the 0% level for a 5 min delay. Note, however, that our attack explicitly assumes no delay whatsoever, therefore this result does *not* mean that a 5-minute random delay safeguards against all sampling attacks.

6   Future Work

For simplicity, we ignored several phenomena that occur in practice, such as different sampling rates and how Tor cells are split over IP packets. Generalizing our analysis to support different known sampling rates at input and output seems straightforward (but an attack by a single adversary with a fixed sampling rate is most likely). Similarly, the effect of packet splitting by Tor nodes seems to be statistically equivalent to different sampling rates. Our analysis could also be modified to take TCP sequence numbers, available from sFlow records, into account, to give more accurate rate calculation.

As reasonable random delays do not protect against our attack, we plan to examine other defenses, such as a moderate amount of dummy traffic. We would also like to measure the effectiveness of our attack against real systems, using an empirically determined prior distribution on durations and rates, for both the analysis (numerical integration required) and the evaluation. Ideally, such an evaluation should be performed for the entire Tor system, with its average 1 million flows per hour.

Furthermore, we are considering how intra-network traffic analysis could be performed. Similar techniques could be used, and are likely to work better than whole-network analysis since the number of flows will be smaller. However, there are complications which must be considered, in particular that multiple flows between the same pair of Tor nodes may be multiplexed within one encrypted TLS tunnel. An improved analysis would take this possibility into account and empirical studies would show to what extent this interferes with analysis.

7   Conclusion

We have demonstrated that Internet exchanges are a viable, and previously unexamined, monitoring point for traffic analysis purposes. They are present on many paths through our sample of the Tor network, even where BGP data would not detect any common points of failure. Furthermore, Internet exchanges are particularly relevant as in some cases they may record, and potentially retain data adequate to perform traffic analysis.

To validate to what extent this was true, we developed traffic analysis techniques which work on the sampled data which is being collected in practice by Internet exchanges. Using a Bayesian approach, we obtained the best possible inference, which means that we can not only attack vulnerable systems, but also declare others as safe under our threat model. Our probability formula is difficult to obtain by trial-and-error, and – as we show – can give orders of magnitude better results than simple intuitive schemes.

We also show that exact "internal" packet timings are irrelevant for optimum inference, so timing-based attacks cannot work with sparsely sampled data. For the same reason, deliberate random packet delays do not protect low-latency anonymity systems against our attack, as the minimum sensible latency (1 min) is unacceptable for web browsing and similar activities.

Acknowledgments. We thank Richard Clayton, Chris Hall, Markus Kuhn, Andrei Serjantov and the anonymous reviewers for productive comments, and also the Tor node operators who collected the data used in this paper.

References

1. Danezis, G., Dingledine, R., Mathewson, N.: Mixminion: Design of a Type III Anonymous Remailer Protocol. In: Proceedings of the 2003 IEEE Symposium on Security and Privacy, IEEE Computer Society Press, Los Alamitos (2003)
2. Möller, U., Cottrell, L., Palfrader, P., Sassaman, L.: Mixmaster Protocol – Version 2. Draft (2003)
3. Dingledine, R., Mathewson, N., Syverson, P.: Tor: The second-generation onion router. In: Proceedings of the 13th USENIX Security Symposium (2004)
4. Berthold, O., Federrath, H., Köpsell, S.: Web MIXes: A system for anonymous and unobservable Internet access. In: Federrath, H. (ed.) Designing Privacy Enhancing Technologies. LNCS, vol. 2009, pp. 115–129. Springer, Heidelberg (2001)
5. Boucher, P., Shostack, A., Goldberg, I.: Freedom systems 2.0 architecture. White paper, Zero Knowledge Systems, Inc. (2000)
6. Serjantov, A., Murdoch, S.J.: Message splitting against the partial adversary. In: Danezis, G., Martin, D. (eds.) PET 2005. LNCS, vol. 3856, Springer, Heidelberg (2006)
7. Serjantov, A., Sewell, P.: Passive attack analysis for connection-based anonymity systems. In: Snekkenes, E., Gollmann, D. (eds.) ESORICS 2003. LNCS, vol. 2808, Springer, Heidelberg (2003)
8. Levine, B.N., Reiter, M.K., Wang, C., Wright, M.K.: Timing attacks in low-latency mix-based systems. In: Juels, A. (ed.) FC 2004. LNCS, vol. 3110, Springer, Heidelberg (2004)
9. Danezis, G.: The traffic analysis of continuous-time mixes. In: Martin, D., Serjantov, A. (eds.) PET 2004. LNCS, vol. 3424, Springer, Heidelberg (2005)
10. Dai, W.: Pipenet 1.1. Post to Cypherpunks mailing list (1998),
    http://www.eskimo.com/~weidai/pipenet.txt
11. Øverlier, L., Syverson, P.: Locating hidden servers. In: Proceedings of the 2006 IEEE Symposium on Security and Privacy, IEEE CS, Los Alamitos (2006)
12. Bauer, K., McCoy, D., Grunwald, D., Kohno, T., Sicker, D.: Low-resource routing attacks against anonymous systems. Technical Report CU-CS-1025-07, University of Colorado at Boulder (2007)
13. Acquisti, A., Dingledine, R., Syverson, P.: On the Economics of Anonymity. In: Wright, R.N. (ed.) FC 2003. LNCS, vol. 2742, Springer, Heidelberg (2003)
14. Feamster, N., Dingledine, R.: Location diversity in anonymity networks. In: Proceedings of the Workshop on Privacy in the Electronic Society (WPES 2004), Washington, DC, USA (2004)
15. Jacobson, V.: Traceroute (1) (1987), ftp://ftp.ee.lbl.gov/traceroute.tar.gz
16. Team Cymru: IP to ASN lookup (v1.0), http://asn.cymru.com/
17. Jacobson, V., Leres, C., McCanne, S.: Tcpdump (1) (1989),
    http://www.tcpdump.org/
18. Claise, B.: Cisco systems NetFlow services export version 9. RFC 3954, IETF (2004)
19. Phaal, P., Panchen, S., McKee, N.: InMon corporation's sFlow: A method for monitoring traffic in switched and routed networks. RFC 3176, IETF (2001)
20. Jasinska, E.: sFlow – I can feel your traffic. In: 23C3: 23rd Chaos Communication Congress (2006),
    http://events.ccc.de/congress/2006/Fahrplan/attachments/
    1137-sFlowPaper.pdf

21. Hughes, M.: LINX news (2006),
    http://www.uknof.org.uk/uknof4/Hughes-LINX.pdf
22. Clayton, R.: spamHINTS project (2006), http://www.spamhints.org/
23. Jaynes, E.T.: Probability Theory: The Logic of Science. Cambridge University Press, Cambridge (2003)

A Appendix

Theorem 1. *Formula* (13) *attains maximum for* $n_y \approx n_x + \frac{1}{2}$.

Proof. Stirling's factorial approximation gives us

$$n! \approx \left(\frac{n}{e}\right)^n \sqrt{2\pi n}.$$

Denoting $a = n_x$, $b = n_y$, and $c = a + b$, we have:

$$P(T_k|\boldsymbol{y}_{1..n}, \boldsymbol{x}) \sim \frac{\Gamma(a+b)}{2^b\Gamma(b)} = \frac{(c-1)!}{2^b(b-1)!} \approx \frac{\left(\frac{c-1}{e}\right)^{c-1}\sqrt{2\pi(c-1)}}{2^b\left(\frac{b-1}{e}\right)^{b-1}\sqrt{2\pi(b-1)}} \sim$$

$$\frac{(c-1)^{c-\frac{1}{2}}}{2^b(b-1)^{b-\frac{1}{2}}} = X. \quad (19)$$

Instead of finding the maximum of X, it is easier to find the maximum of $\log X$:

$$\log X = (c - \tfrac{1}{2})\log(c-1) - b\log 2 - (b - \tfrac{1}{2})\log(b-1). \quad (20)$$

We can find the maximum of $\log X$ by differentiating it w.r.t. b, and remembering that $c' = (a + b)' = 1$:

$$(\log X)' = \log(c-1) + \frac{c - \frac{1}{2}}{c-1} - \log 2 - \log(b-1) - \frac{b - \frac{1}{2}}{b-1}$$

$$= \log(c-1) + \frac{1}{2(c-1)} - \log 2 - \log(b-1) - \frac{1}{2(b-1)} \quad (21)$$

$$\approx \log(c - \tfrac{1}{2}) - \log 2 - \log(b - \tfrac{1}{2}) = \log\left(\frac{c - \frac{1}{2}}{2b - 1}\right).$$

Now, $(\log X)' = 0$ implies $c - \frac{1}{2} = 2b - 1$, which implies $b = a + \frac{1}{2}$, that is $n_y = n_x + \frac{1}{2}$.

Browser-Based Attacks on Tor

Timothy G. Abbott, Katherine J. Lai, Michael R. Lieberman, and Eric C. Price

{tabbott,k_lai,mathmike,ecprice}@mit.edu

Abstract. This paper describes a new attack on the anonymity of web browsing with Tor. The attack tricks a user's web browser into sending a distinctive signal over the Tor network that can be detected using traffic analysis. It is delivered by a malicious exit node using a man-in-the-middle attack on HTTP. Both the attack and the traffic analysis can be performed by an adversary with limited resources. While the attack can only succeed if the attacker controls one of the victim's entry guards, the method reduces the time required for a traffic analysis attack on Tor from $O(nk)$ to $O(n + k)$, where n is the number of exit nodes and k is the number of entry guards. This paper presents techniques that exploit the Tor exit policy system to greatly simplify the traffic analysis. The fundamental vulnerability exposed by this paper is not specific to Tor but rather to the problem of anonymous web browsing itself. This paper also describes a related attack on users who toggle the use of Tor with the popular Firefox extension Torbutton.

1 Introduction

The Internet was not designed with anonymity in mind; in fact, one of the original design goals was accountability [3]. Every packet sent by established protocols identifies both parties. However, most users expect that their Internet communications are and should remain anonymous. As was recently highlighted by the uproar over AOL's release of a large body of "anonymized" search query data [10], this disparity violates the security principle that systems meet the security expectations of their users. Some countries have taken a policy of arresting people for expressing dissident opinions on the Internet. Anonymity prevents these opinions from being traced back to their originators, increasing freedom of speech.

For applications that can tolerate high latencies, such as electronic mail, there are systems that achieve nearly perfect anonymity [1]. Such anonymity is difficult to achieve with low latency systems such as web browsing, however, because of the conflict between preventing traffic analysis on the flow of packets through the network and delivering packets in an efficient and timely fashion.

Because of the obvious importance of the problem, there has been a great deal of recent research on low-latency anonymity systems. Tor, the second-generation onion router, is the largest anonymity network in existence today.

In this paper we describe a new scheme for executing a practical timing attack on browsing the web anonymously with Tor. Using this attack, an adversary can

N. Borisov and P. Golle (Eds.): PET 2007, LNCS 4776, pp. 184–199, 2007.

identify a fraction of the Tor users who use a malicious exit node and then leave a browser window open for an hour. With current entry guard implementations, the attack requires the adversary to control only a single Tor server in order to identify as much as 0.4% of Tor users targeted by the malicious node (and this probability can be increased roughly linearly by adding more machines). The targeting can be done based on the potential victim's HTTP traffic (so, for example, one could eventually identify 0.4% of Tor users who read Slashdot).

2   How Tor Works

Tor [5] is an anonymizing protocol that uses *onion routing* to hide the source of TCP traffic. Onion routing is a scheme based on layered encryption, which was first developed for anonymizing electronic mail [1]. As of December 15, 2006, Tor was used by approximately 200,000 users and contained about 750 nodes (also sometimes referred to as "servers" or "routers") [4].

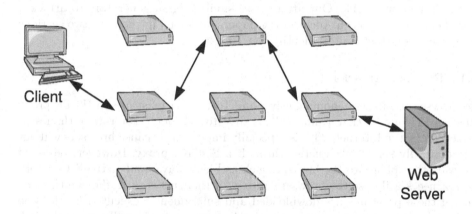

Fig. 1. A Tor circuit. The client chooses an entry node, a middle node, and an exit node, allowing the exit node to fetch content from a web server.

In Tor, a client routes his traffic through a chain of three nodes that he selects from the Tor network, as shown in Figure 1. A client constructs this path of nodes, or "circuit", by performing Diffie-Hellman handshakes with each of the nodes to exchange symmetric keys for encryption and decryption. These Tor nodes are picked from a list of current servers that are published by a signed directory service.[1] To send TCP data through the circuit, the client starts by breaking the stream into fixed sized cells that are successively encrypted with

---

[1] While the directory service is signed, anyone can add an entry, and claim to have a long uptime and high bandwidth. This makes getting users to use a malicious node a little easier, because clients prefer to use servers with good statistics.

the keys that have been negotiated with each of the nodes in the path, starting with the exit node's key and ending with the entry node's key. Fixed size cells are important so that anyone reading the encrypted traffic cannot use cell size to help identify a client [7][9].

Using this protocol, the entry node is the only node that is told the client's identity, the exit node is the only node that is told the destination's identity and the actual TCP data sent, and the middle node simply exchanges encrypted cells between the entry node and the exit node along a particular circuit. The nodes are selected approximately randomly using an algorithm dependent on various Tor node statistics distributed by the directory server, some client history, and client preferences.

3 Related Work

In May 2006, S. Murdoch and G. Danezis discussed how a website can include "traffic analysis bugs"—invisible signal generators which are used to shape traffic in the Tor network [11]. Our attack uses similar signal generators to attack a Tor client. We rely on the ideas of the papers discussed in the next two sections to deliver the attack and to identify the Tor client.

3.1 Browser Attacks

To browse the Internet anonymously using Tor, a user must use an HTTP proxy such as Privoxy so that traffic will be diverted through Tor rather than sent directly over the Internet. This is especially important because browsers will not automatically send DNS queries through a SOCKS proxy. However, pieces of software that plug into the browser, such as Flash, Java, and ActiveX Controls, do not necessarily use the browser's proxy for their network traffic. Thus, when any of these programs are downloaded and subsequently executed by the web browser, any Internet connections that the programs make will not go through Tor first. Instead, they will establish direct TCP connections, compromising the user's anonymity, as shown in Figure 2. This attack allows a website to identify its visitors but does not allow a third party to identify Tor users visiting a given website. These active content systems are well-known problems in anonymous web-browsing, and most anonymizing systems warn users to disable active content systems in their browsers.

In October 2006, FortConsult Security [2] described how to extend this attack so that parties could identify Tor users visiting a website they do not control. The attacker uses a malicious exit node to modify HTTP traffic and thus conduct a man-in-the-middle attack, as shown in Figure 3. In particular, it inserts an invisible iframe with a reference to some malicious web server and a unique cookie. In rendering the page, the web browser will make a request to the web server and will retrieve a malicious Flash application. If Flash is enabled in the browser, then the Flash movie is played invisibly. The Flash application sends the cookie given to the user directly to the evil web server, circumventing

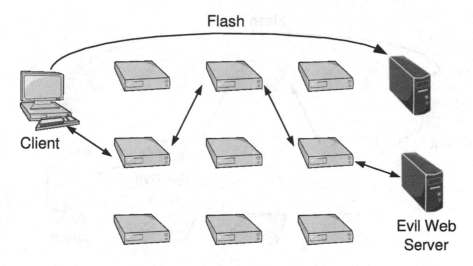

Fig. 2. Prior work: a browser attack using Flash included in a website. The client's web browser executes a Flash program, which then opens a direct connection to a logger machine, compromising the client's anonymity.

Tor. The web server can then identify which webpages were sent to which users by matching the cookies with the Flash connections. In other words, all Tor users who use HTTP through that exit node while Flash is enabled will have their HTTP traffic associated with their respective IP addresses. However, if we assume that the number of malicious Tor servers is small compared to the total number of Tor servers, a normal user will get a malicious exit node only once in a while. As a result, this attack only works to associate traffic with the particular user for the length of time that the user keeps the same Tor circuit, or at most ten minutes by default.

3.2 Finding Hidden Servers

Along with hiding the locations of clients, Tor also supports location-hidden servers, where the clients of a service (for example, visitors to a website) are not able to identify the machine hosting the service. To connect to a hidden server, a client sends a message through an introduction point that is advertised as being associated with the hidden service by the Tor directory. A clever anonymous interaction results in the hidden client and hidden server both opening Tor connections to a rendezvous point (chosen by the client). The rendezvous point patches the connections together to form an anonymous channel between the hidden client and hidden server.

In May 2006, L. Øverlier and P. Syverson [12] described an attack to locate hidden servers in Tor. The attacker begins by inserting a malicious Tor node into the Tor network and using a Tor client to repeatedly connect to the targeted hidden server, sending a distinctive signal over each Tor connection. Since the

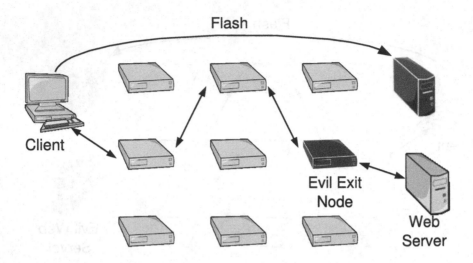

Fig. 3. Prior work: a browser attack executed by an exit node. The client's web browser executes a Flash program inserted into a webpage by the exit node, which opens a direct connection to a logger machine.

hidden server cannot distinguish this from a wave of legitimate clients, each connection forces the hidden server to construct a new Tor circuit. The attacker can do traffic analysis to determine when his Tor node is in the hidden server's rendezvous circuit. He can then identify the hidden server by using a predecessor attack [18].

The paper states that their attack should apply to other clients using an anonymity network, but gives no details for how to do so. In particular, the attack does not immediately apply to clients because they don't make new circuits on demand. The attack relied on requesting a large number of new connections with a hidden server, which is not easy to do with a hidden client.

4   A Browser-Based Timing Attack

We describe a new attack that combines and builds upon the attacks discussed in Section 3. The attack, shown in Figure 4, attempts to discover a Tor client without using invasive plugins like Java or Flash but with JavaScript instead. JavaScript alone is not powerful enough to discover the client's IP address, but combined with a timing attack similar to the one presented by Øverlier and Syverson [12], an adversary has a non-trivial chance of discovering a client in a reasonable amount of time. In Section 4.2 we discuss how to implement this attack using only the HTML meta refresh tag, but the JavaScript version is simpler so we discuss it first. This attack is partially mitigated by *entry guards*, which has become a standard feature of Tor. For clarity, we will defer discussion of the role of entry guards until Section 4.7, after we have explained the basic plan of attack.

4.1   The Attack

Like the FortConsult Security attack [2], our attack uses a malicious Tor exit node that modifies HTTP traffic passing through it, inserting an invisible iframe containing JavaScript into requested webpages. The JavaScript repeatedly contacts a malicious web server, posting a unique ID. This JavaScript continues to run as long as the client leaves the "bugged" browser tab open. The complete attack is as follows:

1. The attacker first sets up the necessary resources.
   (a) The attacker inserts two malicious nodes into the Tor network: one to act as an entry node, and the other to act as an exit node.
   (b) The attacker sets up a web server that receives and logs JavaScript connections.
2. The malicious exit node modifies all HTTP traffic destined for Tor clients to include an invisible JavaScript signal generator that generates a unique signal for each Tor client.
3. The Tor client's web browser executes the JavaScript code, sending a distinctive signal to the web server. This traffic passes through the Tor circuit, and the client is still anonymous.
4. Approximately every ten minutes, the Tor client chooses a new circuit. Eventually, an unlucky Tor client picks and uses the malicious entry node.
5. The attacker performs traffic analysis to compare the signals on each circuit passing through his entry node with the various signals received by the web server. A match reveals the Tor client's identity and its corresponding traffic history during the time it used the malicious exit node.

The entry node only needs to log the traffic pattern that passes through it on each circuit, and the exit node only needs to perform the code injections in the HTTP traffic. Although for clarity we described the attack with multiple machines, the malicious Tor nodes and the web server can all be implemented on the same machine. If the user is browsing the web while using the malicious entry node, the traffic analysis can be difficult because the additional traffic introduces "noise" to the signal. However, if the user stops browsing the web, the channel contains little "noise" and the traffic analysis is easy. A method for simplifying the timing attack even if the user does continue browsing the web is discussed in Section 4.4.

For most traffic analysis attacks, the attacker must control both the exit node and entry node at the same time. For our attack, if a client leaves a browser window open running the JavaScript signal generator, and at any later point chooses a malicious entry node, then the timing attack can reveal his identity. Since this only requires the right choice of an entry node, the probability that the client is compromised each time he chooses a new circuit is roughly $\frac{1}{n_e}$, where n_e is the number of available entry nodes. If the attacker had to get control of both the entry and exit nodes at the same time, the probability would then be $\frac{1}{n_e n_x}$, where n_x is the number of available exit nodes. The signal generator allows us to decouple the need to control an exit node and an entry node at the same time,

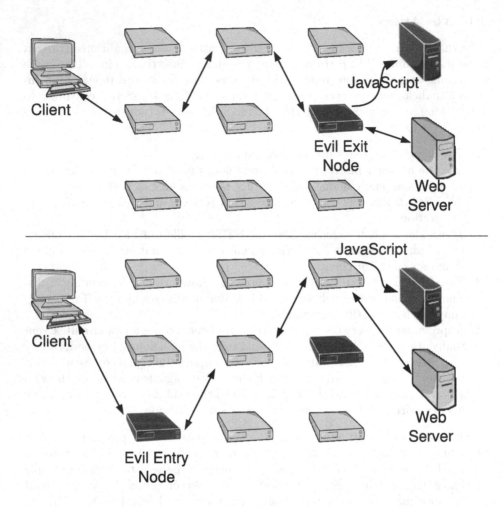

Fig. 4. Our new attack. A malicious exit node modifies webpages, inserting JavaScript code that repeatedly connects to a logger server, sending a distinctive signal along the link (top). If the client then uses a malicious entry node while that JavaScript is still executing, the entry node can detect the signal, and the attacker can thus associate the client with his communications (bottom).

decreasing the expected time to compromise the client. As with any such traffic analysis attack, the adversary can further decrease the time the attack takes by increasing the number of malicious Tor entry nodes [16].

4.2   A Browser-Based Timing Attack Using Only HTML

The attack we just described relies on the victim having JavaScript enabled. This requirement is unnecessary. The same attack can be implemented by using the HTML meta refresh tag. In this version of the attack, the webpage is modified such that it will automatically be refreshed by the web browser after a period of time. The attacker generates the desired traffic signal by dynamically varying the refresh delays or the page size each time the webpage is refreshed.

The HTML meta refresh version of the attack is more conspicuous than the JavaScript version because browsers generally indicate when they are reloading a webpage but not when executing JavaScript XMLHttpRequests. Thus, it is easier for the user to observe the meta refresh version of the attack than the JavaScript one. This could be mitigated by only performing this attack on sites that already have a meta-refresh tag. Even on pages that would not normally have the tag, the HTML meta refresh attack could be made less obvious if the first refresh happens with a large delay, when the user is less likely to be still in front of his computer. After an initial delay of a few hours, subsequent refreshes could happen every few seconds to generate the signal for a timing attack.

4.3 Torbutton

Torbutton is a simple Firefox extension that allows a user to toggle whether their web browser is using the Tor proxy with a single click. This convenient interface makes it possible for users who are frustrated with Tor's slow speed to turn Tor off while browsing websites that they do not feel requires anonymity. It is a popular extension, with more than 251,000 downloads as of February 22, 2007 [19]. Since this number only counts downloads of Torbutton from the official website, it underestimates the number of Torbutton users.

As shown in Figure 5, if a user toggles the Tor proxy off using Torbutton but leaves a tab open with one of our JavaScript signal generators, then he will be discovered the next time the signal generator contacts the adversary's server. In practice, this relatively simple attack is effective at but limited to discovering Tor clients who stop using the Tor proxy while the browser is still open. Torbutton makes it easy for users to be careless in this way.

Torbutton could easily be modified such that when the user chooses to stop using Tor, all JavaScript and automatically reloading webpages are stopped before changing the proxy settings. This may inconvenience the user if he is using sites that heavily depend on JavaScript, but it will protect the user from discovery. A Tor user who wants to browse the web both with and without Tor could also choose to either completely close his browser between uses or use two completely separate browsers for anonymous and nonanonymous communications.

4.4 Tor Exit Policies

Our attack works by adding traffic to a Tor circuit so that a Tor node can identify whether it is, in fact, the entry node of the Tor circuit. If the Tor circuit is carrying no other traffic, this detection is fairly easy—the entry node knows exactly what traffic pattern to look for. On the other hand, a Tor circuit full of unrelated traffic is hard to test for presence of a signal because the entry node does not know what other traffic to expect. For this reason, it is easier to identify a victim during a break than during active browsing. In this section we present

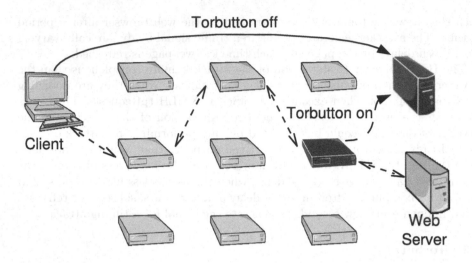

Fig. 5. Our Torbutton attack. A malicious exit node modifies webpages, inserting JavaScript code that repeatedly connects to a logger server, sending an ID number (seen above in dashed lines). If the client later configures their browser to stop using Tor while that JavaScript is still executing, he will connect directly to the logger server.

a novel method of using exit policies to create a clean circuit dedicated to the identifying signal.

A common concern among Tor server operators is the issue of abuse: Tor can be used to anonymously send spam or viruses as well as to anonymously browse the web. In order to make it more attractive to run a Tor server, Tor's protocol dictates that each server advertises an *exit policy* that specifies which (IP address, port) pairs the server is willing to exit traffic to. Because few server operators are willing to exit spam or viruses, there are certain ports that almost every Tor server refuses to exit, as shown in Figure 6.

Port	Number of Exit Nodes	Port	Number of Exit Nodes
22	211	25	4
53	216	119	25
80	226	135–139	6
110	210	445	6
143	208	465	12
443	238	587	13
5190	184	1214	7
6667	172	4661–4666	5
		6699	9

Fig. 6. Number of Tor servers exiting various ports as of December 15, 2006

4.5 Using Tor Exit Policies to Simplify the Timing Attack

Suppose that the signal generator connects to a malicious server over an unpopular port. Most web browsers will refuse to connect to some of the unpopular ports. For example, Mozilla Firefox resists connecting to the SMTP port 25 but not the filesharing ports 4661 through 4666. If the signal generator connects over an unpopular port, the client's existing circuits probably do not have an exit node willing to serve the signal generator's traffic. This likely forces the Tor client to open a new circuit for the signal generator's traffic. In fact, the Tor algorithm for routing traffic over circuits prefers older circuits, so for several minutes, other traffic may use a different circuit than the signal generator's traffic, even if the new exit node is willing to exit other traffic. An attacker can improve the odds that the attack traffic will have a dedicated circuit by inserting exit nodes into the network that will only exit unpopular ports. As we have remarked before, having a dedicated circuit simplifies the traffic analysis substantially.

The Tor exit policy can also be used to decrease the time required for the attack. Suppose that there were zero nodes willing to exit k different ports. Then the attacker could insert k different servers into the Tor network, each of which only exits on one of the k ports. A signal generator that tried to connect on all k ports would force the Tor client to create k new circuits, each dedicated to the signal generator's traffic. Hence the client would have k different entry nodes at a time, rather than only one. This would speed up the attack by a factor of k.

In reality, there are no ports that have zero Tor nodes willing to exit on them, so one would expect a smaller speed increase. Some ports do come close; only five nodes offer ports 4661 through 4666, and at times only one or two of those are operating. If an attacker performed a denial of service attack on these nodes, he could create a situation where these ports do have zero Tor nodes willing to exit on them, and obtain the full factor of six.

Experiments showed that Tor's algorithm was slow to open a circuit to these unpopular ports. It often took several minutes to make a circuit, which can cause browser timeouts in connecting. While this wouldn't be a problem with the JavaScript version of the attack, this error would cause the HTML meta refresh version to fail sometimes.

We believe that this is the first reported method for exploiting the Tor exit policy system in an attack. A reasonable solution to this vulnerability would be to have a client-side exit policy. A client would only send data into Tor destined for selected ports—requests to send data on other ports would be refused. This exit policy should default to only allowing the client to send data via Tor that is destined for popular ports.

4.6 Using TCP Streams to Simplify the Timing Attack

Tor stops sending new connections through a circuit after the first 10 minutes of using the circuit. However, it does not close a circuit until there are no longer any open TCP sessions on the circuit. Thus, an attacker can hold a circuit open for more than 10 minutes by maintaining an open TCP stream on the circuit. After the first 10 minutes have passed, the attacker can start sending a unique signal to the client using that TCP connection. Unless there are other lingering TCP connections on the circuit, the attacker's traffic will now be the only traffic in that direction on the Tor circuit, allowing the attacker to detect the signal using simple traffic analysis techniques.

A defense against this attack is to forcibly close all TCP connections on a circuit after the 10 minutes are up. However, this is perhaps impractical for a couple of reasons. First, if a client is trying to download something that will take more than 10 minutes, the download will always fail. Second, various web applications utilize a perpetually open TCP connection in order to push changes to a webpage (avoiding the delays associated with polling). Killing TCP connections when the circuit becomes stale could prove annoying to users.

An attacker that intentionally keeps a TCP connection open for an extended period of time is difficult to distinguish from the applications that are broken by the defense we just described. We know of no effective way to defend against this version of the attack without losing functionality.

4.7   Entry Guards

Our attack relies on the assumption that eventually, one of the malicious Tor routers will act as the entry node for a client. Since many attacks rely on this assumption, Wright et al. [17] and later Øverlier and Syverson [12] proposed selecting the entry nodes from a small subset of Tor nodes called *entry guards*. This feature is now standard in Tor [20]. By default, each Tor client chooses 3 random Tor nodes to be its entry guards. Thus if none of the entry guards are malicious, the client will never have a malicious entry node. If one or more of them is malicious, the client can be compromised much more quickly than if this feature were not used. Without entry guards, however, our attack would eventually expose all clients if there were even one malicious entry node in the entire Tor network.

Rather than selecting random entry guards, the user can choose a specific set of trusted nodes. This has benefits and drawbacks, which Øverlier and Syverson [12] discuss in detail. We suspect that most users will use the default random choices, so we will assume that henceforth.

One interesting feature of using entry guards is that a timing attack that would find the hidden client will instead find the entry guards. After the attacker identifies the entry guards that a targeted victim is using, he can attempt to execute a denial of service attack against those Tor servers in order to cause the victim to fall back to different entry nodes that the attacker might control.

Entry guards change the probability distribution so that the probability that a malicious server will ever be an entry node for a particular client is $O(\frac{3}{n})$, where n is the number of possible entry nodes in the network. On the other hand, those clients who are unlucky enough to select a malicious router as one of their entry guards will more quickly be discovered. If, for example, the attack targets the visitors of a particular website, the attack will affect up to an expected $\frac{3}{n}$

of the visitors. The use of entry guards then serves to speed up the attack on that fraction of that population. If we take today's numbers into account, n is around 700, one Tor node will be an entry guard for around 0.4% of a targeted population. Adding more malicious Tor nodes to the network is easy and would increase that proportion roughly linearly.

5 Methods

We developed a prototype implementation of this attack, expanding on the techniques discussed in the FortConsult Security paper [2]. FortConsult Security's attack used Linux's iptables filtering to modify the payloads of TCP packets at the exit node. This was a convenient mechanism because it did not require modifications to the Tor source code itself. However, it resulted in a restriction on their attack: they could not change the number of bytes in any TCP packet, because TCP sequence numbers are a byte count. Thus their insertions into the webpages also required overwriting some part of those webpages. We sidestepped this issue by changing webpages at the HTTP level.

Our implementation also uses iptables, but only to redirect Tor's outgoing HTTP requests to a local port. Transproxy, a transparent proxy daemon, binds to this port and adds the appropriate headers to the requests so that a regular HTTP proxy works properly. The requests proceed through a proxy built on the Twisted Python libraries that modify every webpage to insert an iframe. This iframe downloads, from the adversary's web server, a page that contains a simple (25 line) JavaScript program that connects with this server. The size and frequency of these connections can be dynamically modified by the adversary's server in order to produce a distinctive signal.

Because the connections are to a URL containing the unique identifier, the server can ensure that each JavaScript instance sends a unique signal associated with its identifier. This allows the entry node to identify the client that downloaded a specific webpage, rather than one of the clients that downloaded any of the webpages with inserted signal generators. Not only can the attacker attribute the one webpage to this client, but he also knows that client was responsible for all the other traffic sent over its circuit ID at the time that it downloaded the bugged webpage.

When setting up a number of exit nodes to exit ports 4661-4666, we were able to put them all on one machine simply by configuring each Tor instance to use and advertise a different port and IP address. Upcoming Tor releases will not use two routers from the same Class B subnet on a single path, as a weak defense against the Sybil attack [6]. For our attack, the adversary can simply run two computers on different Class B networks, one running a large number of entry nodes, and the other running many exit nodes. Since Tor clients can choose any pair of routers from different subnets, the changes of selecting both entry node and exit node from the adversary's set will still be quadratic in the number of fake routers being used. Since colocation is easily available commercially, we do not believe that this new feature will present an effective defense against a determined attacker with limited resources.

Our experimental entry node required minor modifications of the Tor source to increase logging, most of which were used in Øverlier and Syverson [12]. We tried a Fourier transform to identify circuits with the signal, but could not find a strong enough signal (past the noise of legitimate web traffic) to identify them if they were browsing the web. We then implemented a much simpler recognition system that could find users when their circuit was only carrying attack traffic.

6   Defenses Against Browser-Based Attacks

We have considered a few defenses against these browser-based attacks.

6.1   Disabling Active Content Systems

The most obvious defense against these browser-based attacks is to disable all active content systems, such as Java, Flash, ActiveX Controls, and JavaScript in the browser. The disadvantage of this defense, however, is that disabling the active content systems would preclude the use of many popular web services in the process. Our HTML-only attack using the meta refresh tag also shows that this only exacerbates the problem since it can't be turned off without significant modification to a web browser.

6.2   HTTPS

Modifying a website at the exit node is a man-in-the-middle attack on HTTP. Because HTTPS is secure against man-in-the-middle attacks (assuming that the user has a chain of trust to the website), tunneling HTTP over SSL prevents a malicious exit node from either reading or modifying the data it is transporting.

In practice, this defense is less effective than it might seem, because users will often accept self-signed certificates as valid despite the browser warning. A malicious exit node could thus trick careless users by replacing webpages with malicious versions that are also signed, but with forged certificates.

Using HTTPS provides reasonable security against this attack so long as the client can trust the servers serving the sites he visits and correctly verifies certificates. If the server is not trustworthy, it can include the malicious JavaScript attack code in the website itself, and sign it with a valid SSL certificate. Using the methods we have described, the server could then identify its visitors.

Unfortunately, this defense is not something a Tor client can implement unilaterally; every website that he visits must allow the client to do so. Many sites do not allow a user to communicate with them in a secure fashion; for example, `https://www.google.com` currently (May 2007) redirects to `http://www.google.com`. Using SSL for all web traffic also has performance concerns, which is perhaps the reason why many sites do not support it.

7   Analysis and Results

Let us estimate the probability that our attack will be successful. Suppose that Tor uses k entry guards in a network of n nodes, m of which exit port 80. In our basic attack, the client uses one circuit at a time that changes every ten minutes. Further suppose that the attacker inserts u evil nodes in the network, of which v are exit nodes that modify HTTP traffic. The v exit nodes can be noticed by Tor users, but the other $u - v$ servers only log data, and give no indication of malice. Assume that all Tor nodes are equal—an unrealistic assumption, since some Tor nodes have much better bandwidth than others, but not that relevant if the attacker has average bandwidth. At the moment, the Tor network has $k = 3, n = 700, m = 200$. Setting up an attack with $u = 1$ and $v = 1$ is fairly easy to accomplish, so we will use these values to approximate. We will also assume $n \gg k, u, v$.

Then $\frac{v}{m} \approx 0.5\%$ of all Tor circuits will insert signal generators into webpages, and approximately $\frac{ku}{n} \approx 0.4\%$ of all Tor clients will choose an evil server for an entry guard. Any given bugged page will use one entry guard every ten minutes, so for any Tor user that has an evil entry guard the chance of being discovered in any ten-minute interval is $\frac{1}{k} \approx 33\%$, and the probability of remaining anonymous over time is approximately the exponential distribution $P(t) \approx \left(\frac{k-1}{k}\right)^{t/10 \text{ min}} \approx 0.66^{t/10 \text{ min}}$.

This means that a Tor user has a 0.4% chance of ever being vulnerable to the attack. Every 10-minute interval during which a vulnerable user leaves a webpage open, he has a 0.5% chance of leaving a signal generator running. If he leaves a bugged page open over an hour-long lunch break, he has a 92% chance of having this signal generator go through an evil entry node. At this point, the adversary can associate the user with all the browsing that he did the circuit that he used to download the signal generator. If he leaves a bugged page open for eight hours of sleep, there is a negligible chance he will not be identified.

The probabilities that users are vulnerable or that they will receive a signal generator are low, but this is under the assumption that the attacker only controls a single Tor node. These probabilities are roughly linear in the number of Tor nodes the attacker runs, so he can amplify his probability of success by running several Tor nodes.

The attacker can decide whether to insert a signal generator into websites based on what other websites the potential victim has visited through the same Tor circuit. This allows a malicious exit node to masquerade as an honest machine to most users, a measure which would help the adversary prevent his exit node from becoming discovered as malicious.

8 Conclusion

Current web design presents fundamental problems for maintaining anonymity while browsing the web. Low latency anonymizing systems cannot easily protect their users from end-to-end traffic analysis. Our attack exploits the web browser code execution environment to perform end-to-end traffic analysis attacks without requiring the attacker to control either party to the target communication.

There are two security problems that our attack exploits: HTTP's vulnerability to man-in-the-middle attacks and web browsers' code execution feature. Tor places the exit node as a man-in-the-middle of clients' communications. Thus, using Tor may actually decrease the anonymity of users by making them vulnerable to man-in-the-middle attacks from adversaries that would otherwise be unable to perform such attacks.

Also fundamental to our attack is the fact that web browsers execute (potentially malicious) code within an imperfect sandbox. This code execution allows for arbitrary communication back to the HTTP server. Such communication can include sending network traffic in a pattern designed to be detected by an external observer using traffic analysis. This danger is particularly important when we consider that recent advances in the web are centered around the use of complex programs executed by the web browser. Even if users are willing to disable these technologies, we have shown that mere HTML (through its meta refresh tag) is a powerful enough language to attack the anonymity of Tor users.

Given the current design of the web, neither of these problems can be readily addressed without sacrificing substantial functionality.

Acknowledgements

We thank Lasse Øverlier for sharing his hidden servers timing attack code with us. We also thank Roger Dingledine, Paul Syverson, Frans Kaashoek, and the anonymous reviewers for their helpful suggestions.

References

1. Chaum, D.: Untraceable electronic mail, return addresses, and digital pseudonyms. Communications of the ACM 24(2) (February 1981)
2. Christensen, A., et al.: Practical Onion Hacking: Find the real address of Tor clients. FortConsult (October 2006),
   http://www.fortconsult.net/images/pdf/Practical_Onion_Hacking.pdf
3. Clark, D.: Design Philosophy of the DARPA Internet Protocols. In: Proceedings of the ACM Special Interest Group on Data Communications, pp. 106–114. ACM Press, New York (1988)
4. Dingledine, R.: Tor: anonymity (November 2006), http://tor.eff.org/
5. Dingledine, R., Mathewson, N., Syverson, P.: Tor: The Second-Generation Onion Router. In: Proceedings of the 13th USENIX Security Symposium (August 2004)
6. Douceur, J.: The Sybil Attack. In: Druschel, P., Kaashoek, M.F., Rowstron, A. (eds.) IPTPS 2002. LNCS, vol. 2429, Springer, Heidelberg (2002)
7. Hintz, A.: Fingerprinting Websites Using Traffic Analysis. In: Dingledine, R., Syverson, P.F. (eds.) PET 2002. LNCS, vol. 2482, pp. 229–233. Springer, Heidelberg (2003)
8. Levine, B.N., Reiter, M., Wang, C., Wright, M.: Timing Attacks in Low-Latency Mix Systems (extended abstract). In: Juels, A. (ed.) FC 2004. LNCS, vol. 3110, pp. 251–265. Springer, Heidelberg (2004)
9. Liberatore, M., Levine, B.N.: Inferring the source of encrypted HTTP connections. In: Proceedings of the 13th ACM conference on Computer and communications security, ACM Press, New York (2006)

10. Martin, K.: AOL search data identified individuals. SecurityFocus (August 2006), http://www.securityfocus.com/brief/277
11. Murdoch, S.J., Danezis, G.: Low-Cost Traffic Analysis of Tor. In: Proceedings of the 2005 IEEE Symposium on Security and Privacy (May 2005)
12. Øverlier, L., Syverson, P.: Locating Hidden Servers. In: Proceedings of the 2006 IEEE Symposium on Security and Privacy (May 2006)
13. Raymond, J.: Traffic Analysis: Protocols, Attacks, Design Issues, and Open Problems. In: Federrath, H. (ed.) Designing Privacy Enhancing Technologies. LNCS, vol. 2009, pp. 10–29. Springer, Heidelberg (2001)
14. Serjantov, A., Sewell, P.: Passive Attack Analysis for Connection-Based Anonymity Systems. In: Snekkenes, E., Gollmann, D. (eds.) ESORICS 2003. LNCS, vol. 2808, pp. 116–131. Springer, Heidelberg (2003)
15. Syverson, P., Tsudik, G., Reed, M., Landwehr, C.: Towards an Analysis of Onion Routing Security. In: Federrath, H. (ed.) Designing Privacy Enhancing Technologies. LNCS, vol. 2009, pp. 96–114. Springer, Heidelberg (2001)
16. Wright, M., Adler, M., Levine, B.N., Shields, C.: An Analysis of the Degradation of Anonymous Protocols. In: Proceedings of the ISOC Network and Distributed System Security Symposium (NDSS), pp. 38–50 (February 2002)
17. Wright, M., Adler, M., Levine, B.N., Shields, C.: Defending Anonymous Communication Against Passive Logging Attacks. In: Proceedings of the 2003 IEEE Symposium on Security and Privacy (May 2003)
18. Wright, M., Adler, M., Levine, B.N., Shields, C.: The predecessor attack: An analysis of a threat to anonymous communications systems. In: ACM Trans. Inf. Syst. Secur., pp. 489–522 (2004)
19. Squires, S.: Firefox Add-ons: Torbutton (February 2007), https://addons.mozilla.org/firefox/2275/
20. TheOnionRouter/TorFAQ (November 2006), http://wiki.noreply.org/noreply/TheOnionRouter/TorFAQ

Enforcing P3P Policies Using a Digital Rights Management System

Farzad Salim, Nicholas Paul Sheppard, and Rei Safavi-Naini

[1] School of Computer Science and Software Engineering,
University of Wollongong, NSW 2522, Australia
fsalim,nps@uow.edu.au
[2] Department of Computer Science, University of Calgary,
2500 University Drive, NW, Calgary T2N IN4, Canada
rei@cpsc.ucalgary.ca

Abstract. The protection of privacy has gained considerable attention recently. In response to this, new privacy protection systems are being introduced. SITDRM is one such system that protects private data through the enforcement of licenses provided by consumers. Prior to supplying data, data owners are expected to construct a detailed license for the potential data users. A license specifies whom, under what conditions, may have what type of access to the protected data.

The specification of a license by a data owner binds the enterprise data handling to the consumer's privacy preferences. However, licenses are very detailed, may reveal the internal structure of the enterprise and need to be kept synchronous with the enterprise privacy policy. To deal with this, we employ the Platform for Privacy Preferences Language (P3P) to communicate enterprise privacy policies to consumers and enable them to easily construct data licenses. A P3P policy is more abstract than a license, allows data owners to specify the purposes for which data are being collected and directly reflects the privacy policy of an enterprise.

1 Introduction

Information privacy is regarded as the right of individuals to determine for themselves when, how, and to what extent information about them is communicated to others. The concern about information privacy is growing for consumers who may need to release their personal data to enterprises in exchange for a service. In response to this concern, enterprises publish a *privacy policy* that is a representation of different legal regulations, promises made to data owners, as well as more restrictive internal practices of the enterprise.

Traditionally, privacy policies were written in natural languages. However, informal privacy policies inherit the potential ambiguity and mis-interpretation of natural text [16]. This raises two problems, first, such policies are difficult for consumers to read and understand, and second, controlling the enterprise data practices using such policies is impractical.

To address the first problem, the World Wide Web Consortium has proposed a standard policy language, the Platform for Privacy Preferences (P3P), to enable

N. Borisov and P. Golle (Eds.): PET 2007, LNCS 4776, pp. 200–217, 2007.

enterprises to construct machine-readable privacy policies [6]. P3P policies can be read, summarized and matched against users' privacy preferences by P3P-enabled browser software (*P3P agents*). Therefore, data owners can be prompted on exactly what data is collected, for what purposes this data is to be used and how long it is retained. Background information about the P3P language is provided in Section 2.4.

Although enterprises who have posted P3P policies promise specific data usage, they still require internal mechanisms to enforce those promises. In other words, publishing a P3P policy does not provide any technical guarantee that enterprises act according to their policies once they have obtained user's personal data. To address this problem, privacy protection systems such as *E-P3P* [10], *Tivoli* [3] and *SITDRM* [15] are emerging.

Tivoli, being the commercial version of *E-P3P*, is a privacy protection framework that extends traditional access control systems by adapting a privacy oriented language known as *EPAL* [12]. The language provides a syntax that allows a *policy auditor*[2] to specify privacy rules. In addition, *EPAL* has operational semantics that govern the interpretation of the rules with respect to an access request. Hence, an authorization decision can be made when a data user requests to access a private data.

SITDRM uses another approach to the privacy enforcement problem. It adopts the extended Digital Rights Management (DRM) model that was proposed by Korba et al. [11] and implemented by Sheppard et al. [15]. The core concept in SITDRM is the use of licenses that are formulated by consumers and enforced by a digital rights management system. A license is a digital data file that specifies usage rules for the collected data. A rule may specify a range of criteria, such as the person to whom the right is issued, the frequency of access, license expiry date, restriction of transfer to other devices, etc. Hence, such licenses can express the notions of privacy policies (e.g., obligations or conditions, etc.) under which the data must be used, or the type of actions that can be performed on the collected data. We will give an outline of the relevant components of SITDRM in Section 2.3.

Whilst the SITDRM approach binds the enterprise data handling to the privacy promises made to customers, it has some limitations that we would like to address in this work. First, data subjects in SITDRM are obliged to construct an MPEG REL license. However, this task cannot be handled by an average customer because MPEG REL has a complex syntax and semantics and was designed to be used by policy auditors for specifying concrete access control rules.

Further, to create an MPEG REL license, the consumer must have knowledge of the identity of the user (or role) that the license is to be issued to. SITDRM currently assumes consumers are provided with such information. However, for many real world scenarios this is not practical as such knowledge about the

---

[1] Smart Internet Technology Digital Rights Management.

[2] The policy auditor is a person responsible for writing enterprise privacy policies. In the legal context, this person is referred to as the Chief Privacy Officer (CPO).

roles/employees may reveal the internal structure and data flow of the enterprise. For example, a bank customer would be able to know who in the bank has access to customer's account balances.

In addition, SITDRM needs to handle the dynamicity of the organization's structure. The roles/users within an enterprise change more frequently than the purposes for which the data is being collected. Currently, customers are obliged to provide a new license each time the roles/users (license holders) change.

Finally, SITDRM requires a systematic approach for creating templates for collecting privacy preferences. Currently it assumes that there exists a human user (privacy officer) who is aware of the enterprise privacy policy and can construct license templates. These templates are then used by customers to create a concrete MPEG REL license. However, in an enterprise which may collect data at more than one point with different privacy rules the maintenance and synchronization of the policies with these templates becomes impractical.

To address the above, we extend SITDRM by employing P3P to allow consumers to modify a subset of an enterprise P3P policy for expressing their privacy preferences. P3P preferences are more abstract than a license and allow data owners to specify the purposes for which data is to be collected. Hence, they do not need to know concrete roles, rights or access conditions. Further, P3P preferences reveal less information regarding the enterprise's internal structure and eliminate the need for their re-issuing, when an internal role changes and the purpose remains the same.

Despite these advantages, P3P preferences are not directly enforceable, so they need to be transformed into MPEG REL licenses that can be enforced by SITDRM. In this paper we outline the difficulty of such a translation and propose a practical approach for mapping a P3P statement to an MPEG REL grant.

We have also extended SITDRM's design and implementation by adding two new components, the *P3P Agent* and the *Mapping Console*. The P3P agent provides a systematic approach for collecting an organization's P3P policy and constructing a P3P preference template for data owner's to customize and express their privacy preferences. The mapping console assists CPOs in specifying the mapping rules for constructing MPEG REL licenses.

The rest of this paper is organized as follows: In Section 2 we will provide the necessary background. In Section 3 we will show the architecture of our new P3P-Enabled SITDRM. Section 4 will describe the necessary mapping rules for transforming P3P preferences into an MPEG REL license. Section 5 will discuss how we can systematically automate a preference form from an enterprise's (P3P) privacy policy. We conclude the paper with an a discussion of outstanding issues and conclusions in Sections 6 and 7.

2   Preliminaries

This section will briefly describe the Digital Right Managements (DRM) model for data protection, some components of SITDRM, MPEG REL and the P3P language. Interested readers may refer to [15,6,2] for further details.

2.1 DRM

Digital rights management provides protection for information by making access to information depend on satisfying the conditions imposed by a *license* written in a machine-enforceable *rights expression language*. DRM technology is widely used in copyright protection applications, but can also be applied to privacy protection [11,15] by developing licenses that represent individual's preferences for use of their personal information.

2.2 MPEG-21

The MPEG-21 Framework [2] is a framework for creating, distributing, using and controlling multimedia content currently under development by the Motion Picture Experts Group (MPEG). Of particular interest to us are three components in the MPEG-21 framework: *Digital Items (DI), Intellectual Property Management and Protection (IPMP)* and the *Rights Expression Language (REL)*.

Digital Items. The core notion in MPEG-21 is a digital item [2], which represents a collection of multimedia objects. Digital items are described using the XML-based digital item declaration language (DIDL), which organizes content and meta-data. For the purposes of this paper we consider digital items to be the encapsulation of private data that needs to be protected.

Intellectual Property Management and Protection. Intellectual Property Management and Protection is MPEG's term for digital rights management [2]. MPEG-21 does not define a digital rights management system, but assumes that IPMP functionality is provided by vendor-specific IPMP tools that can be downloaded and made accessible to the terminal as necessary. IPMP tools may implement basic functions such as decryption and watermarking, or may implement complete digital rights management systems in their own right.

Rights Expression Language. Though MPEG-21 does not define a full digital rights management system, it does define a rights expression language known as MPEG REL [2] for creating machine-readable licenses. An MPEG REL license is structured as a collection of *grants* issued by some *license issuer*. Each grant awards some *right* over some specified *resource* to some specified *principal*, that is, user of a resource. Each grant may be subject to a *condition*, such that the right contained in the grant cannot be exercised unless the condition is satisfied.

In order to perform some action on a resource, a user (principal) must possess a license containing a grant that awards the right to perform that action on that resource, and satisfy the associated condition. This must be checked by the terminal prior to exercising the right.

MPEG REL is defined as a collection of three XML schemas, called the core schema (denoted by the XML namespace prefix r in this paper), the standard extension schema (prefix sx) and the multimedia extension schema (prefix mx). In addition, the authors in [15] introduced a *privacy extention schema* with prefix px for use in the proposed privacy protection system (SITDRM). Figure 3 shows an example of an MPEG REL grant allowing a principal (r:keyHolder) identified by his/her public key to print a resource (mx:diReference) identified by a digital item identifier (smartinternet:doc1). The principal is only permitted to print the resource once (sx:ExerciseLimit).

```
<r:grant>
  <r:keyHolder>
     <dsig:KeyValue> ... </dsig:KeyValue>
  </r:keyHolder>
  <mx:print/>
  <mx:diReference>
    <mx:identifier> smartinternet:doc1 </mx:identifier>
  </mx:diReference>
  <sx:ExerciseLimit>
    <sx:count> 1 </sx:count>
  </sx:ExerciseLimit>
<r:grant>
```

Fig. 1. A License

2.3 SITDRM

SITDRM is an implementation of MPEG-21 IPMP for privacy protection. It provides a framework within which content providers can control the use and distribution of personal data (content) through the enforcement of data licenses. In SITDRM each resource that is protected by an IPMP tool is referred to as a *governed* resource. Each governed resource is associated with a plain text identifier and an IPMP information descriptor that associates the resource with a license and describes the IPMP tools required to access the resource. If the conditions of the license are satisfied, the terminal must obtain and instantiate the IPMP tools in order to access the resource.

Figure 2 shows an overview of the SITDRM system, where a data controller (e.g., bank) requires information to be collected from data subjects (e.g., customers). All of this information is stored in some central database. In addition, there are some data users (e.g., employees) that require access to the information in order to carry out their jobs and provide service to the customers.

Customers submit their information via a form on the bank's web site. For example, a document containing the customer's credit card number and postal address are formatted as an XML document. At the same time, customers design an MPEG REL license that describes how this information may be used.

Upon submitting the form, the customer's web browser converts the resulting XML document into the governed resource of an MPEG-21 digital item, and issues a license designed by the customer. The governed item and issued license are then transmitted to the data controller for storage.

Employees who require access to a customer's data may download the governed item from the data controller. Upon attempting to perform some action on the item, the employee's terminal asks the data controller for a license that

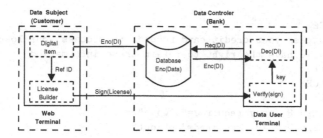

Fig. 2. SITDRM Architecture

authorizes this action. If an appropriate license is found, the action is permitted to continue. Otherwise, the action is rejected.

2.4   P3P

P3P [6] is a standard developed by the W3 Consortium for assisting web users to discover and evaluate the privacy policies of on-line service providers. P3P consists of an XML-based *language* for expressing the privacy policies of service providers, and a *protocol* for associating a P3P policy to collected data and locating the privacy policy file relevant to any particular data collection action. A P3P policy file is composed of a sequence of *statements*, each containing five elements described below. Figure 3 shows a typical statement in a P3P policy.

– a *purpose* for which this data will be used;
– a *recipient* to whom this data may be communicated;
– a *retention* policy according to which the data will be discarded;
– a *data group* of the data to which this statement applies; and
– a *consequence*, being an informal reasoning behind the collection of this data.

Despite many advantages of the P3P language such as providing a standard way of communicating privacy policies to users and allowing for the automation of matching privacy preferences and privacy policies [6,1,9], the language is subject to some criticisms. First, P3P policies are subject to multiple interpretations and different software agents that read them may arrive at different conclusions for the same policy [17]. Second, privacy polices are offered on a take-it-or-leave-it basis by the service provider, and may not reflect the actual desires of users [4]. Third, the policies given in a P3P policy are not automatically enforced [5], requiring dissatisfied data subjects to resort to legal action.

Yu, et al. [17], address the first problem by proposing relational formal semantics for P3P and introducing some integrity constraints. Namely they introduce two types of semantics by which P3P statements can be interpreted, *data-centric* and *purpose-centric* semantics. The term semantics in this context refers to the relationships among the four major components (purpose, recipient, retention and data) of a P3P statement.

```
<STATEMENT>
  <CONSEQUENCE>
    We will access your credit card records to process your loan
    requests. We have the right to retain these information
    for a year.
  </CONSEQUENCE>
  <DATA-GROUP>
    <Credit-Card-History required="always"/>
    <Credit-Card-Number  required="opt-out"/>
  </DATA-GROUP>
  <PURPOSE>
     <loan required="opt-out">Loan and Finance</loan>
  </PURPOSE>
  <RETENTION>  <one-year />  </RETENTION>
  <RECIPIENT>  <ours />      </RECIPIENT>
</STATEMENT>
```

Fig. 3. A P3P Statement

In purpose-centric semantics, a data item along with a purpose determines other elements (i.e., recipients and retention) in a P3P statement. So, each statement takes only one purpose and other elements in the statement are centered around that purpose. The rationale behind the purpose-centric semantics is that certain data is sometimes used for multiple purposes, depending on the specific purposes, the data may be kept for different periods of time. Hence, binding the data and purpose of each statement avoids potential inconsistencies in a statement. For the rest of this paper we assume that our P3P policies have purpose-centric semantics.

3 P3P-Enabled SITDRM Architecture

In order to address the aforementioned limitations of SITDRM, we employed P3P in conjunction with MPEG REL licenses. The P3P protocol is adopted as a standard approach for the communication of privacy policies during data collection[3].

Further, at one end the P3P language is used for presenting privacy policies to customers and collecting their privacy preferences, and at another end, MPEG REL is employed for specifying enforceable licenses (with concrete access control rules). The combined use of these two languages bridge the gap between the abstraction required for consumers to specify their privacy preferences and the precision needed for a license to be enforceable by user's terminals.

As shown in Figure 4 the new architecture for SITDRM introduces the following new components: a *P3P policy*, a *P3P agent* and *mapping rules*. We assume

---

[3] Since we simply adopt the P3P protocol, this paper does not elaborate on the policy communication aspect. Interested readers may refer to P3P specification for more details.

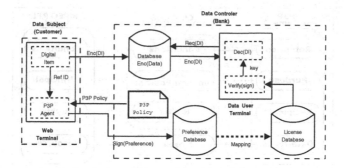

Fig. 4. P3P-Enabled SITDRM Architecture

that there is a Chief Privacy Officer *(CPO)* who writes a P3P policy that specifies the data handling of the enterprise. The P3P policy can then be retrieved and represented to a policy subject by using the P3P agent that is embedded within the data subject's web terminal. In addition, the P3P agent allows the data subject to modify the enterprise policy such that it matches his/her *privacy preferences*. Privacy preferences are then digitally signed and transferred to the enterprise where they are stored. These signed privacy preferences represent the consent of the data subjects. Since the P3P preferences are abstract, they cannot be directly enforced by the data user's terminals, hence, they need to be transformed into their MPEG REL license(s).

In the following section we will explain how a P3P policy can by converted to an MPEG REL license enforceable by SITDRM. We say an MPEG REL license *corresponds* to a P3P preference if the license is constructed using the mapping methodology that we will introduce in Section 4.

4   Constructing a License from a P3P Preferences

In order to convert P3P preferences to an MPEG REL license we will identify the correspondence between the elements in both languages and provide a set of mapping rules that take a P3P policy as an input and return an MPEG REL license(s). However, our aim is not to specify a new standard universal vocabulary for P3P or MPEG REL. Because a particular mapping of P3P elements to MPEG REL elements is enterprise dependent (e.g., role names vary), having a global vocabulary or a generic mapping would be impractical. Rather, we would like to introduce a practical approach to transform a subset of P3P policies into MPEG REL licenses. Figure 5 illustrates the associations that we would like to introduce between the components of a P3P *statement* and an MPEG REL *grant*. Those connections that are represented with dottedlines show the areas where there is no direct relationship between the two components.

In the following sections we will discuss a methodology that permits the conversion of P3P preferences into one or more MPEG REL licenses. We have incorporated the mapping into a tool, the *Mapping Console*, that assists CPOs

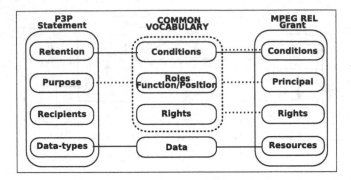

Fig. 5. P3P statement & MPEG-REL grant

by providing the following. First, a central point where the vocabulary necessary (e.g., data elements) for creating an enterprise P3P policy and an MPEG REL license is introduced and stored. This is particularly of interest as the syntax and semantics behind the vocabularies used in P3P and MPEG REL determines the correctness of the mapping rules that are being introduced. Second, like any access control management application, the Mapping Console allows the CPO to specify the *roles*, *principal* and *principal/role* assignments through the role specification window shown in Figure 6. Third, given this contextual information, it allows the CPO to customize the mapping rules as well as automating the process of constructing MPEG REL licenses from P3P preferences.

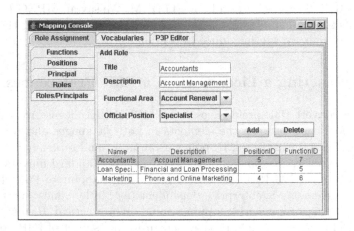

Fig. 6. The Mapping Console: Role Assignment Tab

4.1   Purpose

The most conspicuous difference between MPEG REL and P3P language is the latter's use of **purposes**. In the MPEG REL model, a **purpose** must be interpreted as some combination of a particular **principal** exercising a particular

right under certain **conditions**. In what follows we will describe our approach for determining **principal(s)**, necessary **rights** and **conditions** for a license such that it complies with the **purpose** of the corresponding P3P preference.

Principals: In order to realize the correlation between a **purpose** (in P3P) and a **principal** (in MPEG REL) we need to consider the relationships between data users in an enterprise and the tasks that they perform. The definition of such a relation is directly dependent upon the access control model adopted. Here, we consider access control systems that are based on the Role Based Access Control (RBAC) model [13]. In this model several roles are identified, and associated with them are some rights and conditions, and principals are assigned to roles which enable them to perform certain tasks on data that is predefined for that role.

We adopt the model proposed by Schaad et al. [14], where roles in enterprises are composed of a description of a *function* and an *position* within the organizational hierarchy. Functions represent the type of duties that a role is based on, such as loan processing, promotion & marketing, etc. Typical positions could be that of the ordinary clerk or group manager. An example of a role would be loan processing/group manager, indicating that the principal of the role performs a loan processing function and holds the official position of a group manager. The following table shows some typical roles in a bank.

Table 1. Roles

Role ID	Function	Position
A	Promotion & Marketing	Manager
B	Promotion & Marketing	Officer
C	Loan processing	Officer
D	Finance	Specialist
E	Account Management	Bank Manager

In this model, the job functions indicate the purposes for which a role may use the data. Hence, this indirect relationship between a purpose and a principal (through roles) allows us to determine those data users involved in carrying out a purpose. Since a role is a composition of a function and a position, several roles may be involved in carrying out a purpose. For example, a marketing officer, marketing manager and delivery person may all work under the function "Promotion & Marketing". Figure 7 shows the relationships between purpose, roles, access rights and principals in the system.

Rights: The notion of *right* and *condition* in the P3P language are implicit within the element **purpose**. For example, two P3P purposes email-marketing and telemarketing may be instances of the same right, contact, but imply different conditions.

In a typical RBAC model, there exists a security officer who determines the appropriate rights for each role. We follow the same approach and assume that

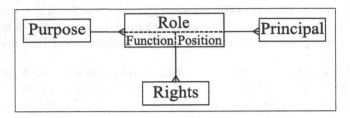

Fig. 7. Role Rights Relationship

the rights for each role are determined by the CPO. Hence, given a P3P `purpose` we can identify (i.e., through roles) the `principal` and the `rights` for the corresponding license.

Conditions: Given a role, there may exist several *conditions* that must be satisfied before a member of the role can carry out an action. We have categorized the conditions into two classes. First, the conditions that are indirectly specified by the data subjects through the purpose for which their data can be used. Such conditions are implicit to some of the P3P purpose element, such as `contact` and `telemarketing`[4]. The first one only asserts that the customer may be contacted and allows for any mode of contact and the second purpose which stipulates the only possible method of contact is phone.

In order to reflect these restrictions in MPEG REL licenses, we use the `ContactMethods` condition. This element contains an arbitrary number of elements of type `ContactMethodUri`, each of which has a mandatory `definition` attribute specifying a URI defining a particular method of contact. A typical contact method might include e-mail, telephone (using voice-over-IP) or the short messaging service (SMS). If the `ContactMethods` child is absent, any available contact method may be used for making contact.

The second class of conditions are those that are imposed by a CPO. These are usually application dependent conditions, derived from the security/privacy policy of the enterprise. Hence, data subjects may not necessarily be informed of the existence of these conditions. An instance of such conditions may impose a constraint that limits the access of principals (with certain roles) to a specific applications within the enterprise. Further, with the advent of wireless devices, location-based access control is also gaining more attention, so the CPO may like to ensure that the data is only accessible within specific zones in the enterprise.

4.2   Retention

The P3P language introduces five elements to specify the retention policy: `no-retention`, `indefinitely`, `stated-purpose`, `legal-requirements` and `business-practices`.

---

[4] Note that due to the shortage of the space we skip providing the definition of the P3P elements. Interested readers may refer to the P3P specification.

```
<r:validityInterval>
  <!-- Time the record is submited -->
  <r:notBefore>2006-12-01T00:00:00</r:notBefore>
  <!-- Destruction time -->
  <r:notAfter>2007-12-01T00:00:00<r:notAfter>
</r:validityInterval>
```

Fig. 8. An MPEG REL condition: Time Interval

Whilst the first two elements specify a destruction timetable, the other three indicate that the retention period is dependent on other factors such as legislation. Since a license requires a concrete time constraint in order to be enforceable, we are only able to map the first two retention elements. In addition to the above standard P3P vocabularies, we have also introduced a sub-element for **retention** that is used in our SITDRM application and allows a CPO to express the exact retention timetable. These elements represent a year, month or day that the data can be retained, (e.g., **one-year** or **one-month**).

For those **retention** sub-elements that specify a time constraint such as one-year we use the **validityInterval** condition in MPEG REL that allows us to specify the duration for which the resource can be used. For example, let us assume a data subject formulates P3P preferences that specify that data may be used for one year. In order to construct an appropriate license condition, SITDRM adds the condition shown in Figure 8 to the corresponding license.

The **no-retention** element means "Information is not retained for more than a brief period of time necessary to make use of it during the course of a single online interaction". We consider the **no-retention** element in a P3P statement to mean that the collected data can only be used once (in a single interaction). Hence, in order to specify this as an MPEG REL condition we use the **Exercise-Limit** element which allows us to specify the number of times that the license can be used. A simplified version of such a condition was shown in Figure 1.

Trivially, when the P3P retention element is **indefinitely** we do not specify any time condition for the MPEG REL license.

4.3 Data-Type

Both a statement in P3P and a grant in a license refer to a piece of information that needs to be protected. In MPEG REL the **resource** element contains a reference to the actual data that the license is about to provide access for. In P3P language the **data-types** consist of sub-elements that specify the type of data that is being collected.

The **data-types** element may include sub-elements at different levels of granularity. It can refer to both aggregate data (categories) as well as more concrete pieces of information, such as, name, e-mail address or credit card number. In P3P, personal data is classified into eighteen categories, including physical contact information, purchase information, demographic and socio-economic data, etc. For example, a person's gender, blood type, and date of birth belong to the category of demographic and socio-economic data. Thus, an organization may only specify the categories of personal data it wishes to collect rather than the concrete data elements. Although such an abstraction simplifies the task of specifying a P3P policy, it will adversely effect the granularity of the licenses. Therefore, in this work, we avoid using categories and only allow the specification of P3P policies with concrete data-types. Currently we use the `user-data` element in P3P base data schema [6], which consists of typical concrete data elements such as, name, birth-date, phone-number and postal-address, etc.

The only major difference between the `data-types` and the `resource` is that the latter contains reference to the particular data that is being collected. P3P `data-types`, on the other hand, do not refer to any particular record, they are only labels of what type of data the enterprise collects. In order to derive a license from a P3P preference we need to determine the reference to the collected data. The reference to the collected data can be trivially identified through the combined use of the unique record identification number that the data subject's web terminals assign to each transaction and the data types (e.g., phone, e-mail) specified in the P3P preferences.

4.4   Recipients

The reason for having the `recipient` element in P3P is to declare the third parties who may receive the collected data. The P3P language defines six possible recipients, `ours`, `delivery`, `same`, `other-recipient`, `unrelated`, `public`.

Although the recipient element may provide abstract information to data subjects regarding the sharing of their data, it does not play a significant role in mapping P3P preferences to an MPEG REL license. This is because the information that it provides can be extracted more precisely from purpose elements. For example, in a P3P statement where the recipient is `ours`, mapping the `purpose` allows us to determine the exact role(s) within the organization for which a license must be constructed.

Other than `ours`, the rest of the recipient classes suggest that the collected data is being shared with other parties. Hence, if there is a P3P statement in which `ours` is not part of its recipients we shall assume that we must not issue any license for the roles inside the enterprise, but only for those outside (within other organizations). However, since the recipient elements (e.g., `delivery, public`) are very abstract, we are unable to determine, whom (which role) within these third parties licenses must be issued to. One simplistic approach would be to assume that the role structure of both parties are identical, in which case, the roles, rights and conditions that were determined through purpose element can be used. But in reality, each organization has its own role model, so a more sophisticated approach must be taken. The current scenario of SITDRM assumes that the collected data is to be protected within the boundary of the enterprise. Hence, we can safely assume that only `ours` is used. Information sharing and cross-organizational privacy control using SITDRM will be our future work.

5   Specifying P3P Preferences

As described in Section 2, the intention of P3P is to provide a standard language to inform data owners of the global privacy practices within an enterprise. In reality, these policies, after being accepted by consumers, can also be considered as their privacy preferences. For example, consider a policy statement that states, the collected phone numbers will be used for marketing purposes. In this scenario, if a consumer (Alice) accepts this policy statement, we can safely consider the statement to be Alice's privacy preferences with respect to the use of her phone number. In the rest of this section we will describe how P3P policies can be used to collect data owner's preferences.

Recall that the elements that constitute a P3P statement may either be optional or compulsory. A policy statement that is composed of *optional* elements can be customized by data subjects to reflect their privacy preferences. For example, consider an arbitrary policy which indicates that Alice's credit card history is accessed to process her loan application and allows her to choose to be contacted via e-mail, telephone or fax. In contrast, those policy statements with *non-optional* elements indicate the areas where the operations that are performed on data are necessary for the enterprise and cannot be changed.

Based on the above concept, we have developed a *P3P Agent* that retrieves the enterprise P3P policy and constructs a template that enables the data subject to modify the P3P policy to create and submit his/her privacy preferences.

The idea of having client side agents that can retrieve P3P policy is not new. There are P3P agents such as AT&T Privacy Bird [7] that can parse the P3P policy and evaluate it against the consumer's privacy preference written in APPEL [8]. Unlike these tools our P3P agent introduces a notion of policy negotiation between consumers and the enterprise by allowing consumers to modify the P3P policy to construct their preference. However, users are not free to express any preference they wish: the scope of the negotiable policy is strictly defined by the enterprise and depends on what optional elements are included in the enterprise's P3P policy.

Our P3P agent collects the relevant P3P policy from the enterprise website and generates a *preference template*. A preference template is a graphical representation of the statements which constitute the enterprise P3P policy. The elements that constitute a statement in the template can either be fixed or modifiable, depending on their attributes (*always, opt-in and opt-out*). This allows the data owners to modify the policy based on their privacy preferences. We refer to the modified P3P policy as *P3P Preferences*. These P3P preferences will be digitally signed by customers (using their web terminal) and sent to the enterprise P3P preferences database. The pseudo-algorithms 1 and 2 in Appendix A show how a preference template is generated from a P3P policy.

Figure 9 shows a P3P preference template that was generated by using the P3P policy shown in Figure 3. As you can see for every statement in the policy, the informal description is followed by a set of modifiable check boxes for

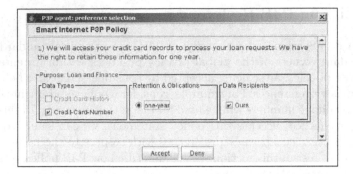

Fig. 9. P3P Preference Template

`data`, `retention` and `recipients`. These elements are centered around the `purpose` of the statement to highlight our purpose-centric semantics of the P3P language.

6   Future Work

The implementation of the P3P agent can be extended by allowing data owners to specify their preferences in the form of APPEL rules. Hence, when the agent receives the P3P policy, it first evaluates the P3P rules with respect to the user's APPEL rules and only shows the rules that do not match the current preferences. This will semi-automate the process of issuing P3P preferences.

Currently, we assume the elements (e.g., purposes) in a P3P statement are atomic elements and there are no hierarchical relationships between them. However, in reality purposes as well as data-types can be structured in a hierarchical form. One extension to the current P3P agent is to allow for the expression of these hierarchies. For example, to allow the data owner to see that the purpose "marketing" may indeed mean *direct marketing* and *online marketing* where direct marketing itself can consist of *phone marketing* or *fax marketing*.

Finally, as an extention to this work we investigate how organizations that implement SITDRM could share sensitive information, whilst ensuring the shared data are used with respect to the privacy policy of the organization that has collected the data.

7   Conclusion

In this paper we have discussed our approach for mapping P3P statements to MPEG REL grants, hence, to construct MPEG REL licenses from P3P preferences. Further, we have adopted this theory to extend the SITDRM architecture with a P3P handling component. Our extension will improve SITDRM and enable us to achieve the following goals. First, to facilitate the communication of P3P privacy policies with data subjects and enabling them to specify enforceable privacy preferences. Second, to provide a systematic way of creating templates, through which data subjects can specify their privacy preferences. Lastly, to ensure that the internal structure of the enterprise (users, roles) remains hidden from data subjects while they are formulating their privacy preferences.

References

1. Barth, A., Mitchell, J.C.: Enterprise privacy promises and enforcement. In: WITS 2005: Proceedings of the 2005 Workshop on Issues in the Theory of Security, Long Beach, California, pp. 58–66. ACM Press, New York (2005)
2. Bormans, J., Hill, K.: International standards organization. Information technology - multimedia framework (MPEG-21) - part 5: Rights expression language. ISO/IEC 21000-5:2004
3. Bucker, A., Haase, B., Moore, D., Keller, M., Koblinger, O., Wu, H.-F.: IBM tivoli privacy manager solution design and best practices. In: Redbooks (2002)
4. Catlett, J.: Open letter to P3P developers and replies. In: ACM Conference on Computers, Freedom and Privacy, pp. 157–164. ACM Press, New York (2000)
5. Coyle, K.: P3P: Pretty poor privacy? a social analysis of the platform for privacy preferences (P3P)
6. Cranor, L., Langheinrich, M., Marchiori, M., Presler Marshall, M.: The platform for privacy preferences 1.0 (P3P 1.0) specification (2002)
7. Cranor, L.F., Arjula, M., Guduru, P.: Use of a P3P user agent by early adopters. In: WPES, pp. 1–10 (2002)
8. Cranor, L.F., Langheinrich, M., Marchiori, M.: A P3P preference exchange language 1.0 (APPEL 1.0). In: W3C Working Draft (2002)
9. Karjoth, G., Schunter, M., Herreweghen, E.V.: Translating privacy practices into privacy promises: How to promise what you can keep. In: POLICY 2003: Proceedings of the 4th IEEE International Workshop on Policies for Distributed Systems and Networks, p. 135. IEEE Computer Society, Washington, DC (2003)
10. Karjoth, G., Schunter, M., Waidner, M.: Privacy-enabled services for enterprises. In: Hameurlain, A., Cicchetti, R., Traunmüller, R. (eds.) DEXA 2002. LNCS, vol. 2453, pp. 483–487. Springer, Heidelberg (2002)
11. Kenny, S., Korba, L.: Applying digital rights management systems to privacy rights management. Computers & Security 21(7), 648–664 (2002)
12. Research Report 3485: IBM Research. Enterprise Privacy Authorization Language (EPAL) (2003)
13. Sandhu, R.S., Coyne, E.J., Feinstein, H.L., Youman, C.E.: Role-based access control models. IEEE Computer 29(2), 38–47 (1996)
14. Schaad, A., Moffett, J., Jacob, J.: The role-based access control system of a european bank: a case study and discussion. In: SACMAT 2001: Proceedings of the Sixth ACM Symposium on Access Control Models and Technologies, pp. 3–9. ACM Press, New York (2001)
15. Sheppard, N.P., Safavi-Naini, R.: Protecting privacy with the MPEG-21 IPMP framework. In: 6th Workshop on Privacy Enhancing Technologies, pp. 152–171 (2006)
16. Stufflebeam, W.H., Antón, A.I., He, Q., Jain, N.: Specifying privacy policies with P3P and EPAL: lessons learned. In: WPES, p. 35 (2004)
17. Yu, T., Li, N., Anton, A.I.: A formal semantics for P3P. In: SWS '04: Proceedings of the 2004 Workshop on Secure Web Service, pp. 1–8. ACM Press, New York (2004)

A Pseudo Codes to Construct a Preference Template

Algorithm 1. createPreferenceForm(policy)

```
 1: while new(statement)  do
 2:    while new(purpose)  do
 3:      create a purpose block
 4:      while new(data)  do
 5:        attribute = getAttribute(data)
 6:        addOptions(data,  attribute )
 7:      end while
 8:      while new(retention)  do
 9:        attribute = getAttribute(retention)
10:        addOptions(retention, attribute )
11:      end while
12:      while new(recipients)  do
13:        attribute = getAttribute(recipients)
14:        addOptions(recipients, attribute )
15:      end while
16:    end while
17: end while
```

Algorithm 2. addOption(element, attribute)

```
1: if  attribute = "always" then
2:    add(element, DISABLED)
3: else if  attribute = "Opt-in" then
4:    add(element, UNCHECKED)
5: else if  attribute = "Opt-out" then
6:    add(element, CHECKED)
7: end if
```

B Security Architecture of P3P-Enabled SITDRM

There are three types of users that interact with SITDRM: a *data user*, who uses a trusted terminal to use the data, a *data owner* who provides the data and the *privacy officer*, who performs the tasks necessary for converting P3P preferences to licenses that can be used by data users.

In SITDRM, digital items are distributed in an encrypted form, and cannot be accessed without a secret key. Hence, the management of keys and licenses is of primary concern. In order to gain access to the content, a data user must obtain a valid license for the terminals that are being used. The license describes the terms and conditions under which the user may use the content, and also provides the user with the keys required to access the content. Hence, terminals must be able to verify the authenticity and integrity of any license that grant rights over content. Every trusted terminal T has a private key $\bar{K}_T$ and its corresponding public key K_T. The private key $\bar{K}_T$ is known only to the terminal; in particular, it is not known to the human user of the terminal. This is to prevent users from accessing the data from any other terminal.

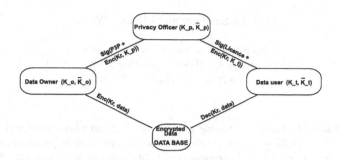

Fig. 10. P3P-Enabled SITDRM Security Architecture

The privacy officer has a private key $\bar{K}_P$ and corresponding public key K_P, and the authenticity of K_P can be verified by terminals using some public key infrastructure. The private key $\bar{K}_P$ is known only to the privacy officer.

The data owner has a private key $\bar{K}_O$ and the corresponding public key K_O. Similarly, the authenticity of K_O can be verified by the privacy officer using some public key infrastructure. In addition, the data owner has a master key $\mathcal{K}$ which is a symmetric key and known only to them. This key is used to encrypt individual resources as described in the following.

Every resource r in the system is associated with a public identifier i_r created by data controller to ensure the uniqeness of the records. All resources in the system are encrypted by a resource key K_r derived via a one-way function of the master key $\mathcal{K}$ and identifier i_r.

After generating K_r, the resources will be encrypted and stored in a resource database. Then the resource key K_r is encrypted with the public key of the privacy officer K_P and embedded to the P3P preferences of the data owner which were constructed using the P3P agent. The P3P preference is signed by the data owner before being sent to the privacy officer.

By having a P3P preference, the resource key and the mapping rules, the privacy officer is in a position to construct a license for data users. These licenses are only issued to the user's trusted terminals, so the user must supply the issuer with the public key K_T of the terminal T on which they wish to use the resource.

In addition to specifying the terms under which the resource r may be used, the license contains the resource key K_r encrypted by the terminal's public key K_T. Since the corresponding private key $\bar{K}_T$ is known only to the terminal T, only T is able to decrypt K_r and therefore decrypt the resource r.

Simplified Privacy Controls for Aggregated Services — Suspend and Resume of Personal Data

Matthias Schunter and Michael Waidner

IBM Research, Zurich Research Laboratory
Säumerstrasse 4, CH-8803 Rüschlikon, Switzerland
{mts,wmi}@zurich.ibm.com

Abstract. The Internet is moving towards dynamic and ad-hoc service composition. The resulting so-called Web 2.0 sites maintain a unified user-experience while interacting and exchanging personal data with multiple other sites. Since the interaction is dynamic and ad-hoc, existing privacy policy mechanisms are not designed for this scenario.

In this article we describe a new lightweight approach towards privacy management. The core idea is to provide a "privacy panel" – a unified and simple entry point at each site that enables consumers to review stored data and manage their privacy. Key aspects were ease-of-use and handling of recursive disclosures of personal data.

1 Introduction

Increased exposure of web services by enterprises has lead to an emerging service aggregation ecosystem. Today, there exists no easily usable concept for distributed privacy controls in such federated service aggregations. As a consequence, today's service aggregations are either limited to applications in which no personal information is handled or to individuals that do not care about their privacy.

In this article, we describe a new concept of privacy panels for end users. We define a powerful yet usable mechanism that enable individuals to control their privacy throughout a network of aggregated services. Our main objectives are

- **Transparency:** Individuals can discover the privacy policy of a site, which data was collected, how it was used, and to whom it was disclosed.
- **Control:** Individuals can control data that is stored about them. This includes deletion or blocking and unblocking of data across all or some of the services that have been aggregated.
- **Usability:** Existing privacy enforcement concepts [5,9] are powerful in an enterprise setting. However, they lack the ease of use and simplicity needed in an end-user-oriented scenario.

The privacy panel (see Figure 1 for an example picture) allows an individual consumer to manage privacy of a given site and all sites to which personal data has been disclosed by that site. The panel provides a single entry point to review the policy ("our policy") and the stored data ("your data"), to block and unblock further usage of portions of personal data ("block identity"), and to delete personal data ("delete identity").

N. Borisov and P. Golle (Eds.): PET 2007, LNCS 4776, pp. 218–232, 2007.

The goal of our concept is to enable enterprises to act as better guardians of their customers' data.[1] Today, enterprises are often limited by the complexity of privacy concepts. As a consequence consumers suffered from limited transparency and control. Note that our concept needs to be augmented by proper auditing and controls to ensure that enterprises correctly deploy the technology and comply with the privacy promises they have made.

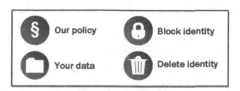

Fig. 1. Privacy panel

Outline. The remainder of the article is structured as follows: Section 2 outlines the basic model of usable privacy control across multiple organizations and provides more details on the proposed privacy panel. Section 3 formalizes privacy controls in a single organization. Section 4 defines our trust management model and expands these concepts to protect personally identifiable information that has been disclosed to other organizations. Section 5 describes how to provide an enhanced level of verifiability to end users. Section 5.4 concludes our article.

2   Usable Privacy Controls in Aggregated Services

Our approach has three main components. The simple user interface to provide transparency and control to end users, the protocols that define how to implement the corresponding privacy controls across multiple organizations, and the policies and their semantics that allow organizations to formalize how data may be used. We use an online retail scenario to illustrate our concepts.

2.1   Online Retail Scenario

Consider the following scenario, involving a typical online bookstore B and a customer C (see Fig. 2). Customer C has an account with bookstore B, and B links whatever it knows about C to his or her account: all purchases made by C, voluntarily provided preferences, which books C looked at in the last few weeks. All in all, B has a fairly complete picture of C, as far as C's reading interests are concerned. By cross-correlating this data B gets a good idea about which books C might purchase in the future, which allows B to offer very precise recommendations to C. Unlike blind mass-marketing, these recommendations are precisely to the point, and thus C is likely to appreciate those recommendations and love this service.

---

[1] Note that this approach augments privacy by means of self-protection [6,7]: While self-protection minimizes the data that is being released and traces accidental disclosures, we focus on data that needs to be released despite minimization.

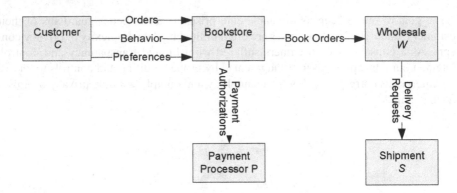

Fig. 2. Online retail scenario

Now assume that C buys a specific book at B, and pays with a credit card issued by a payment processor P. In order to fulfill the order, B sends certain data to P, for payment authorization, and then sends the book and shipping details to a wholesaler W, and finally this wholesaler sends the book plus shipping details to a shipping agent S. At the end, C's data went from B to P and W and from W to S.

Such scenarios raise significant privacy concerns: many people appreciate receiving specific recommendations, but they do not like the idea that others might see their behavior. Particularly critical situations are subcontracting scenarios (B delegates shipping to W, who further delegates to S), and acquisition scenarios. In the latter the fear is that when B' acquires B, and with it all of B's customer data, the business model of B might change, and suddenly the new business owner might decide that the new model will benefit more from selling the customer data to whoever pays most than from keeping them confidential.

2.2 Transparency and Control Using a Privacy Panel

By adding a standardized privacy panel to all participating sites, a single entry point allows individuals to exercise control over their data. The panel is linked from all places where an enterprise collects or displays personal data (e.g., the login page, the page where C can inspect all previous orders), and will also create a specific identity management "portal" at a well known address. Say, if B can be reached at `http://www.B.com` then this portal will be at `http://www.B.com/identity`. The four icons in Figure 1 represent buttons on a web page. Ideally, these buttons and their essential semantics will be standardized so that customers who see them spontaneously and dependably associate the right meaning with them.

"Our policy" will open a window with C's privacy policy (most web sites offer this already).

"Your data" will open a window where C gets a report of all data B stores related to C. A standard should decide what "all data" will mean, but intuitively this is the data itself, plus the history of data (when and from whom and why did B receive data, and to whom and when and why did B send data?), plus links to the privacy panels of all

parties that received data from B. If applicable, the panel should also explain how data was collected or from whom it has been received. Note that this includes direct and any indirect user data an organization plans to collect, i.e., if the collection of indirect data such as clickstream data is not declared, the organization is not authorized to collect this type of data.

"Block identity" will prevent B from using C's data for almost all purposes. All exceptions must be pre-agreed in the policy. Intuitively, these exceptions will only be purposes either required by law or needed to allow C to execute an *"unblock"* command. We call them "mandatory purposes", and if a data element is needed for at least one mandatory purpose we call it "protected data". The set of mandatory purposes is likely to be time-dependent. E.g., a transaction might end such that protected data becomes optional over time. In this case an earlier block (or delete) might have a delayed impact on such data. In our initial scenario we assumed an all-or-nothing scope for "block" and "unblock". A real implementation might give the user some choices. For instance, all data might be sorted into a few categories, and block/unblock and delete might be individually offered for each category. In the most extreme case, each data item can be blocked, unblocked and deleted independently of all other data items. Our technical description covers all cases, but we believe that few all-or-nothing choices for data groups are probably the most usable and thus most relevant case.

"Delete identity" is like "block identity" except that the effect cannot be reversed.

2.3 Related Technologies

Our proposal is related to privacy controls for individuals as well as privacy management based on privacy policy languages. Privacy policies fall into three main categories (see Fig. 3): Privacy notice from enterprise to consumers [12], privacy preferences of individuals [1], and policies governing data handling inside an enterprise [5,9]. The policy formalism used for explaining our mechanisms focuses on privacy notice and only provides high-level constraints for the enterprise internal use. The core goal of the formalism given is to provide an easy-to-understand formalism to describe the data flows between web-sites as well as a high-level summary of their site-internal use. Our simplified approach to policies can be augmented by detailed data types [12] and by mechanisms to validate whether the policies actually enforced satisfy the published promises [11,8,2].

Besides privacy policies, many existing concepts that enhance end-user control relate to our approach. In the sequel, we discuss some of them.

Unsubscribe. Many subscription-based information services, like electronic newsletters, allow customers to unsubscribe explicitly. The meaning is obvious: unsubscribe terminates the service for this customer, and in many cases the basic customer record will be automatically deleted after some time. Unlike *block*, unsubscribe has no reverse operation (subscribing again does not recreate the old customer record such as an interest profile, but generates a new one). It has no transitive semantics (unsubscribe has no impact on other service providers who might have received the subscription information

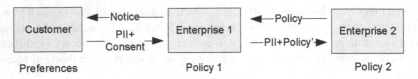

Fig. 3. Privacy policies and negotiation types

– this is actually a very common scenario with free subscription services), moreover, it also has no meaning for data beyond the basic customer record (e.g., if the service is a forum or newsgroup then all postings will still be available to all other subscribers).

Opt-in and opt-out choices. Organizations are supposed to specify the purposes for which they collect personal data. A popular way to specify those purposes is to structure them into a multiple-choice menu. For each menu item the user can say "yes", i.e., opt-in, or "no", i.e., opt-out. Often users can modify their choices at any time. Opting-out from a purpose is very similar to blocking, and subsequently opting-in again is very similar to unblocking. But there are differences:

– Opting in/out has no impact on other organizations. This is the same situation as with *unsubscribe*. One might argue that many proposals for privacy authorization systems suggest that policy changes must propagate ("sticky policies"), and opt-in/opt-out choices are elements of a privacy policy and thus should be sticky, too.
– Opting in/out impacts purposes only. For instance opting out from receiving a newsletter does not make the address inaccessible nor does it touch the history of how the customer reacted to previous newsletters. It just withdraws the organization's right to use the address for sending out a newsletter. Our approach is more general, in that it allows opt-in/opt-out for arbitrary elements of a concrete access control list.
– We also suggest specific implementations for opt-in/opt-out that have not been suggested in this context before. We suggest to off load storing or protecting data needed to unblock or opt-in from the organization to the user.

Several other technologies, such as content management and databases, are related in the sense that they provide functions that would make it easier to implement our concepts.

3 A Simple Policy Model for Local Privacy Enforcement

We now formalize the semantics of the proposed privacy panel. We start with a very basic definition. Consider an organization o that stores data types $D = (d_1, \ldots, d_n)$ about a user U. There is a set of actions $A = (a_1, \ldots, a_m)$ that can be executed on those data, and as a result the data might change, new data might be created, or old data might be deleted.[2] For now we do not assume that data is forwarded (this function will be added in the next subsection).

The access control list $ACL_o \subseteq A \times 2^D$ of an organization o defines the set of data δ items on which each given action a may be performed. We assume that if $(a, \delta) \in ACL_o$ then a has no undesired impact on any data outside δ. This is a very simplified model for access control, but it is straightforward to add details and constraints if needed. We assume that ACL_o is maintained by organization o. Organization o also maintains a subset $ACL_M \subseteq ACL_o$ which contains all pairs the user cannot block (the actions serving mandatory purposes[3]).

The user specifies a set of blocked pairs $block_U \subseteq A \times 2^D$ and permanently shares this list with o. "Blocking" a pair corresponds to moving the pair into $block_U$ "unblocking" corresponds to removing it from $block_U$. The actual access control list ACL_e that is used for enforcement is derived from the inputs provided, ACL_o, ACL_M, and $block_U$, as follows:

$$ACL_e := ACL_o - (block_U - ACL_M).$$

In this abstract model, the impact of "blocking" a pair (a, δ), i.e., adding it to $block_U$, is the following:

– If $(a, \delta) \notin ACL_e$ then there is no immediate impact since the blocked item was either not in ACL_o or else mandatory.
– If $(a, \delta) \in ACL_e$ and $(a, \delta) \notin ACL_M$ then the pair (a, δ) is removed by updating ACL_e, i.e., o can no longer execute this action on this data.

The impact of "unblocking" a pair (a, δ), i.e., moving it out of $block_U$, is the following:

– If $(a, \delta) \notin ACL_o$ then there is no immediate impact. The pair was never in ACL_e or it was in ACL_o but removed by o.
– If $(a, \delta) \in ACL_o$ then the pair is re-added to ACL_e.

Note that $block_U$ is not necessarily a subset of ACL_o, i.e., the user might block and unblock a pair (a, δ) before it is actually added to ACL_o. If o adds a pair to ACL_o that is blocked then this pair will not be added to ACL_e. Whenever any of the inputs change, the resulting ACL_e needs to be recomputed. An update is triggered by changes in ACL_o, ACL_M, or $block_U$. If o removes a pair from ACL_M, but not from ACL_o, then this pair can be blocked in the future. If the pair is also in $block_U$ then the update procedure will immediately remove it from ACL_e.

In our abstract model, $block_U$ is an arbitrary subset of $A \times 2^D$. Listing all elements in $block_U$ is the most obvious way to specify $block_U$, but is unlikely to cover many interesting cases. More practically relevant approaches that can be combined are listed below:

---

[2] Note that purposes can be encoded in actions. If a certain action is a is allowed for one purpose p but not for another purpose p', then action (a, p) and (a, p') would have to be elements of A to enable distinction.

[3] The probably most relevant way to practically define ACL_M is to classify A into mandatory actions A_M and discretionary actions $A_D := A \backslash A_M$, and define $ACL_M := ACL \cap A_M \times 2^D$.

- The all-or-nothing approach can be implemented by setting either $block_U := A \times 2^D$ (everything blocked) or $block_U := \emptyset$ (nothing blocked). Note that this does not block the pairs in ACL_M, which in this case should also include all pairs that are required to perform the unblock operation.
- There might be predefined classes $C_1, \ldots, C_j$ which cover subsets of of $A \times 2^D$, and U can pick any subset of these classes. In this case $block_U$ is the union of all blocked classes. This is similar to the opt-in and opt-out grouping of statements in [12].
- Instead of blocking pairs the user might block data or actions, or classes of data and actions. If the user wants to block all actions in $A*$ and all data in $D*$, then we set $block_U := A^* \times 2^D \cup A \times 2^{D^*}$. The way to deal with classes of actions and data is obvious.

These operations allow users to block portions or all of their data. Note that in a user-centric identity scheme, this blocking/unblocking can be managed by a client-side application. This means that if a user visits a site, the required data is unblocked. Once a user has performed a transaction and logs out, the data is blocked again.

4 Managing Privacy Across Multiple Organizations

Organization o will often share data with other organizations. We now discuss the protocols that allow an organization to disclose data to another entity and maintain the privacy of the disclosed data. This includes disclosure and update of data as well as blocking/unblocking.

Traditional privacy policies allow individuals to specify which actions by which organization are allowed on which data elements. They often do not contain explicit disclosure controls, i.e., they do not specify who is allowed to obtain copies of the data [15]. To simplify data handling, we pursue a simpler and more flexible approach. Our concept is split into two parts. *Disclosure control* prevents data from being disclosed to parties that are not trusted by an individual user. *Usage control* then restricts usage and manages block/unblock for trusted organizations that store data of an individual. An organization is allowed to use data if the organization is trusted and if the required permissions have been delegated to this organization.

4.1 Preventing Disclosure to Untrusted Organizations

The best protection of data against an untrusted organization is not to disclose the data to this organization. This means that either an individual trusts an organization sufficiently to act as a guardian of his or her data or else the organization should not obtain the data in the first place. Since this trust depends on the data types, we specify which parties are *in principle* allowed to handle given data items. Those parties are then trusted to enforce the privacy restrictions as specified by an individual.[4] Special care needs to be taken to

---

[4] This is similar to and can be augmented by the concept described in [10] where parties are only trusted to handle data if they implement a privacy layer that is protected by means of Trusted Computing hardware.

handle the fact that an organization gets the same data via multiple paths. We model this concept as a data-flow matrix DF. Given a set of organizations O and a list of data items D, the data-flow matrix is a subset $DF \subseteq O \times D$ that lists the organizations that are trusted to handle each particular data item.

The corresponding data disclosure can now be specified as follows. Whenever an organization needs to disclose a set D of data to an organization o', it computes a data subset D' such that $d \in D' \subseteq D$ iff $(o',d) \in DF$ and $d \in D$. The recipient should not obtain trust information unless it is trusted to protect the corresponding data. Therefore, the organization computes the subset of the data-flow matrix $DF' \subseteq O \times D'$. The organization o can then disclose D' and DF' to its peer o'. If the trust is not sufficient to pass on critical data for a given transaction, the organization can either cancel the transaction or else ask the user to extend the data-flow matrix. The handling of the data-flow matrix will be discussed in more detail in Section 5.2. Note that cryptographic protection can be implemented on top of this scheme, i.e., if a user releases encrypted data (say for o''), the DF specifies who can get hold of and pass on the cipher text. If it includes o'', then o'' can get hold of the data and actually decrypt it. This concept can be used to tunnel critical data (e.g., SSN, credit cards) through multiple semi-trusted parties to the actual intended recipient.

4.2 Managing Data Usage Permissions for Disclosed Data

Permissions are handled along a dynamically generated directed delegation graph that may have cycles. The organizations are the nodes of this delegation graph. Edges correspond to actual disclosures. Each disclosure (edge) delegates a set of permissions that is a subset of the permissions received. An edge is labeled with the data that has been disclosed as well as the corresponding metadata. The metadata consists of the reduced data-flow matrix DF, a disclosure history, and the associated permissions. The data-flow matrix defines the maximum set of organizations that can obtain subsequent disclosures; the history defines via which intermediaries the data was received, and the permissions are the associated access control lists as defined in Section 3. Blocking blocks a (subset of) a given edge. An action on data can be performed by a node as long as any unblocked incoming edge still permits this action. In practice this, for example, means that a shipment company can use an address as long as some wholesaler still has an ongoing delivery for this customer. We now formalize this intuition depicted in Fig. 4.

In order to receive disclosures, each organization needs to store such a triple (history, data-flow matrix, permissions) for each received disclosure. Note that an organization can receive the same data via different paths and with different or identical permissions. The organization needs to store and maintain received disclosures separately in order to manage the blocking of a single disclosure.

We now explain the permission handling for disclosures that is summarized in Table 1 in more detail. Permissions of a given organization o are formalized by a triple $(ACL_o, ACL_M, block_U)$ that contains the access control list, the list of mandatory permissions, and the blocked permissions.

Disclosure and Delegation: Let us assume that an organization o holds data d with permissions $(ACL_o, ACL_M, block_U)$ received via a single edge, and intends to

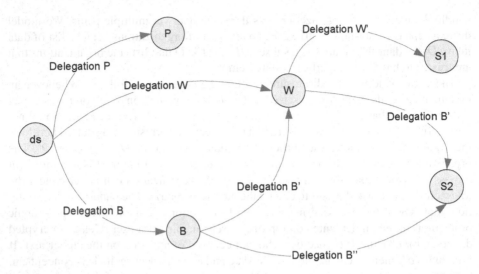

Fig. 4. Dynamic graph of actual delegations for bookstore scenario (S1, S2 are two shipping providers, "ds" is the data subject and edges are labeled with delegated permissions)

Table 1. Computation of metadata for disclosures

Field	Sender o	Recipient o'	Constraint
Data	dat	dat'	$dat' \subseteq dat$ and $(O' \times dat') \subseteq DF$
Data-Flow Matrix	DF	DF'	$DF' \subseteq DF \cap (O \times dat')$
History	$hist$	$hist'$	$hist' := (hist, o)$
Access Control List	ACL_o	ACL'_o	$ACL'_o \subseteq ACL_o$
Mandatory Permissions	ACL_M	ACL'_M	$ACL'_M \subseteq (ACL_M \cap ACL'_o)$
Blocked Permissions	$block_U$	$block'_U$	$block'_U \supseteq block_U$

disclose it to an organization o'. In order to disclose the data, the organization decides on a subset $ACL' \subseteq ACL$ of unblocked permissions to delegate. Both organizations also agree on a set $ACL'_M \subseteq ACL_M$ that defines the mandatory permissions. Once these permissions are defined, the data is disclosed along with the permission vector $(ACL_o, ACL_M, block_U)$, a subset DF' of the data-flow matrix that covers the disclosed data, and the history including sender o and recipient o' as its last two elements. The disclosing organization o also stores the history to enable later updates or blocking of the disclosed data. If an organization wants to delegate a data set of data received via multiple edges, it needs to choose one incoming edge for each data item and break the data down into multiple disclosure messages – one for each incoming edge. This is necessary because the incoming data may have different data-flow matrices or different policies associated with the actual data to be disclosed.

Once an organization has received data of a given data subject ds via one or more paths, it can compute the actual permissions by combining the permissions along all edges. The actual ACL is computed as the union of all incoming sets ACL_e that are computed as specified in Section 3. This formalizes the intuition that data can be used as long as at least a single organization has delegated the corresponding usage. The blocking set $block_U$ and the mandatory permissions ACL_M are maintained separately for all in- and outgoing edges. They are considered when updating the individual ACLs and therefore indirectly influence the corresponding ACLs.

Block/Unblock: There are two types of blocking data. A user can either block information via the organization that collected it or else visit the privacy panel of a particular organization directly to block all or portions of the stored data (no matter where the data was collected). The first type is a user blocking data that has been released to an organization o. In this case, the blocking is recursed along the dynamic disclosure path by updating the policies at each edge. If a user has blocked a set $block_U$ at organization o, then o examines along which paths the given data has been disclosed and discloses an updated $block'_U$. The subsequent parties then update ACL_e for the given edge accordingly. Note that this will only block the data if the organization has not received the same data and permissions via another path. The rationale behind this behavior is that in most cases, from a user's perspective different paths are seen as independent. If, for example, a user blocked all data at a given online retailer, the individual would be surprised if the credit card were rendered unusable also for other online retailers. Unblocking again updates the permission sets and propagates the permission update.

In the second type of blocking, where a user visits an organization directly (i.e., clicks on the privacy panel of an inner node and authenticates), the user will review the information stored at this organization and can also see for what the information is used and where it came from. In this case, a user can again block all or portions of the data usages (except mandatory usages). This is then again propagated along the disclosure graph. Note that in contrast to the first approach, this enables the user to block any non-mandatory usage of data at a given organization, regardless of how and where the data was actually collected.

A special case for permissions and block/unblock are circles in the disclosure graph, i.e., that permissions are delegated along loops. We resolve this by keeping the history. This enables the organizations to effectively distinguish original permissions from permissions that are looped-back.

5   Enhancing User Control

The scheme described so far assumes that the parties in the disclosure set DF correctly implement the proposed scheme. This includes correct policy enforcement as well as blocking and unblocking. In this section, we investigate how these trust assumptions can be reduced to provide a higher level of verifiability and thus security to the individual end user.

5.1   Increased Transparency

The main benefit of our concept is enhanced transparency. A user can review which data is stored by whom and to which organizations it has been disclosed. By default, an individual customer will handle data via the party to whom the data has been disclosed initially. This means that the customer can visit one of the previously visited web-sites and review or block/unblock data. This can include browsing along the disclosure graph. In the special case that a customer decides to distrust an organization further along the graph, he or she should directly visit the corresponding privacy panel and then prune the disclosure tree by blocking or deleting a given branch. Any good implementation of our method should provide feedback to the user regarding the precise meaning of a successful or failed block or unblock operation. Since ACL_o and ACL_M might change over time, blocking and unblocking can have a delayed impact. The user should be given the option to be informed about such delayed impact before as well as at when the impact actually happens.

5.2 Dynamic Trust Management

An important aspect of our concept for multi-organization privacy protection is the trust management that determines who may obtain which data in the first place. There are multiple options that can be mixed in practice:

- *Enterprise Data-Flow Matrix:* A web-site has a fixed set of subsidiaries that are required for a site to work. E.g., all payments are processed through a given payment processor. In this case, the site proposes a fixed data-flow matrix and the individual customer can accept or decline. This is today's solution.
- *Customer Data-Flow Matrix:* The customer proposes a data flow matrix to the enterprise. The enterprise then dynamically selects providers that are in this matrix. This service-oriented approach requires that the customer has at least one service of each type that is required by a given organization. This needs to be validated by the organization.
- *Dynamic Delegation:* For this approach, there is no complete data-flow matrix initially. The customer (via its federated identity management scheme [14] or individually authorized by a party trusted by the customer) is dynamically asked to delegate certain sub-services to providers that are trusted by the individual. This means that the user points to a trusted payment processing service once needed. Once the organization has obtained permission to disclose certain data, this is dynamically added to the data-flow matrix.
- *Role-based Delegation:* The original matrix only contains roles or groups of organizations, e.g., partners certified by auditor X, organizations that satisfy certain privacy requirements, or partners that have signed a privacy protection contract with the user. This concept is similar to the organizations specified by P3P [12]. However, the core difference is that our approach allows later review of the data and the actual organizations that store the data of an individual.

Each of these mechanisms ensures that data disclosure is only permitted to organizations that an individual user trusts. Revoking trust is done by updating the data-flow matrix and the access-control matrix. The consequence is that the corresponding organizations are asked to delete the data they store. If this deletion is not possible legally, one again needs to distinguish between a default and a mandatory data flow matrix DF, where the latter specifies the minimum set of organizations where the data cannot be revoked. Note that the main impact of removing trust is to prevent storage of data corresponding to future transactions. Without additional audits or control, the actual deletion of data cannot be verified in general.

5.3 Verifiable Blocking and Unblocking

The preceding sections assumed that organizations "follow the rules". We now describe a way to increase the auditability of our solution. Our goal is to enable auditors and users to validate that all data that is found at an organization has been obtained legally and has not been blocked. The core ideas are to delete all blocked data, to sign disclosures, to provide receipts for blocking requests, and to require authorization for any data stored at the enterprise.

Our first naïve implementation of unblocking merely modifies the access rights without actually protecting the data. This is a valid implementation approach, but has certain disadvantages:

- Blocking does *not* add a new layer of defense, i.e., this type of blocking does not necessarily reduce the risk of unintentional disclosure.
- Blocked data are of no value to the organization, but the burden of maintaining them is with o. From an economic perspective, a more natural choice would be to put that burden on the individual customer U.

Offloading the burden of maintaining the data to the user can be done as follows: As a result of "block", the organization compiles all data that serves no purpose other than allowing unblock, and send this data token to the user, in some protected fashion (encrypted and authenticated). The user is supposed to store this data, and return it as part of the unblock token. Delayed impact of block might create new tokens, which are all sent to the user. This approach adds a second layer of defense and puts the storage burden on the user. If this storage burden is not considered significant for o, one can use an alternative approach: U can select a cryptographic key and hand the (public) key to o, and o uses that key to protect all this data, i.e., storing the data in its encrypted form without actually knowing the key needed for decryption. Upon unblock, U hands over the (secret) key to o, and o can decrypt all data needed to perform unblock.

In both cases, the user achieves an increased level of control. The most important benefit is that once an honest organization has blocked data, it cannot unilaterally change its mind. This is important in order to prevent that a bankrupt organization sells previously blocked data. Next, we discuss this data token approach as it provides a benefit (and thus an incentive) to the organization that implements this approach. In order to provide accountability for all data that is stored at an enterprise, all disclosures need to be signed (including data, history, and permissions as described above). This enables an enterprise to show that all data has been obtained through a legal disclosure path. When an individual asks an organization to block data, an organization needs to be able to show that it honored the recursive blocking request. This can be done by protecting its own data as described above and requiring blocking proofs from all data recipients.

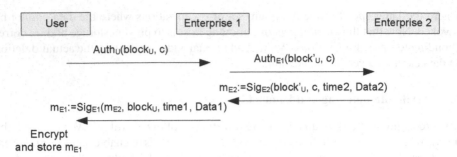

Fig. 5. Example of a blocking protocol

This can be achieved by the protocol depicted in Fig. 5. We assume a confidential channel between the different organizations to prevent data leakage. The customer initiates the blocking protocol by sending an authenticated message containing the updated access control list $block_U$ and a challenge c. If the enterprise has not disclosed the data further, it responds by sending a signed response that contains the updated $block_U$' the time from which it promises to no longer use the data, and the only remaining copy of the actual data that has been blocked. If parts of $block_U$ have been delegated to one or more other organizations $E2$, the organization executes this blocking protocol recursively to block and retrieve the corresponding data. Again, the user will obtain a signed blocking receipt from each organization that held data. Note that the blocking message between different organizations is no longer authenticated by the user. Instead, our concept enables all organizations to block delegations they have previously performed. In the protocol this implies that subsequent blocking messages are authenticated by the sending organization. Furthermore it implies that these blocks can contain a subset of $block_U$ if only a subset has been disclosed. Both enterprises then send signed messages with the blocking time to the user. The user encrypts and stores the data.

To unblock the data, the user returns the blocking token m_{E1} (and m_{E2}) and an authenticated message that allows the organization to unblock the data. The organization then recursively recovers the data from this backup. Note that the authorization to unblock is needed to enable the enterprise to prove that the unblock operation was legitimate, i.e., that it did not cheat the user by sending a blocking token while continuing the usage of the data.

Usually the data used to authenticate U is part of the data protected by our concept (i.e., part of D), and authenticating U is implemented through one or more of the actions in A. To facilitate unblocking it is appropriate to add all pairs (a, δ) representing authentication to the set ACL_M, i.e., to prevent U from accidentally blocking authentication as long as other data can still be blocked. Another approach is to allow blocking of the identity and authentication information. In this case, the user would be required to unblock its identity to perform additional block operations.

Note that without additional assumptions it is impossible to achieve complete verifiability against an organization that is completely untrusted. Known assumptions that enable verifiable deletion are a limited amount of memory [13], or the assumption that data is stored only in a well-defined trusted infrastructure [3], or an infrastructure that supports secret sharing with at least one honest storage server [16].

5.4 Protection of Mandatory Data

In general, data that is mandatory cannot be deleted or blocked. This is either caused by pending transactions that need the data or else by regulatory requirements. In the first case, blocking would terminate the transaction and usually is not desirable. In the second case, usage can be limited to certain well-defined operations such as an annual audit, or following a court order.

We now sketch additional means to offer similar protection for mandatory permissions. The core idea is that the limited amount of mandatory data can be protected by mutually trusted entities. From the enterprise's perspective, this trustee guarantees the legally required availability of the data. From an end-user perspective, the entity ensures that the usage is limited to the pre-defined purposes. Potential options for implementing these trusted third parties are secure hardware (smartcards, secure coprocessors), additional trustees (either for secret decryption keys or the data itself), or special storage devices such as a secondary write-only data store that only reveals data under the conditions specified. One example are log-files that are kept for auditing purposes. In this case, the data can be public-key encrypted and the decryption key is to be escrowed between the user, the organization, and a third party. If the legal pre-conditions are met, the user pre-authorizes this third party to release its key share to the organization in order to meet the regulatory requirements.

6 Conclusion

We have presented a simple concept for increasing transparency and control over the use of data for individual end-users. The core idea is a standardized privacy panel that allows users to review the data that has been stored about them. In contrast to earlier approaches, we describe how to enable temporary suspension of personal information. This blocking renders data unusable while a certain service is not in use. This protects the individual from accidental misuse. Furthermore, we separate data-flow restrictions from data usage restrictions. The rationale is that data should only be disclosed if the recipient is trusted to enforce the associated policies.

Acknowledgments

We thank the anonymous reviewers for valuable comments that enabled us to substantially improve the final version of this paper. We are grateful to Charlotte Bolliger for improving the readability and presentation of this paper. Finally, we would like to thank our colleagues Mike Nelson and Jane Johnson for helpful discussions on privacy in service compositions. This work was partially supported by the OpenTC project www.opentc.net that is funded by the 6th framework programme of the European Commission.

References

1. Cranor, L., Langheinrich, M., Marchiori, M.: A P3P Preference Exchange Language 1.0 (APPEL1.0); W3C Working Draft (April 15, 2002), http://www.w3.org/TR/P3P-preferences/
2. Backes, M., Bagga, W., Karjoth, G., Schunter, M.: Efficient Comparison of Enterprise Privacy Policies. In: 19th Annual ACM Symposium on Applied Computing, Nicosia, Cyprus, March 14-17, 2004, pp. 375–382. ACM Press, New York (2004)
3. Badishi, G., Caronni, G., Keidar, I., Rom, R., Scott, G.: Deleting Files in the Celeste Peer-to-Peer Storage System. In: 25th IEEE Symposium on Reliable Distributed Systems (SRDS 2006), pp. 29–38. IEEE Press, Los Alamitos (2006)
4. Barth, A., Mitchell, J.C.: Enterprise Privacy Promises and Enforcement. In: Proceedings of the 2005 Workshop on Issues in the Theory of Security, Long Beach, California, pp. 58–66. ACM Press, New York (2005)
5. Backes, M., Pfitzmann, B., Schunter, M.: A Toolkit for Managing Enterprise Privacy Policies. In: Snekkenes, E., Gollmann, D. (eds.) ESORICS 2003. LNCS, vol. 2808, pp. 162–180. Springer, Heidelberg (2003)
6. Chaum, D.: The Dining Cryptographers Problem: Unconditional Sender and Recipient Untraceability. Journal of Cryptology 1/1, 65–75 (1988)
7. Dingledine, R., Mathewson, N., Syverson, P.: Tor: The Second-Generation Onion Router. In: Proceedings of the 13th USENIX Security Symposium (August 2004)
8. Karjoth, G., Schunter, M., Van Herreweghen, E.: Enterprise Privacy Practices vs. Privacy Promises - How to Promise What You Can Keep. In: 4th IEEE International Workshop on Policies for Distributed Systems and Networks (Policy 2003), Lake Como, Italy, June 4-6, pp. 135–146 (2003)
9. Karjoth, G., Schunter, M.: A Privacy Policy Model for Enterprises. In: 15th IEEE Computer Security Foundations Workshop (CSFW), pp. 271–281. IEEE Computer Society Press, Washington (2002)
10. Kinateder, M., Pearson, S.: A Privacy-Enhanced Peer-to-Peer Reputation System. In: Bauknecht, K., Tjoa, A.M., Quirchmayr, G. (eds.) E-Commerce and Web Technologies. LNCS, vol. 2738, pp. 206–215. Springer, Heidelberg (2003)
11. Levy, S.E., Gutwin, C.: Improving Understanding of Website Privacy Policies with Fine-Grained Policy Anchors. In: WWW 2005, Chiba, Japan, May 10-14, pp. 10–14. ACM Press, New York (2005)
12. Cranor, L., Dobbs, B., Egelman, S., Hogben, G., Humphrey, J., Langheinrich, M., Marchiori, M., Presler-Marshall, M., Reagle, J., Schunter, M., Stampley, D.A., Wenning, R.: The Platform for Privacy Preferences 1.1 (P3P1.1) Specification; W3C Working Group Note (November 13, 2006), http://www.w3.org/TR/2006/NOTE-P3P11-20061113/
13. Pfitzmann, A., Pfitzmann, B., Schunter, M., Waidner, M.: Trusting Mobile User Devices and Security Modules. Computer 30/2, 61–68 (1997)
14. Pfitzmann, B., Waidner, M.: Federated Identity-Management Protocols. In: Christianson, B., Crispo, B., Malcolm, J.A., Roe, M. (eds.) Security Protocols. LNCS, vol. 3364, pp. 153–174. Springer, Heidelberg (2005)
15. Stufflebeam, W., Antón, A.I., He, Q., Jain, N.: Specifying Privacy Policies with P3P and EPAL: Lessons Learned. In: Proceedings of the 2004 ACM Workshop on Privacy in the Electronic Society, WPES 2004, Washington DC, USA, October 28 - 28, 2004, pp. 35–35. ACM Press, New York (2004)
16. Shamir, A.: How to Share a Secret. Communications of the ACM 22/11, 612–613 (1979)

Performance Comparison of Low-Latency Anonymisation Services from a User Perspective

Rolf Wendolsky, Dominik Herrmann, and Hannes Federrath

University of Regensburg, 93040 Regensburg, Germany

Abstract. Neither of the two anonymisation services Tor and AN.ON clearly outperforms the other one. AN.ON's user-perceived QoS is generally more consistent over time than Tor's. While AN.ON's network latencies are low compared to Tor, it suffers from limitations in bandwidth. Interestingly, Tor's performance seems to depend on the time of day: it increases in the European morning hours. Utilising AN.ON's reporting of concurrently logged-in users, we show a correlation between load and performance. The reported number of users should be adjusted, though, so that it serves as a better indicator for security and performance. Finally, the results indicate the existence of an overall tolerance level for acceptable latencies of approximately 4 seconds, which should be kept in mind when designing low-latency anonymisation services.

1 Introduction and Motivation

Several anonymisation services for low-latency communication have grown up from research projects recently: among them are the well-known systems AN.ON [3] and Tor [17]. This paper focuses on the performance of the services for web surfing from a user perspective.

Although AN.ON and Tor are based on common building blocks (e. g. so called *mixes* [6], which relay multiply encrypted traffic from a client to a server), they differ in various technical attributes such as structure, threat model and application range. AN.ON uses a limited set of *cascades*, each consisting of predefined mixing nodes. In contrast, Tor relies on a large amount of nodes from which random *circuits* are constructed in real-time. As the user base is usually hundreds or thousands of times bigger than the amount of nodes used for relaying traffic, performance issues may arise.

It has been shown that performance, especially latency, is an anonymity-relevant parameter [11]. We can assume that many users are not able to evaluate the real security of an anonymisation service [5]. Therefore, their decision to use a specific service may highly depend on its overall performance: Only few people are willing to use a slow service, and, regardless of any sophisticated cryptographical techniques, such a service might not provide any anonymity at all. Consequently, the performance from a user perspective might serve as an important indicator for the overall quality. Moreover, performance evaluations can be used to identify characteristics of the different approaches, and – obviously – they allow the evaluation of tuning measures.

N. Borisov and P. Golle (Eds.): PET 2007, LNCS 4776, pp. 233–253, 2007.

In this paper, we will provide an empirical study regarding the relation between performance and the number of concurrent users. Based on that we will present the results of a comparison of AN.ON and Tor from a user perspective and try to explain the source of any differences found. We will show that a naïve comparison of average throughputs and delays is hardly sufficient, but conclusions can be drawn with the help of inferential statistics nevertheless. Our results indicate the existence of an overall *performance threshold*. This means that users are not willing to use a service which fails to meet this threshold.

We will introduce the evaluation scenarios for our performance tests in section 2 and present our methodology for data collection in section 3. Section 4 contains a short description of the statistical methods used during analysis. The results of our evaluation of AN.ON and Tor are presented in section 5. We suggest areas for future research in section 6, while section 7 summarizes our findings.

2   Performance Indicators and Evaluation Scenarios

In this section we will present the relevant performance indicators and our evaluation scenarios. For the performance evaluation of the anonymisation services, we simulate the behaviour of a typical WWW-user who (1) requests web sites and (2) downloads files. We identified two performance indicators, namely *latency* and *bandwidth*.

The *bandwidth* (KBytes/s) indicates how fast data packets may be transmitted on a communication channel. The *latency* (milliseconds) corresponds to the roundtrip time of a network packet. Ideally, the latency is independent from the bandwidth. For large files it is almost irrelevant, whereas retrieving a web site (with many small objects) can be slowed down by high latencies substantially.

In order to profile the aforementioned indicators, we set up different *scenarios*. A scenario is characterised by two parameters: *type of simulation* and *URL language*. The *type of simulation* is either (1) a test with different web sites containing a (large) number of small objects {WEB}, or (2) a test with fixed-size downloads {DL}. The separation into different *URL languages* is a heuristic method to measure system performance in a local area, e. g. Germany, or world-wide. For our research, we split the tests into German {DE} and English {EN} content language. While the English pages can be used for a fair comparison of different anonymisers, the German sites allow profiling the AN.ON service from a local perspective.[1] The URLs were chosen from the most popular web sites according to Alexa [2] and the downloads according to downloads.de/downloads.com respectively (cf. table 7). Table 1 lists the basic scenarios.

3   Data Collection Methodology

In this section we will describe our methodology for collecting performance data from anonymisation services based on an example of the Tor network and

---

[1] All current AN.ON servers reside in Germany, whereas Tor is distributed throughout the world.

Table 1. General attributes of the basic scenarios

| | Simulation | WEB | | DL | |
	Language	DE	EN	DE	EN
Total URLs / scenario		11	14	3	3
Average requests / scenario		398	309	3	3
Average requests / URL		33.17	20.6	1	1
Average KBytes / scenario		1267	987	1520	1702
Average KBytes / URL		105.58	65.8	506.67	567.33

AN.ON. We will start off with an overview of our evaluation setup and the evaluated services. The major part of this section will present our data quality measures.

3.1 Test Suite Overview

There are some free tools available to measure proxy or server performance [10,15]. Unfortunately, they proved not suitable for the evaluation of anonymisation services. They focus on other applications and consequently lack important features such as failure tolerance. In the end, we decided to write a test suite specifically designed to meet our needs.

As we evaluate the services from a user perspective, the two performance parameters mentioned, *bandwidth* and *latency*, cannot be determined exactly: There are too many influences not under our control. Therefore, we approximate the performance of the services with the help of the two observable parameters *throughput* and *initial delay*. The throughput is calculated by dividing the amount of received bytes by the time needed for the data transmission. The initial delay is the time difference between sending the HTTP request and receiving the first chunk of the response.

Our test suite perfeval[2] is written in Perl (about 2.500 lines of code)[3]. The scripts retrieve a set of URLs via HTTP (non-recursively) and calculate throughput and initial delay for each HTTP request. All recorded data of a session is aggregated into a *test case*.

We utilise the Perl library *LWP::ParallelUA* [12] which can handle simultaneous connections. Thus, we are able to simulate the behaviour of a web browser: First, perfeval downloads the HTML page, and then it fetches all the embedded objects in parallel. In order to prevent proxies or web caches from influencing the results we send a *Cache-Control:no-cache* HTTP header [14] along with the request.

---

[2] We were running the test suite on two WindowsXP workstations with ActivePerl v5.8.7.815 [1]. The workstations were connected to the Internet directly and had public IP addresses.

[3] http://www.jondos.de/downloads/perfeval.zip

3.2 Scope of the Evaluation

Table 2 lists the three services we evaluated with `perfeval`. In the rest of this paper we will refer to them with the presented acronyms. We also use a control connection (DIRECT) for assessing the performance of the Internet connection used during testing.

Table 2. Evaluated systems

DIRECT	Direct web access without any proxy
TOR	Tor client v0.1.0.16, Privoxy v3.0.3
DD	AN.ON cascade *Dresden-Dresden* (JAP v00.05.078)
CCC	AN.ON cascade *Regensburg-CCC* (JAP v00.05.078)

Privoxy was configured with the option *toggle 0* in order to disable all of its filtering rules. The two mentioned AN.ON cascades were chosen because of high stability and high number of users at the time when we started the test.[4] The test run started on February 15 2006, 6:00 p. m., and ended on February 26 2006, 11:59 a. m. (both Berlin local time [5]) by manual interruption. Thus, we got test data for 10 complete days and 18 hours, that corresponds to 258 hour-based test cases for each combination of scenario parameters and tested systems. We therefore have 4128 test cases altogether.

For the scope of this article an individual web site or a file download is represented by its URL. Each URL may lead to a number of HTTP requests: Typically, a web sit causes additional requests (for the HTML page and all its embedded objects), whose number typically differs over time, whereas a download causes exactly one HTTP request.

3.3 Data Quality Measures

In order to get statistically utilisable results for measuring the tested services, the collected data should not be considerably influenced by

(a) external factors jeopardizing the validity of the test cases like downtimes of the network, downtimes and failures of services, HTTP errors reported by web sites, and errors in the evaluation software itself,
(b) bias introduced by the observation itself like concurrent tests on the same anonymisation service, concurrent test requests of the same resource, and performance fluctuations on the computer where the test software runs,
(c) influences through fluctuations during the test like performance fluctuations of requested resources and fluctuations of the total amount of requested data,

---

[4] At that time the remaining two AN.ON cascades were used for testing purposes only, and were neither stable in structure nor in code.
[5] Note that Germany has one single time zone.

(d) performance tampering through HTTP redirects,
(e) performance limit introduced by the Internet conection,
(f) varying performance throughout the day.

These influences have to be mitigated before and during the test. After that, the collected data must be examined for influences by the aforementioned factors. If at least one of those has a *non-negligible* influence, the corresponding data is probably not usable for any statistical analysis. We assume an influence as *non-negligible* if the ratio of (possibly influencing) "critical" cases to "good" cases is higher than 5%.[6]

In short, we found that our test data is of high quality regarding these measures. A more detailed description of our approach to measure data quality is presented in the following sections.

External factors. Single erroneous test cases resulting from a bad implementation of the test software may be discovered by looking for extreme values in the number of HTTP requests (which should be the same for each test case), the initial delay and the throughput.

HTTP errors, service failures, network and service downtimes may lead to missing or unintentionally influenced cases. For each unsuccessful HTTP request (i. e., the status code of the HTTP indicates a failure), we have to determine whether the source of the problem is the webserver or the network (i. e., the anonymisation service or the Internet connection). We will refer to the former as *errors*, to the latter as *failures*. This differentiation is important to measure the "quality" of an anonymisation service. Our software implements a sophisticated algorithm to differentiate errors from failures:

An unsuccessful HTTP request will be flagged as an *error*, if all of the following conditions apply immediately after the HTTP response has been received:

- a connection to the webserver/proxy can be established successfully
- a HTTP test request can be sent over the network
- a corresponding HTTP response is received
- the HTTP status code is not *200 OK* (or something similar)
- the HTTP status code is not *502 Service temporarily overloaded*, or *503 Gateway timeout*

Otherwise, the unsuccessful request is probably a *failure*, but further examinations are necessary. This is especially true for responses with status codes *502* and *503*, which can be issued by the webserver as well as by the proxy server. If the webserver is the originator, the request should be flagged as *error*, otherwise as *failure*. Timeouts, i. e., delays exceeding 60 seconds, are the most common type of *failures*.

Table 8 lists the number of cases missing either due to software errors or because of network or service downtimes. Compared to the total number in the

---

[6] Note that this is a heuristic approach. The quality measures are **ratios** and not probabilities as in statistical tests.

sample, they are negligible. It also shows that almost all *failures* occur for DD, but as less than 5% of all requests are affected, we still treat external influences as negligible. This finding indicates hardware or network problems on the AN.ON DD cascade, though. Its operators have not been aware of that until now.

The number of *errors* is uncritical for all but one case: the error ratio on the CCC cascade for English downloads is about 9%. That means that a lot of downloads were skipped, probably due to service-specific blockings by the web site operators (e. g. by blacklisting the IP of the last mix of the cascade). Nevertheless, this influence is limited to reducing the sample size for this service.

Bias introduced by the observation itself. The tests for web surfing / downloads together were composed to be completed in less than 30 minutes for each language. In order to force comparable and periodic hour-of-day-based time intervals from 0 to 23 (Berlin local time), we put a hard limit of 60 minutes on the total duration of a language test. For each test case, all URLs were processed sequentially so that no interference between them was possible[7]. As the DE and EN tests should not interfere with each other, we performed these test cases on two separate machines, the latter one starting with a time offset of 30 minutes. Figure 1 shows the course of events during the performance evaluation.

Table 8 shows that the hard limit of one hour was never reached in our experiment and that a 30-minute-overlapping did not occur more often than in 5% of the test cases. These influences are therefore not seen as critical.

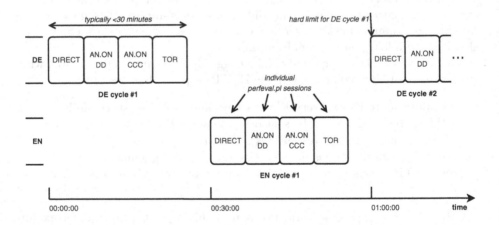

Fig. 1. Test sequence for performance evaluation

Influences through performance fluctuations. In order to avoid performance influences from slow web servers that could lead to wrong conclusions in the analysis, the measurements of the individual URLs are aggregated into one *test case* for each scenario. Accordingly, we do not try to evaluate the service

---

[7] Note that HTTP requests for each requested web site are done concurrently, but this is what a typical web browser would do as well.

performance regarding single URLs (although this would be possible with our result files, of course).

Another possible influence is related to the amount of data received in each test case. To make the cases of one scenario comparable, they should be of equal size. We compared the median and the interquartile range[8] (IQR) of the downloaded bytes for each service with the median and IQR of all services to analyse this influence.

Table 8 shows that the ratios of all medians are negligible. Although there are some problems with English downloads (causing a huge IQR ratio for the CCC cascade), they do not affect the median. Therefore, our analysis suggests that we have indeed collected similar amounts of data for the different services.

Note that measuring performance fluctuations within the infrastructure of the anonymisation service is beyond the scope of this paper. In particular, we are not trying to measure the performance of individual nodes or one anonymity service as a whole. For Tor, we have to trust the node selection algorithm of its client software – we are looking at performance from a user perspective after all.

HTTP redirects. Our evaluation software honours HTTP *301* and *302* redirect status codes. Although this behaviour is necessary for the imitation of a web browser, it introduces a new challenge: Our test might be influenced by server-side redirects *(geolocation)*, which would undermine the geographic separation introduced by the *URL language* scenario parameter.

It is rather difficult to rule out this influence completely as we cannot control the behaviour of the web servers. Of course, our software does not send any *Accept-Language* headers which would give away any information about its location or preferred language, nor does it interpret JavaScript code in the HTML pages which could be used to query language-specific browser attributes. But there are still more sophisticated ways for geolocation, for example by querying the WHOIS database for the IP address of the sender of the HTTP request. Obviously, it is impossible to fully prevent a webserver from delivering adapted versions of the requested content to the client. It has been observed that Tor (with its world-wide network of exit nodes) is subject to this phenomenon [18]. We screened the evaluation data to make sure that no geolocation was employed, though.

Note that language adaption is not as big a problem as it seems. HTTP requests which are automatically being redirected to a server located in close vicinity of the client are a far more intriguing threat. We have examined the URLs for the [EN] scenario and could not find any indication that this form of redirection was employed by any web site. Of course, some sites utilise *round robin* DNS entries in order to distribute the load on several webservers (e. g. google.com). But such procedures shouldn't affect the performance evaluation because their influence is averaged by the large amount of test cases.

Performance limit introduced by the Internet connection. If the local area network suffers from performance fluctuations, it may influence the observed

---

[8] The interquartile range is the difference of the upper 75% and the lower 25% quartile. It is a robust measure for the standard deviation of frequencies.

$$I(S_t) = \begin{cases} 0 & if \ Th_{\text{crit}}(S_t) \geq 0, \ \text{small or no influence} \\ 1 & if \ Th_{\text{crit}}(S_t) < 0, \ \text{possible high influence} \end{cases}$$

w.r.t

$$Th_{\text{crit}}(S_t) = Th(\text{DIRECT}_t) - Th(S_t) - \frac{IQR_B(\text{DIRECT})}{2}$$

where

$$S \in \{\text{DIRECT, TOR, DD, CCC}\}$$

$$t := \text{time (day and hour)}$$

$$S_t := \text{test case of } S \text{ at the time } t$$

$$IQR_B(\text{DIRECT}) := \text{Interquartile range of throughput of DIRECT}$$

$$Th(S_t) := \text{measured throughput of } S_t$$

$$Th_{\text{crit}}(S_t) := \text{critical throughput of } S_t$$

$$I(S_t) := \text{possible influence of DIRECT on } S_t$$

Fig. 2. Evaluating performance influences of the network connection

data as well. Network-caused performance breaks in all systems could be mis-interpreted as a common attribute. For example, if the network is not faster than the slowest anonymisation service, all systems would look the same. There is no influence if the local area netwok offers better performance than the fastest system at all times.

The basic idea to estimate the possible influence of the network (DIRECT) is to analyse all single test cases of all tested systems for this possible influence. We call the ratio of the number of all cases with a non-negligible influence to the total number of cases *critical influence ratio*. If this ratio is, for a scenario, higher than 5%, we call the influence of the network on the scenario *non-negligible*. Otherwise, we assume that there is no influence of the network on this scenario.

To calculate a *level of non-negligibility*, we suggest to evaluate all test cases by their throughput, separately for each scenario, by the formula presented in figure 2. This approach basically calculates the difference between the through-put measured for the network at a given hour and the throughput of a given test case in this hour. As a measure for the standard deviation of the network's bandwidth, we also provide the interquartile range for its througput. We sub-tract half of its value, as only the diminishment of the network's bandwidth is critical, and call the resulting value *critical throughput* for this test case. If the *critical throughput* is greater than zero, we assume a low possibility for network interference. Otherwise, the network influence is assumed to be non-negligible for this test case. As shown in table 8 (critical throughput influence ratio), we found a non-negligible network influence for 5 out of 12 scenarios. This means that care must be taken when these scenarios are analysed, as at least some clipping phenomena[9] are expected.

---

[9] Clipping means that some performance curves will have a hard break in the peaks.

Varying performance throughout the day. An anonymity service saturated with a big and distributed user group is expected to show a normal distribution in user numbers, bandwidth and latency for each hour and day. In reality, though, the user groups may be heterogenous and therefore have a strong influence on performance over time. Before statistically analysing and comparing services, it is therefore useful to exploratively identify time-dependend trends in the user behaviour.

During the performance evaluation we retrieved the real-time number of concurrent users provided by the AN.ON services for further analysis. We identified two major trends:

1. The user numbers seem to follow a sinusoidal curve with vertex at 11 a.m. (cf. figure 5). Given that most users of AN.ON are located in Europe [8], this means that the majority of them is using the service during the day and not during the night.
2. The variables *throughput* and *delay* seem to be normally distributed between 1 p.m. and 9 p.m. Therefore, the influence of varying loads on the AN.ON services is expected to be minimal in that time period.

Therefore, we decided to introduce a new scenario parameter *daytime* to simplify the comparison of AN.ON with Tor, which is more equally distributed over the whole day. *daytime* has the values *morning* (M) and *afternoon* (A), defined as the hour-of-day intervals 1-9 a.m. and 1-9 p.m. (Berlin local time). All test data from the remaining time periods was discarded.

4 Statistical Methodology for Analysis and Comparison

For distinguishing differences in our sample from "random noise", we performed thorough statistical analyses. This section provides a short explanation of the statistical background needed to understand the results presented in section 5.

4.1 t-tests

In order to compare two samples, we use *Student's t-test*, which is very robust against violations of the *normality assumption*. In this paper we will use t-tests to compare the mean value of a given parameter (i.e., throughput or delay) of two samples (i.e., two anonymisation services). The t-test checks whether the means of the tested parameters *differ significantly* (hypothesis H_1).

t-tests can only be applied under the following assumptions [16]:

1. normal distribution of data
2. homogeneity of variances
3. independent, randomly selected samples

The last assumption is already addressed by the data quality measures mentioned in section 3.3. As we cannot expect the data in our samples to be normally distributed, we employ the *Kolmogorov-Smirnov test*. If the result of this test is significant, the data of the sample is not normally distributed and the t-test may draw incorrect conclusions. Similarly, the equality of the variances is proven with the *Levene test*. Even if the Levene test shows significantly differing standard deviations, the t-test can still be applied. In this case a modified version of the t-test has to be applied, though.

In the following sections the results of the the t-tests are shown in the column labelled "Sides". The higher the number of asterisks (*, **, ***), the more significant is the evaluated difference of mean values. A dash (-) indicates that the test found no significant difference (e. g. table 3).

4.2 Regression Analysis

We analyse possible correlations of two or more metric parameters by a *Linear Regression Analysis*. It tests the assumption of a linear correlation between the dependend parameter y_i and the independent parameters x_i of the form

$$\hat{y}_i = b_0 + \sum_{j=1}^{m} b_j x_{ij}$$

for all test cases $i = 1, 2, \ldots, n$ and the independent parameters $j = 1, 2, \ldots, m$. In the following sections the confidence in the regression analysis is shown in the row labelled "Terms". The higher the number of asterisks (*, **, ***), the more significant is the estimated influence of the parameter (cf. table 6).

In order to be able to perform a regression analysis, the basic assumptions of *linearity, independence, homoscedasticity* and *normality* must be fulfilled for the data [7].

5 Evaluation

As mentioned earlier we decided to split the gathered data points into two data sets according to the time of day. The graphs in figures 5 and 6 show that user numbers, delay, and throughput follow a typical course for the two AN.ON services: between 1 p. m. and 9 p. m. the curves are approximately at the same level, whereas they resemble a quadratic function with a minimum at about 5 a. m. between 1 a. m. and 9 a. m. For the comparison of the services, we focus on the first of these periods which we call 'afternoon', as the AN.ON cascades are obviously not under full load during the latter one – most users are asleep during the 'morning' hours (cf. figure 6). Combining both the morning (M) and afternoon (A) data of the AN.ON services and comparing that with the results of Tor would unduly favor the AN.ON services, as Tor seems to be much less dependent on daytime.

Anyway, splitting the samples offers another benefit: As described in section 4.1 t-tests operate under the assumption of normally distributed data.[10] We

---

[10] Following common practices we use logarithmically transformed values for this purpose.

found that *within each of the two periods* the samples are either normally distributed or closely resemble a normal distribution. This is not the case if the samples include data of the whole day, though.

Note that we will only provide results on latencies for the WEB scenarios as they are irrelevant for downloads.

5.1 Descriptive Statistics for DD, CCC and Tor

Descriptive statistics can provide some first hints regarding the characteristics of a sample. Our results show that the evaluated systems *differ* in offered bandwidth and latency. We suspect that the differences are partly due to varying *loads* (amount of concurrent users) on the anonymisation services. In the rush hours of the afternoon period, DD has very high user numbers (about 1,700 concurrent users on average). In contrast, CCC, which had to be selected manually in order to use it, is used by only 650 users on average. Figure 3 shows the mean values of delay (a) and throughput (b) together with the observed standard deviations for the individual services.

In terms of average delays, CCC offers best performance. The mean values for DD and Tor are considerably worse, but they are too close together for a meaningful graphical comparison. We will provide more concrete results utilising t-tests in section 5.3 and 5.4.

On the other hand, Tor might outperform the AN.ON services in terms of bandwidth. Due to the comparably high standard deviations a comparison without thorough analysis is difficult, though. The AN.ON services tend to offer a more constant QoS. From the user perspective, this may be an advantage, as users might not be interested in performance peaks, but rather in adequate performance every time they use the service.

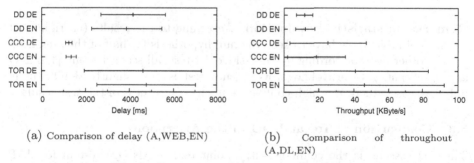

(a) Comparison of delay (A,WEB,EN)   (b)   Comparison   of   throughout (A,DL,EN)

Fig. 3. Comparison of latency in the afternoon

5.2 Tor over Daytime

While performance differences between the morning and afternoon periods are rather obvious for the AN.ON services (cf. figure 6), this is not that clearly visible for Tor. As Tor has a global network of nodes and a distributed user base, this is very reasonable. Looking at the descriptive statistics, though, we found that the mean values of delay and throughput differed a lot between the morning and the afternoon period.

The results of the t-test suggest that there is indeed a difference between the two time periods (cf. table 3 and statistical remarks). Local time may therefore have a significant influence on local measurements, and Tor might not only prefer nodes with the highest bandwidth as found in a recent study [4], but also the nearest (low-latency) nodes. This may be due to an implicit attribute of its implementation, although there is no sign of such a strategy in the source code. If so, Tor's practical anonymity would be affected: The difficulty of mounting a collusion attack to capture the connections of specific local user groups would be substantially reduced. Another reason for the observed pattern might be that the initial assumption of a distributed user community is false. This is difficult to prove, though, as the Tor network does not provide information about the location and the number of its users. Accordingly, further research is needed to explain our observations.

Table 3. Tor: Performance differences morning/afternoon

Scenario			Means (exp)		Kol.-Smir.			T-Test	Sides	
Sim	Lang	Measure	M	A	M	A	Levene	T (df)	2	1
WEB	DE	Log(Delay)	3472	4097	-	-	3.2(177)	-2.3(177)	*	*
WEB	EN	Log(Delay)	3790	4231	-	*	1.0(178)	-1.8(178)	-	*
WEB	DE	Log(Thr)	8.7	6.3	*	-	6.9(177)*	2.4(170)	**	**
WEB	EN	Log(Thr)	5.9	4.9	-	-	0.6(178)	2.1(178)	*	*
DL	DE	Log(Thr)	43.9	34.7	-	-	0.0(176)	1.9(176)	-	*
DL	EN	Log(Thr)	45.7	39.1	-	-	1.5(176)	1.6(176)	-	-

Significance codes: *** $p<0.001$, ** $p<0.01$, * $p<0.05$.

Remarks on statistical evaluation. According to the results (cf. rightmost columns of table 3) we have to keep the null hypothesis for half of the scenarios. On the other hand, according to the 1-sided[11] t-test, all scenarios but {DL,EN} are significant. As the Kolmogorov-Smirnov test is only slightly significant in only two cases, there is a high confidence in the correctness of the test result.

5.3   Comparison of Tor and DD in the Afternoon

The DD cascade is the common entry point to the AN.ON system for JAP users. As there is (at the time of measurement) no automatic switching function between different AN.ON cascades, most unexperienced users (who do not know how to switch cascades) use the DD cascade. In terms of latency the statistical

---

[11] If there is a good reason – not concluded from the collected data – that one of the means should be higher or lower than the other one, the p-value (not shown in the tables) of the t-test may be halved, as only one side of the test is of interest, and the test returns a higher significance.

results from table 4 show that there is little difference between DD and Tor in the afternoon period. This may indicate that there is a tolerance level for this kind of unexperienced users regarding latency of approximately 4 seconds. A constant latency above this level seems to deter from using the system.[12] This supplements the results of [11] who found that there is a linear relation between user numbers and latency by altering the internal delay of the DD service.

Remarks on statistical evaluation. Looking at table 4 we observe that DD seems to have a slight advantage over Tor in regard to latency, but the difference is only significant for the {WEB,EN} scenario. But then, Tor obviously offers higher channel capacities by far (as shown by the {DL} scenarios) and thus is able to outrun DD in the {WEB} scenarios. The significant difference in bandwidth shows up in the {WEB,EN} scenario once again: Here, the difference in bandwidth is not as clear as in the {WEB,DE} scenario however.

Table 4. Comparison of Tor and DD in the afternoon

Scenario			Means (exp)		Kol.-Smir			T-Test	
Sim	Lang	Measure	Tor	DD	Tor	DD	Levene	T(df)	Sig
WEB	DE	Log(Delay)	4032	3689	-	**	31.7(178)***	-0.3(131)	-
WEB	EN	Log(Delay)	4238	3427	*	*	19.4(178)***	2.1(153)	*
WEB	DE	Log(Thr)	6.30	4.30	-	*	22.2(178)***	3.8(140)	***
WEB	EN	Log(Thr)	4.92	3.75	-	-	17.6(178)***	2.7(150)	**
DL	DE	Log(Thr)	34.71	10.31	-	*	46.1(176)***	7.7(119)	***
DL	EN	Log(Thr)	39.13	10.25	-	***	53.8(176)***	6.7(122)	***

Significance codes: *** p<0.001, ** p<0.01, * p<0.05.

Units: throughput [KBytes/s], delay [msecs].

5.4 Comparison of Tor and CCC in the Afternoon

While the DD cascade is the default in AN.ON's client software (JAP), the CCC cascade has to be explicitly selected by the user. Obviously, most users stay with the default (cf. figure 5). Consequently, this situation leads to lower latencies on CCC than on DD. Nevertheless, compared to Tor the bandwith of the CCC cascade is still lagging behind as shown in the {DL} scenarios in table 5. This is true even for the German downloads, where CCC presumably has an implicit advantage. Nevertheless, CCC outperforms Tor in the {WEB} scenarios, which is quite interesting. Apparently, for web surfing extremely low latencies (CCC) are more critical than sheer bandwith (Tor).

5.5 Correlations of User Numbers and Performance

In this section we will evaluate the influence of *load* on performance. AN.ON cascades provide the number of concurrent users at a given time. We will use

---

[12] Note that using the system and being connected to it are two different perspectives.

Table 5. Comparison of Tor and CCC in the afternoon

Scenario			Means (exp)		Kol.-Smir.			T-Test	
Sim	Lang	Measure	Tor	CCC	Tor	CCC	Levene	T (df)	Sig
WEB	DE	Log(Delay)	4032	1091	-	-	98.4(178)***	17.5(96)	***
WEB	EN	Log(Delay)	4238	1191	*	-	91.2(178)***	18.9(105)	***
WEB	DE	Log(Thr)	6.30	10.07	-	-	25.0(178)***	-9.1(137)	***
WEB	EN	Log(Thr)	4.92	9.15	-	-	23.3(178)***	-11.4(143)	***
DL	DE	Log(Thr)	34.71	21.40	-	-	8.4(177)**	2.4(161)	*
DL	EN	Log(Thr)	39.13	15.84	-	**	25.0(176)***	4.3(142)	***

Significance codes: *** $p<0.001$, ** $p<0.01$, * $p<0.05$.
Units: throughput [KBytes/s], delay [msecs].

this information to investigate the correlation between *user number* of both AN.ON cascades and the performance parameters. We expect a strong positive correlation between user numbers and latency and a strong negative correlation between user numbers and throughput. Figure 4 shows this graphically in two scatter plots.

The performance parameters have been scaled logarithmically as we expect an exponential influence of the load. The correlation is especially explicit in the selected *morning period* which contains data points with widely varying user numbers, whereas the afternoon period consists of fairly uniform data that is not suitable for further analysis.

The results of a regression analysis confirm the graphical observations. While both cascades are similar in terms of delay, their characteristics differ a lot in terms of throughput. Apparently, user numbers have a much greater effect on the performance of CCC than on DD. This observation cannot be explained by a gerenally inferior infrastructure (i. e., less capacity) of CCC, which still has plenty of unused resources (cf. figure 3). Instead, we assume that users on DD are considerably less active than those on CCC. A constant and inactive user

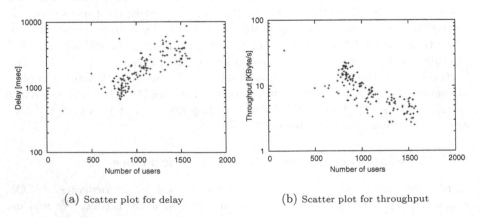

(a) Scatter plot for delay   (b) Scatter plot for throughput

Fig. 4. Influence of number of users on performance (M,WEB,DE,DD)

Table 6. Regression model for performance and user numbers for language DE

			Scenario			
	WEB				DL	
	DD	CCC	DD	CCC	DD	CCC
Param. ($\hat{y}_i$)	Log(Delay)	Log(Delay)	Log(Thr)	Log(Thr)	Log(Thr)	Log(Thr)
Terms						
Const. (B_0)	2.708***	2.655***	1.49***	1.66***	2.11***	2.871***
	(0.04)	(0.02)	(0.04)	(0.03)	(0.05)	(0.05)
Users	5.075***	5.802***	-5.215***	-10.235***	-6.781***	-25.170***
Model						
N	258	256	258	256	256	256
R^2	0.612	0.522	0.623	0.626	0.631	0.774
F	404.2***	277.1***	422.8***	426.0***	433.4***	870.8***
df	1/256	1/254	1/256	1/255	1/255	1/255

Significance codes: *** p<0.001, ** p<0.01, * p<0.05 .
Standard errors in brackets (). Users: $B_1 * 10^4$.

base would correspond to the findings in [11] where still some hundred users were counted on DD even when the service had been made unusably slow.

According to these findings raw user numbers are no suitable predictor for load and expected performance on a cascade. We therefore suggest that AN.ON services should only report the number of *active users*. Otherwise, users might be deceived in terms of the provided anonymity, which is shown in JAP's *anonymeter*. As adjusted user numbers would correspond to the actual load they could serve as suitable performance measure. Due to their different characteristics finding a uniform regression model for multiple cascades can be a daunting task, though.

Remarks on statistical evaluation. As we assume exponential correlations, all performance parameters are transformed by log_{10}. For the DE scenarios, we could clearly identify normally distributed (transformed) residuals, while this

Table 7. Domains chosen from Alexa's[2] top 20 and Downloads.de/.com top 200

Simulation	Language	Domains
WEB	DE	google.de spiegel.de amazon.de t-online.de msn.de mobile.de leo.org freenet.de arcor.de heise.de
WEB	EN	yahoo.com msn.com google.com passport.net amazon.com myspace.com microsoft.com bbc.co.uk aol.com blogger.com go.com alibaba.com cnn.com craigslist.org
DL	DE	virenschutz.info gratisgames24.de neuesvon.de
DL	EN	morpheus.com freewarefiles.com macromedia.com

To minimize space requirements, the domains are listed here only, not the downloaded files or the protocol identifier. Files were requested by HTTP only.

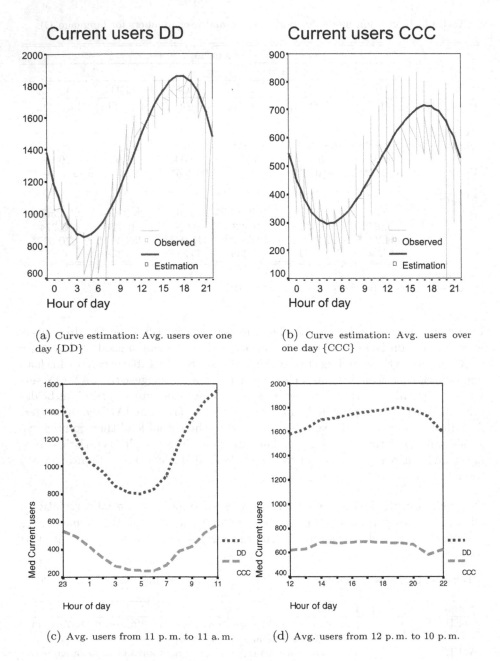

(a) Curve estimation: Avg. users over one day {DD}

(b) Curve estimation: Avg. users over one day {CCC}

(c) Avg. users from 11 p. m. to 11 a. m.

(d) Avg. users from 12 p. m. to 10 p. m.

Fig. 5. User behaviour in AN.ON cascades

is not the case for the EN scenarios, though. As shown in table 6 the exponential correlation is highly significant and explains most of the spread of the performance parameters ($R^2 > 0.5$).

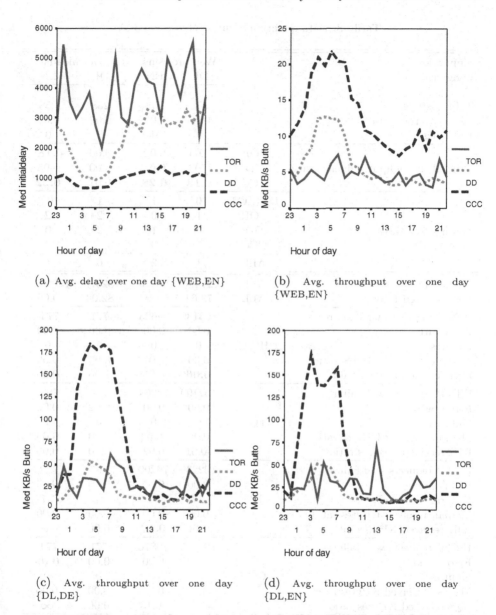

(a) Avg. delay over one day {WEB,EN}

(b) Avg. throughput over one day {WEB,EN}

(c) Avg. throughput over one day {DL,DE}

(d) Avg. throughput over one day {DL,EN}

Fig. 6. Graphical comparison of different anonymity services

6   Future Work

Maybe our methodology for collecting performance data can be further improved concerning the robustness of the collected data. As measurements took place always in the same interval, this might give rise to inherent biases due to repeated network phenomena being in time with the test cycles. A simple solution might

Table 8. Data quality measures (cf. section 3.3)

Simulation Language		Web browsing DE	EN	Downloads DE	EN
Total test cases		258	258	258	258
30min overlap ratio		0.02	0.05	0.02	0.05
1h breaks		0	0	0	0
	TOR	0.04	0.02	0.00	**0.18**
Critical throughput influence ratio	DD	0.03	0.04	0.00	0.05
	CCC	**0.13**	**0.28**	0.01	**0.22**
	DIRECT	0	1	1	0
	TOR	1	0	2	2
Missing test cases	DD	0	1	2	0
	CCC	0	0	1	0
	ALL	1	2	6	2
Median received KBytes	ALL	1274.65	997.1	1529.44	1759.69
IQR received KBytes	ALL	73.64	56.50	82.00	0.00
HTTP Requests w/o failures		103130	79623	771	774
Error ratio		0.00	0.00	0.00	0.00
Failures	DIRECT	0	0	0	0
Median received KBytes ratio		0.00	0.01	0.00	0.00
IQR received KBytes ratio		**0.06**	0.05	0.00	0.00
HTTP requests w/o failures		102199	79264	768	768
Error ratio		0.00	0.00	0.02	0.02
Failures	TOR	0	0	0	**1**
Median received KBytes ratio		0.00	-0.02	0.00	0.00
IQR received KBytes ratio		-0.01	0.02	0.00	0.00
HTTP requests w/o failures		102236	79200	767	772
Error ratio		0.00	0.00	0.00	0.00
Failures	DD	**17**	**11**	**15**	**27**
Median received KBytes ratio		0.00	0.00	0.00	0.00
IQR received KBytes ratio		**0.06**	**0.17**	0.00	0.00
HTTP requests w/o failures		102845	79876	771	774
Error ratio		0.00	0.00	0.00	**0.09**
Failures	CCC	**3**	0	0	0
Median received KBytes ratio		0.00	0.00	0.00	0.00
IQR received KBytes ratio		-0.01	-0.13	0.00	∞

involve randomly changing session time slots or delays (cf. section 3.3), e. g. using a Poisson distribution as proposed in [13].

Moreover, extending the measured time frame would allow for interesting long term analyses and could help the developer community to understand the impact of newly introduced features. Besides, more AN.ON cascades with high load should be investigated in order to confirm the findings about a user tolerance level, and for building a common regression model for the cascade performance depending on user numbers. This will be more promising in the future, as AN.ON now has a client-based load balancing, and may take this study as a reason for only counting active users.

Finally, the time-dependent performance differences of Tor should be further analysed.

7   Conclusion

Evaluating the performance of Tor and two AN.ON cascades, we have shown that Tor, a large scale implementation of a free-route mixing protocol, is subject to unpredictable performance, while AN.ON, implementing typically more central mix cascades, is able to offer more consistent performance in general.

The suggestions of the Tor community regarding tuning the connection handling policy of the web browser to mitigate Tor's rather high network latencies [19] are a reasonable approach. Anyway, the overall performance of Tor is already sufficient for fast web surfing and downloads. The reason for the performance differences between morning and afternoon periods remains unclear for now. If Tor's routing strategy was really lured into selecting close-by nodes, this would have considerable implications for the anonymity provided.

In contrast, AN.ON's advantage in latency is restrained by its limited bandwidth and its lack of a load balancing mechanism. Apparently, the DD cascade of AN.ON suffers from high loads (up to 2,000 concurrent users observed). Therefore it cannot deliver satisfying performance during the busy afternoon period where it behaves comparable to Tor regarding latency. The less frequently used CCC cascade is able to offer low-latency web surfing, but at the price of a smaller user base and therefore less anonymity.

An important finding is the supposed user tolerance level for latency: Tor, as a distributed network with many entry points, may automatically adapt to user expectations regarding latency, and therefore pick up as many users as possible with the given network structure. Its performance is not expected to suffer noticeably from single new users connecting to the system. AN.ON, on the other hand, deters a lot of users by offering a single entry point for new users right at the tolerance level, as the performance of this entry point is much more affected by new users than that of Tor.

As this relatively high latency seems to be tolerated by most privacy-aware users, i. e., the ones using Tor or AN.ON, this level may serve as a foundation for a new definition of *low-latency* in the context of anonymity services. Accordingly, this observation might be useful for designing new and more secure anonymity protocols. Further experiments should verify this level and whether it changes over time.

Acknowledgement

We thank Rainer Boehme for his priceless help concerning our statistical analysis, the reviewers for their valuable hints and remarks, and Simson Garfinkel for helping us as shepherd to give the article the final cut.

References

1. ActiveState ActivePerl: (2006),
   http://www.activestate.com/Products/ActivePerl/
2. Alexa Top Sites: (2006-02-06), http://www.alexa.com/site/ds/top_sites
3. AN.ON: Protection of Privacy on the Internet (2006),
   http://www.anon-online.de
4. Bauer, K., et al.: Low-Resource Routing Attacks Against Anonymous Systems.
   Technical Report (2007),
   http://www.cs.colorado.edu/department/publications/reports/docs/
   CU-CS-1025-07.pdf
5. Boehme, R., et al.: On the PET Workshop Panel Mix Cascades vs. Peer-to-Peer:
   Is One Concept Superior? In: Martin, D., Serjantov, A. (eds.) PET 2004. LNCS,
   vol. 3424, pp. 243–255. Springer, Heidelberg (2005)
6. Chaum, D.: Untraceable electronic mail, return addresses, and digital pseudonyms.
   Communications of the ACM 4(2) (1981)
7. Draper, N.R., et al.: Applied Regression Analysis, p. 17. Wiley, New York (1966)
8. Federrath, H.: Privacy Enhanced Technologies: Methods - Markets - Misuse. In:
   Katsikas, S.K., Lopez, J., Pernul, G. (eds.) TrustBus 2005. LNCS, vol. 3592, pp.
   1–9. Springer, Heidelberg (2005)
9. I2P: (2006), http://www.i2p.net
10. JMeter: (2006), http://jakarta.apache.org/jmeter/
11. Köpsell, S.: Low Latency Anonymous Communication - How long are users willing
    to wait? In: Müller, G. (ed.) ETRICS 2006. LNCS, vol. 3995, pp. 221–237. Springer,
    Heidelberg (2006)
12. LWP: ParallelUA 2.57 (2006),
    http://search.cpan.org/~marclang/ParallelUserAgent-2.57/
13. Paxson, V.: End-to-end routing behavior in the internet. In: Proceedings of the
    ACM SIGCOMM Conference on Applications, Technologies, Architectures, and
    Protocols for Computer Communications, pp. 25–38 (1996)
14. RFC2616 Hypertext Transfer Protocol - HTTP/1.1. Section 14.9 (2006)
15. Servertest: (2006), http://softwaregarden.com/products/servertest/index.html
16. Sheskin, D.J.: Handbook of parametric and nonparametric statistical procedures,
    2nd edn., p. 247. Chapman & Hall/CRC, Boca Raton (2000)
17. Tor: An anonymous Internet communication system (2006), http://tor.eff.org
18. Tor FAQ: Why does Google show up in foreign languages? (2006),
    http://wiki.noreply.org/noreply/TheOnionRouter/TorFAQ#GoogleLanguage
19. Tor Wiki: (2006),
    http://wiki.noreply.org/noreply/TheOnionRouter/FireFoxTorPerf

Appendix

The criteria for our choices of URLs were

- server performance much better than performance offered by anonymisation
  service, so that the results are not biased by slow servers[13]

---

[13] As we can never be sure that all servers have an adequate speed during the measurement, we aggregate the download performance of a set of URLs to a *test case* in order to mitigate possible influences.

- comparable number of URLs and downloaded bytes within the same scenario
- low number of HTTP errors produced by the requested web servers
- average total download time for web sites plus downloads of one language is much smaller than 30 minutes
- for web site URLs: plausibility of ranking in the Alexa top list

Geolocation detection. As stated in section 3.3, the separation of the EN/DE scenarios might be jeopardised through geolocation of the client based on its IP address. Geolocation is performed by the webserver in order to (1) provide a localised version of a web site, or to (2) enhance the user-view performance by redirecting the request to a "nearer" webserver.

Localised versions of web sites do not influence our tests unduly, because latency and bandwidth are not affected. However, if requests are re-routed to another server, this will change. We applied the following checks to check whether any form of request re-routing took place:

- We utilised the Unix *dig* utility and examined the DNS records for the individual hosts. We found multiple IPs and short TTLs, which indicates that several sites employed *round robin* IP rotation. Typically, web sites under high load use this approach for load balancing, but not for geolocation.
- We requested the individual URLs from our {EN} scenarios with the Unix *wget* utility and looked for HTTP redirects, which the webserver might send during geolocation: No URL used in the scenarios employed HTTP redirects for their homepage.

Anonymity in the Wild: Mixes on Unstructured Networks

Shishir Nagaraja

Computer Laboratory
JJ Thomson Avenue, Cambridge CB3 0FD, UK
shishir.nagaraja@cl.cam.ac.uk

Abstract. As decentralized computing scenarios get ever more popular, unstructured topologies are natural candidates to consider running mix networks upon. We consider mix network topologies where mixes are placed on the nodes of an unstructured network, such as social networks and scale-free random networks. We explore the efficiency and traffic analysis resistance properties of mix networks based on unstructured topologies as opposed to theoretically optimal structured topologies, under high latency conditions. We consider a mix of directed and undirected network models, as well as one real world case study – the LiveJournal friendship network topology. Our analysis indicates that mix-networks based on scale-free and small-world topologies have, firstly, mix-route lengths that are roughly comparable to those in expander graphs; second, that compromise of the most central nodes has little effect on anonymization properties, and third, batch sizes required for warding off intersection attacks need to be an order of magnitude higher in unstructured networks in comparison with expander graph topologies.

1 Introduction

As governments pursue large scale surveillance and censorship programs, anonymity in online communication mechanisms is an increasingly important requirement. Anonymous communications are also useful in building resistance against a global passive adversary who can subject the targets to traffic analysis. Often, an attacker will try to destabilize a network by building a dossier of the most central nodes, and attacking ones on the top of the list. Traffic analysis of inter-node communication offers basic tools to collect necessary intelligence in order to plan an attack.

Seminal work by Chaum [Cha81] introduced mix networks as a technique to provide anonymous communications where messages are relayed through a sequence of intermediate nodes called mixes, to make the task of tracing them through the network as difficult as possible. The essential idea is to make the inputs of each mix bit-wise unlinkable to its outputs.

Anonymity research conducted since, can be classified into low-latency or real time systems primarily for Internet browsing such as onion routing [STRL00] and high-latency or non-real time systems such as mixminion [DDM03].

N. Borisov and P. Golle (Eds.): PET 2007, LNCS 4776, pp. 254–271, 2007.

The topology of a mix network plays an important role in its efficiency and traffic analysis resistance properties. The mainstream design paradigm that has emerged so far is that of structured network topologies based on regular graphs. The theory is that such topologies are amenable to theoretical analysis that proves they have optimal expansion properties. This leads to a mix network design that is highly efficient and resistant to traffic analysis. Examples are onion-routing systems such as TOR [DMS04]that use a complete graph topology, where a mix can contact every other mix in the network. While such models are theoretically elegant, the assumption that every node in the network is equally resourced (as regular graphs necessitate) to handle network traffic loads is their main drawback.

An alternate paradigm is topology based on unstructured networks, such as those inspired from social networks. The argument in their favor being that the incentive to carry traffic is clear and simple - friends carry each-others traffic. Moreover, no additional resources go into constructing an overlay network since the pre-existing topology is used by the mix network as well, which works well for power constrained environments such as adhoc networks and sensor networks. Legal considerations play an important role too. It is not enough to merely have a large number of mixes. When hassled by legal requests (such as a subpoena to hand-over mix server logs to the police), a mix-network where friends route each others traffic, is likely to have a higher proportion of servers in operation, as opposed to a synthetic network.

A comparison between the two paradigms needs to address mix-network efficiency, resilience to corrupt nodes and the loss of anonymity from statistical disclosure attacks.

In this paper we analyze various types of unstructured networks, especially social networks and evaluate their suitability as mix topologies. We discuss the reasons behind using social networks to route mix traffic and we analyze the suitability of various types of model networks to routing mix traffic and offer a comparison between them. We also analyze the theoretical bounds on anonymity such networks can provide in terms of mixing speed and resistance to traffic analysis. We apply concepts from spectral graph theory to derive the route length necessary to provide maximal anonymity.

This paper is organized as follows: Section 3 discusses the various topologies used in our analysis. Section 4, lays out the evaluation framework to measure the traffic analysis resistance of various topologies. Section 5 discusses the application of the framework to various topologies and the results obtained. Finally, we offer our conclusions in section 6.

2   Related Work

Danezis [Dan03] explored the anonymity provided by expander graph topologies, this is one of the main sources of inspiration for our work. He established the thoretical bounds of anonymity for expander graphs, and also showed that they were optimal.

Borisov [Bor05] analyzes anonymous communications over a De Bruijn graph topology overlay network. He analyzes the deBruijn graph topology and comments on their successful mixing capabilities.

3   Network Models

In this section we give a brief introduction to the network models we wish to analyze as candidates for mix network topologies.

3.1   Erdös-Rényi Model of Random Networks

One of the earliest models for heterogeneous networks is the Erdös-Rényi (ER) model [ER59]. Although seldomly found in real world networks, their use has been popularised by the work of Eschenauer and Gligor [EG02] in designing a key management scheme for sensor networks.

Here, we start from N vertices without any edges. Subsequently, edges connecting two randomly chosen vertices are added as the result of a Bernoulli trial, with a parameter p. It generates random networks with no particular structural bias. The average degree $\langle k \rangle = 2L/N$ where L is the total number of edges, can also be used as a control parameter. ER model networks have a logarithmically increasing average shortest path length l with increasing N, a normal degree distribution, and a clustering coefficient close to zero.

3.2   Scale-Free Networks with Linear Preferential Attachment

A number of popular peer-to-peer systems are found to have heterogeneous topologies with heavy tailed degree distributions. The work of Ripeanu [RFI02] shows that two popular systems, Gnutella [KM02] and Freenet [CSWH00], have power-law degree distributions.

A variable X is said to follow a heavy tail distribution if $Pr[X > x] \sim x^{-k} L(x)$ where $k \in \Re^+$ and $L(x)$ is a slowly varying function so that $\lim_{x \to \infty} \frac{L(tx)}{L(x)} \to 1$. A power-law distribution is simply a variation of the above where one studies $Pr[X = x] \sim x^{-(k+1)} = x^{-\alpha}$. The degree of a node is the number of links it has to other nodes in the network. If the degree distribution of a network follows a power-law distribution it is known as a scale-free network. The power-law in the degree or link distribution reflects the presence of central individuals who interact with many others on a continual basis and play a key role in relaying information.

We denote a scale-free network generated by preferential attachment, by $G_{m,N}(V, E)$ where m is the number of initial nodes created at time=t_0 and N is the total number of nodes in the network. At every time step $t_i, i \geq 0$, one node is added to the network. For every node v added, we create m edges from v to existing nodes in the network according to the following linear preferential attachment function due to Barabasi and Albert [AB02]:

$$Pr[(v, i)] = k_i / \sum_j k_j$$

where k_i is the degree of node i. We continue until $|V| = N$.

3.3 Scale-Free Random Graph Topology

An alternate way of constructing a large scale-free network is to create a network with a given power-law degree sequence that is random in all other aspects. Aiello et al. [ACL00] propose such a random graph model inspired by massive AT&T call graphs, with two parameters α and β. Where, α gives the fraction of nodes with degree 1 and β defines the exponent of the power-law function. Then, if y be the number of vertices of degree $x > 0$, x and y satisfy $log(y) = \alpha - \beta log(x)$.

3.4 Klienberg-Watts-Strogatz(KWS) Small World Topology

Our next network model is inspired by the network of social contacts. It is well known that any two people are linked by a chain of half a dozen others who are pairwise acquainted – known as the 'small-world' phenomenon. This idea was popularised by Milgram in the 60s [Mil67].

The KWS graph topology models a small world network that encapsulates the following: a network rich in local connections, with a few long range connections. The network generation starts from a N by N lattice each point representing an individual in a social network. The lattice distance $d((i, j), (k, l)) = |k-i|+|l-j|$. For a parameter p, every node u has a directed link to every other node v within $d(u, v) \le p$. For parameters q and r, we construct q long range directed links from u to a node v with a probability distribution $[Pr(u, v)] = \frac{(d(u,v))^{(-r)}}{\sum_v (d(u,v))^{(-r)}}$.

Low r values means long-range connections, whereas higher values lead to preferential connections in the vicinity of u.

3.5 LiveJournal (LJ)

In order to test our ideas on a real world unstructured network, we turned to a large-scale social network called LiveJournal (LJ). LiveJournal is a social networking and blogging site with several million members and a large collection of user defined communities. LiveJournal allows members to maintain journals, individual and group blogs, and – most importantly for our study here – it allows people to declare which other members are their friends. Using a web crawler called touchgraph (http://www.touchgraph.com), we traced the LJ network to the online friendship network. The snapshot of the network we use in our analysis has 3,746,240 nodes and 27,430,000 edges.

A mix server bundled along with a future LiveJournal client acts as the basis of mix deployment. Mix circuits are built on top of the social network topology.

3.6   Expander Graphs

Danezis [Dan03] previously analyzed the use of expander graph topologies to construct mix networks. Expanders are well known to have excellent expansion properties. We include this as a baseline comparison against theoretical structured topologies. An expander graph $G_{N,D}$ has a homogeneous topology with N nodes each with a degree D.

4   Evaluation Framework for Measuring Traffic Analysis Resistance

Before we set out the evaluation framework, we first clarify what we mean by "anonymity" in this paper. The focus of this work is on message receiver anonymity [SD02]: given a message, the attacker should not be able to determine who sent it to whom, leading to both sender and receiver anonymity requirements. Sender anonymity is determined by the probability that a specific node is the originator of a given message. Receiver anonymity, also an important requirement in a number real world situations, is the probability that a specific node is the recipient of a given message whose sender is known. There are other definitions such as relationship anonymity defined by Pfitzmann et. al. [PH00]. We also note there that the evaluation framework is the contribution of Danezis [Dan03].

The objective of our analysis is to determine how the topology of a mix network affects the amount of effort on the attacker's part to uniquely identify communication endpoints using traffic analysis attacks alone. The effectiveness of such attacks depends heavily on the topology of the underlying network. If the attacker is not able to reduce anonymity beyond his or her initial knowledge then the mix network is said to be resistant to traffic analysis attacks under the given threat model.

The attacker might also employ side channel analysis on the end-points before the data enters the mix network, we do not consider such attacks here. Side channel information might be timestamps or other information related to the protocol or mechanism in use. Attacks using such information can be used to link messages to the communication end-points, and are known as *traffic confirmation attacks* [RSG98], their effectiveness depends on the mixes' batching and flushing strategy.

4.1   Threat Model

Throughout this paper we consider the adversarial context of a global passive adversary.

4.2   Measuring Anonymity

There are several ways one can express the anonymity a system provides. In our analysis we use a quantitative method due to Serjantov and Danezis [SD02], based on the following definition: "Anonymity of a system may be defined as the amount of information the attacker is missing to uniquely identify an actor's link to an action". In information theoretic terms, the anonymity of the system $\mathcal{A}$, is the entropy $\mathcal{E}$, of the probability distribution over all the actors α_i, that they committed a specific action.

$$\mathcal{A} = \mathcal{E}[\alpha_i] = -\sum_i Pr[\alpha_i]log_2 Pr[\alpha_i] \tag{1}$$

This gives the number of bits of information, with a negative sign, that the attacker is missing before they can uniquely identify a sender or a receiver.

4.3   Modeling Mix Route Selection

In order to understand the maximal anonymity provided by a mix network we use Markov chains to model the route selection process, as they closely match the way mixes are selected to form a mix route.

The process of selecting a mix route of length k by selecting k random nodes in the mix network, is equivalent to first selecting a random mix node, and, then a random neighbour of the first mix, repeating this process $k - 2$ times. Hence we may model the route selection process as a random walk on the underlying graph, with the various states of the Markov chain process being the mix nodes of the network.

4.4   Measuring Mix Network Efficiency

Receiver Anonymity

In analyzing the receiver anonymity provided by a particular network topology we need to examine the probability that a specific message is at a particular node at a certain time. In order to link the sender and the receiver to a particular message, the attacker must retrace the steps taken by the message through the mix network starting from the receiver. Let the mix network be an undirected graph $G(V, E)$. If messages m_{ij} are inserted at node i destined for j, then for a message m_x^t at node x at time t, the attacker must link m_x^t to m_{ij}. Note that m_x^t might either be in the edge or the core of the mix network.

Applying the above mentioned information theoretic metric we have:

$$\mathcal{A} = \mathcal{E}(p_{ij})$$

where $p_{ij} = Pr[m_x^t \ is \ m_{ij}]$ is the probability distribution over all the nodes in V.

Suppose a message is inserted into the mix network through a randomly chosen node. Then after an infinite number of steps, the probability that the message is present on any randomly chosen node in the network is given by stationary distribution of the Markov chain π. Let $q^{(0)}$ be the initial probability distribution describing the node on which message m is introduced into the mix network, this is equivalent to the distribution of input load across the nodes in network. $q^{(t)}$ then, is the probability distribution of the node on which the message is present after t steps. (this is also known as the state probability vector of the Markov chain at time $t \geq 0$). With increasing t one would like to see that $q^{(t)}$ merges with π. The rate at which this takes place is known as the *convergence rate* of the Markov chain, and the difference itself is called the *relative point-wise distance* defined as:

$$\Delta(t) = max_i \frac{|q_i^t - \pi_i|}{\pi_i} \tag{2}$$

The smaller the relative point-wise distance, faster the convergence, and more efficient the mix network. It is now easy to see that the maximum receiver anonymity $Pr[x = receiver|y = sender]$ the network can provide is the entropy of the stationary distribution of the chain.

$$\mathcal{A}_{network} = \mathcal{E}(\pi). \tag{3}$$

When P is the transition matrix of the chain it is well known that P has n real eigen-vectors π_i and n eigenvalues λ_i [Wes01].

By using the relation $q^{(t)} = q^{(0)} P^{(t)}$, we calculate the probability distribution of a message being on a node after having transited a mix route of length t.

Sender Anonymity

Next, we consider the probability distribution of potential originators of a given message recipient. This may also be modeled by a Markovian random walk. For a destination node y, consider all random walks terminating at y. In order to achieve maximal sender anonymity, all these walks must be long enough for the respective state probability vector to converge with the stationary distribution. Since this applies equally to all sender nodes in the network [Bor07], the sender anonymity is given by:

$$Pr[X = x|y] = \frac{1}{N = |V|}.$$

Hence, both maximal sender and receiver anonymity are achieved when the random walk reaches convergence.

Also, the stationary distribution vector gives the normalized fraction of traffic load on each mix [Dan07].

4.5   Compromised Mixes

Suppose a subset of mixes are taken over by an adversary. Then a compromised mix route is defined as a mix circuit that is solely composed of compromised mix nodes. Then, what is the probability that a randomly chosen mix route is compromised?

A network topology with poor expansion properties (or lower *eigen-value gap* $\epsilon = 1 - \lambda_2$) tends to have relatively 'localized' mix routes, so that, given the first mix of a route, there exists a subset of mixes within the network that have a higher chance of being on the route than others.

The spectral theory of graphs lends us a few tools, namely chernoff bounds, in quantifying this risk. Suppose S is the set of subverted nodes, and π_S the corresponding probability mass of the stationary distribution π. The upper bound of the probability that a mix route (random walk) of length t goes through t_S nodes of S is given by Gilbert [Gil98]: $Pr[t_A = t] \leq \left(1 + \frac{(1-\pi(A))\epsilon}{10}\right) e^{-t\frac{(1-\pi(A))^2\epsilon}{20}}$. However as Danezis [Dan03] notes, given that this probability exponentially decreases with increase in t, a small increase in route length will successfully mitigate this risk.

What is more relevant in the context of unstructured networks, is the presence of 'hub' nodes and 'weak-ties'. Hubs [New03b] are special nodes that owing to their position in the network topology handle large amounts of traffic. Similarly, weak-ties [Gra73] are edges responsible for significantly reducing average path-lengths in networks of tightly knit communities such as social networks. The risk of compromised mix routes is significantly higher in a topology where hubs only connect to other hubs, and handle most of the network traffic. If an attacker can locate and strategically target mix nodes that also play the role of a hub, then the percentage of mix routes under risk can be significant. This property is known as assortativity [New03a], defined as the affinity of a node to link to others that are similar or different in some way.

Hence, we simulated a large number of random walks for various topologies presented in section 3, of different lengths, and make a recommendation on the route length to mitigate this risk in section 5.1.

4.6 Intersection Attacks

The term *intersection attack* was introduced by Berthold et al. [BPS00]. These attacks involve the detection of the preferential use of a mix route. If for some reason, a sender under attack sends more traffic along a specific route much more often than other routes, then a simple intersection attack is carried out by intersecting the set of possible next-hop mixes of every mix with the set of possible next-hop destinations of previous messages. The actual path of a message will then become apparent unless the network has countermeasures against observability.

If each link from a mix node is used to flush messages to its neighbours, then the potential for the simplest of intersection attacks can be greatly reduced [KAP02]. So, for a given node i, we wish to calculate the probability that any out going link remains unused during a flushing cycle. If each mix node receives b messages per batch, then each of these will appear on a particular outgoing link j with a binomial probability distribution $p_i = 1/deg_i$. Danezis [Dan03] then calculates the volume of incoming traffic required so that the probability of any out going link being unused is negligible.

$$b = \frac{9}{f^2}\left(\frac{1 - p_i}{p_i}\right) \tag{4}$$

where f is the percentage deviation of traffic output on a particular link of i in a given flushing cycle from the mean traffic output.

Combining this with p_{min}, the probability associated with the highest degree node in the mix network, we can derive the amount of genuine traffic to be mixed together.

The prevention of basic intersection attacks as a system design criteria is first found in the work of Pfitzmann and colleagues on ISDN mixes [PPW91], and more recently to the work of Reiter and Rubin [RR98].

5   Results and Discussion

5.1   Simulation Parameters

In all the synthetically generated networks we considered, we have $N \approx 5000$ nodes. The parameters used for each of them are listed below.

We model scale-free networks with linear preferential attachment with m links per node and average node degree $\langle d \rangle$; $2 \leq m \leq 7$ and $4 \leq \langle d \rangle \leq 14$.

Next we model scale-free random networks which have a scale-free degree sequence but which are random in all other respects. Generated with parameters $\alpha = 0.25$, $\beta = 0.25$ and Average node degree $4 \leq \langle d \rangle \leq 14$. See section 3.3 for an explanation of α and β.

Klienberg-Watts-Strogatz model of directed social network ties is analyzed next, generated with parameters r, the lattice radius within which each node creates direct links to all its neighbors. q is the number of weak ties. We used $1 \leq r \leq 4$ and $2 \leq q \leq 10$.

Our next network is based on our primary source data, obtained by web-crawling the LiveJournal site. The snapshot of the network we use in our analysis has 3,746,240 nodes and 27,430,000 edges.

Finally we analyze two theoretical topologies, one degree heterogeneous and the other degree homogeneous, to offer a baseline comparison against ER graph and constant expander graph topologies.

The ER graph is created with each edge formation as the result of a Poisson distribution of $p = 0.0028$ with $\langle d \rangle = 14$.

The constant expander graph is created with each node having $D = 14$ edges. Motwani et.al. [MR95] prove a relation between the second eigenvalue λ_2 of the transition matrix of a constant expander graph and the degree D of a node $\lambda_2 \geq \frac{2\sqrt{D-1}}{D}$. We can then use the result of Sinclair [Sin93] connecting λ_2, random walk length t and convergence rate $\Delta(t)$, namely $\Delta(t) \leq \frac{\lambda_2^t}{\min_{i \in V} \pi_i}$. For $D = 14$, we have a constant expander graph with theoretical minimum second eigen-value of $\lambda_2 \geq 0.5527708$, converging to maximal anonymity state in approximately 4 steps. This forms the baseline against which we compare all the other topologies.

5.2   Efficiency

We can now comment on the efficiency and recommended mix route lengths for various network topologies by comparing them to our baselines.

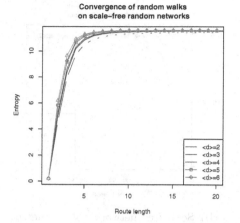

Network ($N = 5000$)	$\langle d \rangle$ or D	t	$\mathcal{A}_{network}$
SFR	4	8	11.4383
	6	7	11.5626
	8	6	11.5958
	10	6	11.6135
	12	5	11.6351
ER	14	7	12.2339
Expander	14	4	12.2877

Fig. 1. Convergence rates: Efficiency and maximal receiver anonymity for Scale-free random, ER and Constant expander graph topologies

The efficiency of mix topologies based on a scale-free random network is shown in Figure 1. It plots the anonymity achieved against increasing random walk lengths. Maximal receiver anonymity is calculated using equation 3 is the entropy of the probability distribution of the chain at convergence, while maximal sender anonymity is $\frac{1}{N}$.

Our calculations show that maximal anonymity is reached in just 6 steps in the medium density case $\langle d \rangle \geq 4$, as opposed to 4 steps in to 4 steps in an expander graph topology. It turns out that social collaboration networks [New01a,New01c, New01b] with scale-free characteristics have average degrees in the range of $4 \leq \langle d \rangle \leq 18$. This suggests, firstly, that efficient mix networks can be designed using scale-free random networks, and second, that mildly denser scale-free networks are more suitable for building mix networks than sparser ones.

While this is an encouraging initial result, it is important to strike a note of caution. Scale-free random graphs only model the scale-free aspect of degree distribution, while being random in every other way. However most real world unstructured networks have several other non-random characteristics apart from their degree distributions.

A number of real world unstructured networks are not scale-free, hence we included the Klienberg-Watts-Strogatz(KWS) network topology, as it explicitly models the presence of weak ties in a network. We experiment with a number of parameter configurations; selecting $r = 1$ and $r = 4$ to model low and high richness in local links or 'strong ties' between nodes; and $2 \leq q \leq 10$ the number of short cuts or 'weak ties', between mix nodes. Figure 2-a plots mix-route length vs mix network anonymity, for the KWS topology. When the topology is poor in local links, it seems to converge in 7 to 8 hops, given enough short cuts. However, if the network invests a large amount of resources into local connections forming relatively tightly knit communities, then regardless of the amount of shortcuts, convergence is not achieved until 62 hops!

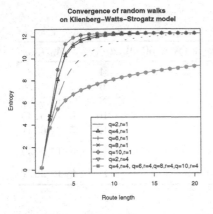
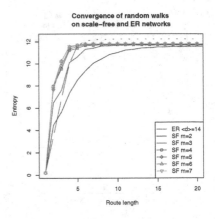

(a) Klienberg-Watts-Strogatz model

(b) Scale-free network with preferential attachment

Fig. 2. Mean entropy vs mix-route length

Our final model network topology is the scale-free network based on linear preferential attachment, which has attracted much attention in the complex networks literature. This topology models a scale-free network where hubs are connected to other hubs, a pattern that is repeatedly observed in many real world scale-free networks. The parameter m controls graph sparsity, random walk and convergence results are shown in figure 2-b. Our simulations show that while very sparse topologies converge in 10 to 15 hops, topologies that are relatively dense converge within 6 or so hops, this is comparable to the optimal 4 hops of a constant expander graph.

Next, we considered our primary data source the LiveJournal graph with a little less than 4 million nodes. Figure 3 shows the convergence rate of mix routes, which we note converges to the stationary distribution in around 11 hops. While this seems a high number in comparison to expander graphs (converging in 4 hops), we also note that the entropy achieved by the random walk in 4 hops in LJ is $\mathcal{A}_{LJ}^4 = 15.56$. To obtain the equivalent on an expander graph topology we would only need $2^{15.56}$ or 48309 nodes. On the face of it the design decision seems really simple, to go for a structured expander graph topology. We argue a different view: A successful mix network design must also consider liability management issues arising from running a mix. Considering that aspect, topology links backed up by social capital are likely to be more robust than those of an optimal topology, but where nodes quickly buckle under legal pressure. We propose, running mixes on the nodes of the LJ topology bundled along with a future LiveJournal client. Nodes only allow incoming traffic from their neighbors, and will only direct outgoing traffic to their neighbors.

In this context, an interesting question is why nodes would process traffic that didn't originate from their neighbors, and especially so in the face of legal hassles?

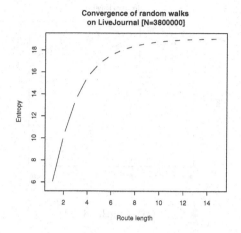

Convergence of random walks on LiveJournal [N=3800000]

Network	m	t	$\mathcal{A}_{network}$
SF	2	15	11.5852
	3	10	11.6961
	4	6	11.7293
	5	6	11.7687
	6	6	11.7953
	7	6	11.8090
KWS	$q=2, p=1$	11	12.2945
	$q=10, p=1$	5	12.2939
	$q=2, p=4$	63	11.6440
	$q=10, p=4$	63	11.6380
ER	$\langle d \rangle = 14$	7	12.2339
Expander	$D = 14$	4	12.2877

Fig. 3. Mean entropy vs mix-route length for LiveJournal

Fig. 4. Convergence rates: Efficiency and maximal receiver anonymity for linear Scale-free, KWS, ER and constant expander graph topologies

We offer the following reasoning: Humans making decisions on whether or not to run a mix server, will have to consider the following costs. They benefit in the long term, from processing traffic for unknown nodes in order to generate a diverse user base, the need for which is well illustrated in Dingledine and Mathewson [DM06]. However this only holds if other mixes cooperate accordingly. Then there is the immediate social benefit of having processed traffic for your friends. The success of the system then depends on the extent to which individual nodes perceive the costs of litigation pressure to be less than the total of immediate social benefit and the long term benefit of a diverse user base. Psychology studies tell us that humans involved in taking security decisions weigh short and long term benefits differently. It should also be interesting to investigate whether the idea of running a mix to primarily process traffic for your friends is an effective tool for seeding indirect reciprocity in a mix network where cooperation flourishes.

5.3   Compromised Mix Nodes

As explained in our evaluation framework, compromised nodes can lead to compromised routes. This presents a special challenge in unstructured networks where π_A, the probability mass of the stationary distribution π, corresponding to set of compromised nodes A, can be significant for topological reasons.

To measure the robustness to nodes being strategically compromised by an attacker, we simulated 100000 random walks of different lengths, for each of our network topologies, in the range indicated by efficiency considerations of

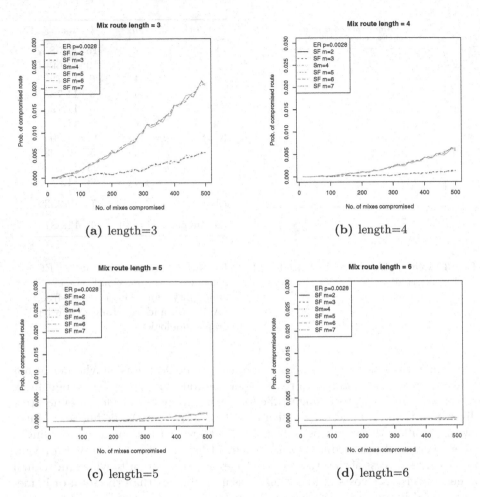

Fig. 5. Probability of mix-route compromise vs no. of corrupt nodes

the previous section $3 \leq t \leq 6$, and measured the fraction that passed through compromised nodes. The set of compromised nodes is chosen to consist of the nodes with the highest degrees in the network. In each case, for mix routes greater than 4 hops the probability of existence of a compromised mix route is negligible. Fig 5 in the appendix confirms that the threat of mix route compromise can be successfully reduced by suitably increasing the mix-route length.

5.4 Intersection Attacks

Using equation 4 we consider the required batch sizes for a threshold mix, so that the traffic output on any link in the mix network does not deviate by more than 5% from the mean traffic output on that link. For $f = 5$ we calculate the number of messages that must be received in each mixing cycle in table 1.

Table 1. Batch sizes required to prevent intersection attacks

Network	$\langle d \rangle$	p_{min}	Batch size
SFR	4	0.0344	10.08
	6	0.0222	15.84
	8	0.0243	14.4
	10	0.0192	18.36
	12	0.0135	26.28
	14	0.0125	28.44
KWS	27 ($q = 1, r = 1$)	0.0294	11.88
	43 ($q = 10, r = 1$)	0.0169	20.88
	26 ($q = 1, r = 4$)	0.0333	10.44
	28 ($q = 10, r = 4$)	0.0294	11.88
SF-linear	4	0.0048	74.16
	6	0.0048	74.16
	8	0.0041	86.04
	10	0.0038	93.6
	12	0.0037	96.12
	14	0.0031	112.32
LJ	7.3221	0.00857	41.64
ER	14	0.0333	10.44
Expander	14	0.0714	4.68

From table 1 it is clear that scale-free random networks and KWS both require a batch size that is 4-5 times that of expander graphs. Whether social networks can produce enough 'chatter' to feed genuine traffic into the mix network is an open question.

Our theoretical base line of ER network topology does slightly better at a little over twice that. More significantly, the LJ network has a batch size of almost 9 times the required batch size for expander graphs. Scale-free networks with linear preferential attachment are the worst performing, requiring a batch size almost 20 times larger than expanders. We think that the exceptionally high value of batch size in LJ network is due to its size of four million or so nodes. While does not mean that LJ is inherently unsuitable as a mix network topology, but it certainly indicates a scalability limit with the deployment of mixes on LJ nodes, as proposed earlier.

6   Conclusions

We have analyzed a comprehensive set of network topologies from the perspective of efficiency, maximal anonymity, compromised nodes and simple intersection attacks in comparison with (provably optimal) expander graphs.

To the standard threat model of the global passive adversary, we have added real world issues such as liability management and the need for clear incentives for carrying traffic under the pressure of legal threats, and discussed our simulation results in this context.

We have considered topologies with two important characteristics found in the empirical studies of large-scale unstructured networks: scale-freeness (scale-free random graph) and the small-world property (Klienberg-Watts-Strogatz (KWS) graph). In both the topologies, we can recommend mix route lengths for achieving 95% of maximal anonymity, that is only a few hops larger than the optimal route length found in expander graph topologies. Currently deployed mix networks such as TOR have around 540 volunteers. To increase the scale of such mix deployments the Internet, we believe the way forward (for high latency systems only) is to use online social networks. The minimum mix route must have two mixes to allow sender and receiver anonymity. For this length, a mix network constructed by placing mixes on the nodes of a social network such as Live-Journal can achieve far higher maximal anonymity as per the entropy metric we have used. We argue that including network incentives within a framework does not allow the construction of structured overlay mix topologies that can robustly withstand the threat of legal action. By moving to social networks, we make a start on tapping the social capital underlying node-node interaction to encourage users to deploy and run mixes with policies that reflect this aspect.

We also found that subverted nodes, either compromised randomly, or by strategic choice, on the basis of their degrees has little effect on the efficiency of a mix network. This is because the route length required to mitigate that risk is less than the recommended length for achieving efficient convergence rates.

We also analyzed scale-free and the small-world topologies for their robustness to attacks based on traffic load patterns observable on their out-going and incoming links. Both the scale-free random graph topology and the KWS topology turn out to require almost 5 times as much traffic as corresponding expander graph topology. This suggests the need for further tests to see if enough genuine traffic is generated in online social network interaction, to satisfy the minimum batch sizes required for preventing the most basic versions of these attacks.

We conclude that, unstructured networks based on large-scale topologies are indeed very promising, we have outlined the merits and challenges these topologies present to the design of mix networks for anonymous communication.

Acknowledgements

The authors are grateful to Ross Anderson and Nikita Borisov for reviews on early versions of the paper, and to George Danezis and Roger Dingledine, for thought provoking discussions.

References

[AB02]   Albert, R., Barabási, A.: Statistical mechanics of complex networks (2002)
[ACL00]   Aiello, W., Chung, F., Lu, L.: A random graph model for massive graphs.
           In: STOC 2000: Proceedings of the thirty-second annual ACM symposium
           on Theory of computing, pp. 171–180. ACM Press, New York (2000)

[Bor05]   Borisov, N.: Phd thesis: Anonymous routing in structured peer-to-peer overlays (April 2005)

[Bor07]   Borisov, N.: Private communication (June 2007)

[BPS00]   Berthold, O., Pfitzmann, A., Standtke, R.: The disadvantages of free MIX routes and how to overcome them. In: Federrath, H. (ed.) Designing Privacy Enhancing Technologies. LNCS, vol. 2009, pp. 30–45. Springer, Heidelberg (2001)

[Cha81]   Chaum, D.: Untraceable electronic mail, return addresses, and digital pseudonyms. Communications of the ACM 4(2) (February 1981)

[CSWH00]   Clarke, I., Sandberg, O., Wiley, B., Hong, T.: Freenet: A distributed anonymous information storage and retrieval system. In: Federrath, H. (ed.) Designing Privacy Enhancing Technologies. LNCS, vol. 2009, pp. 46–66. Springer, Heidelberg (2001)

[Dan03]   Danezis, G.: Mix-networks with restricted routes. In: Dingledine, R. (ed.) PET 2003. LNCS, vol. 2760, Springer, Heidelberg (2003)

[Dan07]   Danezis, G.: Private communication (July 2007)

[DDM03]   Danezis, G., Dingledine, R., Mathewson, N.: Mixminion: Design of a type iii anonymous remailer protocol. In: IEEE Symposium on Security and Privacy, pp. 2–15 (2003)

[DM06]   Dingledine, R., Mathewson, N.: Anonymity loves company: Usability and the network effect. In: Proceedings of the Fifth Workshop on the Economics of Information Security (WEIS 2006), Cambridge, UK (June 2006)

[DMS04]   Dingledine, R., Mathewson, N., Syverson, P.: Tor: The second-generation onion router. In: Proceedings of the 13th USENIX Security Symposium (August 2004)

[EG02]   Eschenauer, L., Gligor, V.D.: A key-management scheme for distributed sensor networks. In: CCS 2002: Proceedings of the 9th ACM conference on Computer and communications security, pp. 41–47. ACM Press, New York (2002)

[ER59]   Erdos, P., Rnyi, A.: On random graphs. Publicationes Mathemticae (Debrecen) 6, 290–297 (1959)

[Gil98]   Gillman, D.: A chernoff bound for random walks on expander graphs. SIAM J. Comput. 27(4), 1203–1220 (1998)

[Gra73]   Granovetter, M.S.: The strength of weak ties. The American Journal of Sociology 78(6), 1360–1380 (1973)

[KAP02]   Kesdogan, D., Agrawal, D., Penz, S.: Limits of anonymity in open environments. In: Petitcolas, F.A.P. (ed.) IH 2002. LNCS, vol. 2578, Springer, Heidelberg (2003)

[KM02]   Klingberg, T., Manfredi, R.: "gnutella 0.6" (June 2002)

[Mil67]   Milgram, S.: The small world problem. Psychology Today 2, 60–67 (1967)

[MPS03]   Mihail, M., Papadimitriou, C., Saberi, A.: On certain connectivity properties of the internet topology. In: FOCS 2003: Proceedings of the 44th Annual IEEE Symposium on Foundations of Computer Science, p. 28. IEEE Computer Society, Washington, DC (2003)

[MR95]   Motwani, R., Raghavan, P.: Randomized Algorithms, vol. 1. Cambridge Univ. Press, Motwani (1995)

[New01a]   Newman, M.E.: The structure of scientific collaboration networks. Proc. Natl. Acad. Sci. 98(2), 404–409 (2001)

[New01b]   Newman, M.E.J.: Scientific collaboration networks. ii. shortest paths, weighted networks, and centrality. Phys. Rev. E 64(1), 016132 (June 2001)

[New01c]   Newman, M.E.J.: Scientific collaboration networks. i. networks construc-
            tion and fundamental results. Phys. Rev. E 64(1), 016131 (June 2001)
[New03a]   Newman, M.E.J.: Mixing patterns in networks. Physical Review E 67,
            026126 (2003)
[New03b]   Newman, M.E.J.: The structure and function of complex networks. SIAM
            Review 45(2), 167–256 (2003)
[PH00]   Pfitzmann,   A.,   Hansen,   M.:   Anonymity,   unobservability,   and
            pseudonymity: A consolidated proposal for terminology. Draft (July
            2000)
[PPW91]   Pfitzmann, A., Pfitzmann, B., Waidner, M.: ISDN-mixes: Untraceable
            communication with very small bandwidth overhead. In: GI/ITG Confer-
            ence on Communication in Distributed Systems, pp. 451–463 (February
            1991)
[Ran06]   Randall, D.: Rapidly mixing markov chains with applications in computer
            science and physics. Computing in Science and Engineering 8(2), 30–41
            (2006)
[RFI02]   Ripeanu, M., Foster, I., Iamnitchi, A.: Mapping the gnutella network:
            Properties of large-scale peer-to-peer systems and implications for system
            design. IEEE Internet Computing Journal 6(1) (August 2002)
[RR98]   Reiter, M.K., Rubin, A.D.: Crowds: anonymity for web transactions. ACM
            Trans. Inf. Syst. Secur. 1(1), 66–92 (1998)
[RSG98]   Reed, M.G., Syverson, P.F., Goldschlag, D.M.: Anonymous connections
            and onion routing. IEEE Journal on Selected Areas in Communications
            16(4) (1998)
[SD02]   Serjantov, A., Danezis, G.: Towards an information theoretic metric for
            anonymity. In: Dingledine, R., Syverson, P.F. (eds.) PET 2002. LNCS,
            vol. 2482, Springer, Heidelberg (2003)
[Sin93]   Sinclair, A.: Algorithms for random generation and counting: a Markov
            chain approach. Birkhauser Verlag, Basel, Switzerland (1993)
[STRL00]   Syverson, P., Tsudik, G., Reed, M., Landwehr, C.: Towards an Analysis
            of Onion Routing Security. In: Federrath, H. (ed.) Designing Privacy En-
            hancing Technologies. LNCS, vol. 2009, pp. 96–114. Springer, Heidelberg
            (2001)
[Wes01]   West, D.B: Introduction to Graph Theory, 2nd edn. Prentice Hall, Engle-
            wood Cliffs (2001)

A   Mix-Route Compromise on Linear Preferential Attachment Scale-Free Networks

In this section we sketch a few analytical results concerning mix-route compromise in BA scale-free networks.

Let B be the set of compromised high vertex-order centrality nodes. For a
route to be fully compromised, all intermediate nodes must be in B. We then
wish to calculate,

$$P(C_l) = [Pr(Random - Walk(v_1....v_l))]\forall v_1...v_l \subseteq B.$$

It is straightforward to see that if $l > |B|$ then P(C)=0. In BA scale-free networks, all hubs(high vertex-order) nodes are connected to each other. Hence,

$$P(C) = \frac{|B| - 1}{\prod_{j \in B} k_j}.$$

B   Convergence Rate and Network Size in Scale-Free Random Networks

Simulations conducted in this paper have not accounted for the effect of varying network size on the convergence rate of the respective topologies. We address this, by offering a simple conductance based proof that the second eigen-value of a scale-free network is a independent of the network size. See [Ran06] for a review of the conductance based technique as well as others.

We denote a scale-free network generated by preferential attachment, by $G_{m,n}(V, E)$ where m is the number of initial nodes created at time=l_0 and n is the total number of nodes in the network. At every time step $t_i, i \geq 0$, m nodes are added to the networks. For every node added, we create m edges from the node to existing nodes in the network. We continue until $|V| = n$.

Next, there is an intimate relationship between the rate of convergence and a certain structural property called the *conductance* of the underlying graph. Consider a randomly chosen sub-graph S of $G(V, E)$. Suppose a random walk on the graph visits node i $i \in S$. What is the probability that the walk exits S in a single hop. If conductance is small, then a walk would tend to "get stuck" in S, whereas if conductance is large it easily "flows" out of S.

Formally, for $S \subset G$, the *volume* of S is $vol_G(S) = \sum_{u \in S} d_G(u)$, where $d_G(u)$ is the degree of node u. The *cutset* of S, $C_G(S, \overline{S})$, is the multiset of edges with one endpoint in S and the other endpoint in $\overline{S}$. The textbook definition of conductance Φ_G of the graph G is the following:

$$\Phi_G = \min_{S \subset V, vol_G(S) \leq vol_G(V)/2} \frac{|C_G(S, \overline{S})|}{vol_G(S)} \tag{5}$$

[MPS03] prove that the conductance of a scale-free network is a *constant*. Specifically, $\forall m \geq 2$ *and* $c < 2(d - 1) - 1$, $\exists \alpha = \alpha(d, c)$ such that

$$\Phi = \frac{\alpha}{m + \alpha} \tag{6}$$

From [Sin93] we have the following bound for λ_2:

$$1 - 2\Phi \leq \lambda_2 \leq 1 - \Phi^2/2 \tag{7}$$

Substituting for Φ from equation 6 in equation 7, it is easy to see that λ_2 is a constant.

Author Index

Lecture Notes in Computer Science

Sublibrary 4: Security and Cryptology

Vol. 4236: L. Breveglieri, I. Koren, D. Naccache, J.-P. Seifert (Eds.), Fault Diagnosis and Tolerance in Cryptography. XIII, 253 pages. 2006.

Vol. 4219: D. Zamboni, C. Krügel (Eds.), Recent Advances in Intrusion Detection. XII, 331 pages. 2006.

Vol. 4189: D. Gollmann, J. Meier, A. Sabelfeld (Eds.), Computer Security – ESORICS 2006. XI, 548 pages. 2006.

Vol. 4176: S.K. Katsikas, J. López, M. Backes, S. Gritzalis, B. Preneel (Eds.), Information Security. XIV, 548 pages. 2006.

Vol. 4117: C. Dwork (Ed.), Advances in Cryptology - CRYPTO 2006. XIII, 621 pages. 2006.

Vol. 4116: R. De Prisco, M. Yung (Eds.), Security and Cryptography for Networks. XI, 366 pages. 2006.

Vol. 4107: G. Di Crescenzo, A. Rubin (Eds.), Financial Cryptography and Data Security. XI, 327 pages. 2006.

Vol. 4083: S. Fischer-Hübner, S. Furnell, C. Lambrinoudakis (Eds.), Trust and Privacy in Digital Business. XIII, 243 pages. 2006.

Vol. 4064: R. Büschkes, P. Laskov (Eds.), Detection of Intrusions and Malware & Vulnerability Assessment. X, 195 pages. 2006.

Vol. 4058: L.M. Batten, R. Safavi-Naini (Eds.), Information Security and Privacy. XII, 446 pages. 2006.

Vol. 4047: M.J.B. Robshaw (Ed.), Fast Software Encryption. XI, 434 pages. 2006.

Vol. 4043: A.S. Atzeni, A. Lioy (Eds.), Public Key Infrastructure. XI, 261 pages. 2006.

Vol. 4004: S. Vaudenay (Ed.), Advances in Cryptology - EUROCRYPT 2006. XIV, 613 pages. 2006.

Vol. 3995: G. Müller (Ed.), Emerging Trends in Information and Communication Security. XX, 524 pages. 2006.

Vol. 3989: J. Zhou, M. Yung, F. Bao (Eds.), Applied Cryptography and Network Security. XIV, 488 pages. 2006.

Vol. 3969: Ø. Ytrehus (Ed.), Coding and Cryptography. XI, 443 pages. 2006.

Vol. 3958: M. Yung, Y. Dodis, A. Kiayias, T.G. Malkin (Eds.), Public Key Cryptography - PKC 2006. XIV, 543 pages. 2006.

Vol. 3957: B. Christianson, B. Crispo, J.A. Malcolm, M. Roe (Eds.), Security Protocols. IX, 325 pages. 2006.

Vol. 3956: G. Barthe, B. Grégoire, M. Huisman, J.-L. Lanet (Eds.), Construction and Analysis of Safe, Secure, and Interoperable Smart Devices. IX, 175 pages. 2006.

Vol. 3935: D.H. Won, S. Kim (Eds.), Information Security and Cryptology - ICISC 2005. XIV, 458 pages. 2006.

Vol. 3934: J.A. Clark, R.F. Paige, F.A.C. Polack, P.J. Brooke (Eds.), Security in Pervasive Computing. X, 243 pages. 2006.

Vol. 3928: J. Domingo-Ferrer, J. Posegga, D. Schreckling (Eds.), Smart Card Research and Advanced Applications. XI, 359 pages. 2006.

Vol. 3919: R. Safavi-Naini, M. Yung (Eds.), Digital Rights Management. XI, 357 pages. 2006.

Vol. 3903: K. Chen, R. Deng, X. Lai, J. Zhou (Eds.), Information Security Practice and Experience. XIV, 392 pages. 2006.

Vol. 3897: B. Preneel, S. Tavares (Eds.), Selected Areas in Cryptography. XI, 371 pages. 2006.

Vol. 3876: S. Halevi, T. Rabin (Eds.), Theory of Cryptography. XI, 617 pages. 2006.

Vol. 3866: T. Dimitrakos, F. Martinelli, P.Y.A. Ryan, S. Schneider (Eds.), Formal Aspects in Security and Trust. X, 259 pages. 2006.

Vol. 3860: D. Pointcheval (Ed.), Topics in Cryptology – CT-RSA 2006. XI, 365 pages. 2006.

Vol. 3858: A. Valdes, D. Zamboni (Eds.), Recent Advances in Intrusion Detection. X, 351 pages. 2006.

Vol. 3856: G. Danezis, D. Martin (Eds.), Privacy Enhancing Technologies. VIII, 273 pages. 2006.

Vol. 3786: J.-S. Song, T. Kwon, M. Yung (Eds.), Information Security Applications. XI, 378 pages. 2006.

Vol. 3108: H. Wang, J. Pieprzyk, V. Varadharajan (Eds.), Information Security and Privacy. XII, 494 pages. 2004.

Vol. 2951: M. Naor (Ed.), Theory of Cryptography. XI, 523 pages. 2004.

Vol. 2742: R.N. Wright (Ed.), Financial Cryptography. VIII, 321 pages. 2003.